New England Natives

A New England Elm

NEW ENGLAND NATIVES

Sheila Connor

Harvard University Press

Cambridge, Massachusetts

London, England · 1994

This book is printed on acid-free paper, and its binding materials
have been chosen for strength and durability.

Library of Congress Cataloging-in-Publication Data

Connor, Sheila.

    New England natives : a celebration of people and trees / Sheila
Connor.

        p.   cm.

Includes bibliographical references and index.

    ISBN 0-674-61350-3 : $39.95

    1. Trees—New England. 2. Trees—Utilization—New
England. 3. Forest plants—New England. 4. Ethnobotany—
New England. 5. New England—Industries. 6. Natural
history—New England. 7. Arnold Arboretum.   I. Title.

QK121.C66 1993

582.160974—dc20   93-6306

                                          CIP

RD21

Frontispiece: This illustration, "A New England Elm," is taken from
a study of the native flora by George Russell Shaw (1848–1937)
entitled *On the Identification of the Trees and Shrubs of Massachusetts at All Seasons of the Year.* Although Shaw is most famous
for his two botanical works on pines, *The Pines of Mexico* (1909)
and *The Genus Pinus* (1914), both published by the Arnold
Arboretum, this collection of watercolors, pen-and-ink drawings,
and pencil sketches, which he compiled during the years 1891–1893
and bound by hand in hand-tooled leather, captures both the identity of each native species and its special place in the New England
landscape. The Shaw family generously donated this unique work to
the Archives of the Arnold Arboretum in 1983. Shaw was an
architect as well as a botanist, practising architecture with Henry
Hunnewell in Boston from 1873 to 1902.

Contents

Foreword

A rare word now (and one not immediately understood, despite its superficial simplicity), *woodcraft* more than echoes throughout this book. It resonates, indeed booms, as a last felled tree booms in an otherwise silent winter woodlot, just at the end of the day, in the falling light and gathering cold that make woodsmen suddenly careful.

For centuries, *woodcraft* has denoted skills of the chase, of exploration, of survival in forest, and especially in forest wilderness, the sort of wilderness Europeans encountered in the New World. Nineteenth-century lexicographers typically emphasized that denotation. In his first unabridged dictionary, Noah Webster defined woodcraft almost starkly: "skill and practice in shooting and other sports in the woods." That definition endured in almost every major American dictionary from 1828 to the 1930s, often as the only definition. "Skill is anything which pertains to the woods or forest; skill in the chase, especially in hunting deer, etc.," opined the massive *Century Dictionary* in 1911. "Skill and practice in any thing pertaining to the woods, esp. in maintaining oneself and making one's way, in hunting or trapping, or in tracking and studying wild life of the woods," offered Webster's *New International Dictionary of the English Language* in 1934. But "Webster's Second," as lexicographers call the gigantic 1934 edition, offered a far briefer secondary definition: "skill in shaping or constructing articles from wood." That secondary definition had long flitted in and out of American dictionaries, appearing in nascent form in Joseph Worcester's *Dictionary of the English Language* as early as 1859, "skill in anything which pertains to the woods or forests," in localism in the 1928 New Standard Dictionary, "the business of lumbering," and in contemporary, always secondary form in the 1961 *Webster's Third New International Dictionary*: "skill in shaping or constructing articles from wood." British dictionaries tend toward the primary definition, although many late-eighteenth-century and early-

nineteenth-century dictionaries eschew the term completely, and as late as 1934 the *Oxford English Dictionary* emphasized the "colonial" notion that woodcraft proved useful for exploration as well as for sport. While clearly English enough in origin, the primary definition has coexisted with another, far looser one since the colonization of North America, a second definition emphasizing not the uses of woods but the uses of wood.

Today, *woodcraft* lingers chiefly in the firelit talk of hunters, backpackers, and other recreational users of the forest, although it and kindred terms, such as *lore*, become less common by the decade. And *woodworker*, with all its connotations of factory work supplanting home crafts, almost overwhelms the secondary definition of woodcraft, which itself lingers only in such wilderness-related activities as the carving of decoys, perhaps, or the carving of birds to grace tables and mantels. At the close of the millennium, *woodcraft* might acquire a third, far more subtle definition, the one implied throughout *New England Natives*. Perhaps woodcraft might come to mean sophisticated appraisal of the forest, of woodlots, of trees growing forlornly in shopping-center parking lots.

New England Natives demonstrates beyond measure the overwhelming significance of wood in the history of the Republic, as well as the abyss that separates contemporary Americans and such technological wonders as particleboard, flakeboard, waferboard, and oriented-strand board from the native Americans moving north with a warming climate three thousand years before European contact. But this book does more: it delineates the use of the forest as more than mere scenery.

Today, for most people, the woods are screen only, a green screen in summer, a darker, less dense screen in winter, perhaps, but always a screen, something essentially visual. Just beyond the mowed berm of the interstate highway, a few yards beyond the commuter-train window , almost part of the haze in the long-distance view from the low-flying airliner, trees are scarcely recognizable as individual specimens now, let alone as specimens with specific uses. Many otherwise educated Americans find themselves hard pressed to distinguish more finely than between obviously deciduous woods and those obviously coniferous, and even clear scenic change—say, the way birches suddenly appear along interstate highways probing north into New Hampshire or the way conifers suddenly seem different along highways leading north into Maine—perplexes them as it pleases. But use, beyond visual delight, more than perplexes—it befuddles them. If that tree is indeed an oak, and soaring aloft from the center of a cow pasture, then obviously "a pasture oak," what use is it to a boatbuilder, one of the "woodcrafters" of colloquial American English? What does the clockmaker see in maple, the wagonmaker in hickory, the farmer in chestnut, the cabinetmaker in cedar? What they see, they see through the screen so easily accepted by the uninitiated.

So *woodcraft* might possibly serve to designate a sophisticated way of looking at trees, a knowing way of looking, the sort of attention so many educated people give to paintings. What New England Natives offers us is not the explorer's way of looking nor that of the craftsmen setting out to shape a bowl or a mast or a chair, but the regard of one acquainted with trees, on speaking terms with them. The gift of this book is the gift of speech, the gift of being able to say some intelligent words about a stunning assortment of trees far more useful than as green screens against the sun.

John R. Stilgoe
Cambridge, Massachusetts

Preface

New England Natives was written with the goal of revealing the evolving interaction between the people and the plants of New England. By describing the wide range of uses, during different eras, to which men and women have put the various species of trees and shrubs that grow in this region and describing the qualities of these plants and noting their distributions, I have attempted to provide a glimpse into the cultural and natural history of New England. Although this book is about the trees and shrubs that populate the New England forest, I hope that it will also serve as an introduction to the native trees and shrubs that can be seen every day on the way to work or to the store, or even in one's own back yard. Today, with close to eighty percent of New England reforested, it is almost impossible to find a landscape devoid of trees. Yet, our modern urbanized society has become so separated from nature that information about our natural surroundings that once was common knowledge has been largely lost. Perhaps this book will bring new meaning to street names such as Candlewood Lane and Tarkiln Road, to the look of the figure and grain in the cherry drop-leaf table inherited from grandmother, or to the texture of the pages in the morning newspaper.

This volume grew out of a number of discussions held by Arnold Arboretum staff members to explore how the nature, content and arrangement of the Arnold Arboretum's living collections of trees and shrubs might best be interpreted for our visitors. We soon agreed that we wished to go beyond the guidebooks typically written for arboreta and botanic gardens, which simply identify each notable plant and its location and may perhaps include a line or two describing a noteworthy characteristic of the species. We wanted instead to capture the imagination of our visitors by telling them something about the history of the plants and their interactions with people—stories of how people have sought out plants and used them for various economic, cultural, and esthetic purposes.

Within the Arnold Arboretum's 265-acre landscape grow plants from all the north-temperate areas of the world. Although the natural ranges of the plants covered in *New England Natives* extend beyond political boundaries, this book focuses on the native species that can be found growing within the six-state region. I have been selective, rather than encyclopedic, in my coverage of species, and I readily admit to some bias in my choices. I have selected plants according to my own personal preferences, plants that can be tied to specific, well documented uses, and plants whose historical or current uses I thought were inherently interesting or unusual. I hope that, in the bargain, the trees and shrubs that made the cut provide a representative sampling of our folkways and material culture.

Although this book is not intended to serve as a manual for the identification of native New England trees and shrubs, given the nature and design of the Arnold Arboretum's living collections and the strength and depth of its library and herbarium, I chose to emphasize the taxonomic characteristics of each species rather than, except to a very limited extent, to chronicle the ecological dynamics of the New England forest. This is not to underplay the importance of the ecology of these plants; rather, it is simply an attempt to provide the reader with sufficient taxonomic clues to recognize the species being discussed. I hope also that, by introducing taxonomic concepts, the book will function as a resource for interpreting the scientific arrangement of the Arboretum's collections, which provide a backdrop in which living examples of New England forest species can be seen growing side by side with introduced or exotic species.

Throughout the text, common and botanical names have been used more or less interchangeably. However, the first time a common name is mentioned, it is followed by the botanical or Latin name set off by commas or parentheses. A plant can have several common names, and because these vernacular names often were coined and adopted because they were descriptive of important features of the species, I have tried to include the most frequently used names, along with whatever plausible explanations of those names may be available.

Acknowledgments

Principal support for the research, writing, and publication of this book has come from the National Endowment for the Humanities through grants to the Arnold Arboretum for the implementation of a three-volume series based on the Arboretum's living collections. Grateful acknowledgment is made to Andrea Anderson of the National Endowment for the Humanities for her guidance and help in making this project a reality. I offer my special thanks to Peter S. Ashton, past director of the Arnold Arboretum, who believed in and championed this undertaking, and also to his wife, Mary Ashton, who was equally supportive of the project.

While researching and writing this book, I received assistance from many people. Foremost among all those who contributed their knowledge and gave of their time are my colleagues at the Arnold Arboretum: Jack Alexander, Genie Braasch, Carin Dohlman, Alfred Fordham, Ethan Johnson, Edmund Schoefield, and Richard E. Weaver, Jr. Jennifer Quigley read and commented on parts of the manuscript, retrieved information from the plant-records database, and solved the numerous problems I experienced with computers while working on the manuscript for this book. To Karen Kane, my able assistant, I owe a special debt. I cannot imagine how I could have accomplished all that needed to be done without her extraordinary help.

Sandy Anagnostakis provided me with an overview of her research on chestnut blight at the Connecticut Agricultural Experiment Station, and Barbara Luedtke, who identified and typed the Arnold Arboretum's collection of prehistoric artifacts, read and commented on my first chapter as well. I thank both for so willingly sharing their expertise with me. Hollis Bedell, Happy Spongberg, and three anonymous readers read the manuscript and offered valuable corrections and suggestions. I thank them all, both for their encouragement and for their comments. Throughout the project, I have benefitted greatly from the advice of Charles Carroll, William Cronon, Sam Bass Warner, and John Stilgoe, scholars who have shared their research and insights with me. Their participation helped to determine the project's direction and their knowledge helped to shape the book's content and form. John Stilgoe's foreword provides an added dimension to the book, and his encouragement has meant much to me.

Peter Del Tredici and Stephen Spongberg provided photographs from their own collections, and Albert Bussewitz, Barth Hamberg, and Istvan Racz spent countless hours photographing specimens within the Arnold Arboretum's landscape; each one of their exceptional photographs included here enlivens the text. For help on the illustrations, I would particularly like to thank Christopher Burnett, the photographer for the project, whose skill in photographing material in the collections of the library and archives of the Arnold Arboretum, the Harvard Botany Libraries, Houghton Library, and the Kummel Library clearly shows in the outstanding quality of the images reproduced in the book. Unlimited access to material in these collections and permission to photograph on site was cheerfully provided by Judy Warnement, Librarian of the Botany Libraries; James Lewis, Curator of the Reading Room, Houghton Library; and Constance Wick, Librarian of the Kummel Library of the Geological Sciences.

Several institutions allowed materials in their care to be used as illustrations. I extend my appreciation to the directors and the staffs of the American Philosophical Society; *The Boston Globe*; the Century Association; the Commonwealth of Massachusetts, Department of Environmental Management, Division of Forest and Parks, Region 5; the Founders' Society, Detroit Institute of Arts; the Hitchcock Museum; the Gray Herbarium of Harvard University; Houghton Library, Harvard University; the Museum of Fine Arts, Boston; the Massachusetts Historical Society; the Museum of Comparative Zoology, Harvard University; the Metropolitan Museum of Art; the Morton Arboretum; the National Museum of American Art, Smithsonian Institution; The Pilgrim Society; the Public Records Office, Surrey; the Society for the Preservation of New England Antiquities; the United States Department of Agriculture, National Agricultural Library; the United States Department of Agriculture, Forest Service, Northeastern Forest Experiment Station; the United States Department of the Interior, National Park Service, Cape Cod National Seashore; the Weare, New Hampshire, Public Library; the Woodstock Historical Society; and the Yale University Art Gallery, Mable Brady Garvin Collection.

I am appreciative of the generous hospitality that has

been extended to me by the staffs of the following institutions: Plimoth Plantation; Old Sturbridge Village; the Maritime Museum, Bath, Maine; the New Bedford Whaling Museum; the Museum of Early American Science and Technology; the Lumberman's Museum; the Slater Mill Historic Site; and the Cape Cod National Seashore.

To Howard Boyer, who assisted me from the early stages of the book through to submission of the manuscript to Harvard University Press, I express my warm thanks. Andrew Kudlacik magically transformed my manuscript pages and many photographs into a beautiful book. I am particularly indebted to my editor, Gunder Hefta, whose editorial abilities are surpassed only by his civilized patience, kindness, and wit. His enthusiastic support never wavered; for this I shall be eternally grateful.

While writing this book, I have had the opportunity to accompany a timber cruiser as he surveyed part of a forest, to tour a mill that turned pulpwood into paper, and to watch as birch bolts were transformed into toothpicks. I have admired the workmanship that turned basswood into canoe paddles, beech into saw handles, and maple into butcher blocks. I have interviewed artisans of all sorts, from basketmakers to shipbuilders, and have the acquaintance of foresters, loggers, and tree wardens. So many people have given so freely of their time that, although I know that I cannot name them all, I wish to acknowledge all the men and women working with wood throughout New England who have shared their work experiences with me.

To my colleagues and cherished friends Ida Hay and Stephen Spongberg, both of whom worked with me on the grant from the National Endowment for the Humanities, no expresssion of appreciation can really be adequate. Each contributed so generously to the development of my own understanding of the nature and science of New England's trees that I am certain that, without their help, this book would never have reached fruition. I also wish to acknowledge Stephen Spongberg for his invaluable assistance with identifying, locating, and photographing the botanical illustrations reproduced here as color plates.

Finally, to James McGrath—who listened, advised, and encouraged me—I give my most heartfelt thanks.

To aid visitors to the Arnold Arboretum, specimens of each of the plants in the Arboretum's living collection that are featured in this book are marked with a small logo that appears on the display label attached to the specimen.

New England Natives

1. Hemlocks and oaks in winter at the Arnold Arboretum.

CHAPTER ONE

A Place in the Forest

Initially, only subtle changes were evident in the long, broad valley. The short winter days grew slightly colder. The first frost came a few days earlier, and often the land remained frozen until later in the spring. The sap in the forest trees rose later, and a late cold spell often froze the early flowers of the silver maples growing along the stream. Few winged maple seeds matured in those years. The summer growing season also shortened, and the leaves of the birches and oaks growing on the hillsides turned gold and scarlet earlier in the year. The cool, short summers aborted many of the nuts produced by the chestnut trees, which flowered much later in the growing season than most forest trees.

Overall, the cold lengthened and deepened. Dogwood buds that held the next year's flowers fell to the ground unopened. Only farther south did the dogwoods flower and set seeds. Fewer and fewer seedlings sprouted on the forest floor, and the cold winds stunted the growth of saplings, yellowed the needles of the conifers, cracked limbs and trunks, and killed many of the older trees. Early snows fell on deeply frozen land, and no midwinter thaws interrupted the months of cold. Each spring, the snow took longer to melt than it had in previous years.

On north-facing slopes, the snow cover stayed late in the hemlock groves. Beneath its bark, the hemlock's annual growth rings became thinner every year. Heavy snowfalls smashed the crowns of pine trees, broke large limbs from hickory and ash, and stripped twigs and branches from the dogwoods, alders, and viburnums and from the other small trees and shrubs that grew in the understory. One spring, the snow-covered ice on the pond at the head of the valley remained frozen. Under the ice, a thin trickle of water flowed down the brook bed through a white landscape. Only a great distance to the south, after the brook left the valley, did it swell with runoff from melting snow.

In the Grip of Glacial Ice

About two million years ago, the temperature dropped and the climate changed worldwide. The most recent ice age, the Pleistocene epoch, had begun. In colder regions, rain was replaced by sleet and snow, which accumulated faster than it could melt. In the Canadian highlands of northern Quebec, east of Hudson Bay and west of the Saint Lawrence River, the climate of the Laurentian Mountains provided optimal conditions for the development of a glacier. The west winds blew cold, polar air across the waters of Hudson Bay and brought more snow to the mountains. With lower summer temperatures interrupting the cycle of freezing and thawing, much of each year's snow remained through summer, gaining depth with each winter's storms. Snowfields increased their extent, meeting and covering the land. As the accumulating snow reflected back more of the sun's rays, the atmosphere began to cool, and more precipitation fell as sleet and snow. Each successive snowfall compacted the snow that had fallen earlier until the great weight of centuries of accumulating snow compressed the lower layers into ice. The glacier grew heavier, its weight pushing downward in the middle and outward toward the edges, until the whole mass began imperceptibly to move.

The glacier spread in all directions, joining others that had formed west of Hudson Bay. The Laurentian glacier grew, merged, and flowed—south and east into New England and the Atlantic Ocean, and north and west to the Arctic Ocean and the interior of the continent. Throughout the two million years of the Pleistocene epoch, glaciers formed and decayed, advanced and retreated, as many as eighteen or twenty times. The interglacial stages, periods of retreat, gave only brief respites from the cold. At the time of greatest glaciation, roughly five million square miles of ice—an area larger than the size of the present Antarctic ice sheet—covered Canada,

2. Bussey Brook Valley in the Arnold Arboretum, photographed by T. E. Marr in 1900. In 1692, an inventory of Samuel Gore's estate, which included part of this valley, described an old mill and a broken-down dam that spanned the narrowest part of Bussey Brook. In 1708, the area was described as being made up of "meadow, pasture, and orchard," while an inventory taken in 1771 identifies this parcel as the "Saw Mill pasture & Meadow."

parts of the northern Great Plains, and a section of the Northwest.

Twenty thousand years ago, so much of the earth's water was locked up in glacial ice in northern Europe and in North America that the oceans dropped at least 350 feet below their present level. During this last great ice age, new land bridges connected continents, islands joined adjacent mainlands, and great migration routes opened up. Along the southern Atlantic seaboard, expanses of the continental shelf dried out, and the shape of the North American continent changed.

The cold and snow preceding the glacier triggered a slow migration of plants. The range of a plant species is determined by the dispersal of its seeds and the ability of its seedlings to survive. In order to avoid extinction, each new generation of plants needed a warmer climate or a more sheltered location. The species that constituted the forest of the Northeast were gradually displaced southward. Some moved far down the Appalachian Mountains to Florida, others migrated south and southwest along the Gulf of Mexico, while still others drifted southeast along the Atlantic coastal plain onto the newly exposed continental shelf. Species that failed to outrun or to adapt to the rigorous climatic changes were eliminated. During the short interglacial periods, those that remained moved

north again, only to be forced to retreat with each new advance of the ice.

In the Northeast, the greatest and last glacial advance began 70,000 years ago, with the maximum reaching many areas between 18,000 and 20,000 years ago. New England lay buried, its shoreline obliterated by the extension of ice southward and eastward over the seabed. In central New England, the ice lay 5000 feet thick, and it may have approached a depth of 10,000 feet elsewhere. Beneath the ice, all plants had been exterminated, and the land had been drastically altered.

The final retreat of the glacier produced a land scrubbed clean, an open frontier awaiting the return of plants and animals and the coming of human beings. Over millennia, the cold, barren landscape evolved into a temperate forest able to sustain prehistoric human cultures, to attract European colonists, to fuel an industrial society, and to shelter the present-day human population. While the glaciers have long since disappeared, the changes that the ice made as it slid and ground its way across the face of New England can still be seen today. The repeating patterns we recognize in our topography are as much a part of New England's scenery as is its landscape of plants, villages, homes, churches, factories, office buildings, and roads. The glaciers smoothed and rounded mountains and created valleys. They made hills, both large and small; they formed lakes, ponds, and low depressions in which bogs would develop; their force scored, scratched, and gouged bedrock, broke pieces from mountains, and removed topsoil. The soil that remained was made up of a jumble of clay, silt, sand, and stones of all sizes, from small pebbles to huge, rounded boulders— a mixture known as glacial till. New England's ubiquitous stone walls, now often dividing forests where they once bounded fields, are monuments to the New England farmer's harvest of glacial souvenirs.

A special vocabulary identifies the pieces of the Pleistocene puzzle. Large hills that look like inverted spoons or overturned canoes are called drumlins. Kames are small, rounded hills made up of stratified sand or gravel, while eskers are long, sinuous hills or ridges formed as streams flowed under or beside fingerlike extentions of the ice. Drumlins, kames, and eskers are among the glacial features that make up parts of the landscape of what is now the Arnold Arboretum. Peters Hill—at 235 feet, the highest point in the Arboretum—is a drumlin. Most likely formed as the glacier piled debris around and over an obstruction in its path, it is one of a group of drumlins that occur throughout the greater Boston area.

As the climate moderated, returning vegetation softened the stark landscape. An article by David White in the journal *Pennsylvania Forest Leaves* in 1924 promoted early, popular ideas of the effects of the ice age upon plants. He wrote, in images of fast-moving time changes, of prehistoric forests "subjected to forced marches to and fro in front of the great ice sheets." In reality, however, the individual trees remained firmly rooted in place, and the return of plants was as slow and complex a process as the original retreat; only through the stepwise northward progress of generations of successful seedlings did plants reforest the deglaciated land.

The plants "migrated" north at different rates and by different means. Wind, water, gravity, self-propulsion (seeds expelled from their pods), animals, and people were the agents of seed dispersal. Before its seeds or fruits could be transported, needless to say, a plant had to be old enough to produce them. Fast growing, early maturing, heavily fruiting species held an advantage. Light seeds or winged fruits were able to move farther in a generation. If the majority of the seeds that a plant produced germinated, and if the plant's seedlings were adapted to a variety of microclimates and soils, then the ability of that species to occupy new territory was greatly enhanced.

Huge decaying glacial masses remained where the ice had been particularly thick, and a deep cold still permeated the land. Plant species that could endure these hostile conditions were the first to reestablish themselves.

3. This photograph of Dixville Notch, New Hampshire, was made in the nineteenth century. The "notch" was created by a huge ice mass moving through a narrow V-shaped gap that a stream had eroded through this mountainous region. When a glacier was formed, it filled this valley with ice, and, when it gained a thickness sufficient enough to press its way over the mountains, grinding away the sharp peaks and making smooth, rounded summits, it also depressed the floor of the valley and ground away its original V shape, turning the valley's profile into a U. The notch's sidewalls of exposed bedrock and its rounded floor (caused by glacial scour) are typical of glaciated valleys in northern New England.

4. Rock fragments transported by glaciers range in size from microscopic particles to boulders, some of which were (like these glacial "erratics" photographed in New Hampshire), if not the size of a house, at least as big as a cottage. Many of the smaller rocks and stones that the glacier gouged and cracked out of bedrock were carried great distances, some of them for hundreds of miles. Although most huge boulders were transported only short distances from their original locations, erratics, by definition, were deposited in very unlikely places far from their points of origin. If the geological point of origin of an erratic can be ascertained, its location can be used to trace glacial movements. The last glaciation of New England produced the "Mount Ascutney Train," which consists of a great number of identifiable boulders that were moved from Mount Ascutney in southeastern Vermont into Massachusetts.

5. A serpent kame of unconsolidated till being mined near Hilldale Avenue in Haverhill, Massachusetts, during the first part of this century. These men are in the process of sorting out the sand, gravel, and boulders that collected between the melting edges of two glaciers.

6. Two excursionists, perhaps a father and son, looking out over the islands formed by drumlins near Bar Harbor, Maine. Drumlins are usually small, smooth, tear-shaped hills that are highest at the rounded edge and lose elevation as they slope down and taper off to a tip. The length of a drumlin is often twice its width, and the orientation of this elongated shape can also be used to track the glacier's path: a drumlin's long axis is parallel to the glacier's direction of movement. Drumlins can occur singly or in groups called swarms. Peters Hill in the Arnold Arboretum is one of more than a hundred drumlins, including many of the Boston Harbor islands, in the Boston Basin. Although geologists agree that drumlins are shaped by glacial movement, they are still debating about their formation. Some geologists think that drumlins are caused by the erosion of glacial drift, while others think they occur when a clayey portion of the glacier's debris adheres to an obstacle in its path.

The composition of the community of plants that assembled in the glacier's immediate wake exists nowhere on earth today. However, we can reconstruct the vegetational history of the landscape in our imagination or with computer models based on paleoecological research that has disclosed the amounts and kinds of pollen deposited over thousands of years in core samples taken from bottom sediments of lakes and ponds or from bogs. Like fossilized plants, pollen grains are durable bits of evidence that can tell us which plants once grew in a given area.

The pollen evidence indicates that the first plants to return were tundra plants—low-growing, ground-hugging plants, such as grasses, sedges, willows, alders, dwarf birches, and small flowering herbs that probably grew interspersed with mosses and lichens. Made up of only a few species, this new flora existed in a precarious balance with the environment. The Arnold Arboretum, like the rest of New England, was covered with a close-cropped mat of stunted and dwarfed trees and shrubs. With tundra plants covering the landscape, the view from Peters Hill would have been unobstructed in all directions. This band of tundra appeared at different times in the Northeast. Arriving first in deglaciated southern areas, it moved in tandem with the retreating ice, taking years to work its way northward. Some of this tundra vegetation still persists on New England mountain tops. Plants that occur in the far north can also be found in the alpine zone of the Presidential Range in the White Mountains and on Maine's Mount Katahdin.

7. Cones of the three species of spruce in New England from the Arnold Arboretum's herbarium. The two cones at the top of the illustration are from a red spruce (*Picea rubens*). Typically, the cones of red spruce are from one and one-half to two inches long. When they are closed, they are narrow, egg-shaped, and pointed. The cones open in fall and usually remain attached to the branchlet for almost a year. Their brown scales have toothed or rough margins. The cone at the bottom left is from a black spruce (*P. mariana*). The cones of black spruce are approximately one inch long, and they are the smallest and the most rounded of the three. The scales are a dull purplish brown, and their margins are very roughly toothed; the edge of each scale looks chewed. The remaining cone is from a white spruce (*P. glauca*). When closed, they are about two inches long, slender, and cylindrical. The light-brown scales are smooth-edged and are often indented. The cones of white spruce detach from the tree soon after they shed their seeds in the fall.

Taiga: Forests of Spruce, Cedar, Larch, and Jack Pine

About 12,500 years ago, the emerging barren uplands and the lowland tundra, checkered by glacial remnants, began to support the growth of larger trees. Cold-adapted cone-bearing plants, which had proved successful at living close to the margins of the great ice sheets of the Pleistocene epoch, appeared first, because most of eastern North America that had not been covered by ice or by a narrow belt of tundra had been covered by a forest of Boreal, or northern, cold-tolerant conifers. (The term Boreal—from Boreas, the god of the north wind in Greek mythology—designates one of the three major ecological life zones in the Northern Hemisphere, the other two being the Temperate and the Tropical.)

As spruce and pine first invaded the tundra, they created a parkland environment—a broad, grassy plain with scattered stands of trees. Pollen samples indicate that black, red, and white spruce were some of the first conifers to return. All three were adept at reforestation. Their seeds were light, winged, and easily dispersed by the wind; they grew rapidly and began to produce seeds while relatively young. Black spruce (*Picea mariana*), the most dominant of the three species, begins forming cones in its third year of growth and is also able to reproduce by "layering," which occurs when lower branches become partly covered by soil or moss and take root, thereby forming new, independent trees. Black spruce succeeds best on wet land, and the abundance of ponds and bogs left behind by the glaciers offered a wide variety of likely new sites. White spruce (*P. glauca*) also prefers wet land, and it grows faster than either black spruce or red spruce, but its life span is shorter than those of the other two spruces. Red spruce (*P. rubens*) can tolerate much drier conditions than the other two. All three would eventually grow in pure stands (acre after acre of the same species), intermingled with one another, or side by side with trees of unrelated species.

Two species of pine grew on land unfavorable to the growth of spruces. Jack pine (*Pinus banksiana*) can grow on nearly pure sand. A prolific tree, it can bear cones as early as its third year. Pitch pine (*P. rigida*) also favors dry conditions, can live on nearly sterile soil, and produces cones in its third or fourth year. As the tundra was slowly replaced, these conifers and a few deciduous plants made up New England's forest cover. The blazing colors of autumn, along with the soft tints of the spring flowers of many of the broadleaf trees, were absent from what

8. The unopened cones of a black spruce (*Picea mariana*) can persist on the tree for four or five years. Although some cones will open during winter to shed their seeds, most will remain closed until a fire stimulates them to release all of their seeds at once.

9. The white spruce (*Picea glauca*) dominates areas in northern New England where the soils are deep, moist, and well drained. Stands of white spruce are common in northernmost Vermont and New Hampshire and north of Casco Bay in Maine. It is a widely distributed tree in Canada, occurring in every province from Newfoundland to the Yukon Territory and from sea level to the northern limit of trees. In addition to its distribution in northern New England, this spruce crosses the Canadian border into the United States in northern Minnesota and Wisconsin, in central Michigan, and in northeastern New York. The white spruce attains a height of between forty and and eighty feet in New England, but trees 100 to 120 feet tall are common in other parts of its range.

would one day become the landscape of the Arnold Arboretum.

However desolate and forbidding the land, the presence of plants enabled a variety of herbivores to survive. In the cold and stormy climate of the tundra, the woolly mammoth, with its strong, pillarlike legs supported by broad feet that allowed it to move about on boggy land, grazed in solitude on grasses, arctic willows, and lichens. South of the narrow belt of tundra habitat, where the windswept landscape was beginning to dry out, leaf litter and humus or organic matter had begun to accumulate in the lee of small obstructions and in depressions. Before long, in such places, herds of mastodons browsed on the emerging coniferous forest. The pursuit of game must have outweighed any hesitation men and women had about entering the postglacial environment, for archeologists date the coming of a group of people—now called the Paleo-Indians—to New England around 12,500 years ago, soon after the flora could support the huge, now extinct herbivores.

To supplement their diet of plants, small mammals, and birds, Paleo-Indians sought not only mammoths, mastodons, huge bears, and giant beavers but other large grazing or browsing animals, such as bison, elk, moose, and musk oxen. By comparison with the dense, more stable coniferous forests to the south, the evolving forests of New England may have provided better hunting grounds for the small bands of people who could enjoy days of feasting from the success of bringing down one of the large game animals. Our fascination with the mysterious extinctions of the mammoths and the mastodons often overshadows our knowledge that the Paleo-Indians usually relied on a more dependable diet of plants. Perhaps these early people gathered food on the hills and in the valleys of today's Arboretum or stalked their game by the Arboretum's streams and ponds, but the land was still inhospitable, and they left us no traces of their passage.

A unique, fluted projectile point, found only at a few scattered riverine sites in New England, identifies the ancient culture of these people. Mounted on lances or on throwing spears, this versatile hunting point served a multitude of purposes and was a major component of the tool kit of the Paleo-Indians. Although the absence of grinding stones indicates that they did not count on reliable or abundant plant resources to process into meal or grain, other cutting, scraping, and boring tools chipped from stone enabled them to work in wood, bone, and leather. Objects created from these less durable materials—baskets to carry their goods, snowshoes for

10. The jack pine (*Pinus banksiana*), one of the most northern of all pines, was named in honor of Sir Joseph Banks (1743–1820) by a colleague, the English botanist Aylmer Bourke Lambert (1761–1842). Banks had explored and collected plants in Newfoundland and Labrador during 1766 and 1767, and he later accompanied Captain James Cook on the *Endeavour* on the first of his around-the-world voyages. Lambert made pines his specialty, and he published his *Description of the Genus Pinus* in 1803. Jack pines are slow-growing, short-lived, small to medium-sized trees. Grown in the open, they are more more likely to have a short, twisted trunk than a straight one. This old specimen, photographed in the Arnold Arboretum's conifer collection, has this species' typical open crown, slender spreading branches that turn upward at the tips, and curved reddish-brown trunk. The jack pine and the red pine (*P. resinosa*) are the only two-needled pines in New England. The ranges of these two conifers overlap, and both grow in sandy soils, but they are very different in the length and shape of their needles. The needles of jack pine are stout and twisted and less than two inches long. The red pine has needles that are slender, straight, and needle-shaped and that are twice as long as those of the jack pine.

11. Pitch pines (*Pinus rigida*) with an undergrowth of scrub oak (*Quercus ilicifolia*) on Cape Cod, Massachusetts. Pitch pine dominated the Cape's woodlands a century ago, but a mixed-oak association, consisting of black, white, and red oak as well as sassafras and red maple, is slowly replacing the pitch pines where fire and cutting have been minimized.

winter travel and hunting, hides for clothing, and bark- or skin-covered tree limbs used for shelter—have all disappeared. Only their beautifully crafted stone artifacts remain.

As more and more land was freed from the ice, plants and animals extended their ranges northward. With increasingly larger hunting and gathering areas, the Paleo-Indians perfected different strategies and hunting methods and often used fire to control naturally occur-ring environmental change. Fires intentionally set to drive herds of prey animals or to stimulate plant growth altered the landscape to the advantage of these people.

For about two thousand years, the climate remained stable, and conifers continued to dominate the landscape. A few cold-tolerant deciduous plants, such as alders, birches, poplars, and arctic willows, grew along with the conifers. Alders, whose bark provides sustenance and whose stripped branches provide building material for today's beavers, often grow, as every trout-fishing enthusiast knows, in dense thickets along the margins of streams and rivers and at the edges of ponds and lakes. Melting ice created more streams and rivers, more water-ways on which the now extinct giant beaver could travel and inadvertently spread the alder's seeds when felling and transporting its branches. Birch, too, grew in profusion. One pound of the nutlets of white or paper birch (*Betula papyrifera*) can contain more than a million seeds. Light and easily dispersed by the wind, these seeds can be transported great distances from the parent tree. Arctic willow (*Salix arctica*), a dwarf, prostrate species, had its own specialized habitat; it colonized gravelly moraines with a dense carpetlike cover.

A dramatic change occurred about 9500 years ago. The climate became first wetter and warmer, then drier and even warmer. Known as a thermal maximum, this period of warming lasted about 3000 years. In response to this change, the established plants of the spruce parklands gave way to a vegetation of temperate climates, one of deciduous hardwoods and pines. Unlike the coniferous forest that it replaced, this new forest was made up of a great variety of food-rich species. The arrival of beeches, hickories, oaks, pines, and hemlocks increased the availability of substantial and dependable food resources in the Northeast, and the Paleo-Indians devised more complex subsistence patterns to utilize these new resources.

The temperate hardwoods and pines that began to return to New England had been displaced far to the south and west or had survived in isolated remnant populations scattered throughout the Boreal Forest's broad "temporary" southern range. Many deciduous species, long thought by paleobotanists to have retreated to the southern Appalachians during the Pleistocene epoch, survived only in very small sheltered locations in those mountains. Most now are thought to have survived in sparsely populated refugia (singular, *refugium,* an area of relatively unaltered climate during a period of glaciation) deep in the Southwest or far out on the then-exposed continental shelf. As these Temperate Zone plants again pushed northward, some species leapfrogging others, the coniferous forest moved even farther north along with the colder Boreal climate.

Many of the deciduous (or broadleaf) trees in this group are "mast" species, trees that produce large quantities of edible seeds on a cyclical basis. At two- to three-year intervals, American beech (*Fagus grandifolia*) produces large crops of seeds enclosed in woody burs. Depending upon the species, hickory trees produce either bitter or sweet nuts at intervals of one to four years. The common names used for *Carya cordiformis* and *C. glabra,* bitternut hickory and pignut hickory, leave no doubt about the taste of their nuts, but, every other year, two to three bushels of delicious nuts can be harvested from one mature shagbark hickory (*C. ovata*). Among the oaks, longer intervals usually occur between years when heavy acorn crops are produced. This association of different types of trees, each with its own cycle of nut production, insured that at least some food was available during every fall harvest season.

Small mammals and birds benefited from a greater variety of nut-producing deciduous trees and were important agents of seed dispersal for those species. Even though acorns and hickory nuts are round enough to roll a short distance from the tree, it is likely that many of these heavy seeds and nuts were carried away from the parent tree by animals foraging for food. The Paleo-Indians' selection of foods that suited their tastes and needs resulted in the dispersal of some species over even greater distances. Timing their seasonal rounds to include forays to productive or convenient collecting areas, they carried away with them great quantities of seeds and nuts. During their extended journeys, some seeds surely escaped the grinding stone or were lost during the leaching process that was employed to wash away toxic tannins, and groves or individual trees thus became established at new locations.

Climatic warming, the decrease in the numbers of large game animals and in the extent of the parkland habitat in which they roamed, the emerging deciduous forest with its abundance of food plants and higher population of small animals—all of these factors were reflected in a change in the Paleo-Indian culture. It is unclear whether a migration of people, or a diffusion of ideas and tools, or a combination of the two reshaped or replaced the established culture. Never present in great numbers, the Paleo-Indians seem to have abandoned New England. Better adapted to hunting large animals and to living in a colder climate, this small population may have either followed the retreating spruce parkland northward or become intermingled with the new peoples that began to arrive from the south and west.

Warming temperatures, along with a greater diversity in plants and animals and a growing human population, typify the entire Archaic time frame, a cultural era that lasted about 6000 years, from 9000 to 3000 years B.P. ("before the present"), twice as long as the Paleo-Indian Period.

Because their stone artifacts are not abundant, little is known about the very earliest Archaic Indians; but the pieces that have been found vary greatly in style and type from those of their Paleo-Indian predecessors and suggest a multitude of new uses. Like the Paleo-Indians, the men and women who entered this area between 9000 and 8000 years B.P. were pioneers; they were infiltrating into a place either recently or only sparsely inhabited and one in which the landscape itself was undergoing critical

12. American beech (*Fagus grandifolia*) ordinarily begins producing nuts when the tree reaches the age of forty years. By the time a tree is sixty years old, it produces large quantities of beechnuts at two- to three-year intervals. Cross-pollination is usually necessary for seed production because, although male and female flowers occur on the same tree, beeches are usually self-sterile. The beechnuts mature in one season and begin to ripen in late September. The first hard frost causes the burs to open and shed their nuts. Some of the opened burs will remain on the tree over the winter, but most will fall after their seeds have been shed. Seeds and husks continue to fall for several weeks, until the ground under the tree is littered with a combination of small, prickly burs and shiny, triangular, sweet, edible nuts that are no larger than a fingertip. American farmers, following the age-old custom of allowing animals to forage for pannage, once turned their hogs loose in the forest to feed on beechnuts. The great flocks of passenger pigeons also once relied on beechnuts: during the fall migration, thousands of these birds would alight in beech groves to feed on their mast. Beechnuts are a source of food for pheasants, grouse, squirrels, raccoons, and deer. Bear, too, eat beechnuts, and occasionally they leave long claw marks inscribed in the smooth, gray bark of beech trunks.

changes. Through the traditions and technologies of their culture, the people of the Early Archaic Period took advantage of the diversity of the changing deciduous–coniferous forest and were able to draw subsistence not only from the animals that populated the forest but increasingly from the plants of the forest itself.

With plants and animals more plentiful, the need to travel great distances in search of food was diminished. The Archaic Indians found choice hunting and gathering areas along the shores of estuaries, and they established living sites at these locations. Although they still led a migratory existence, they followed a loosely constructed round of hunting and gathering in more familiar territories. Bifacially chipped celts and adzes—large chopping and digging stones used for gathering roots and tubers—and anvil stones made for processing nuts indicate the development of new methods of food preparation and preservation.

The warming trend continued. By 6000 years B.P., during the middle part of the Archaic Period, New England was even warmer and drier than it is today, and a temperate deciduous forest covered the land. The long and complex evolution of New England forests was nearing an unsteady equilibrium, and most of the species that we know today were present. Seasonal migrations of birds and fish were set in modern patterns, and people settled along the borders of rivers, meadows, and marshes to take advantage of spring spawning runs and the flyways used semiannually by migrating birds.

Evidence suggests that it was during this era, the Middle Archaic Period, that men and women first spent extended periods of time on the land we now know as the Arnold Arboretum. The Arboretum's landscape, like the rest of New England's, had been dominated by different groups of plants at different times. Once the ice had receded, it had taken more than 8000 years of northward migration to produce the meeting of plants and people that occurred on the Arboretum's lands during the Middle Archaic Period. Eight projectile points identified from the Middle Archaic Period have been found in the Arboretum. It was probably the first time that this landscape could support a community of animals, plants, and fish that could provide enough variety to attract and support a small human population. What did the landscape of the Arboretum look like when men and women first built shelters from saplings and bark in the clearings among its trees? From a vantage point high on Peters Hill, where even today the individual plants spread out below are hard to identify, it would look much the same as it does at present—an almost continuous canopy of forest cover made up of deciduous and coniferous trees. Because of the warming trend, the Archaic Indians visiting this site could select the plants they needed from a forest that would look very similar to one growing just

13. The nut, with its sharp ridges, and, below it, the half-inch-thick husk of the shagbark hickory (*Carya ovata*) appear on the left. The husks of the shagbark split open to their base to reveal the large, finely flavored, thin-shelled kernels. The group of three fruits on the right are those of the pignut hickory (*C. glabra*). The nuts are small and rounded and enclosed in thin leathery husks that are hard to crack. The husks usually split open only to the middle, and the taste of the kernel is strong, bitter, and "fit only for pigs." The single kernel at the top represents the bitternut hickory (*C. cordiformis*). The meat of this nut is oily and extremely bitter. The nuts were once pressed to extract the oil, which was used by the early settlers as a remedy for rheumatism. They also burned the oil in their lamps.

south of New England today. The broadleaf trees that grew on the land that would become the Arnold Arboretum included species of oak (*Quercus*), elm (*Ulmus*), beech (*Fagus*), ash (*Fraxinus*), hickory (*Carya*), basswood (*Tilia*), and maple (*Acer*). The many species of oaks and the two species of elms were early arrivals, while the different maples and hickories appeared later. The American chestnut (*Castanea dentata*) was not to be found; it would take an additional 2000 to 3000 years for this tree to enter the New England flora. While some spruces and larches remained at higher elevations, the dominant conifers were white pines (*Pinus strobus*) and hemlocks (*Tsuga canadensis*). Both of these trees had expanded their ranges north from eastern Coastal Plain refugia, both arriving in the Northeast at about the same time. Because of the warmer temperatures that prevailed during this era, these two conifers grew over a much greater area, including the more mountainous regions of New England, than they do today.

Perhaps the first small group of people that camped on the Arboretum's lands may have been following a spring spawning run of anadromous fish, such as shad, salmon, or herring. The Northeast's first boat builders, these explorers could have easily reached the Arboretum by dugout canoe. Today, a leisurely walk of two to three hours will take you from Boston's waterfront to the Arboretum, a distance of about four miles, if you follow the Emerald Necklace, the chain of Boston parks designed by Frederick Law Olmsted. While it is no longer possible to make the trip entirely by water, it was once the easiest mode of travel. The inland journey would have begun on the area's largest river, a river once known as the Massachuset, but more recently known as the Charles. This major waterway emptied into a large estuary that extended far out into Massachusetts Bay. About three miles inland, a smaller river, our Muddy River, flowed into the Charles. This river wound its way across the flat bottom land of the Boston Basin. A tributary brook, named the Stony River by the area's later settlers, entered the Charles from the south. This waterway, now called Stony Brook, rises in the Dedham Highlands, and it once passed by the southern edge of the land that would become the Arnold Arboretum, where an even smaller stream joined it. In the Arboretum, Sawmill Brook, renamed Bussey Brook after the founding of the Arboretum, flowed through the valley lying between Hemlock Hill and Bussey Hill and emptied into Stony Brook. This serpentine route from the sea to the Arboretum presented few obstacles. The land was relatively flat, and there were no falls that required portages

or overland detours—difficult passages for the heavy dugout craft—and the journey from the coast may have taken less than a day. Stony Brook, a critical link in the route, was diverted underground during the last century in an attempt to improve the drainage of the area. Today, because of further engineering "improvements," the Arboretum's Bussey Brook, even in the spring, carries only a small flow of water, much less than is needed for travel by canoe.

Groups of Indians continued to visit the Arboretum throughout the remainder of the Archaic Period, camping for a few days or weeks to hunt, fish, and gather food. Thirty-eight artifacts dating from the Late Archaic Period (5000–3000 B.P.) have been found at several locations in the Arboretum. These projectile points, drills, and scrapers provide evidence of their domestic chores and indicate recurring visits to preferred areas. No longer home to mastodon or mammoth, the rich woodland that included the Arboretum lands harbored deer and smaller game along with the plant foods the Archaic Indians sought. They used trees for shelter, fuel, and tools, drawing on generations of knowledge garnered about the special qualities each plant possessed that made it suitable for making the various articles they required. More solitary in their hunting practices than their predecessors, Archaic Indians had diversified hunting techniques and caught small game with traps and snares they made using strong, supple tree limbs and saplings. Different plant species were available to them, depending upon where they lived, and cord for their hunting devices and for fishing nets was fashioned either from the pliable roots or from the inner bark of trees. These men and women had learned which nuts, fruits, and berries needed processing to remove toxins and how to store seeds, roots, and nuts that could be ground or milled. They boiled, broiled, or roasted food over small, intensely hot fires. They knew which twigs and bark would burn in the rain and which branches would produce a quick, spark-free, and smokeless fire. Lacking ceramic and metal vessels, they cooked either directly on the fire or by plunging heated "fire stones" into water held in finely woven baskets, soapstone bowls, or bark containers. With axes, adzes, wedges, and pounding stones, they shaped bowls from burls, made dishes from bark, and processed plant fibers into gathering baskets or storage containers.

One of the village sites in the Arboretum that was used many different times is located on the north side of Bussey Brook. Here, near the center of the present-day Arboretum, there is a slight rocky ledge, the upper part of which even today is carpeted with lowbush blueberries

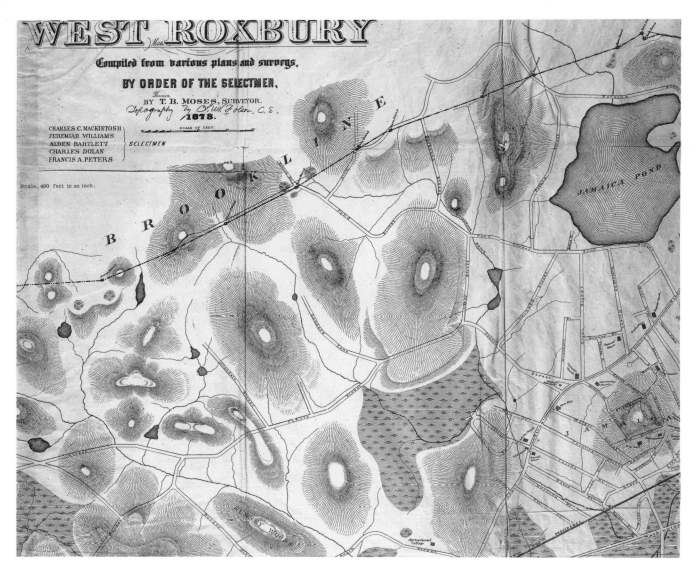

14. This map of West Roxbury, dated one year after the founding of the Arnold Arboretum, shows Harvard College's newly built Agricultural College, the Bussey Institution, at the bottom center of the photograph. The initial 135 acres of the Bussey property that had just been transferred by Harvard from Bussey Institution holdings to the Arnold Arboretum occupied the area bounded on the west by Bussey Street, on the north by Centre Street, on the south by South Street, and on the east by the soon to be constructed Arborway. The hill labeled Bussey Woods would become known by the name Hemlock Hill, and the section of the unlabeled brook, known as Sawmill Brook, that traversed its edge and flowed south through the Arnold Arboretum into Stony Brook, would become Bussey Brook. Just east of the brook is the unlabeled summit of what would become Bussey Hill.

15. This projectile point, from the Late Archaic Period, is made of white quartz and is of a type known as a "Squibnocket triangle." One hundred thirty-six Native American artifacts, including pounding stones, perforators, edge tools, and abrading stones, as well as chipping waste and tool fragments, have been found on the Arnold Arboretum's grounds. Most have been discovered at the surface of the ground in areas where cultivation has been intense, such as the land formerly occupied by the shrub collection, or in the former planting beds at the Bussey Institution. Others have been found in soil disturbed by the planting of trees and shrubs

and a remnant of the native forest of beech, birch, oak, and pine. This natural woodland extends to Centre Street, the northern border of the Arboretum. Ledges of conglomerate rock, called Roxbury puddingstone, occur on the higher land near the street. At the southern end of these woods, an intermittent spring flows towards Bussey Brook. The small plateau between the spring and the brook made an excellent village site. Being on level ground near a navigable stream, having fresh drinking water nearby, and providing a vantage point from which to see up and down the valley, it was a perfect place to camp. In the early spring, while snow still covered the

ground under the hemlocks on the north side of the hill, the sun warmed this small valley. Shaded from the summer heat by open oak or mixed woods and protected from the winter winds, the site offered shelter throughout the seasons. An abundance of Native American artifacts found here at the Spring Brook site by the Arboretum staff attests to the enduring appeal this place held over the centuries.

Less than three thousand years remained before Native Americans would come in contact with European society. Archeologists have documented that a great diversification occurred within the native cultures during this period. Many different schemes and systems are used to describe and classify the variety of cultures that developed in the Woodland Period, the name for the period that covers the final stage in prehistoric eastern North America before European settlement. Geographic areas, each with a unique environment, help to delineate the many cultural patterns that evolved among the native peoples during this time.

New subsistence patterns and social adaptations developed during the Woodland Period. The construction of semipermanent houses and villages changed daily life. Along with the forest, the New England coastline was reaching stabilization. Now that the coastline's long recovery from the effects of glaciation was almost complete, shellfish beds became established. Villages appeared along the coast as the Woodland Indians increased their exploitation of these shellfish beds and rich coastal fishing areas. The climate was more like that of today, the warming trend having been reversed. The forest settled into its present composition, with a discernible difference between the floras of northern and southern New England. The lifestyles of the Indians that inhabited each area differed, and this difference in the management and selection of resources would last beyond the arrival of European explorers and colonists.

The winter's heavier snows made the interior villages that had been occupied by previous inhabitants less useful to the Woodland Indians. The smaller number of artifacts from this period that have been found on Arboretum soil testify to this change. A growing reliance on marine fisheries made coastal sites more attractive, and a location like the Arboretum's would have been used as an easily accessible fall and winter hunting ground rather than a more permanent village site.

During the Late Woodland Period, the people of the Northeast added pottery and horticulture to their cultural traditions. Not only were new plants introduced into the area from other regions but familiar ones were prepared

16. This photograph of an outcrop of Roxbury puddingstone was taken near the "Spring Brook Village" site, an area frequently visited by small groups of people as early as the fourth millennium B.C.

in different ways. The use of pottery and the practice of horticulture were not adopted simultaneously; in both northern and southern New England, the art of making ceramic vessels preceded the art of growing plants. Southern New England lay closer to the source of introduction of both skills, and this area was better suited for gardening. Spending summers in coastal villages or in river valleys, where they had cleared fields for planting, allowed the men to take advantage of fishing or shellfish harvesting and enabled the women to gather plants and to tend gardens of corn, beans, sunflowers, and squash. Storage pits for wild and cultivated food products became important: although groups of families traveled in fall and winter to temporary camps used for nut harvesting and hunting, they now spent longer times at one location than their predecessors had done. The new cultivated plants—the corn, beans, and squashes—were easily stored, and they helped the people survive the winter season without extended travel in search of additional food to be collected from the wild. During this era, the native people that lived in southern New England made

spring and fall base camps along large streams, often at a waterfall or at the head of an estuary—the very kinds of places that would later attract settlement by European colonists for very different reasons. In northern New England, the technology of pot making was adopted, but the dense woods and short summers resulted in only marginal success with horticulture. Without the additional duty of caring for many cultivated plants, these men and women were free to structure their lives to follow more closely a yearly round that featured travel to hunting, fishing, and gathering grounds.

"Newe Founde Lande"

Throughout the East, the Native Americans who first encountered Europeans were the Woodland Indians. These were the people whom European fishermen sighted and traded with, and whom French, Portuguese, and English explorers encountered and described as they were searching along the northeastern coast for an alter-

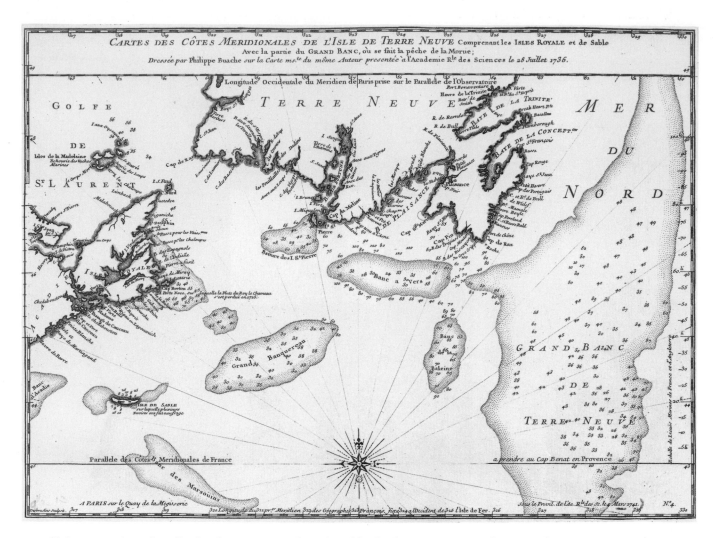

CARTES DES CÔTES MERIDIONALES DE L'ISLE DE TERRE NEUVE Comprenant les ISLES ROYALE et de Sable Avec la partie du GRAND BANC, où se fait la pêche de la Morue; Dressée par Philippe Buache sur la Carte ms.^{te} du même Auteur présentée à l'Academie R.^{le} des Sciences le 28 Juillet 1736.

17. Off the coasts of Newfoundland and Nova Scotia, where the cold Labrador Current meets the warmer Gulf Stream, lie the great fishing areas known since John Cabot's time as the Grand Banks. The Grand Banks are made up of a number of separate areas or banks; the Grand, Green, and St. Pierre banks are the three most important fishing grounds.

native trade route to Asia. It was economic gain rather than scientific curiosity that motivated exploration. On or about May 20, 1497, John Cabot, with the backing of merchants in Bristol, England, merchants, set sail in the *Matthew* on a voyage he hoped would shorten the trade route to "Cathay." Instead, the voyage resulted in the discovery of "the newe founde lande."

After the vast North American continent had been discovered by Europeans, it was for many years the riches of the offshore waters, rather than the land itself, that lured succeeding visitors to the northeastern coast. The Grand Banks, once one of the most productive fishing grounds for cod in the world, drew fishermen like a mag-

net. During the early sixteenth century, while exploration continued along the northeastern coast, Norman, Basque, Breton, and Portuguese fishing fleets plied these coastal waters in ever increasing numbers. The voyage from Europe could take as little as twenty-one days or as much as five weeks, but—like today's modern, self-contained Japanese and Russian trawlers—the earliest fishing boats from Europe, especially those of the Portuguese, with their abundant supplies of salt, needed no landfall; the catch was processed on board, and the ships quickly returned to home port.

At the same time, European preoccupation with the fashion of gentlemen's felt hats put increased pressures

Tab. III

B C a

f g h i

Pinus Banksiana

Fer.d Bauer del.   Wamer sculp.

Plate 1.   The jack pine (*Pinus banksiana*), one of the most northern of all pines, was named in honor of Sir Joseph Banks (1743–1820) by a colleague, the English botanist Aylmer Bourke Lambert (1761–1842). Banks had explored and collected plants in Newfoundland and Labrador during 1766 and 1767, and he later accompanied Captain James Cook on the *Endeavour* on the first of his around-the-world voyages. Lambert made pines his specialty, and he published his *Description of the Genus Pinus* in 1803.

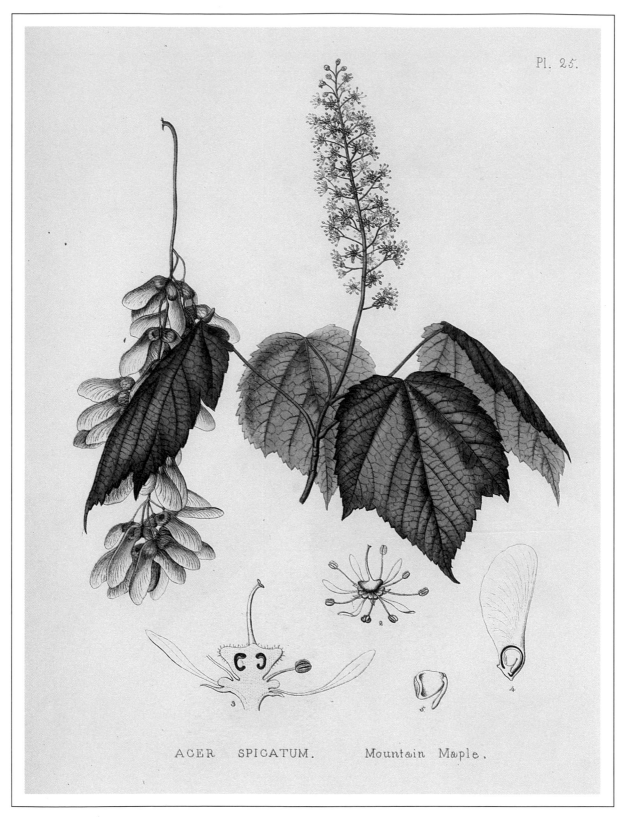

Pl. 25.

ACER SPICATUM. Mountain Maple.

Plate 2. This illustration of the mountain maple (*Acer spicatum*) shows the tree's narrow, long-stemmed, and many-flowered upright raceme, to which the Latin epithet *spicatum* ("spikelike") refers. The pale yellowish flowers appear when the leaves are fully grown. In the fall, the winged fruits (which are three-quarters of an inch long) often turn a brilliant red before fading to a yellow or a pinkish brown. The mountain maple, an understory tree, is the smallest of the eastern maples. It very seldom reaches a height of twenty-five feet. This plate, by Isaac Sprague, is one of a few that were prepared to accompany a report on the forest trees of North America by Asa Gray.

Plate 3. This illustration of the highbush blueberry, *Vaccinium corymbosum,* is one of 170 beautifully colored plates published between the years 1823 and 1825 in *Dendrologia Britannica, or Trees and Shrubs That Will Live in the Open Air of Britain Throughout the Year: A Work Useful to Proprietors and Possessors of Estates, in Selecting Subjects for Planting Woods, Parks, and Shrubberies, and Also to All Persons Who Cultivate Trees and Shrubs.* A retired tradesman, the work's author, Peter William Watson, helped to found, lay out, and manage the Hull Botanic Garden in Yorkshire, England, which was established in 1812. The text that accompanies the plates in *Dendrologia Britannica* consists of very detailed and complete descriptions of native and exotic plants that Watson observed growing on the grounds of the botanic garden.

Tab. 160.

Juglans nigra
Schwarze Wallnuß.

Plate 4. The black walnut (*Juglans nigra*) is characterized by its pinnately compound leaves and its edible nuts (technically, the cotyledons or "seed leaves"), which are gathered in the fall and then freed from the husk of the fruit that encloses them. Once the peculiar odor of a mature walnut husk has been experienced, it is not soon forgotten. Equally memorable is the brownish stain the husks impart to fingers, hands, and clothing, as well as to driveways and sidewalks, a stain that persists far longer than those who cultivate walnuts and those who merely gather their nuts would wish.

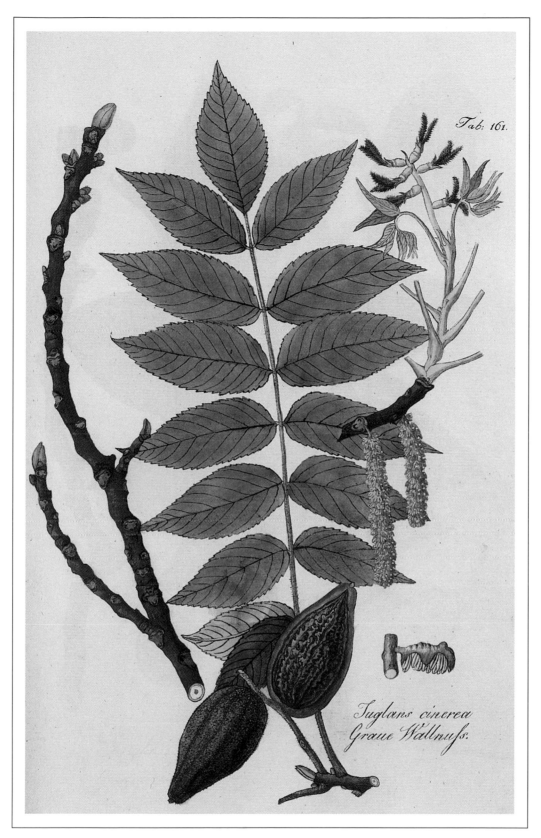

Tab: 161.

Juglans cinerea
Graue Wallnuß.

Plate 5.   Only two species of walnut occur in New England, the black walnut (*Juglans nigra*) and the species illustrated here, the butternut or so-called white walnut (*J. cinerea*). In addition to these two species, another four species of walnut (all of which have relatively limited ranges) occur in North America. Two are found in the southwestern states—Texas black walnut (*J. macrocarpa*) and Arizona walnut (*J. major*)—while the remaining two species—the California walnut (*J. californica*) and the Hinds walnut (*J. hindsii*)—are confined to California.

N 2586

Plate 6. According to Messrs. Whitley, Brame, and Milne, the three gentlemen who contributed the description of *Vaccinium macrocarpon* that accompanied this colored plate in *Curtis's Botanical Magazine* in 1825, "American Cranberries are larger and fairer to the eye than the European, and by some they are preferred in tarts and preserves; but in our opinion the taste of the English Cranberry is pleasanter than that of the American."

Plate 7. The dark green foliage of eastern arborvitae (*Thuja occidentalis*) is flat and lacy, and the branchlets overlap in fanlike sprays. The minute, scalelike leaves occur in pairs on opposite sides of the twig and, when crushed, are pungently aromatic.

Plate 8.   Sassafras (*Sassafras albidum*): *Top,* a rather idealized representation of the habit of sassafras that also includes the three leaf types that typically appear on mature trees. *Bottom,* botanical details of sassafras. Both illustrations are from the same work, *Plantae Selectae,* written by Christoph Jakob Trew (a German botanist and physician who practiced in Nuremberg), and both were drawn by the celebrated German botanical illustrator Georg Dionysius Ehret. The son of a market gardener, and as a young boy a gardener himself, Ehret learned the art of drawing plants, as well as the art of cultivating them, from his father. He traveled extensively in Europe, and a meeting with Linnaeus led to a commission to illustrate Linnaeus's *Hortus Cliffortianus.* Ehret is often thought of as an English painter, for he eventually settled down in England (marrying the sister-in-law of the famous plantsman Philip Miller), where his skill caught the attention of botanists and patrons and where he went on to produce some of his greatest works.

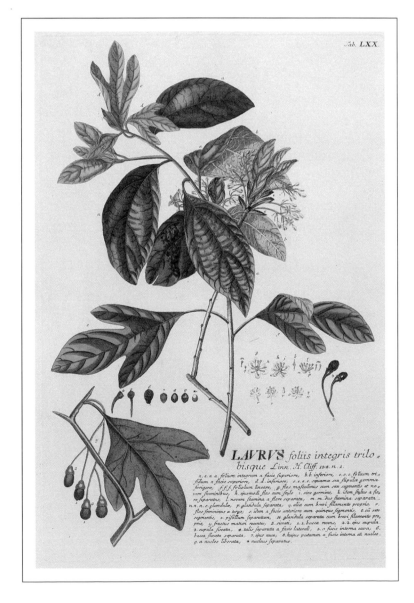

on the fur trade. When the insatiable demands for beaver pelts (the raw material used by furriers to make the hats) caused traders to turn to North America, the impact it made on the Woodland Indians of northern New England was devastating. Their seasonal round of hunting and fishing was disrupted as they spent more time and energy trapping small game and storing and transporting pelts to trade for kettles, knives, hatchets, bells, cloth, and clothing. Gardening, a risky and tenuous experiment in the north, almost completely disappeared as Indian women spent large amounts of time processing more and more beaver, martin, otter, mink, and muskrat pelts rather than coaxing produce from their garden plots.

As regular contact grew—marred by insensitivity on the part of the explorers, by misunderstanding on the part of the native inhabitants, and by the spread of disease between them and the fishermen and fur traders from Europe—the balance between the Woodland Indians and their environment shifted. In the Northeast, typhoid fever, diphtheria, measles, chicken pox, whooping cough, tuberculosis, and other European diseases killed thousands of the native people before they had even laid eyes on the white men. The Woodland Indians, who had once hunted only for food and clothing, began to hunt for material gain, and overexploitation of game, coupled with a decline in the limited success they had had with horticulture, caused starvation and death.

Information about New England's flora, fauna, and people that was brought back to Europe in the journals, diaries, and ship's logs of the sixteenth-century explorers

18. By the late sixteenth century, as the fishing industry expanded down the northeastern coast of North America, the more economical method of "dry fishing" became common practice. This curing process required only small amounts of expensive salt, but it required a base on shore to land where the lightly salted, split cod could be laid out on spruce-bough platforms, or flakes, to dry slowly in the sun. This illustration is taken from Henri Louis Duhamel du Monceau's *Traite general des peches,* which was published in Paris between the years 1769 and 1782.

described a society reacting to the onslaught of European culture. These early accounts provided the Old World inhabitants with an introduction to the names, faces, language, and lands of the people of the Northeast and paved the way for the successful colonization by Europeans that followed in the next century. Later, more complete descriptions of Native American settlements, tools, gardens, boats, chores, and leisure pursuits—the common realities of their daily life—were recorded by curious interlopers of various sorts. These people, who more often came to stay rather than to hunt and fish and return home, accelerated the pace of change in the native people's 12,000-year-old heritage. Because the Native Americans had no written language of their own, their story was revealed to us through observations made by missionaries, soldiers, and political leaders—people whose cultural (and especially religious) outlook often biased their narratives. As the practice of native crafts diminished and the adoption of European economic values increased, these accounts came to contain mere glimpses of precontact life and a sketchy, prejudiced record of colonization.

What the Europeans viewed as a simple existence, whether it was the lifestyle of the hunter-gatherers of the north or of the horticulturists of southern New England, was really a complex set of activities based on decisions that utilized the wide variety of natural resources that were available. The kinship systems, concepts of ownership, division of labor, seasonal rounds, and subsistence patterns of Native Americans were developed to take advantage of the cycle of seasons, the quality and quantity of marine and freshwater life, and the plant and animal species that occurred in the different climates, terrains, and forest types.

Forest Tapestry: Overlapping Patterns

While many plant species can be found growing together throughout New England, a species common in one climatic zone often exists with more limited success in warmer or colder locations and, although these plants are an important part of the forest in such locations, they are found in much more limited numbers. With the multitude of species and their associations, it is the abundance of the dominant trees that defines major forest types and that once set the human cultural boundaries.

The land north of an imaginary line extending from northwestern Connecticut to the coastline of southern Maine supports two distinct forest types. In the far north,

the Boreal Forest covers the land; south of the Boreal Forest and extending south as far as the line is the Hemlock–White Pine–Northern Hardwood region. Forming a broad swath 500 miles wide across the North American continent, most of the Boreal Forest region occurs in Canada, but in the east it ranges into New York and into the mountains and northern parts of New England.

The Beothuk tribe of Newfoundland, the Micmac of Nova Scotia and New Brunswick, and the Malecite and Passamaquoddy of eastern Canada and Maine lived surrounded by cool-climate trees and shrubs whose appearance changed little from season to season. The species in this forest can tolerate a growing season that lasts only three to four months, a climate that is cold and moist, and a deep snow cover that comes early and stays late. The trees that thrive under these conditions are some of the species that are recorded in pollen samples as being the first to enter the tundra after glacial retreat. Because six cone-bearers, all evergreen but one, constitute the majority of forest trees, it is also called the Northern Conifer Province. White and black spruce (*Picea glauca* and *P. mariana*), balsam fir (*Abies balsamea*), jack pine (*Pinus banksiana*), and eastern aborvitae (*Thuja occidentalis*) are evergreen. Only tamarack (*Larix laricina*) loses its soft, feathery needles, which turn a golden yellow before they fall. There are few large deciduous trees that can tolerate these conditions. Only two aspens, balsam poplar (*Populus balsamifera*) and quaking aspen (*P. tremuloides*), and the paper birch (*Betula papyrifera*) grow in great abundance. Their leaves turn translucent shades of yellow in the fall, creating pockets of sparkling brightness in the deep green forest. Likewise, in winter, the light-colored trunks of these three trees stand out against the dark boughs of the conifers.

Pierre Biard, a Jesuit missionary who spent eight months with the Micmac in 1611, called these people "the offspring of Boreas and the ice. . . . " Another visitor recorded that "their food is whatever they can get from the chase and from fishing; for they do not till the soil at all." They did not need to hoe or till. The plants they gathered for food and the trees that provided the materials for shelter, weapons for hunting, nets for fishing, boats for travel, and baskets for belongings were less diverse than those of the forest farther south, but these materials were used with great versatility. The Boreal Forest appears limited, harsh, and unforgiving; to the native people, it was a rich woodland that provided everything they required. They were able to take advantage of the wide range of resources that occur in an environment that appears to be most impressive in its simplicity.

The white or paper birch (*Betula papyrifera*), a major component of the transcontinental Boreal Forest, was the deciduous tree most often used in the technology of the northern Indians. It is the most widely distributed of the native birches and one of the few hardwoods found growing near timberline on New England's highest mountains. One of the five birches that grows in New England, *Betula papyrifera* is a short-lived, quick growing tree that often reaches a height of 80 feet. While the paper birch can sometimes be found on dry uplands, it occurs more often on moist slopes and on the borders of lakes and streams. Its waxy and lustrous white bark sets it apart from other birches, which have bark that ranges in color from the reddish brown or almost black of the sweet birch (*B. lenta*) to the pale, golden bronze of the yellow birch (*B. alleghaniensis*). It was the bark of the paper birch, rather than its wood, that was the prized raw material used by the Native Americans in a multitude of ways.

The adoption of cultural traditions was not always one-sided. The Indians' fascination with European metal objects was matched by the explorers' admiration of the natives' canoes. The dense stands of conifers that grew in the northern woods presented an obstacle to overland travel, and the Indians had developed a style of travel that depended upon the use of light, portable, bark-covered canoes. Skillfully made with stone tools for cutting, boring, and scraping, the design, construction, speed, and ease of handling of these craft immediately impressed the seafaring French and English.

Fortunately, we know much today about the old ways of canoe building, largely through the sketches, notes, and personal experiments of a man who, before the skill was lost, dedicated the better part of a lifetime to learning the handicrafts of the Native Americans. Edwin Tappan Adney, an Ohioan born in 1868, was an artist and naturalist who began his study when canoe makers still practiced a skill learned from their forefathers and bark canoes glided across the lakes and ran the rivers of North America. Adney's sketches and interviews, as well as the canoes he made himself, provide a detailed record of the methods and materials used in canoe making. For a contemporary account of one man's dedication to the ancient methods of the Indians, John McPhee, a master of documenting the objects and folkways of our age, fashions a tale as fine and well fitted as the canoes he admires in his 1975 essay *The Survival of the Bark Canoe.*

To make a canoe, large sheets of bark were sewn together. Each tree species has an identifiable outer covering—bark—that becomes more distinct as the tree matures. This covering is a living tissue—only the outermost layers are dead. As a tree grows, its trunk and limbs expand and grow in circumference, and the bark, its protective cover, grows at the same pace. Usually, as bark expands to accommodate the increasing girth of the trunk, its outer layer becomes deeply furrowed, ridged, or scaly. Only a few tree species have outer layers of bark that remain smooth. The bark of many species was used to make canoes, but the Indians determined that none was superior to that of the white or paper birch. The rough-surfaced bark of other trees was less suitable, and usually used only in emergencies or for temporary needs. Furrowed only at the base of older trees, the trunk of the paper birch is smooth from snow line to its largest lower limbs. The bark is resinous and flexible, and its grain encircles the tree, making it easy to remove. To select the best paper birch, tall, straight trees were examined closely for blemishes—only clear sheets of bark at least one-eighth of an inch thick were suitable.

In winter, the bark could be loosened only during a prolonged thaw or by applying heated water to the trunk, and summer bark, with its darker layers, was thought to be inferior. Consequently, it was usually in the spring, when the sap was rising, that the sheets of bark were peeled from the trunks of the chosen trees. If construction was not to begin immediately, the easily damaged sheets of bark were carefully rolled and submerged in a nearby stream or lake to insure that they would remain flexible enough to be worked.

During the winter, the canoe maker would have cut long notches in the trunks of spruce trees. *Picea*, the generic botanical name for the spruce, comes from the Latin *pix*, meaning pitch, and it refers to the resin produced by these conifers. Spring also would be the season to scrape the resin, or "spruce gum," from the scars made earlier in the year and to collect it from damaged or fallen trees. To make a canoe watertight, this sticky resin would be reconstituted by heating before it was applied to every seam.

Spruces supplied another essential material. The long, thin roots of the black spruce (*Picea mariana*) were used as thread to sew the seams and lash the canoe together. Tough, durable, and flexible, these roots grow close to the surface of the ground and are easily pulled from the soft, boggy soil where black spruce usually grows. Easily harvested, the roots were split with a sharp stone, coiled, and kept in water until needed. Two of the black spruce's other common names—bog spruce and swamp spruce—denote its ability to grow on floating islands of sphagnum moss, which it sometimes shares with tamarack

A Place in the Forest

19. Known also as the canoe, white, or paperbark birch, the paper birch (*Betula papyrifera*) is probably not only the most familiar birch but also one of the most well known trees in the northern United States and in Canada. There are about forty species of trees and shrubs belonging to the genus *Betula*. It is a circumboreal genus, and there are white-barked birches widely scattered throughout the colder regions of the Northern Hemisphere. *B. pendula*, also known as white birch, is found throughout Europe, Asia Minor, and Siberia. This species is the Old World equivalent of *B. papyrifera*. In 1838, J. C. Loudon, author of the multivolume *Arboretum et Fruticetum Britannicum*, reported on the many uses to which birch had been put across the cold north: "Sandals are also made of [birch], and thin pieces of the epidermis are placed between the soles of the shoe, or in the crown of the hat, as a defence against humidity. . . . The bark is also extensively used in Sweden and Norway, in roofing houses. The rafters are first covered with boards, on which plates of birch bark are laid in the same way as slates are in England; and the whole is covered with turf and earth." In 1810, in his *Sylva*, F. A. Michaux had made note of similar uses of birch bark that he had encountered in northeastern North America: "In Canada, and in the District of Maine, the country people place large pieces of it immediately below the shingles of the roof, to form a more impenetrable covering for their houses; baskets, boxes and portfolios are made of it, which are sometimes embroidered with silk of different colors; divided into very thin sheets, it forms a substitute for paper; and, placed between the soles of the shoe and in the crown of the hat, it is a defence against humidity."

(*Larix laricina*), whose roots were also a source of sewing material. The roots of both trees never come in contact with the soil at the bottom of the pond. Growth is slow under these conditions, and small, straight trees only a few feet tall are often very old. Tamarack prefers these wet conditions, but the black spruce is so adaptable that it can also grow on the thin soil of barren, wind-swept mountainsides.

The frame of the canoe—its thwarts, ribs, gunwales, and other structural members—could be made of spruce, but the builder knew that, with the tools at his disposal— stone celts, adzes, chisels, and beaver-tooth knives—the light wood of the eastern aborvitae (*Thuja occidentalis*) was readily split along its annual growth rings and could be worked with ease. *Thuja occidentalis* becomes commonplace in the Boreal Forest in the Great Lakes region, and in New England its range extends southward into Connecticut, well beyond the limits of most cold-climate conifers of the Boreal Forest. Its foliage is different from the needlelike leaves of the spruce, fir, tamarack, and pine. Short and blunt, its flattened, scale-like leaves overlap each other, forming fan-shaped, frondlike branchlets.

In addition to gathering the proper canoe-making materials, it was necessary to select a building site with a smooth, shady area free of stones and roots. Because construction took a long time, involved the whole family, and required that food and water be easily obtained,

generations of Indians reused particularly good canoe-building areas. The men felled the trees, stripped the bark, gathered the gum, paced off the length of the canoe, cut and bent the thwarts, and constructed the frames. The work of sewing or lacing the sheets of bark together, and then lashing the pieces onto the frame, depended on the skilled hands of the women.

American Indian women were artisans in birch bark, spruce, and larch roots, and canoe "wrapping" was just one facet of their skill. Their spruce-root baskets were so compactly woven that they could hold water. Deftly cut, folded, and sewn, pieces of bark became pails, dishes, and baskets in which to cook, carry, and store a family's food and possessions. By scraping away the dark layers of "summer bark" or by attaching cut-out pieces of bark or quills, the women decorated these vessels with images of the plants and animals of their world.

If you want to acquire a canoe today, unless you are as persistent and determined as John McPhee, you'll find yourself choosing from brightly colored fiber-glass, polyethylene, laminated plastic, and aluminum models. Sometimes, held reserved in a special cradle, lies the satiny hull of a wooden canoe. This craft, along with other small, handmade wooden boats, represents what might be the last chapter of an art, and the price tag gives some indication of how much we value natural materials and craftsmanship. For with all the obvious advantages of twentieth-century plastics and metals, they lack the

20. While still a student at the Howard Pyle School, N. C. Wyeth emerged as one of America's best-known painters of the unspoiled wilderness after "The Moose Call," which he painted in 1904, was reproduced in *Scribner's Magazine*, in October 1906. At the same time, Scribner's offered a mounted print of the picture to its readers, and "The Moose Call" soon became one of Wyeth's most popular Indian canvases. Wyeth went on to paint other pictures of Native Americans, five of which were published as a series in *Outing Magazine* in 1907. "The Indian in His Solitude," which was also published by *Scribner's*, may be one of his most beautiful studies of Indian life. Although Wyeth is perhaps best known today as an illustrator of children's books, his portraits of Native Americans are considered to be some of his finest work.

21. This grove of paper birches (*Betula papyrifera*) in the Arnold Arboretum was photographed early in this century only a few years after the trees had been planted. Unfortunately, infestations by two very serious insect pests, the bronze birch borer (*Agrilus anxius*) and the birch leaf miner (*Fenusa pusilla*), have decimated many of the white-barked birches in the Arboretum's collections. The bronze birch borer is a native beetle that lays its eggs in cracks in the bark. After hatching, the grublike larvae tunnel into the cambium, where they feed for one or two years. During this period, they make long channels between the bark and the wood that can girdle the limbs, causing them to die. Often, the first sign of borer damage is dieback in the crown of the tree. The birch leaf miner is a small, black sawfly, introduced from the Old World, that was first discovered in Connecticut in 1925. The sawflies lay their eggs directly on the leaves, upon which their maggotlike larvae then feed. The leaves first appear papery, then brown. Repeated attacks cause the tree to decline and make it more susceptible to other pests, including the bronze birch borer.

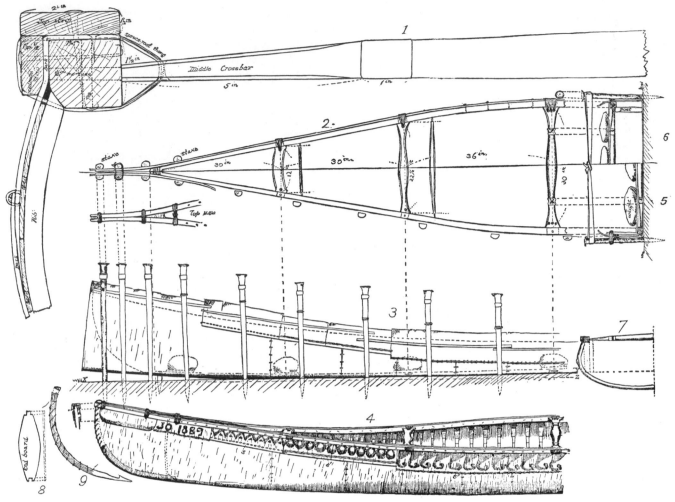

FIGS. 1–9.

22. This illustration of the construction of a birch-bark canoe was drawn by Edwin Tappan Adney for his article "How an Indian Birch-Bark Canoe Is Made," which was published in the Supplement to *Harper's Young People* on 29 July 1890. In just nine drawings, Adney took his young readers through the entire process of building this impressive canoe (which was nineteen feet long and thirty inches wide) with such attention to detail that they must have felt that, given the necessary materials, they too could easily build one.

marriage of the canoe builder's spirit with the spirit of a living tree.

Variety and abundance of species usually increase as climate moderates, and the Native Americans who occupied land south and west of the Boreal Forest could gather foods, medicines, and other products from a wider range of plants and animals. The more southern, and more diverse, White Pine–Hemlock–Northern Hardwood Forest covers almost all of Vermont, most of New Hampshire, the hills of western Massachusetts, and much of Maine north of the coastal city of Portland. This is the forest that glows with the colors of flame in fall, and the transition between it and the Boreal Forest depends on soil, elevation, and temperature, with the Boreal Forest restricted to the poorest soils in the wettest, coldest regions. The change from one forest to the other is often gradual. Travel through woods becomes easier as the almost solid walls of conifers become broken by deciduous trees. Footing becomes firmer, as mosses and lichens are replaced by understory trees and shrubs, with more sunlight reaching the forest floor through the canopy of the hardwoods.

As boggy areas give way to drier upland, stands of white and black spruce (*Picea glauca* and *P. mariana*) are invaded by red spruce (*P. rubens*). Balsam fir (*Abies balsamea*) and black spruce remain in cooler mountain sites, but eastern aborvitae (*Thuja occidentalis*) is joined by eastern hemlock (*Tsuga canadensis*) and eastern white pine (*Pinus strobus*), which become the dominant conifers. The hardwood trio of beech, birch, and maple also begins to appear. The smooth blue-gray bark of *Fagus grandifolia*, the American beech, makes this tree's presence easy to notice. Large groves of paper birch (*Betula papyrifera*) persist, but substantial stands of yellow birch (*B. alleghaniensis*) become more common. American basswood (*Tilia americana*) and species of ash (*Fraxinus*) begin to appear where the environmental conditions meet their requirements. *Acer rubrum*—swamp, soft, or red maple (the most common tree east of the Mississippi River)—occurs throughout New England except in far northern Maine. In the hardwood forest, red maple begins to appear frequently and is often joined by three additional species of maple. Sugar maple (*A. saccharum*) also called rock maple because of its extremely hard wood, is the largest of the maples that grow in these woods; two smaller ones, *A. pensylvanicum* and *A. spicatum*, are understory trees that are usually found growing on the slopes under the canopy of larger trees. The common name mountain maple refers to the the preferred habitat of *A. spicatum*, while the three common names used to identify *A. pensylvanicum* describe three of this tree's characteristics: striped maple, goosefoot maple, and moosewood refer, in turn, to this small tree's bright green bark inscribed with sharp, vertical white lines; its large three-lobed leaves, which look like the footprints of an oversized goose; and the preference moose have for browsing on its branches and leaves. Other small trees, such as the American mountain ash (*Sorbus americana*) and the hop hornbeam (*Ostrya virginiana*), also appear in the understory, along with shrubs such as witch hazel (*Hamamelis virginiana*), and a host of viburnums.

The Penobscot, Kennebec, Arosaguntacook, and Pigwacket—the four major subdivisions of the Woodland Indians known as the Eastern Abnaki, the "dawn land people"—lived among the northern hardwoods. The four tribes spoke different dialects of a single language and each defined its homeland in terms of a river drainage. Canoe transportation reinforced the territorial, political, and linguistic subdivisions associated with the principle waterways used by each tribe, and, by following the area's major rivers upstream, they could acquire

23. The greenish-brown bark of the striped maple (*Acer pensylvanicum*) is thin and smooth and marked by long, vertical, greenish-white stripes, or lenticels. As the maple matures, these stripes darken to a grayish white. It grows best in mountainous regions, where the soil is cool and moist, in deep valleys or on northern slopes. As an understory tree, it is often shrublike, or it develops a short main trunk with many irregular branches. As a lumber tree, it has no commercial value, and, unfortunately, it has also long been overlooked by the nursery trade. When grown in the open, it becomes a small but very handsome, many-branched tree. With its attractive bark, arching branches, and large drooping leaves, this small native maple can add year round interest to the cultivated landscape.

24. This American basswood (*Tilia americana*) which grows beside Meadow Road in the Arnold Arboretum, was photographed in early spring, just as its leaves were beginning to unfurl. The American basswood is a symmetrical, compact tree. The species once occupied large tracts of rich land, before the New England woods were cleared for farming. Its range includes all of the northeastern United States; in Canada, it occurs in the southern parts of Ontario, Quebec, and New Brunswick. Its wood is among the whitest, softest, and lightest of the hardwoods, and it was often used to make numerous products in which those qualities were very important. Crackers and chocolates were shipped in basswood boxes. Candy pails and jelly pails, as well as pails for pickles and fish, had sides and covers made of basswood—their bottoms were made of pine, maple, or birch. Beekeepers used basswood for beehives, bee boxes, and honey crates; poultrymen preferred incubators and coops made of basswood, and they shipped their dressed poultry and eggs in basswood crates; and dairymen once used basswood butter churns and cheeseboxes.

other forest products through trade with more northern tribes.

As skilled in boat building as the Indians of the far north, the Eastern Abnaki also favored paper birch for constructing canoes. It was the canoe's design—its profile, curves, width, ends, and other important details, including sewing materials and lashing methods that identified each tribe's canoes. To sew canoe seams, the Eastern Abnaki often used twine made from basswood rather than the roots of spruce.

American basswood (*Tilia americana*), the only native species of linden that grows in New England, is a sizable tree that has large, asymmetrical, but almost heart-shaped leaves that are toothed along the margins. Beneath these dark green leaves hang 4- to 5-inch-long, smooth edged, lighter green, leaflike blades. These are not true leaves—they are bracts, modified leaves that occur as part of the inflorescence or flower cluster.

In late June and early July, the American basswood's creamy white flowers emit a heavy fragrance that per-

25. Bracts are curious structures. Sometimes, as in the case of *Tilia* species, they are easily mistaken for leaves, while on other plants, such as our native flowering dogwood (*Cornus florida*) they appear to be large, showy flower petals. On basswood trees, as this illustration shows, the long, pendulous stalk that holds the cyme (or cluster of flowers), and later the seeds, is attached to the middle of the bract. What function these bracts play in summer is unclear, but, late in the fall, the propellerlike blade acts like a whirligig and transports the hard brown seeds that dangle beneath it away from the parent tree.

fumes the air. Drawn to the sweet nectar that almost drips from the flowers, the native North American bumblebees seek out the basswood. The colonists were familiar with a species of basswood, the so-called lime tree, that grows in Europe, and by 1750 the honeybees they imported (the Iroquois called them "English flies") had discovered the American species, and the name "bee tree" came to be used by the colonists for the basswood. Whether alerted by the fragrance of its flowers or by the sound of a swarm of bees, the Indians noted the basswood's location as a source of rope, thread, and twine.

Throughout New England, Indian place names indicated where this important tree could be found. Wicopee Hill in Vermont, Wecoachett Meadows on Cape Cod, and Wecuppemee Stream and Wecobemeas in Connecticut translate from the different dialects to signify "basswood place," "tying bark place," or "place to gather basswood."

The name basswood—originally "bastwood"—derives from the bast, the woody fibers from the phloem of the tree, which are the strongest of any North American tree. Herbaceous members of this family that grow in India and Pakistan are cultivated to produce jute, the durable material used in making twine, burlap, and a backing material for rugs. In North America, successful fishing once depended on line and nets made of *wuskwabi*, the Penobscot name for the tree's inner bark.

Basswood bark was gathered in almost the same manner as birch bark. A blunt wedge would be inserted between the bark and the wood of the trunk. Instead of peeling the bark from around the tree, the gatherer would pull a long vertical strip down the length of the trunk. The condition of the outer bark wasn't critical; it was the protected inner layers that provided the fiber for making rope. A freshly peeled piece of bark was workable, but a good soaking made the rough outer bark (which was often used by the Indians to cover the arched roofs of their houses) easy to detach. Most importantly, it made the inner fibers soft, slippery, and easy to separate. Depending on how she processed the bast, an American Indian woman could make many different grades of twine—from fine sewing thread for bags and pouches to coarse cord for strong, durable baskets. Beginning with two strands of fiber, and using the soft surface of her upper thigh, she would first roll two strands back and forth, then join them by rolling them together. The length of the cord grew by splicing new sections of fiber onto the strand already in progress. The thickness of the rope could be controlled by increasing the number of fibers being joined together at one time.

Because, for the most part, collections of trees at the Arboretum are grown in groupings by genus, each collection assumes a distinct pattern that reflects the architecture of the various species that constitute the genus. Thus, there are vignettes within the Arboretum's landscape that reflect the spirit and characteristics of groups of closely related species. The *Tilia* collection consists of large, regularly shaped, and very densely foliated trees whose architecture implies a rather formal design. This group or collection of trees occupies a prominent area beside Meadow Road that was once a wet meadow. The combination of large, regular trees sited in an expanse of very level ground creates a landscape reminiscent of a manicured English parkland.

To replenish their supplies of meat, hides, fish, shellfish, bark, roots, rope, tubers, berries, and nuts, the Indians travelled to their temporary camps in canoes during the summer and on snowshoes in winter. For many North American tribes, as well as other inland inhabitants of circumpolar regions, snowshoes were one solution to winter transportation. Early cultures in northern Europe, Asia, and North America developed snowshoes and turned the snow to their advantage. The first snowshoes were simply solid pieces of wood lashed to the feet with strips of uncured hide, and the earliest examples of this kind—and of the open frame types—are from central Asia. The ancestors of the American Indians carried the knowledge of this important development in the advancement of transportation with them across the Bering Land Bridge from Siberia to Alaska. In the words of the Danish historian Kaj Birket-Smith, the invention of the snowshoe "meant nothing short of a cultural revolution in the boreal regions."

On snowshoes, Paleo-Indians could track herds of caribou, reindeer, and bison through snow-covered postglacial landscapes and overtake any that foundered. Without such footgear, the Paleo-Indians would have found New England uninhabitable, except on a seasonal basis. Today's wood-frame snowshoe has changed little from the basic design that evolved thousands of years ago. The short, rounded, familiar bear-paw shape was first made in Asia, but it was the North American Indians who elaborated upon its simple design. By bending the wood into different shapes, they made square, pointed, and upturned toes. They added a toe hole, tapered the ends, and made a snowshoe that looked like a beaver's tail. They added netting and crosspieces to the frame and learned to weave patterns with *babuchi,* the lacing material made from the skin of caribou and deer. For the frame itself, they sought wood that would hold its shape and that would not snap once it was steamed and bent. Different styles, each frequently associated with only one tribe, were well developed by the time the European explorers —especially the fur traders and trappers—adopted them for their own use. By then, depending upon their availability, ash, cedar, and beech had become the woods preferred for frame construction.

Today, aluminum and plastic snowshoes laced with polyurethane and neoprene-coated nylon have gained a foothold in the western mountains of North America, but, in conservative New England, snowshoes made of native white ash (*Fraxinus americana*) continue to be manufactured and used to the exclusion of almost any other kind. Not only tradition but terrain makes wood a wise choice. Snowshoes take a worse beating on New England's rocky, steep, and often only lightly snow-covered trails than anywhere else in America's snow belt, and the hard but flexible wood of *F. americana* holds up very well under these conditions.

After the Indians used snowshoes and sleds for inland hunting during the fall and winter, the spring runs of anadromous fish entering the rivers drew them back to their camps on the coast. During summer, fishing and hunting turned to marine species, with harbor seal, porpoise, crab, and lobster being taken along with cod, sturgeon, and other fish. Also during the summer, the array of berry plants growing almost everywhere, from cool, lowland bogs to mountain tops, were important in the diet of Native Americans.

Men, women, and children ate their fill of each type of berry as it came into season; then the women prepared the remainder for the lean winter months. Almost any berry could be pounded or crushed by hand, boiled, and dried. Later, these dried berries would again be pounded in wooden or stone mortars, made into a fine meal, added to dried meat or animal fat, shaped into cakes, and consumed on long winter hunting forays.

Although pemmican (the Cree name for this mixture of berries, meat, and fat) is a North American Indian invention, we more frequently associate the mixture with Norwegian, English, and American polar explorers. Containing ascorbic acid (vitamin C) and fat, both of them essential to the good health of an active person on a limited diet, it was the Indian precursor to modern dehydrated and freeze-dried foods. In his book *The Secrets of Polar Travel*, published in 1917, Rear Admiral Robert E. Peary declared pemmican to be "the absolute sine qua non" for polar exploration. Perhaps his high opinion of pemmican—he likened it to "dried mincemeat" and insisted that it could be eaten twice a day for a whole year and the last bite would taste as excellent as the first—was not shared by the rest of the members of his crew, but a list of supplies for a typical journey attests to the amount that they ate: ". . . flour, 16,000 pounds; sugar, 5,000 pounds; pemmican, 30,000 pounds"! It is only fair to mention that Admiral Peary thought that pemmican was the best food for his sled dogs as well; perhaps that fact accounts, at least in part, for the size of the rations.

When the days lengthen and the spring sun begins to warm the brackish waters of New England's tidal rivers, the anadromous fish are drawn in from the sea to spawn in the freshwater rivers and streams. The alewife, *Alosa pseudoharengus*, and the American shad, *A. sapidissima*, both members of the herring family that share the same range, begin gathering offshore along the Atlantic coast in preparation for their annual migration from salt water to fresh water. Attracted to the warmer currents of freshwater outlets, the fish circle and race along the shore, until they finally gather in great schools at river estuaries. Governed by temperature, tide, daylight, and perhaps the press of their own numbers, the alewives leave the ocean waters first.

During those first rare days of spring, when the pussy willows (*Salix discolor*) swarm with bees eagerly working over their large, gray, furry catkins, the alewives begin their run. Turning, darting, and doubling back, their dorsal fins slice the surface of the water in unison as they leave the wide, deep rivers for increasingly narrow and shallow streams and brooks. The alewife is a smallish, one-pound fish, but what it lacks in size it makes up for in numbers. When "the herring are running," schools of these silver-sided, bluish-backed fish can turn a stream bed black.

Meanwhile, the American shad have been biding their time. Milling about in tidal pools, they are frequently

26. The same characteristics that make the wood of ash trees good for snowshoes—flexibility, great tensile strength, and resilience—make it a perfect wood for baseball bats. The Hillerich and Bradsby Company of Louisville, Kentucky, makes the famous Louisville Slugger (used by such notable home-run hitters as Babe Ruth, Shoeless Joe Jackson, Joe DiMaggio, Ty Cobb, Ted Williams, and Hank Aaron) from white ash lumber from trees in northern and eastern Pennsylvania. The company prefers to use white ash trees with straight, tall boles that grow where the soils are rich and retain moisture. Trees in such locations grow at a steady, moderately rapid rate, and they develop the clean, straight, and narrow-grained wood that is best for bats. This white ash with its multiple trunks, although a handsome specimen, would clearly not meet the batmaker's standards.

swept out into the deeper waters as the tide ebbs, only to return with the incoming tide. The American shad is the largest species of the herring family; although it is not uncommon for fishermen to land eight- and nine-pounders—even thirteen-pounders have occasionally been taken—the average shad weighs between three and five pounds.

At one time, the waters of every large river along the Atlantic coast would roil for days—often even weeks—from the immense schools of shad that invaded them each spring. Today there are far fewer, but, in New England, the Connecticut, North, Palmer, and Merrimack rivers still play host each spring to substantial numbers of these migrating fish. Shad spawning runs begin as early as January in Florida and Georgia and occur progressively later in the season farther north along the coast. The males precede the females as the schools of fish move up the rivers in waves. The main body of shad ascends when the temperature of the river water reaches between 62 and 67 degrees and when, along the river banks, the frost-hardy flowers of a small shrubby native tree of the genus *Amelanchier* burst from their buds. In New England, late April to early May is the time to watch both for the silvery-scaled shad as they flash through the water and for the frothy white flowers of the *Amelanchier* as they brighten the pale-blue sky. The arrival of these fish in the rivers was a cause for celebration among the Native Americans. Thomas Morton described the spring festivities in his *New English Canaan*: ". . . when the fish comes in plentifully . . . they exercise themselves in gaminge and playing of jugling trickes and all manner of Revelles. . . ."

While there are a variety of common names both for native and for exotic species in the genus *Amelanchier,* because of the vernal association of the trees with the fish, the native species have become known by the common name "shadbush." The genus name is probably derived from *amelanche,* a common name for a European species that grows in France. Shadblow, serviceberry, sarvisberry, and Juneberry are all common names that are used for these trees either in North America or in Europe. As the Native Americans stretched their basswood-fiber nets across the streams to trap the shad, they knew that it would be less than two months before the fruits of the shadbush would ripen—some would even be ready to eat by the middle of June. These vitamin-rich pomes were the first prizes of a long season of berrying for the women. Welcome they were, since last summer's harvest, preserved by drying, was likely to have been depleted before winter was over.

Amelanchier is but one genus of approximately 120 genera in the rose family, and there is a total of roughly 3600 species within these genera. In addition to roses, such familiar orchard trees as apples, cherries, pears, peaches, and plums, as well as such ornamental trees as hawthorns and mountain-ashes, belong to the Rosaceae, or rose family. Both edible and ornamental shrubs, vines, and herbaceous plants are also well represented: blackberries, raspberries, and strawberries delight the palate, while spiraea and potentilla delight the eye.

The remarkable variety in the type, size, and shape of the fruits that rosaceous plants produce seems all the more amazing when the striking similarity of their flowers is considered. Whether the resulting fruit is a follicle, an achene, a drupe, a hip, or a pome, each evolves from a five-petaled, five-sepaled flower that displays only minor variations in its structure from genus to genus. On the other hand, a spiraea fruit is a woody capsule; cherries are berrylike drupes; apples, quinces, and pears are pomes; and strawberries are aggregate fruits that are not unlike apples turned inside out.

The shadbushes are the first showy-flowered native trees and shrubs that flower in each year's new growing season. As such, they constitute New England's first, succinct floral declaration of spring. Depending on the weather, their small, numerous flowers (which appear just before or as the leaves emerge) may last as long as a week, but a warm spell can shorten that time period by half.

The petals of the shadbush flower are long and narrow, and each has a five-lobed, bell-shaped calyx and a five-parted pistil. The individual flowers are attached by stalks to a central axis that elongates as it develops; this type of inflorescence is called a raceme. The fruit is a round (or sometimes pear-shaped) drupe that contains between five and ten chestnut-brown seeds. Because *Amelanchier* flowers resemble those of the pear, and because their small, pulpy fruits are berrylike, the colonists referred to these trees not only as the shadbush but also as Juneberry, wild sugar pear, swamp pyrus, and swamp sugar pear. Because they reminded some settlers of other members of the rose family, *Amelanchier* species were also called sugar plums and swamp cherries.

Most shadbushes are as shrubby and bushlike as their name implies. *Amelanchier canadensis,* the thicket shadbush, is a good example. Although it can grow quite tall—up to 25 feet—it is always a multistemmed shrub that grows in dense clumps or thickets in bogs, swamps, and other wet, low-lying areas. The fruits of the thicket shadbush are delicious; however, not all species of shadbushes produce fruits that taste as sweet as "sugar plums." Moreover, the shadbushes are not easy to tell apart—even taxonomists quibble over their identification. Although there are only two native arborescent (or "treelike," rather than shrubby) shadbushes in New England—*Amelanchier arborea* and *A. laevis*—one is often confused with the other. A clue to identifying *A. arborea* lies in one of its common names, downy shadbush. For a brief time in early spring, a silvery white sheen is visible on all its new growth: leaves, sepals, pedicels, and the rachis (the main flower stem) are covered with silken hairs, and a dense covering of matted hairs also coats the undersides of the leaves.

The word *laevis* means smooth, and *Amelanchier laevis*, the so called Allegheny shadbush, is devoid of these silken threads. However, *A. laevis* does have a readily observable characteristic that helps to signal its identity. From the time they begin to unfold until they are fully developed, its leaves are colored a distinct purplish bronze. Despite the diagnostic differences between the two shadbushes, the Native Americans probably learned to recognize them by the taste of their fruits. The purplish fruits of *A. arborea*, which will do in a pinch of hunger, are dry and dull, while the slightly darker, almost black fruits of *A. laevis* are a sweet delight.

The Cree Indians of western North America called the fruits of *Amelanchier alnifolia*, a western American species, *mis-sask-qua-too-min*, which was shortened to "saskatoon" by the Hudson's Bay Company fur traders. The Canadian city founded on the banks of "a swiftly flowing river," the Saskatchewan (in the prarie province known by the same name), became Saskatoon.

The Eleanor Cabot Bradley Garden of rosaceous plants is one of the Arnold Arboretum's gardens within a garden. After five years of planning, preparation, propagation, and planting, this garden was dedicated in June 1985. Eight acres have been devoted to displaying approximately eight hundred different species of the rose family. By growing such a wide selection of closely related species in juxtaposition, the similarities as well as the differences within this enormous and interesting family can be observed and, it is hoped, comprehended. Rosaceae is such a large and complex family that it has been subdivided into subfamilies. In this subdivision, the genus *Amelanchier* is placed in Maloideae, a subfamily "blessed" with some unconventional reproductive techniques. *Amelanchier* species are capable of producing viable seed without adhering to normal sexual conventions; that is, the egg, an ovule, develops without fertilization by a male gamete. This process of asexual

propagation is known as apomixis, and it amounts to a form of cloning in which genetically identical plants result. Frequently, microspecies—taxa that are recognized as distinct from others only by virtue of minute differences—occur in plants that grow in isolated locations. There are approximately two dozen species, including several microspecies, of *Amelanchier* that are hardy in Boston. In the Bradley Garden, our native species are joined by others that hail from western North America, Asia, northern Africa, and Europe. In Great Britain, the vernacular names for these plants are serviceberry and sarvisberry, because their fruits resemble those of another genus in the rose family, the European service-tree, a species of *Sorbus*. In the Bradley Garden, there is also a specimen of *Amelanchier nantucketensis*, a species—or perhaps a microspecies, depending on your taxonomic bent—found only on the islands of Nantucket and Martha's Vineyard.

Among the multitude of woody shrubs that produce berries, perhaps those whose berries are the most flavorful and the easiest to collect are the blueberries. Stoneless and thornless, the fruits have numerous, but almost unnoticeable, tiny soft seeds inside. There are several species of blueberry, but, because of their delicious fruits, the lowbush and highbush blueberries, *Vaccinium angustifolium* and *V. corymbosum*, stand out from the others. The genus *Vaccinium* belongs to the heath family, Ericaceae, and it is from this family that berries are harvested for food as far north as the Arctic, in the Old World as well as in North America. Like all members of the family, both lowbush and highbush blueberries grow in acid soils, but each thrives in a slightly different environment. Found most often in swamps and moist woods in coastal lowland areas, or around the margins of ponds, highbush blueberries form large, multistemmed shrubs that can sometimes reach ten to twelve feet in height. While the lowbush species can grow in bogs—especially in alpine areas—these low-growing, woody shrubs most often inhabit arid and sandy plains, which are transformed by them into "blueberry barrens." Their dwarf stature enables the shrubs to grow as far north as the Canadian tundra, where winter snows cover and insulate the plants from the cold. Both lowbush and highbush blueberries are endemic to North America. The native range of the highbush species is the more extensive; it grows as far west as Wisconsin and as far south as Louisiana and northern Florida. The more northerly lowbush blueberry, *Vaccinium angustifolium*, extends southward into northern Virginia in the Appalachian Mountains. In New England, the wild, treeless heathlands of the southeastern

27. Because lowbush blueberries can be found growing in so many places—from the sand-plain community on Cape Cod to the barrens of Maine—it is probably the most familiar species of blueberry in New England. This plant can grow in full sun in open, rocky pastures, under the shade of pitch pines and scrub oaks, in the middle of a cart path, and at a road's edge. A many-branched, plant that seldom exceeds two feet in height, it has finely bristle-toothed leaves less than two inches long. The leaves are bright green above and light green below, and they are attached to the stem by a short stalk. In May and June, their small, pinkish-white, urn- or bell-shaped flowers open at the same time as the leaves or slightly earlier. Ninety to a hundred days later, the flowers, if pollinated, will have become small, sweet berries that can be either a dark blue that is almost black or a lighter blue with a whitish bloom.

28. The highbush blueberrry (*Vaccinium corymbosum*) is a parent of many of the cultivated blueberies grown today. It occurs along the edges of swamps, in openings in moist woodlands, and occasionally in wet areas in upland fields. Its distribution reaches into the Maritime Provinces, but it becomes more common from southern Massachusetts southward. Highbush blueberries grow ten to twelve feet high, and they begin to bear fruit when they are eight to ten years old. Their smooth-margined leaves are elliptical in shape and green both above and beneath. Flowering begins in May or June, and it takes from fifty to ninety days for the fruit to mature. The fruits of lowbush and highbush blueberries remain on the bush after they are fully ripe, providing a source of food for wildlife. Grouse, bobwhites, mourning doves, and wild turkeys feed extensively of them, as do many songbirds. The black bear, red fox, New England cottontail, and striped skunk, as well as the white-footed mouse, all eat the fruit, and white-tailed deer eat the fruit and browse on the branches and foliage.

part of Maine constitute "the barrrens," an area that today exceeds 150,000 acres of wild blueberries.

While Native American men laid claim to hunting territories, the blueberry barrens were the women's domain. The right to collect in particular places belonged to the women of the family, and this privilege was often passed down from one generation to another. On a cool, clear morning in late July, women and children would rise early, line special collecting baskets or bark pails with basswood leaves to protect their harvest from the heat that would come later in the day, and set off for the barrens to gather the first blueberries of summer. Roger Williams noted in 1643, in his *Key to the Language of America,* that the Native American's name for blueberry was *sautaash* and that the berries were "dried by the natives and so preserved all the year; which they beat to powder and mingle it with their parched meal, and make a delicate dish which they call Sautauthig, which is as sweet to them as plumb or spice cake to the English." The Indians had observed that there were many more blueberries to harvest for several years after a fire had swept through the barrens, and they therefore used fire to increase blueberry productivity. Burning the barrens to stimulate the growth of blueberries and to eliminate weeds and seedling trees is an ancient method that is still practiced today.

Northern Boundary, Southern Line

The northern boundary of the territory of the Native Americans that inhabited southern New England (and relied more on horticulture than did their northern counterparts) coincided with a change in the flora that occurs in central New England. A gradual shift from a cooler climate to a slightly more moderate one separates the characteristic trees of the northern part of the hardwood forest from those of the southern hardwood forest, which consists of oaks, hickories, ashes, and, until the early 1900s, chestnuts. The southern limits of many conifers and other cool-climate trees are reached in this area, but some northern species do penetrate into southern New England, and beyond, along the mountains, hills, and uplands—places where the climate remains cooler. Southern species, in turn, invade the northern forest in the sheltered river valleys and the ravines of their tributaries, on southern, less exposed slopes and in protected lowland areas.

Just as the wild beauty of New England's far north owes its existence to the vegetation of the transcontinental Boreal Forest, the open woodlands of our southern New England landscape are populated by the trees associated with another great forest region. Beginning in Georgia, the Oak–Chesnut Forest sweeps to the northeast, up along the mountains and east to the coastal plain, until it reaches its northern limits in southern New England. This is the forest of James Fenimore Cooper's "oak openings," the western edge of which meets America's tall-grass prairie.

The Oak–Chesnut Forest region was named before an exotic fungal blight killed the forest's most magnificent tree. The American chestnut, *Castanea dentata,* was so common that this one species shared in the dominance of the region with more than a dozen different species of oaks. Today, the oaks remain, while the chestnut survives only as a leggy understory tree or a large shrub, and the region has been renamed the Oak–Hickory Forest.

Along the New England coast from the Saco River in southern Maine south to Rhode Island, including Cape Cod and the offshore islands, the Oak–Chesnut Forest was the home of several native tribes collectively known as the Massachuset. It was also home to the Mohegan and Pequot, who dwelt inland in western Massachusetts and Connecticut, and to the Mahican, who lived in areas of New England that now border on the state of New York. All of them hunted, yet they were also horticulturists; their survival depended as much upon the plants they could cultivate in their gardens as on the game they could kill and the plant food they could collect from the wild. In this warmer and drier but more humid environment, these tribes were fortunate in being able to grow plants as well as to collect an abundant selection of roots, herbs, berries, fruits, and protein-rich nuts. Along with the plants that they cultivated, the sweet meat of chestnuts, the flavorful hickory nuts, the delicious walnuts, the smaller, tasty hazelnuts and beechnuts, and the meal that could be ground from somewhat bitter but dependable acorns—all played an important part in the diet of southern New England Indians.

Anyone who has attempted to conquer a nut just harvested from the tree has discovered that the seed, or nutmeat, has several protective coverings. The outer part—the husk or hull—can be spiny or smooth, shiny or dull, bone hard or brittle, leathery or even slightly soft and fleshy. Beneath the husk lies the shell. The shell—which can either dry and split open by itself or remain whole and, like that of the black walnut, seem impossible to crack—protects the inner nutmeat, or kernel, which usually is enclosed within a papery wrapping.

Five hickories (species of *Carya*) and two walnuts

29. While the so-called English walnut (*Juglans regia*) is widespread in Eurasia, where it has long been cultivated for its edible nuts, four or five additional species occur in eastern Asia, reputedly the original home of the English walnut. The Romans and the Greeks regarded the walnut as a symbol of fecundity, and British herbalists of the sixteenth century saw in walnuts a likeness of the human head—the skull being the shell and the nutmeat the brain. Because of this similarity, they prescribed ground walnut shell for head wounds and walnut meat for mental illness.

(species of the related genus *Juglans*) reach their northern limits in southern New England and in a few hospitable locations further north. The name *Juglans*, from which the family Juglandaceae derives its name, has its roots in the ancient Latin *Jovis glans* ("nut of Jupiter"). The range of the eastern black walnut, *Juglans nigra*, whose bright green husk does indeed enclose food fit for the gods, is limited not only by climate but by its need to grow on rich, fertile soils less acid than those usually found in New England. Its large, heavy fruits persist on the trees after the leaves have fallen. As they age, the fleshy, tannin-rich husk darkens from green to almost black. The shells inside are thick and hard, and they require a good pounding to crack them open and expose the sweet nutmeat. *J. cinerea*, the butternut or white walnut, New England's second species in this genus, is more tolerant of a wider range of soils and temperatures than *J. nigra* and is found throughout southern New England and in substantial areas of Maine, New Hampshire, and Vermont. The sticky husk of the butternut and its rough shell enclose a nut that tastes like a mild version of the walnut. Its shell is also hard to crack, and great care must be taken to shatter only the shell and not the delicious kernel.

The Native Americans knew the value of being able to tell the five species of hickory apart: Unlike the dependable walnuts, not every species of *Carya* produces nuts that contain an edible kernel. *Carya tomentosa*, the mockernut hickory, has the smallest range and is the hardest to find. Rare in the north, it grows in Connecticut, in a small part of Rhode Island, and in the eastern part of Massachusetts. Perhaps disappointment led to its common name; its exceedingly hard shell encloses a very sweet but very tiny kernel. *C. glabra* and *C. ovalis*, pignut hickory and red hickory, which some taxonomists treat as a single species, together have the next largest range.

Both can be found as far north as the Massachusetts border with New Hampshire and Vermont and in coastal portions of New Hampshire and Maine. Bitternut hickory, *C. cordiformis,* has the greatest and most even distribution of all the hickories. In New England, its range extends north into the hardwood forest, where it can be found growing in the rich, moist soils of the river valleys. In southern New England, it is found almost everywhere except in higher, colder areas, where the soil is too dry for its survival. Its abundance may be due to the fact that many of its seeds are left to germinate: Although its smooth shelled nuts crack open when they dry, even the squirrels seem to disdain their bitter taste.

It was *Carya ovata,* the shagbark hickory, that the Native Americans held in highest esteem, and we owe our common name for trees of this genus to the Algonquian language. Hickory is a contraction and Latinization of *powcohicora,* the "hickory milk" the Indians made from its nuts. The similarities among the hickories and between the hickories and the walnuts led to much confusion when these new American trees were first discovered by Europeans. The explorers and colonists knew only one species of walnut—*Juglans regia,* the "English" or "Persian" walnut—and they were not at all familiar with hickories; those that once grew in Europe had been eliminated by the glaciers. In 1791, William Bartram (the son of John Bartram, America's first native-born botanist, and an eminent botanist in his own right) wrote about his country's plants and animals in *Travels through North & South Carolina, Georgia, East & West Florida,* and made "observations on the manners of the Indians." He described their cultivation of groves of shagbark hickories as "an ancient practice," and wrote about the way they processed their harvest of shagbark hickory nuts.

The fruit is in great estimation with the present generations of Indians . . . they store it up in their towns. I have seen above a hundred bushels of these nuts belonging to one family. They pound them to pieces and then cast them into boiling water, which, after passing through fine strainers, preserves the most oily part of the liquids, this they name hickory milk; it is as sweet and rich as fresh cream.

In the north, the native people of New England planted orchards of fruit trees and groves of nut-bearing trees around their villages, but they seldom cleared large tracts of land. Needing only small areas for their dwellings, these northern hunters made less of an impact on the landscape than did their southern counterparts. Also in the north, the Native Americans gathered food and medicinal plants along with other plant products, but their hunting camps were moved frequently and, with the exception of a limited number of trees taken down for construction and canoe building, the northern tribes most often used only the bark, roots, or branches of trees.

The horticulturists in southern New England imposed greater changes upon their surroundings. The explorers and settlers from Europe wrote of seeing large sections of forest burning, from Massachusetts Bay south—the area most suitable for horticulture—and they often found large areas that had been cleared for fields. Farther north, gardening could succeed only where there were at least 130 frost-free days. Even though the Indians of southern New England practiced intensive (rather than extensive) horticulture, gardening was such an important part of their lifestyle that the open nature of the Oak–Chestnut Forest may have been caused, in part, by their practice of clearing and burning fields for crops.

The entire population of a village would join together to burn the forest and clear the land. Roger Williams, after being banished from the Massachusetts Bay Colony because of his political beliefs, traveled south and founded Providence, Rhode Island, on lands occupied by the Narraganset Indians. His fascination with their language and customs and his sincere appreciation of their culture led him to write *A Key into the Language of America* (1643). In this book, which was written with more sensitivity than most such accounts of the day, he noted the communal effort that went into preparing a garden.

When a field is to be broken up, they have a very loving sociable speedy way to dispatch it: All the neighbors men and women forty, fifty, a hundred &c, joyne, and come in to help freely. With friendly joying they break up their fields, build their Forts, hunt the woods, stop and kill fish in the Rivers.

Through the use of a slash-and-burn method of clearing, underbrush could easily be collected and burned; but with stone tools alone, and without the help of domesticated animals, the most expedient way to remove large trees was to mimic the beaver's method of removing a strip of bark from around the trunk. Girdled in this manner, the trees quickly dried out and died, and later they too could be burned or simply left to decay. The European settlers, although armed with sharp metal axes and hatchets and sometimes with a yoke of oxen to remove the trees, often adopted the Indian method of planting

30. The common name of *Carya ovata*, unlike those of the other hickories, refers not to its nuts but to its most outstanding characteristic—its shaggy, smoke-gray bark. Not only is the shagbark hickory the easiest hickory to identify, but, because of its uniquely exfoliating bark, it is one of the most distinctive of New England's trees. Throughout its large northeastern range, it grows best on the edges of streams, swamps, and ponds, but it can also be found growing in southern New England's dry woods. Hickories rarely grow in pure stands, being more commonly found in a mixture with other trees, especially oaks. Covering sixteen million acres from the prairie border eastward, the Oak–Hickory Forest is the largest timber type in the United States. The hickory collection at the Arnold Arboretum is on the right side of Valley Road, beginning at the Centre Street gate. Eleven of the fifteen extant species of *Carya* are native to the New World, the remaining four species being found in Southeast Asia. Most of the New World species are found in the eastern United States, and the Arboretum's collections contain, not only the Asian species, but, with the exception of one or two species from the deep south, almost all of the other hickories—even the southern pecan (*Carya illinoensis*).

their crops among roots, rocks, scorched lands, fallen timber, and dangerous stands of dead trees.

Although seasonal rounds remained important in the rhythm of tribal life, villages grew up around these valued clearings as planting fields became the focus of the seasonal round. A worn field might be allowed to lie fallow for several seasons, but, before being reused, the area would be burned to eliminate any seedling trees and to increase fertility. Each year, the native people would visit these gardens regularly during the spring, summer, and fall, and, after using up dead wood and underbrush that had been sacrificed to create the field, they began to have difficulty finding enough fuel wood. More and more small trees and shrubs were cut or destroyed in order to feed their domestic fires and enlarge their fields. These practices led to increasingly large open areas around the villages, and eventually these cleared spaces changed the appearance and ecology of the forest.

After preparing an area for planting, the women maintained the gardens. In the spring, they watched the leaves of special species of trees expand and checked the position of the stars. On cue, when oak leaves attained the size of a mouse's ear or became as large as a red squirrel's foot, and when the three hunters had chased the Great Bear (Ursa Major) into the center of the night sky, they planted their seeds. Using the shells of horseshoe crabs for trowels, sharpened pieces of wood for spades, and pieces of deerhorn or sharp rocks lashed to strong shafts of wood for hoes, they hilled up the soil amid the trunks and stumps and began to tend their gardens. They grew their main food plants together. Dropping several corn seeds into each hill of soil—an old folk rhyme came to suggest at least four: "One for the squirrel, one for the crow, one for the cutworm, and one to grow"—they then added seeds of beans, squash, and gourds. As the corn grew tall, its stalks supported the scrambling bean vines, and the large-leaved vines of the cucurbits—the squash and gourds—carpeted the garden, effectively shading out many weed seedlings.

The southern New England Indian's calendar consisted of thirteen lunar months, six of which were named for their connections with horticultural activities. The month of *squannikesos*—"corn-setting time"—introduced the agricultural round. By *matter la haw kesos*—when "squashes are ripe and beans begin to be eatable"—the yellow flowers of the cucurbits had been transfigured into squash, and the corn's large knife-edged leaves, their spring-green color dulled by summer's heat and dust, hid ears topped with silk. *Pa[s] qui taqunk kesos*, "the moon comes at summer's end," ushered in a season of plenty, a

31. The young leaves and male flowers of a shagbark hickory photographed at the Arnold Arboretum in May. The large, buff to reddish-brown bud scales have folded back to accommodate the rapidly expanding catkins and the unfurling compound leaves. The yellow-green leaves will become approximately fourteen inches long, and will have five (or rarely seven) leaflets. The leaflets are opposite, but the leaves themselves are arranged alternately. The male catkins will expand to a length of four to five inches.

time when harvest and hunt overlapped. Again, as in the spring, it was a time of ceremonies and social gatherings. During the waning days of summer, black bear and white-tailed deer, as well as skunks, raccoons, and other creatures of the woods, were bolstering their reserves of winter fat. The men took to the woods for days at a time in search of game; the women and children, who remained close by the camps, brought in the garden harvest and collected the fruits and nuts of wild plants.

32. It is almost impossible to harvest a hickory nut before a squirrel has left its mark, and a tree can often be entirely stripped by squirrels long before the nuts are even ripe. Hickories are such a significant source of food for squirrels that the squirrel population often fluctuates according to fluctuations in the production of hickory nuts. Squirrels abound in the Arnold Arboretum, but they appear to occur in exceptionally high numbers, and to exhibit uncommon industriousness, where the hickories grow. This part of the Arboretum is squirrel heaven: not only is it the site of the family Juglandaceae, which includes the walnuts as well as the hickories, but also located nearby is the beech family, Fagaceae, which is made up of beeches, chestnuts, and oaks.

Women's contributions to laying in provisions did not end with the harvest; the cultivated plants, along with the collected wild foodstuffs, had to be processed and, in some cases, stored in baskets and bark containers in secure underground caches. Before being ground into flour, acorns had to be subjected to several boiling water baths to leach away the bitter tannic acid. Beech nuts had to be separated from their burs and their shells had to be split, while hickory nuts and walnuts had to be hulled—not an easy task—and their nutmeats had to be picked out. The

men's success at hunting added other tasks. Meat brought home had to be smoked and dried, and the skins had to be readied for garment making.

Yet, before the snow came down, there remained one last tart, ruby-red treasure to collect. From plants in the heath family (Ericaceae), from the genus *Vaccinium*—the same genus that produced summer's sweet blueberries—came the red berries of the mountain cranberry (*V. vitis-idaea*), and the bog cranberry (*V. oxycoccos*). These two low, mat-forming evergreen shrubs are species that

Vaccinium macrocarpon.

33. Like its circumboreal relatives, the American cranberry (*Vaccinium macrocarpon*) has a low, trailing, prostrate form, and its small, waxy leaves are evergreen. The leaves are a dark, glossy green during summer, but they turn bronze late in the fall and remain so colored over winter. Their small, four-petaled, white to pinkish flowers are tightly reflexed—that is, the petals turn back on themselves, exposing the stamens, the pollen-bearing parts of the flower. The flower stalks curve downward, causing the flowers to tip toward the ground. If given only a cursory glance, these nodding blossoms resemble the profile of a bird, with the stamens forming the beak, the petals forming the head, and the curved stalk forming the neck. Tradition suggests that cranberry, the colonist's name for the American species, was a contraction of "crane" and "berry."

---

are able to survive in a stringent environment. The mountain cranberrry, the plant Linnaeus chose to name *Vitis idaea foliis subrotundis non crenatis, baccis rubris* —loosely translated, the rounded, smooth-leaved, red-berried grape of Mount Ida—thrives not only on the mountains of Europe and the highlands of the British Isles, but as far north as the Arctic Circle. Equally adaptable to Siberian tundra or to Canadian muskeg (the sphagnum bogs of northern North America), it is a plant that can take root on moss-covered boulders and stumps

as well as on bare and treeless mountaintops. *V. oxycoccos*, the bog cranberry, is true to its common name. Throughout its range in the North Temperate Zone, it is a species consistently associated with wet places, whether bog, fen, or sump.

There is, however, a third acerbic, red-fruited *Vaccinium* species that is found only in North America. This species has the largest, finest berries of all three. The true American cranberry, *V. macrocarpon*, (from the Greek *macro*, "large," and *carpon*, "fruit") produces berries that are twice as big as those of the mountain cranberry.

Plymouth and Barnstable counties—respectively, the shoulder and the arm of Cape Cod—are the nation's premier cranberry-growing areas. Beginning at the eastern end of Plymouth County and extending throughout Cape Cod, the soil is extremely sandy and infertile. A thin cover of humus underlain by a grayish-white layer of sand characterizes the Cape's soil type as a "podzol," from the Russian word *zola,* meaning "ash." The grayish-white or ash-colored layer is a remnant of the dense coniferous forest that slowly revegetated the Cape's infertile glacial till.

The advancing ice brought the till—the heterogeneous glacial debris—and, when the ice stalled and melted, the meltwater fashioned those sands and gravels into terminal moraines and outwash plains. Another geologic form—roundish, regular, sometimes seemingly bottomless basins that indicate places where something huge once had been—bear witness to the final passing of the ice age. As the glaciers retreated, they left behind huge blocks of ice that had calved away from the main ice sheet. Covered and insulated by the alluvium spawned by the melt, these immense, landlocked icebergs lay strewn about on the recessional moraines and outwash plains. Such ice blocks eventually melted, but not without leaving their mark. The depressions they made in the landscape are called kettles or kettleholes. Most kettles hold water (and many of the local people claim that there is a kettlepond on the Cape for each day of the year), peat has collected in others, and some are perfectly dry, shallow, bowl-like hollows. Wild cranberries can be found along the margins of kettleponds and also in the peaty wetland kettles. They also grow in company with sphagnum moss, sedges, and other wetland species in the moist, low-lying, little "dune bogs" that are tucked in among the older coastal sand dunes. Mineral enrichment from the sea, in the form of salt spray, enables the dune-bog communities to persist, but the kettles and wetlands contain some of the Cape's richest soils, a fact that was not overlooked when the cranberry industry began.

The medicinal and culinary attributes of the new American berry were noted by the colonists. As John Josselyn pointed out in 1672, in *New England's Rarities Discovered,*

> They are excellent against the Scurvy. They are also good to allay the fervour of hot Diseases. The Indian and the English use them much, boyling them with Sugar for Sauce to eat with their meat; and it is a delicate sauce, especially for roasted mutton; some make tarts with them as with Gooseberries.

The berries were thought to be so fine that, in 1677, when the Massachusetts colonists fell into disfavor with Charles II for issuing their own, unauthorized coins, they sent—along with 3000 cod and two hogsheads of samp (corn, boiled and beaten to a pulp)—ten barrels of cranberries to temper his anger.

In order to take advantage of the diversity and seasonality of the wild harvests, the Native Americans often changed the location of their small movable communities. By late fall, when the cranberry blazed with bronze leaves and ripe, red berries, they traversed the low, boggy areas, gathering the tart berries. In the Naranganset dialect, *sasemineash* meant "very sour berry." *Ibimi,* "bitter berries," was a Wampanoag word, and cranberries were known to the Hurons as *toca* or *atoca,* the "good berry." Used for medicinal purposes as well as for food, cranberries provided a rich source of vitamin C that could be dried and stored for use during the lean winter months.

Lowbush blueberries (*Vaccinium angustifolium*), highbush blueberries (*V. corymbosum*), and American cranberries (*V. macrocarpon*) were counted among the naturally occurring species in a catalogue of ligneous (woody) plants growing in the Arnold Arboretum on 1 September 1874, two years after its inception. Today, a mass planting of highbush blueberries can be found in the Arboretum just off Meadow Road at the edge of a natural area called the North Woods. Run-off from the low knolls and ridges feeds a small bowl-like area and a swale that runs parallel to the road, which keeps the area moist and suitable for wetland species. It is very likely that blueberries, perhaps even the very plants catalogued in 1874, have persisted here for years.

As abundant as the harvest was, whether it was blueberries collected by the hunter-gatherers from the dry heathlands of northern New England or the cranberries gathered from the wetland heaths of Cape Cod by the horticulturists, the Native American practice of cyclic resettlement insured the least impact on the land and the resources they relied on. The locations of their settlements were as fluid and as changeable as those of their hunting and gathering places. The Native Americans' claim to the land was vested in the resources the land supported and was not measured by physical bounds. Nor were territorial rights to hunt, or fish, or forage for food assigned to an individual. It was through the authority of the governing sachem (the tribal leader) or through family lines that the collective members of the village or

34. "All the women wore sun bonnets that covered their faces from the sun's gleaming rays. Big blue denim aprons with a patch of oil cloth across the front enveloped them from the waistline to their toes. The oil cloth came down under their knees when they knelt to pick and, if the bog was wet, kept them dry. On their fingers were stalls made of white cloth, and over these were drawn mitts made of cast-off stocking legs. These were to prevent them from [being injured by] the sharp vines. Everybody carried a six quart measure, their lunch and the inevitable bottle of tea." This description of the annual cranberry harvest, written by Geneva Eldridge and published in the July edition of *Cape Cod Magazine* in 1915, differs little from the scene portrayed in *The Cranberry Harvest, Island of Nantucket,* which was painted in 1880 by Eastman Johnson. As late as 1927, children were excused from school to take part in the harvest. Early cranberries are ripe by the beginning of September, and during "picking time," which could last through to the first hard frost, all other work ceased until the harvest was in.

family held these rights. The European colonists, intent on establishing fixed settlements and "permanent" agricultural fields, viewed the Indian's mobility and their apparent lack of sense of possession and of any interest in "improving" the land as being a detriment to productive land management rather than an asset to a lifestyle.

Not until 1810—long after stone walls had bounded plowed fields and doomed the Native American's seasonal rounds—did a farmer from Dennis by the name of Henry Hall "improve," by accident, a portion of Cape Cod's sandy plain, and, according to the noted horticulturalist Liberty Hyde Bailey, "the cranberry, the most unique of American horticultural products, was first cultivated, or rescued from mere wild bogs."

It was, wrote Bailey in 1890, in a summary of the cranberry industry, "an arduous duty to subdue a wild bog."

But, despite the difficult work required, by the middle of the nineteenth century, the industry had taken off. With ditch and dike, the Cape's barren wastes were squared off into civilized plantations. Even seafaring men, when they retired ashore, joined with the farmers in the culture of cranberries. In the 1850s, when Lettice Cahoon, the wife of Captain Cyrus Cahoon, discovered a dark-colored cranberry that had matured earlier than the others growing on the family's bog in Harwich, she named the first of the cultivated varieties. Mrs. Cahoon's selection, *Vaccinium macrocarpon* 'Early Black,' has remained to this day a mainstay among the cultivars developed by the industry. For more than one hundred years, the lowly wooden scoop epitomized the zenith of mechanization in the bogs. In the 1930s, dry-harvest machines took over much of the labor-intensive, backbreaking work. By the

35. The employment of small, homemade wooden cranberry scoops with short, straight wooden tines supplanted the more tedious hand-picking method. Long handles were attached to some scoops, and the cranberries could be harvested with this rakelike tool without requiring the harvester to bend down. On many bogs in southeastern Massachusetts, scoops were used until the 1970s. This photograph, taken in the town of Carver, shows a modern scoop—and it also shows how little its design has changed since Colonial times. The scoop has been widened, and the tines curved to facilitate combing the berries from the vines.

36. Most hand-held scoops were replaced by the Darlington picker, a machine that resembles a power lawn mower. Until recently, Massachusetts cranberries were picked by these machines when the bog was drained and dry, but now most bogs are flooded, and huge waterwheels churn up the water and dislodge the berries from the vines. The berries float to the surface, are corralled by booms, and are brought to the edge of the bog, where a chute sucks them out of the water.

37. On the starkly beautiful blueberry barrens of Maine, experimental harvesting machines, designed and built in New Hampshire, are being tried out alongside the time-honored methods of agricultural hand labor. Although the blueberry industry contributes about thirty-five million dollars to an extremely economically depressed area, workers are hard to find, and newspaper ads calling for "rakers" and "winnowers" run constantly during the six week harvest that begins in late July and lasts into early September, or until the first heavy frost. Initially, the large blueberry processors, whose canneries are capable of freezing up to 400,000 pounds of berries a day, thought that mechanical harvesters would be cost-saving investments, but, as bumper crops that can exceed forty million pounds of berries are becoming common, mechanization may well become the only way the crop can be harvested. This young girl holding the traditional metal-tined blueberry scoop may soon be replaced by a machine, but, until harvesting blueberries from the barrens of Maine can be mechanized on a large scale, it will remain extremely labor-intensive, back-breaking work.

1960s, a new generation of machines had been introduced—"beaters," which separated the cranberries from the plants after the bogs were flooded.

In comparison with cranberry bogs, whose ramrod-straight lines of dikes bisect the level, carpetlike expanses of cranberry plants, there are no obvious manmade bounds to the treeless blueberry barrens "Down East." As late as 1872, long after Cape Cod's sea captains had financed the acquisition of land and the construction of

bogs, as they had their ships, by selling sixty-fourths interests in their ventures, the people of Maine considered the blueberry barrens to be common land. William Freeman, a landowner and a lawyer, deemed this public use of the barrens to be trespassing. A bitter legal battle, which eventually reached the Maine's Superior Court, settled the dispute by allowing owners of barrens land to collect "stumpage," or a royalty on the plant products (in this case, berries) harvested from their land.

Although there are parallels in the development of these two New England industries, innovative technology has been slow to come to the barrens. Even though mechanized harvesters loom on the horizon (these prototype machines have been nicknamed "bigfoot"), pickers still wield blueberry rakes—basically, cranberry scoops with metal tines—to harvest the blueberries. And, unlike the native cranberry, and even the highbush blueberry, whose growers have adopted "improved" cultivated varieties to replace the native species, *Vaccinium angustifolium* and its environment remain virtually unchanged.

38. Figured in the border of this map, published in Amsterdam in 1671 (in *De nieuwe en onbekende weerreld; of, Beschryving van America en 't zuid-land . . .* by Arnoldus Montanus), are illustrations not only of the indigenous peoples, complete with their weapons, canoes, and shelters, but also of a selection of the native flora. In the land areas not occupied by names, mountains, or forests, there are small, but delightful, representations of bears, turkeys, rabbits, beavers, birds, and deer.

CHAPTER TWO

This Wooden World

Early descriptions of North America as a place whose off-shore waters were teeming with fish and whose land was covered by endless forests probably stirred the imaginations of European mapmakers more than those of the financiers who funded the New World expeditions. After all, it was not the fabulous Cathay that had been found. That rich and exotic land remained just beyond the reach of the merchants, the bankers, and the kings and queens of Europe, who had hoped to find a measure of the success of their ventures in the acquisition of cloves, pepper, nutmeg, and ginger. Convinced of the existence of the elusive Northwest Passage, mariners continued to make their way, with compass card, wooden quadrant, and marine astrolabe, through the labyrinth of islands, false bays, and narrow inlets of northeastern North America that they believed concealed the "Strait to the Indies." By the first quarter of the sixteenth century, these navigators had taken enough measurements and soundings for cartographers (who disdained maps with empty spaces) to create, if not an absolutely accurate map, at least a somewhat fanciful and approximate image of the edge of the new continent.

It is easy to understand the impact that a land so covered with trees made on Europeans. In many places, forest was all that could be seen, and it grew in scope and diversity with each succeeding voyager's recollections. John Cabot saw the Boreal Forest and wrote of a forest of tall trees that stretched unbroken for hundreds of miles. Sailing in more southern latitudes in 1500, Gaspar Corte Real described "luscious and varied fruits" growing in "a large and delightful country, well watered and covered with pines of mast-tree length." To commemorate trees he saw during his 1524 voyage, Giovanni da Verrazano bestowed the names, now long forgotten, *Selva di Luri* (forest of laurels) and *Campo di Cedri* (field of cedars) on headlands he sighted on the coast of present-day Georgia or South Carolina. The next year, Charles V, Holy Roman Emperor (who, as Charles I, was also King of Spain) bade Estévan Gomez search for "el Cathayo oryental," promising him a reward based on the value of his discoveries. Gomez found a "temperate" country "well forested with oak, birch, olive, and wild grape" but, as for precious metals, only iron pyrite ("fool's gold") was found.

The Americas may not have been the land of spice and silk, but the tales the mariners told slowly changed the perception that this new land stood as an obstacle to an easy route to the Orient. It would soon become a destination in its own right. It was fine to continue to gamble on discovering yet another new sea route to Asia, but, to the Spanish and French, the acquisition of lands in the New World was equally attractive. Spain moved quickly; her conquistadores swept across the southern latitudes, creating a fabulous empire. In 1524, Jacques Cartier set sail to claim a northern territory for France.

"L'Arbre de Vie"

Cartier's first voyage accomplished the exploration and mapping of the Gulf of Saint Lawrence and the west side of Newfoundland. There he ventured on land "to see the trees, which are marvellously beautiful and sweet smelling." On Cartier's second voyage, the small fleet sailed inland until winter closed in around their ships. Locked in "four fingers' breadth of ice" for five months, Cartier and his men endured bitter cold and the swollen limbs, rotting gums, loose teeth, and excruciating pain of scurvy. They survived by drinking a decoction that their Huron guides provided that was made from the bark and leaves of a tree. Cartier recorded the turning point in their suffering in his account of the voyage: "They brought back from the forest nine or ten branches and showed us how to grind the bark and boil it in water, then drink up the potion every other day and apply the residue as poultice

PORTRAIT DE LA MAISON RO: YALE DE FONTAINE BELLEAV.

1. La Cour du cheual blanc a 80. toises de long et 58. de large.
2. La grande gallerie a 76. toises de long et 3. de large.
3. Le pauillon des poiles.
4. La Cour de la fontaine a 30. toises de long et 28. de large.
5. La sale de la belle chemnee a 20. toises de long et 5. de large.
6. La petite galerie a 30. toises de long et 5. de large.
7. Le glise de la trinite a 20. toises de long et 4. de large.
8. Les Ieux de paulmes.
9. Le Iardin de la Roÿne a 50. toises de long et 38. de large.
10. La voliere a 38. toises de long et 3. de large.
11. La galeries des cerfs et de la Roÿne ont 28. toises de long et 3. de large.
12. Le logemant du Roÿ et de la Roÿne.
13. La conciergerie.
14. La cour du donjon a 40. toises de long et 20. de large.
15. La sale du bal a 15. toises de long et 4. de large.
16. Chappelles haute et basse.
17. La cour des offices a 45. toises de long et 40. de large.
18. Le grand portail.
19. Le logis de Monsieur Zamet.
20. Le grand iardin a 190. toises de long et 154. de large.
21. Le logis de Monsieur de Suly.
22. Le iardin de letant a 34. toises de long et 34. de large.

23. Lestan a 150. toises de long et 114. de large.
24. La vielle conciergerie.
25. La fontaine dons fontaine belleau prant son nom.
26. Le iardin des pins a 160. toises de long et 80. de large.
27. Le iardin des fruis a 84. toises de long et 80. de large.
28. Le bois des canaye a 88. toises de long et 80. de large.
29. Le chenil.
30. La Capitainerie.
31. Le paste-mail a 300. toises de long et 3. de large.
32. Le circuit de tout le Chasteau a 1450. toises de tour.

39. Of all of the châteaux of France, Château de Fontainebleau is one of the most magical. Begun by Francis I, the palace has grown over time to the impressive complex of buildings and gardens that greets today's tourist who ventures south of Paris. It was here in the gardens of Fontainebleau, where the parterres were designed by the famous French landscape architect André Le Nôtre, that the humble arborvitae from French America was first brought under cultivation (in 1536). The arborvitae was also the first North American tree to be introduced into European gardens.

to swollen and infected legs." Relief was almost immediate. Not only did the aromatic and bitter-tasting brew cure scurvy, the men claimed that it cured various other afflictions that had been plaguing them for years! Valued for its wood by canoe makers, this conifer was also an important plant in the Native American's materia medica. To dispel scurvy and pain, to enhance their sweat baths, and to treat coughs and fevers, they steeped sprays of its pungent foliage in boiling water. In 1536, in recognition of its curative properties, Cartier brought back to his king, Francis I, a gift from the Boreal Forest, the first North Temperate tree introduced into Europe. The Indians called this plant *annedda*; the French, *l'arbre de vie*, "the tree of life." It is commonly known in English by the New Latin version of its name, arborvitae.

The seedlings of arborvitae (*Thuja occidentalis*) that Cartier collected were set out in the royal garden at Fontainebleau, where the small, narrow, pyramidal conifer with lacy foliage and a clipped-looking conical form quickly gained recognition not for its wood nor for its medicinal attributes but as an ornamental. *T. occidentalis* was introduced into Europe just as the decorative qualities of exotic plants were first being exploited. No longer were plants being sought only for their utilitarian value; gardens of novel aliens and of curious and attractive trees and shrubs had joined the orchard and the kitchen and herb gardens.

A very easy plant to propagate, arborvitae made a good garden specimen. After about ten years of growth, each plant produces enormous numbers of small, narrow, pale-brown, slightly winged seeds that germinate readily, and cuttings stuck into damp sand are almost always successful. Progeny from one of the original trees in the Royal Gardens, which are believed to have survived for many years, were transplanted into other gardens on the Continent. One of the circuitous routes arborvitae followed as it made its way across Europe can be traced to the journeys of a widely traveled plantsman from the Netherlands, Charles de l'Escluse (1526–1609). A student of the native flora, he botanized the wilds of Europe and also

40. At age sixty-eight, Carolus Clusius (1526–1609) assumed the role of directing the Leiden Botanical Garden. Although the garden, the sixth oldest botanical garden in the world, was founded in 1587, planting did not commence until after he had been appointed to the faculty of Leiden University in 1594. During his tenure at Leiden, Clusius introduced two New World members of the family Solanaceae into Holland—the potato and the tomato—but perhaps his most important contribution to Holland's future was his introduction of a flowering bulb that was purely ornamental—the tulip. Clusius's *A Treatise on Tulips* remained for many centuries the major source of information for Dutch bulb growers.

41. This photograph of relatively young specimens of eastern arborvitae (*Thuja occidentalis*) illustrates the symmetrical, conical habit of the tree when individuals are grown in open, sunny sites and with freedom from competition. Because of this growth habit, the tree is often used as a hedge. At maturity, individuals can attain a height of nearly sixty feet. The common name arborvitae, Latin for "tree of life," was given to this tree by Jaques Cartier on the second of his three expeditions to Canada, where he and his crew came down with scurvy and twenty-five crew members died. As a consequence of drinking tea made from the arborvitae, they found that the debilitating symptoms of the disease (which is caused by a deficiency of vitamin C) were alleviated, and they justly credited the tree with having saved their lives.

visited his friends' estates and gardens searching for the rare and exotic. By 1573, at the age of forty-seven, Carolus Clusius (he had by then Latinized his name) had been appointed by Maximilian II, Holy Roman Emperor, to take charge of the new Imperial Gardens in Vienna. Clusius remained at the garden for twenty years before moving on to Leiden, where he held the chair of botany and oversaw the first plantings at the University's Botanical Gardens, which he directed until his death in 1609. "Through my own effort," Clusius wrote in 1601 in his *Rariorum Plantarum Historia,* "the tree that I had first laid eyes on at Fontainebleau was brought to Belgium." Later, he saw to it that seedlings from the plant in Belgium were transplanted into gardens in Germany. By 1597, *Thuja occidentalis* was reported to be thriving in England, and there, a century later, the English naturalist John Ray noted that it was a commonplace plant often used as a windbreak or a hedge.

Having recovered from his bout with scurvy and his winter's imprisonment in ice, Cartier returned once again to the New World. He devoted his third, and what was to become his final, voyage to establishing a crown colony for France. The settlement, Bourg Royale (now called Charlesbourg), failed; it would take an additional sixty years for the founder of New France, Samuel de Champlain, to succeed in that undertaking.

"To Go to Cataia"

England remained blissfully unconcerned with developments in the New World. For many years after John Cabot's visit, only English fishermen joined the craft that sailed the waters off the northern coast of North America. Unlike the French, who added trading in furs to fishing for cod, they seldom tarried long enough to barter for skins and pelts. England's interest lay elsewhere. Not mariners but merchant adventurers (banded together in powerful trading cartels called companies) dictated the course of English seamanship, which ran to the southeast, to Africa and the Mediterranean. Slowly, Elizabethan England awoke to the certainty that, if its indifference to controlling the seas and the lucrative trade routes continued, the sun would never rise on a British empire. A new generation took up a new cause—expansionism. Merchants joined forces with noblemen, and the Queen cautiously loosened her purse strings and lent not only money but prestige to the ventures. If, speculators reasoned, the southern trade route to the west found by Ferdinand Magellan was controlled by the Spanish and the Dutch, and if the Portuguese used Vasco da Gama's way east around Cape Horn, a northwest passage must be found. It was hardly a new idea, but it now became England's.

The last quarter of the sixteenth century found English scholars and sailors engaged in unraveling the mysteries of maritime science. While ancient maps were being unrolled and consulted, early travel accounts were collected, translated, and studied. Subscribers supported carefully planned voyages, but experienced navigators were at a premium. Years behind their competitors in cartography, geography, and charting the courses of their ships, English seamen had been sailing without benefit of navagational tools long used by the Italians, Portuguese, and Spanish. But now the English seamen, who had learned to navigate with new "precision" instruments, set sail to the west and began to record their own voyages of discovery.

Although the eighty-year-old riddle of a northwest sea route to Asia remained unsolved and early colonizing expeditions had failed, persistent and articulate advocates for the discovery of this northern passage had turned English attention from the Old World to the New World. The end of the sixteenth century found the English in possession of accurate new maps, a generation of master mariners, a strong fleet, and social and economic pressures for overseas expansion.

The failure of their attempts to colonize either Newfoundland or Roanoke Island—by, respectively, Humphrey Gilbert and his half brother, Walter Raleigh, each of whom had held in turn the Crown patent for establishing an English colony in America—focused interest on the intervening latitudes. The coastline that extends from present-day Maine to Long Island, New York, had been viewed by the sailors of five nations during at least twenty-five recorded voyages. Now, at the beginning of the new century, those shores fell under the scrutiny of English adventurers. Each of the men who set sail was entrepreneur, colonizer, explorer, and promoter; and many were also plant hunters hoping to make their fortunes from the roots and bark of the miracle plant of the day.

42. Nicholas Monardes (1493–1588) was born in Seville and studied medicine at Alcalá de Henares, a center of medical research during the sixteenth century, a time when Spain was considered to be a leader in medical science in Europe. Monardes published his findings on the medicinal attributes of New World plants in two volumes. The first, published in 1569, contained no illustrations, except for a portrait of Dr. Monardes on the title page. The 1571 volume contained illustrations of the plants he described. He combined the two books into a single volume in 1574; this was the edition that John Frampton translated into English. Frampton was not the only translator of Monardes; there were French and Italian editions also, and Carolus Clusius published a Latin edition in 1593. Frampton, who translated Monardes' book after he was no longer "pressed with the former toils of my old trade" as a British merchant in Spain, went on to publish a translation of Marco Polo's account of his travels in Asia and, later, a discourse on a voyage to China by Bernardino de Escalante.

"A Tree of High Price and Profit"

Sassafras (*Sassafras albidum*) first gained its European reputation as a cure-all when a published account of its virtues appeared in Spain in 1569. The author, Nicholas Monardes, an inquisitive and successful Spanish

43. Born on 26 April 1785 at Les Cayes in Saint Domingue—now Haiti—and baptized Jean Jacques Fougere, the illegitimate son of a French lieutenant and his Creole mistress became one of America's most well-known ornithologists. At about the age of ten, Jean Jacques was formally adopted by his father, Jean Audubon, and approximately ten years later, after spending several years at Mill Grove, his family's farm in eastern Pennsylvania, he Americanized his first and middle names, becoming known as John James Audubon. Audubon used the sassafras (*Sassafras albidum*) as a backdrop for his portraits of the small green-crested flycatchers (now known as Acadian flycatchers, *Empidonax virescens*) in his monumental *Birds of America*. Seen in this illustration, plate 62 of the 1840 edition published in New York, are the sassafras's small, dark blue fruits. The few fruits that do develop on sassafras trees at the Arnold Arboretum disappear quickly because they are devoured by birds even before the fruit is fully ripe.

No 13   Pl. 62

Small Green-crested Flycatcher!
Sassafras Laurus Sassafras
1 Male. 2 Female.
Drawn from Nature by J. J. Audubon, F.R.S. F.L.S.   Lith? Printed & Col? by J. T. Bowen, Philad?

physician who lived in Seville, had become interested in the medicines and herbs brought from the New World by the conquistadores from hearsay evidence of cures attributed to the new plants. He began to prescribe these new drugs for his own patients. The doctor's publications, which included guidelines for preparing the different drugs and descriptions and illustrations of the plants, caught the eye of John Frampton, a merchant "returning home into Englande out of Spaine," and Frampton brought the news of sassafras with him. Frampton "Englished" Monardes' books, calling his own translation *Joyfull Newes out of the Newefounde World Wherein Is Declared the Rare and Singular Virtures of Diverse and Sundry Herbs, Trees, Oils, Plants, and Stones with Their Applications as Well for Physic as Chirurgery, the Said Being Applied Bringeth Such Present Remedy for All Diseases, as May Seem Altogether Incredible.*

According to Frampton, the familiar and timeless ills of

Monardes' patients had ranged from complaints "of the liver, griefs of the head, the breast, the toothe ache, the weakness of the stomacke, the stone of the kidneis, the burnying of the Urine, the Goute to the 'evill of the Poxe'." The doctor had treated each affliction with various concoctions of one or another of the new plants. Of all the botanicals tried, the one from Florida, the sassafras, seemed to cure almost everything. He stopped short of declaring that it enabled the blind to see or the deaf to hear, but he did claim that it healed "them that bee lame or crepelles" and made barren women able to conceive. News of such a cure-all surely brought joy to other English merchants who read of Monardes's "cures," and they quickly realized that the newly discovered American plants, especially sassafras, would command a very high price.

The plant hunters were seeking a tree that was not easily mistaken. When Monardes wrote that the sassafras "Hath leaves aftere the maner of the Figge Tree, with three points, and when thei are little, thei be like to the leaves of a Peare Tree," he provided the clue that, from spring to fall, quickly reveals this tree's identity. For of all North American trees, only the sassafras and the mulberry, a relative of the fig, bear leaf blades of three distinctly different shapes on the same plant. Thanks to the Romans, who brought seeds or seedlings of many edible plants (and weeds as well) with them during their invasions, the English were familiar not only with the grape, walnut, plum, medlar, and sweet chestnut but also with both the fig and the mulberry. Like the fig—but unlike the mulberry, whose leaves have toothed edges—sassafras leaves have smooth edges. The three-lobed leaf blade is shaped like the silhouette of a mitten with thumbs on each edge. The second leaf shape, with two smooth lobes, one large and one much smaller, looks like a right- or left-handed mitten. The third leaf shape—a simple, unlobed elliptical blade—looks as if the knitter had become distracted and forgot to include any thumb at all.

When Bartholomew Gosnold, one of the first of the sassafras hunters to visit New England, set sail in the *Concord* in 1602 to explore "the north part of Virginia," the price of sassafras in England was 336 pounds sterling per ton. Gosnold was hoping to "plant" some colonists and reap some profits, but he knew that Sir Walter Raleigh held the rights of government over the territory of Virginia, which at that time included all of the East Coast not in the hands of the French in Canada or the Spanish in Florida. Raleigh thus controlled a monopoly over all settlements and commodities, including the wood, bark, and roots of sassafras. Apparently motivated by the prospect of riches, Gosnold sailed without the patent-holder's knowledge or blessing.

Gosnold could find no sign of the sassafras tree until he sailed south from his first landfall in Maine to the shores of Massachusetts, for this plant is really a tree of the Middle Atlantic and southeastern region, and it is the only tree of the spicy and aromatic laurel family hardy enough to withstand New England winters. In New England, its range closely follows that of the Oak–Hickory Forest, and in southwestern Maine, southeastern New Hampshire, and southern Vermont it grows only in scattered locations; it is far more abundant throughout Massachusetts, Connecticut, and Rhode Island.

In spring, when the sassafras leaves first unfold, they are light green. At maturity they darken, and in autumn these sassafras "mittens" can take on a range of colors from pale yellow to ruby red. If you stop to look at a leafless tree in winter, other characteristics become obvious. The dense and craggy crown is made up of short, stout branches that grow at right angles to the stem. The young shoots and twigs, and even the sucker growth, are smooth, lustrous, and bright green; as the branches age, they turn a light reddish-brown. On older specimens, the much darker, reddish-brown bark of the trunks, often more than an inch and a half thick, becomes so deeply and regularly furrowed that the broad flat ridges at the surface look like diamond-shaped lattice work.

At the tree's northern limits, fruit production is sporadic, and propagation most often occurs when underground branches form roots and send up stems, called suckers, that can become independent plants if the connection from the parent tree is severed. If undisturbed, many generations of plants share the same root system, which may become very old, much older than even the oldest trees that it supports. Sassafras seldom reaches heights of thirty feet in New England, and this, along with its slender form and dense suckering habit, often makes a mature grove look like a thicket of saplings.

Dispite its ability to clone itself, sassafras is a difficult plant to propagate and a hard one to transplant. Look for *Sassafras albidum*—a pioneer tree apt to colonize disturbed areas—not in gardens, or in parks, or planted along highways but on the edges of old cart paths and logging roads or at the borders of clearings and abandoned fields. From Florida to southern Maine, it inhabits sandy woodlands along the coast, the type of habitat where once, nearly four centuries ago, the sassafras hunters found and collected its roots and bark.

Gosnold found the object of his voyage growing in

44. Across from the Arnold Arboretum's lilac collection on Bussey Hill Road, there is a quiet retreat. A bench, shaded by a canopy of leaves, faces into the "North Woods," a bowl-shaped area that is populated by many native New England trees. Beneath the soil around the bench lies an extensive network of thick, fleshy, roots covered with a fragrant, light yellow bark; this root system nourishes the stand of sassafras that provides much of the shade. It is likely that the older trees that make up this grove of sassafras were living on the hillside before the founding of the Arboretum.

45. A sassafras tree is either male or female, and only the carpellate (or female) flowers, which are illustrated in this photograph, develop into clusters of deep blue, aromatic, egg-shaped drupes (a fleshy, one-seeded fruit like a cherry). In the Arnold Arboretum, however, these fruits are rarely seen, because the majority of the sassafras trees in the collection produce only staminate (or male) flowers.

great abundance on a small group of islands off the headland he named Cape Cod. He called one island Martha's Vineyard (perhaps for his wife); another he named Elizabeth Isle in honor of his queen. The second island —now called Cuttyhunk—became the site of what he hoped would become a permanent camp. Within three weeks, he and his men had built a flat-bottomed punt and a sedge-thatched house, planted wheat, barley, and oats, and had begun collecting sassafras roots and trading with the natives, who had greeted the party with "signs of joy." Unfortunately, this fragile friendship turned into a hostile conflict after Gosnold's men stole one of the Indian canoes. Soon, relations with the Indians had deteriorated to such an extent that the twenty sailors (including Gosnold) who had planned to remain on the island for the winter thought better of the idea, and the entire party quickly packed up and departed.

An account of the voyage written by crew member John Brereton included a line on the title page that read "by the permission of the Honorable Sir Walter Raleigh, Knight." This acknowledgment, although somewhat after the fact, apparently appeased Raleigh, who had seen the price of sassafras, and his profits, plummet when the *Concord's* abundant cargo of the medicinal plant glutted the market. From afar, Brereton's *The Brief and True Relation of the Discoverie of the North Part of Virginia* described a rock-strewn countryside as a land "full of all sorts of stones for building . . . many of them glistering and shining like mineral stones." Not only were there "many springs of excellent sweet water" but these springs ran "exceedingly pleasantly through woody grounds." As for the likelihood that the land could be successfully planted, the visitors had quite obviously been smitten: "We stood a while like men ravished at the beauty and delicacy of this sweet soil."

"The Natural Commodities of the Country"

After Gosnold's return to England, and until the Pilgrims established themselves by chance in Plymouth Bay, not a sailing season went by without one or more English adventurers contemplating the northeastern coast with an eye to settlement. The handful of publications that told of these journeys formed the preface to a body of literature, carried on by later visitors, dedicated to describing the goodness of the land and the region's abundant assets. Limited to prospects from hills near the coast and short inland journeys, these accounts—often little more than lists of plants and animals that ignored natural

relationships—fired the imagination of the English and made the New World seem just like home but much, much better:

> Trees both in hills and plaines, in plenty be,
> The long liv'd Oake, and mournefull Cypris tree,
> Skie towring pines, and Chestnuts coated rough,
> The lasting Cedar, with the Walnut tough:
> The rozin dropping Firre for masts in use,
> The boatmen seeke for Oares light, neate growne
>   sprewse,
> The brittle Ash, the ever trembling Aspes,
> The broad-spread Elme, whose concave harbours
>   waspes,
> The water spungie Alder good for nought,
> Small Elderne by th' Indian Fletchers sought,
> The knottie Maple, pallid Birtch, Hawthornes,
> The Horne bound tree that to be cloven scornes;
> Which from the tender Vine oft takes his spouse,
> Who twinds imbracing armes about his boughes.
> Within this Indian Orchard fruites be some,
> The ruddie Cherrie, and the jettie Plumbe,
> Snake murthering Hazell, with sweet Saxaphrage,
> Whose spurnes in beere allayes hot fevers rage.
> The Diars Shumach, with more trees there be,
> That are both good to use, and rare to see.

This description is taken from *New Englands Prospect*, by William Wood. One of five men who, in 1629, had founded the town of Lynn, Massachusetts, the third oldest town in New England, Wood wrote his detailed chronicle of life in the colonies after returning to England. By his estimation, New England was a bountiful forest that contained each and every tree and shrub known and needed by man, continued the tradition of promotional literature that had described the region in the most glowing of terms. All that was needed, according to Wood, were skilled men—"an ingenious Carpenter, a cunning Joyner, a handie Cooper, such a one as can make strong ware for the use of the country." Although the species Wood identified were new, he cited them by the common names that his fellow countrymen used for similar plants that grew in England.

Compared with the scarcity of wood in England, the abundance and variety of trees in the new lands made an enumeration of all the different genera virtually a requirement. The roster read like the inventory of a present-day lumber yard, with oak, ash, elm, pine, and fir seemingly stacked up and waiting to be turned into houses and barns, while the descriptions of the edible plants approached the inflated prose of a supermarket advertisement. The fruits, nuts, and berries were more plentiful, juicier, sweeter, larger, and better than any that had been seen before. Ground nuts (*Apios americana*) "big as hens eggs and good as potatoes" competed with "fields of wild corn" (meaning wild cereal grains in general, not Indian corn or maize in particular), and "the peas that scrambled everywhere." They thought the climate to be good (they sailed during the summer months), the fish plentiful ("even more so than in New-foundland"), the birds bigger, and the animals diverse. Other commodities, such as the "sweet turpentine and gum that smelled like frankincense" and the "excellent clay so suitable for making bricks and tiles," were not overlooked. Even the grasses, sedges, and rushes, as well as all the rest of the indigenous plants, appeared to be greener than those of Europe.

From Wildwood to Pasture Land

Unfortunately, the New World grasses did not match the lushness of those at home, and, in truth, the fields and woods of seventeenth-century England bore little resemblance to the land that John Smith, in his voyage of 1614, had so carefully described, mapped, and christened New England. Yet after the retreat of the glaciers, which had covered much of northern Europe, the denuded land, like its North American counterpart, had regained many of its displaced trees. Fifty to seventy species of trees and shrubs, almost all of them deciduous species, slowly reforested Great Britain's newly made drumlins, moraines, combes, and escarpments; they encircled ket-tleholes and glacial lakes. Diversity within this forest, called the wildwood by Britain's woodland historian, Oliver Rackham, had been curtailed by local extinctions. North America's forest had met with far fewer obstacles as it retreated from the advancing glaciers, but, as the European forest communities migrated southward during the Pleistocene glaciations, major continental mountain ranges (such as the Pyrenees and the Carpathians), which ran east to west, and the great expanse of the Mediter-ranean Sea proved to be formidable barriers. These obstacles prevented the survival of many thermophilous (or warmth-loving) plants and dramatically reduced the number of species available for the reforestation of Great Britain. One more obstruction blocked the pathway of the natural dispersal of seeds of plants returning north. Once the rising seas, caused by the climatic maximum that occurred worldwide about five thousand years ago, created the English Channel and cut Great Britain from

the continent, few species could return to the newly formed island without human intervention.

Other forces, in addition to the retreating and advanc-ing glaciers and the corresponding climatic shifts, restructured the landscape. People lived at the glacier's edge, in what is now southern England, 17,000 years ago—the same time that artisans, using the light of juniper-twig and tallow lamps, painted figures of animals on the cave walls at Lascaux and at many other cave sites in France and Spain. Even before open woodlands and, later, forests of birch, oak, ash, elm, and linden replaced the ice and tundra, men and women had begun to exert dominion over the environment.

These sophisticated hunter-gatherers used many of the same ecological controls to manage natural resources as did the Native Americans. A slow process had begun that created a land of heaths, downs, chalks, fens, hedgerows, pastures, and farms from what had been an island of trees.

When a new social order, an immigrant agrarian society, packed the skin-covered boats (so similar to Irish curraghs and Welsh coracles still in use today) that carried them across the English Channel, they included items that would change England's flora forever: domesti-cated animals and cultivated crops. The seeds of annual wild grasses endemic to the Fertile Crescent of the Near East had provided the agricultural legacy for the new migrants to the British Isles. Over millennia, as people cultivated wheat, barley, rye, and other grains in the grass family (Gramineae), they recognized and selected better strains. Farmers transported these improved cereals (named for the Roman goddess of agriculture, Ceres) throughout the Mediterranean region. A westward migra-tion of farming people opened up the forests of Europe, because the husbanding of cereal crops required land cleared of its trees. The arrival of these colonists, with their breeding and milking stock, winter fodder, seed grain, and agricultural tools, made as great a change on the patterns of land use employed by hunter-gatherers in Great Britain as English colonists, five thousand years later, imposed on the lifestyle of the natives of the New World.

Nomadic farmers wielding sharp axes of polished stone felled trees to make small, temporary clearings. They then cut, stacked, and burned the timber. Working the warm wood ash into the soil released nutrients and prepared the ground for their seeds. Each society that followed brought new technologies that hastened the inroads being made on England's wildwood. During the Bronze Age, greater numbers of people needing even larger settlement areas increased the size of permanent

clearings. Browsing or foraging on different species, their cattle, goats, and pigs ate their way through the forest and decimated different habitats. Wooded areas on heavy soils, which had remained untouched, fell under the Celt's new iron plows, and, later, large tracts of forest fueled Roman ironworks. The Romans actually exported grains grown in the British Isles, and their exceptional road system allowed easy dissemination of domestic seeds and plants throughout Great Britain. By the time the first survey of the British countryside in 1086, instigated by William I (the Conqueror), recorded land use and holdings in the *Domesday Book* (1086), only fifteen percent of the island was forested, and the true "wildwood" no longer existed. Southern England was by then densely inhabited, and most of its population lived in hamlets and villages separated from one another by mountain, down, heath, and moorland, not by forest.

William's reign saw another innovation: Tracts of land located in the wilder parts of the countryside that often included privately owned woods and that encompassed moorland, pasture, open wastes (forests overgrazed by cattle or pigs, or formerly cultivated land returning to scrub), and commons—even villages—became Royal Forests. These were forests in a legal (if not always a vegetational) sense, and they existed primarily as habitations for the King's red deer and wild boar. They provided the King, his court, and his professional hunters not only with grounds over which to hunt and acquire meat for the King's table but also to acquire shillings for the King's coffers, because the Crown often held the timber, grazing, pasturing, and mineral rights to the land as well. A whole cadre of officials protected those rights—from the Chief Forester to the officials of the individual forest, with its warden, lieutenant, verderers, walking and riding foresters, woodwards, agisters, rangers, parkers, palers, and regarders. By protecting game, these men insured a stable and controlled environment, and they helped indirectly to conserve forested areas. In the span of two centuries, with the exception of exacting monetary profits and meat for special celebrations from his holdings, the Crown lost interest in the Royal Forests. The bureaucracy that collected the fines and meted out the punishments became corrupt, and English society had by then doubled in size, requiring more arable land, more pastures, and more forest products. England's pell-mell growth was finally halted, and the population was halved by a scourge of famine and disease. When the Black Death swept across Europe in the great pandemics of the fourteenth and fifteenth centuries, more than a million English people died. In the sixteenth century, when the population again began to increase, the distance had widened between the displaced and homeless poor and the merchant, tradesman, landed gentry, and even the yeomen class. It was more profitable to use land to raise sheep than to engage in any other venture. The wealthy enclosed common land to consolidate their holdings and converted more and more of the dwindling forest either to arable land or to pasture.

By the beginning of the seventeenth century, four-fifths of England's population lived south of an imaginary line running from the bustling Atlantic Coast seaport of Bristol northeast across the country to the great estuary in the east known as The Wash. Although England's society was still agrarian, one-quarter of the people inhabited urban areas. With the Thames Valley the home to more than a million people, two hundred thousand people resided in the city of London alone.

In the south, along the coast, beside the rivers, and in the principal sheep-raising areas, the landscape had been given over to fields. The wooded areas held few trees suitable for timber, and mostly "underwood" remained. This underwood consisted largely of coppice trees—trees whose roots, once the main trunk had been cut, developed sprouts that grew to be dense clumps of secondary shoots. To fuel the furnaces and to fulfill the everyday needs of firebote (fuel wood), hedgebote (fencing material), and housebote and cartbote (wood used in the repair of buildings and equipment), people pollarded, lopped, or topped coppice trees, treating the wood as a crop to be harvested in cycles. As more woods disappeared, tradesmen suffered: the cobbler and the cooper, the carpenter and brickmason, the tanner and dyer—to a man, all users of wood—saw their livelihoods threatened. Manufacturers, too, were at a loss; everything from soap, salt, and sugar

POLLARDING WILLOWS.

47. Managing a tree so that, over time, successive cuttings of wood can be obtained from the same root system can be accomplished in several ways. Trees that have a propensity to sucker can be cut at the ground, leaving a stump, or coppice stool, that will continue to produce shoots. A tree can be shredded (or shrouded) which is a method that consists either of removing limbs first from one side of the tree and then, after the tree has regenerated limbs on that side, removing them from the other side, or of removing all limbs on both sides except at the very top. This illustration of men pollarding willows shows a very common method of managing trees for wood production. Pollarding, otherwise known as lopping or cobbing, is a process that begins with cutting a mature tree at seven to eighteen feet above the ground. The trunk that remains is called a bolling. The sprouts obtained by pollarding are similar to those produced by a coppice stool, but animals (such as deer) are not able to browse on the shoots when the tree is cut this high above the ground. John Evelyn, the famous English diarist and the author of *Sylva, or a Discourse of Forest-Trees, and the Propagation of Timber in His Majesties Dominions* (1664), offered this advice on timber management to estate owners: "Therefore if you would propagate trees for timber cut not off their heads at all, nor be too busy with lopping: but if you desire shade and fuel, or bearing of masts alone, lop off their tops, sear, and unthriving branches only."

---

to charcoal and clothes required fires of either long duration or great intensity made by burning vast amounts of wood. Populous southern England, no longer a society of subsistence farmers, fueled its industry with a raw material that was becoming both scarce and dear.

Soon, in East Anglia and the southwestern counties, the poor and the wealthy—the country gentlemen, yeomen, husbandmen, and village craftsmen, as well as the city's merchants and tradesmen—began to pay attention to the books being written and the stories being told about the rich lands and golden opportunities that lay across the Atlantic.

"The Newe-Come English Planters"

It is ironic that the first tenacious foothold gained in New England, the first "plantation" to succeed in a land so touted for its economic riches, was made by a small band of people motivated more by spiritual than by material gain. Virginia, with its warmer climate, may have been the Pilgrims' destination, but their sails had carried them to the colder northern limits of the Oak–Chestnut Forest. Though their numbers were halved during the four difficult winter months that followed their arrival, members of the Plymouth colony—the saints and the strangers, the Pilgrims from Leyden and the volunteers from London who filled out the plantation's quota—survived the "starving times," the cold, and even their own unpreparedness and frailties.

Their arrival in New England in the late fall of 1620 made erecting a shelter an immediate necessity. If the tradesman, gentleman, and servant (and the proportionately large number of wives and children that accompanied and probably inspired them) had any hope of surviving, they had to learn quickly the skills of the woodsman and the carpenter. It did not matter that Isaac Allerton, William White, and Samuel Fuller boarded the *Mayflower* as tailor, wool comber, and boot dealer; by the end of December, each had journeyed ashore to "fell some timber, some to saw, some to rive, and some to carry," as all able-bodied men labored cooperatively to construct the first of the colonists' frame dwellings.

These buildings presented a problem. The last place the Pilgrims wanted to set up housekeeping was in the forest. It did not matter that, in most cases, these southern New England woods were clear and open; in the minds of the Pilgrims, who had come from a land almost denuded of trees, the forest was dark and a wilderness home not only to dangerous and mysterious birds and beasts but also to fearsome Indians. With careful deliberation, they had chosen (as did many that followed in their footsteps) an open area, an abandoned Indian field, upon which to lay out their road and build their houses. Unfortunately, this choice placed them some distance from the very materials they required for building their houses. The hard and slow work of felling trees and hauling timber provided many a Pilgrim with the first opportunity to hold an ax, much less to heft one. The new environment presented yet another problem: the many different kinds of trees were not the familiar ones of home.

48. An assemblage of "typical" leaves from different species of oak. Of the twelve oaks represented, only one, *Quercus robur*, the English oak, is an introduced or exotic species. The remaining eleven line drawings represent the leaves of native oaks that can be found growing in the woods of New England. *A,* bear (scrub) oak, *Q. ilicifolia; B,* white oak, *Q. alba; C,* black oak, *Q. velutina; D,* English oak, *Q. robur; E,* dwarf chinkapin oak, *Q. prinoides; F,* post oak, *Q. stellata; G,* pin oak, *Q. palustris; H,* chestnut oak, *Q. prinus; I,* bur (mossy-cup) oak, *Q. macrocarpa; J,* scarlet oak, *Q. coccinea; K,* swamp white oak, *Q. bicolor; L,* northern red oak, *Q. rubra.*

"The Long Liv'd Oak"

English adventurers had been pleased to send back news of acorn-bearing trees growing in the New World forests; they held their English oak (*Quercus robur*) in high regard, and they hoped that one or more of the oaks that grew in these new forests possessed its qualities. They did not know that species of this large family of trees occupy every temperate region in the world, and that, although the exact number of species is a matter of debate, taxonomists would eventually identify close to 450 different species, almost two-thirds of them in the Americas. A complex taxonomic puzzle, oaks exhibit extreme variability and hybridize freely. They take on many different guises: they can be deciduous or evergreen, trees or shrubs. Often their leaves look similar to those of other trees, giving rise to such common names as laurel oak, willow oak, and chestnut oak. To cope with the large number of species and hybrids, a wide range of characteristics are used in identifying the different kinds of oaks. There is, however, one aspect common to all: no other tree in eastern North America bears fruit like an acorn.

Most of the acorn-bearing trees the Pilgrims encountered in the new environment grew to be fairly large, and, although many of them retained their leaves throughout winter, all were deciduous. The shape of oak leaves varies so greatly, even on the same tree, that determining an individual's identity by its leaves alone is a risky business. Because the acorns of each species are unique, and the bark of different species is almost as distinctive, it is likely that, in telling one species of oak from another, the colonists relied more upon the habit of the tree and on the characteristics of its acorns and bark than on the shape of its leaves. The first oaks they became familiar with were the white (*Quercus alba*), the red (*Q. rubra*), and the black (*Q. velutina*). Over time, they would become familiar with others, and botanists would later examine and compare flowers, fruits, leaves, bud scars, and winter buds in determining that thirteen different species of oaks grow in the forests of southern New England.

Once the settlers identified *Quercus alba* and *Q. rubra*, they had unknowingly become acquainted with the trees that typify the two major groups, or subgenera, into which the American oaks are divided. Taxonomists assign species to either the white oak group or the red oak group, depending on whether or not the lobes of the leaves end with a bristle, a small spinelike projection, and by the length of time required for the acorns to mature. Leaves of the white oak group have smooth, rounded lobes; their acorns mature in just one season. The red oaks have bristle-tipped lobes, and two years are needed for their acorns to ripen fully. Wood anatomists have added another character to distinguish the two groups: the shape and thickness of the pores developed in the wood during the summer growing season. White oaks have summer (or new) wood pores that are angled, small, and thin-walled; these same pores in red oaks are large, rounded, and thick-walled.

The first product made and shipped from the Plymouth colony consisted of barrel staves fashioned from the wood of oaks. As soon as a cooper began to ply his trade, he noticed that the characteristics of oak wood differed. The wood of white oaks, with its smaller pores, made the best staves for wet cooperage, pipes, casks, and hogsheads for holding liquids. Dry provisions—flour, sugar, nails, and even sticky molasses—could be transported safely in slack cooperage, barrels made from the more porous wood of red oaks.

New England desperately needed manufactured goods. Ships laden with the colony's most exportable commodities—dried cod, corn, peas, and forest products—called at the wine-making islands off the coast of North Africa and on wine ports in southeastern Europe. As a consequence, trade in white oak staves grew so briskly (not only did this wood hold wine, it improved its flavor) that credit generated from transactions with winemakers was applied to the purchase of guns, gunpowder, glass, salt, and clothes made in England. The different degrees of porosity of the wood of American oaks had proven to be an important economic discovery. Had the finished product been prone to leak, the winemakers of the Azores and the Canary Islands and those in Spain and Portugal would not have been so willing to continue to purchase the "shooks" (pieces of unassembled casks) that the colonists exported.

Once they had learned the value of many of the new trees and had become aware of each one's finer points, the colonists would occasionally resort to slight exaggerations when appropriate opportunities arose. A Mister Thomas More—known as "the Pilgrim Botanist"—had been sent from England to collect specimens and to gather information about New England's flora and fauna. The settlers told More that the pores of the red oak were so large that "a beam of this wood 40 feet long you may blow at one end and a man shall perceive your breath at the other end." He believed them and wrote home with the news. Once he swallowed that piece of information, this piece followed: hogs in New England grew so tall that "they could eat the top leaves of an Oak." Only later did More discover that there existed in the New World a very small oak, *Quercus ilicifolia*, whose height at maturity can be less than two feet. Perhaps "the Gullible Botanist" would have been a better title for Mr. More.

"Orderly, Fair, and Well Built Houses"

The Pilgrims' survival at Plymouth and the Puritans' success at Boston encouraged others to immigrate. Potential for economic growth and political freedom outweighed fear of the unknown, and increasing numbers of English men, women, and children boarded ships destined for New England. Just as the spiritual and political leaders brought their visions of utopia to the New World, so the craftsmen carried their tools. Despite lofty ideals, the building of New England was shaped by the skills and traditions of a society determined to recreate the familiar patterns of European life in an undeveloped land.

Among the thousands of emigrants who arrived during the Great Migration of the 1630s, there were some who relied temporarily on makeshift shelters for housing. Contemporary accounts tell of families that lived in "tents of Cloath" and "canvas boothes"—accommodations reminiscent of the temporary dwellings thrown up by itinerant charcoal makers in England. However, as soon as land could be cleared, building skills acquired, or carpenters engaged, these families abandoned their rude hovels and made permanent homes built in the style of contemporary English frame construction.

In England, notched joints and wooden pegs held houses together; the strength of oak timbers supported heavy roofs made of thatch, tile, or slate, and the huge size of the supporting members enabled carpenters to cut into them without fear of weakening the structure. In the New World, the tradition of post-and-beam construction was continued, and the colonists cut tons of white oak to supply the preferred wood for beams, joists, rafters, and braces. Only when mass-produced nails became available early in the nineteenth century could American carpenters take advantage of the vast quantities of nails, planks, and boards made by mechanical means to develop two new building techniques: Called balloon-frame and platform-frame construction, these techniques utilized many smaller timbers and thinner boards.

Young men apprenticed to the carpentry trade in England at the end of the sixteenth century had learned their craft from masters who had worked during a time when nearly everyone who could afford to build, rebuild, or add on to their dwellings did so. This surge of construction, which culminated in Britain's great Housing Revolution, wreaked havoc on the island's remaining forests, but it produced a remarkable carpentry tradition. The young carpenters who migrated were expected to know which type of timber suited each job, to estimate the volume, weight, and running feet of wood contained in each live tree, and (now in the New World) to recognize and select the appropiate kinds of trees needed from among the many unfamiliar species available. Builders chose the wood of the white oak (*Quercus alba*) to be their mainstay for the huge and heavy timbers needed for framing buildings. For durability and strength, they had selected what would prove to be the best all-round hardwood tree North America possessed. Carpenters and potential homeowners learned to seek a tree with a light, ashy-gray bark, sometimes tinged with red or brown. This oak bore a relatively small (one-half to three-quarters of an inch long) acorn whose cap, with its warty scales, covers about a quarter of the nut. It is next to impossible to ignore its fall crop of acorns—in a heavy fruiting (or mast) year, one mature white oak can produce as many as three thousand. As builders searched the

forest, they saw how deceptive the leaves of this species can be. Anywhere from five to nine inches in length and three to four inches in width, the leaves of white oak can have five, six, or seven lobes. Most misleading is the extent to which the leaf may be divided. Some are so deeply divided that very little leaf surface remains on either side of the midvein, and the leaves look more like the skeleton of a leaf than a leaf itself; others have only slight indentions and appear hardly lobed at all.

Like many other tree species, the white oak reaches the limits of its northern range in central New England. Most of Maine has conditions unfavorable for the growth of white oak, but some trees do occur in the southern tier of counties. White oaks can be found along the Connecticut River valley in New Hampshire and Vermont. In New Hampshire, they grow in greater abundance in the eastern part of the state; in Vermont, they are most often found west of the Green Mountains. However, there are few places in Massachusetts, Connecticut, and Rhode Island where *Quercus alba* does not occur. In the Ohio and Mississippi river valleys, individual trees can exceed heights of 150 feet, but even in New England the sight of an old and solitary white oak is impressive. The short, stocky trunk, with bark that looks a bit like worn, oversized, wide-wale corduroy, can support massive, wide-spreading branches that are larger than many full-grown

49. Although Frederick Law Olmsted was the designer of the Arnold Arboretum's road system, the system of pathways that wend their way through the collections is the creation of Charles Sprague Sargent, the Arboretum's first director. Sargent felt that the paths would allow the visitor more intimate access to the collections than was possible with roadways. Oak Path leads through the largest and one of the oldest of the original plantings. Along this path, Sargent's "groups" (groves of trees of a single species) were most highly developed. This photograph was taken in 1979, at the beginning of a restoration of the Arnold Arboretum's path system. The path and its surroundings have been greatly altered since the days of Sargent and Olmsted; the oaks have been thinned, and only remnants of Sargent's groups are evident. However, the large white oak (*Quercus alba*) that appears on the left hand side of the path was probably a seedling tree when the virgin forest covered the land that became the Arnold Arboretum. An estimate by a staff member who traced the evolution of the Arboretum's landscape places this oak's age at more than 300 years.

50. A view taken in June 1908 of the lower section of Bussey Brook valley with the mountain laurels (*Kalmia latifolia*) in full bloom in the middle distance. The sawmill that was powered by the brook and the dam that once flooded the valley were both located in front of the dark line of trees that appear in the distance on the left side of this photograph. For many years, the meadows in the Arnold Arboretum were allowed to go to hay, and wildflowers, such as the black-eyed Susans (*Rudbeckia hirta*) and ox-eye daisies (*Chrysanthemum leucanthemum*), both seen blooming in the foreground, provided such a display that W. J. Bean of the Royal Botanic Gardens, Kew, made special mention of the Arboretum's meadow plants in a published report on his visit in 1910: "Another beautiful feature of the Arboretum, and one which makes a special appeal to the foreigner, is the native undergrowth. In place of the lawns and grass which cover so much of the ground in English gardens and parks, there is here a very interesting ground-covering consisting of native plants, amongst which are various species of Vaccininum, Aster, Rubus, golden rod and asclepias, *Baptisia tinctoria*, sweet fern and the poison ivy." Although much of the meadow alongside Bussey Brook is now mowed regularly, the spontaneous flora that occurs along its margins still contains a colorful assortment of native and naturalized plants.

trees. When competing for space in the forest, a white oak grows up, not out, and the trunk, often free of branches until just below its summit, tapers little and supports a small crown. In Colonial times, the potential homeowner felled these giants with an ax, then cut and hauled timbers that could weigh upwards of 48 pounds per cubic foot.

About halfway up Bussey Hill, to the left of the Arboretum trail known as Oak Path, grows a thick-boled tree with a conspicuous burl at its base. Had the acorn from which this tree grew fallen on the deeper and more fertile valley soil, a tree that matched or exceeded champion proportions might have resulted. Still, tall and wide by comparison with many others of its kind, the majesty of this specimen lies in the girth of its burly trunk and in the shape of its stout, gnarled limbs. A mere seedling in the virgin forest that covered the land in 1681, when John Weld acquired some 60 acres of "partly plowland part meadow and pasture and woodland" from his father, Joseph, the less-than-perfect hillside site helped to insure this tree's longevity. In the valley on Saw Mill Brook —now known as Bussey Brook—the dam that held back its waters and the sawmill that straddled its banks had both fallen into disrepair before the young, slender sapling had grown large enough to be sawn into boards. By 1763, when it was almost a century old—spared by its hillside location from being made into part of a house or a barn for the family or from being sold as lumber to a neighboring farmer—most of the valley had been cleared of timber trees. Too steep for cultivation, the hill probably served as pastureland, and perhaps this now formidable white oak, being one of only a few mature trees that remained in the area, was left to provide the next generation of farmers with shade for their cattle. Eleazer Weld, the last of a long line of Welds to work the farmland that had been in the family's hands since 1640, died during the first year of the nineteenth century. Six years later, Benjamin Bussey, a gentleman and a "scientific" farmer, purchased Eleazer's estate. The parcel included this sturdy white oak, as well as the hill and the brook that would both come to bear Bussey's name. During the next thirty years, Bussey added other contiguous farms to his holdings and acquired much of the surrounding countryside. He willed his land to Harvard University in 1842, and 210 acres of his extensive farm became the nucleus of the Arnold Arboretum. Today, Arboretum visitors can walk or drive along Bussey Street, then ascend Bussey Hill and rest for a while in the shade of a tree that cast its shadow over many of the area's earliest settlers.

The Lasting Cedar

Not long after home building began, the colonists realized that the exteriors of their homes required modification. Their houses may have been designed and constructed with methods well proven in an English climate, but, when the rains and winds of the Pilgrim's second winter caused "much daubing of our houses to fall down," they discovered the need to adapt to a harsher environment than England's, one that fluctuated between greater extremes. To withstand the cold as well as winter thaws, and as protection against drifting snow and freezing rain, warm, dry, and secure houses could not continue to be built with half-timbered plastered walls or to be roofed with thatch. Surrounded by the wealth of New England's raw materials, venturesome carpenters and novice homeowners experimented with native tree species to find new exterior sheathing materials. They adapted to their own needs some of the tools and methods coopers used to rive barrel staves, and they covered the exteriors of their houses with vertical weatherboards or clad them with overlapping, horizontal, unpainted clapboards or shingles. Cut in lengths of five to six feet and nailed with their ends overlapping one another, wedge-shaped oaken clapboards were a mainstay; but the colonists found, through trial and experience, that a very light and long-lasting clapboard or a smaller, tapered shingle could be made from the white wood of a rot-resistant tree that grew in freshwater swamps, wet depressions, and bogs. The colonists called this tree (which we know as the Atlantic white-cedar, *Chamaecyparis thyoides*) the swamp, post, or white cedar. Its wetland habitat gives the wood of *C. thyoides* a quality possessed by many other trees that grow with their roots submerged in water—durability. Considered to be the most durable of all wetland species of trees, its wood is also one of the lightest in weight.

Soon, both the sides and the roofs of the colonists' houses were covered with shingles. Originally, the roofs had been pitched at an angle of sixty degrees so rain would quickly run off the heavy bundles of thatch; the lighter cedar shingles allowed builders to modify those steep slopes. Shingles proved to be less susceptible to fire, and thus thatched roofs, along with chimneys made either of logs plastered with clay or of reeds and mortar, were outlawed, sooner or later, in almost every town.

So popular was the wood of this swamp-loving conifer for home building, for small boat construction, and for making poles, ties, yards, topmasts, and bowsprits for larger ships that the tree had become scarce by 1750.

51. This pilgrim at Plimoth Plantations is at work with a maul and a wedge turning Atlantic white-cedar logs into clapboards. To make a clapboard, a log is split in half, then each half is split again to make quarters, then eighths, and so on, until many thin pieces have been produced. Because the log is split radially, each piece is wedged-shaped in section. The "feather" edge, the thinnest part of the clapboard, begins at the center (or pith) of the log; the "butt" or thicker edge ends at the bark (or outer face) of the log. According to the *Dictionary of Architecture*, the word clapboard may have been derived from the German *Klapholz*, or *Klapperholz*, translated as "barrel-staves, clapboards" in Ludwig's *Lexicon* of 1789. While thatched roofs were very common in the Massachusetts Bay Colony, other materials, such as boards or shingles, were also used. However, because fire posed such a danger, thatched roofs and platted chimneys were abandoned rather quickly. In 1631, Thomas Dudley, commenting on construction in "our new town" (Cambridge, Massachusetts), makes note of the fact that "we have ordered that no man there shall build his chimney with wood, nor cover his house with thatch."

52. These houses, also at Plimoth Plantation, with their shingled roofs, clapboarded sides, and substantial fieldstone chimneys, reflect the carpenter's, joiner's, and stonemason's adaptation of local materials. Although shingles and clapboards could be found in England, the colonist's early and widespread use of Atlantic white-cedar and eastern white pine for these two purposes had significant effects on local timber resources. In 1663, John Josselyn reported in his book *New England Rarities Discovered* that "the colonists used white cedar to make shingles to cover their houses with instead of tyle, it will never warp." By 1685, *The Acts and Resolves . . . of the Province of the Massachusetts Bay . . .* had regulations governing the size of shingles: "That all shingles exposed to sale, shall . . . bear eighteen or fifteen inches in length, and not under three and a half inches in breadth . . . [nor] under full half an inch thick, and [be] well shaved." Apparently, these specifications were taken seriously, at least in Boston. The *Boston News-Letter* for 23/30 March 1713 reported: "On Wednesday last, . . . a Bonefire was made on King-Street below the Town-House, of a parcel of Shingles, (upwards of Eight thousand out of Ten thousand,) found defective by the Surveyors both as to length and breadth prescribed by the Law." The article continued with this warning, that "both makers and sellers of Shingles had best conform to the Law and prevent any more such Bonefires."

53. The quarter-inch female cones of the Atlantic white-cedar (*Chamaecyparis thyoides*) resemble pock-marked, globe-shaped raisins. As they mature, their color changes from bluish purple to a dark reddish raisin brown.

54. Eastern redcedar (*Juniperus virginiana*) produces cones that look unlike those of either *Chamaecyparis* or *Thuja*. In fact, they do not look like cones at all, but appear to be berrylike. Called juniper berries (no one seem to find it strange that juniper berries grow on cedar trees), their soft, fused scales rarely open by themselves, and the one or two wingless seeds contained within are released and dispersed most often by birds. Cedar waxwings find the dark blue, fleshy cones particularly attractive, and they feed on them voraciously in the fall.

55. Eastern arborvitae (*Thuja occidentalis*) releases its seeds from small structures that look somewhat like the typical cones of pines. Oval, with four to six scales, these fruits are light brown and are held upright on short, curved stalks. After ripening and shedding their winged seeds, they remain attached to the branches, looking almost flowerlike.

When the English nurseryman, agriculturist, and author William Cobbet crisscrossed the new nation in the years following the Revolution, he came away with the impression that "all the good houses in the United States were covered with white cedar shingles." He may have exaggerated, but the disappearance of cedar forests had already been noted by Benjamin Franklin, who wrote, in *Poor Richard's Almanac* for the year 1749, of the need for Americans to plant other trees to take its place.

The tree the colonists called the swamp cedar (*Chamaecyparis thyoides*) is not a cedar at all. The true cedars, four species in the genus *Cedrus* of the pine family (Pinaceae), are Old World plants found in the mountains of Africa or Asia, on the island of Cyprus, or in the hills of Lebanon. *C. thyoides* is a small coastal conifer in the cypress family (Cupressaceae). The family also includes two other eastern North American conifers, *Thuja occidentalis* and *Juniperus virginiana*. All three have wood that has a slightly spicy, aromatic "cedar"

fragrance, somewhat the same shape as the Old World cypress, and thin, easily peeled shaggy bark. Unfortunately, because of these similarities, each has come to be known by one or more names that include the word "cedar." There are other conifers in America's southern and western states that are also called cedars, and designations that imply regional distributions have been added to the already befuddled common names. Thus, in addition to swamp cedar, post cedar, and white cedar, Atlantic white-cedar is known also as northern white-cedar, southern white-cedar, false-cypress, and juniper. Alas, arborvitae, *Thuja occidentalis,* is also often called white cedar and northern white-cedar, and *Juniperus virginiana* is known as red cedar, eastern redcedar, pencil cedar, and sometimes aromatic redcedar. Even botanists took a long time to agree upon the classification and family placement of these plants, yet, to this day, lumbermen persist in lumping almost all fragrantly scented conifers under one form or another of the name "cedar."

Unrestricted to either the North or the South, the common name "Atlantic white-cedar" most clearly identifies the range of *Chamaecyparis thyoides*. Rarely found anywhere but in swamps, it grows within a narrow coastal belt 50 to 130 miles wide that stretches from the gulf coast of Louisiana to northern Florida and north into southern Maine. Usually reaching 20 to 50 feet in height with a trunk up to two feet thick, Atlantic white-cedars form such solid stands that they can exclude other trees and make the dense swamps and miry marshes they inhabit all but impenetrable. For the colonists, cutting cedar wood was a winter chore; only when the boggy ground was frozen could they hope to penetrate into the gloomy and featureless cedar swamps that were often held in common and set aside for public use. They harvested the cedars but could find no use for the wet and untillable land on which they grew. The remaining Atlantic white-cedar swamps of Massachusetts, Rhode Island, and Connecticut may well represent the last vestiges of the awesome "wilderness" that the colonists confronted and the Native Americans savored.

More than 150 years later—as preparations were being made to celebrate the country's centennial in 1876—Americans paused and reflected on the qualities and lifestyles of earlier times, and a revival of all things Colonial became fashionable. Architects seized on the form and materials of Colonial dwellings, and shingles became more than an impervious weather seal—they became stylish. In the northeast, in the 1880s, the Shingle Style came into its own as Henry Hobson Richardson, Boston's master architect, launched a renaissance in domestic architecture utilizing stone and wood. Following his lead, New England architects began to weave rich patterns of cedar shingles over the porches, gambrels, towers, turrets, and gables of new seaside "cottages," turning what had been a Colonial hodgepodge of additions and lean-tos into massive, streamlined mansions.

Atlantic white-cedars grow in the Arnold Arboretum's conifer collection, but they have also been planted in a more suitable ecological habitat. Just inside the Arboretum's main entrance, the Arborway Gate, and across from the Visitor Center lies a wetland meadow several acres in size. Willow Path skirts its edge on the Arborway side. Along with other native and exotic wetland trees and shrubs, several Atlantic white-cedars collected in 1980 and 1981 from Massachusetts bogs grow beside the path.

Only 47 feet above sea level, this meadow (the lowest land in the Arboretum) was once covered by water; this area served as part of a catchment basin for run-off from

56. The bark of Atlantic white-cedar (*Chamaecyparis thyoides*) is usually quite thin over the entire tree, but on mature trees, such as this one photographed at the Arnold Arboretum, the bark can become nearly two inches thick at the base of the trunk, decreasing in thickness farther up on the tree. The bark can range in color from ashy gray to a reddish brown. When a piece of bark is peeled off, the inner side is a bright cinnamon brown. On young trees and on small branches, the fibrous bark is usually quite smooth. Mature trees have bark that is irregularly furrowed into narrow, flat, connected ridges that separate into loose scales that can be peeled off in long, fibrous strips. Throughout its range, natural stands of Atlantic white-cedar are usually pure, even-aged, and very dense. In the swamps of the Southeast, where *Chamaecyparis thyoides* trees reach heights of between 100 and 120 feet and can have diameters between three and five feet, large pure stands, called "juniper glades" or "cedar glades," are so dense as to be almost impenetrable. In New England, the maximum height of this conifer is sixty feet, but most trees grow only to a height of forty feet. On Cape Cod, The White Cedar Swamp Walk in South Wellfleet at the Cape Cod National Seashore allows visitors to penetrate a relatively unspoiled cedar swamp by means of an elevated boardwalk that spans the tea-colored water and skirts the straight trunks of Atlantic white-cedar trees that arise out of raised hummocks.

---

melting glaciers. Peat deposits extending to a depth of 38 feet attest to its slow evolution from pond to swamp. Here, in prehistoric times, Native Americans may have gathered the young asaparaguslike shoots of milkweed (*Asclepias syriaca*) for a spring meal, dug the edible roots of cattail (*Thypha latifolia*) in winter, and returned later in the season to collect the cottonlike fluff of its flower heads for bedding, insulation, or even "disposable" diapers or dressings.

Old maps, including one that Charles Sprague Sargent and Frederick Law Olmsted used in planning the Arboretum, show this area covered by a large swamp fed by a meandering stream. The stream, Goldsmith Brook, had its source near the summit of Moss Hill, a large drumlin to the northwest of the Arboretum, and it followed a downhill course roughly parallel to the present-day Louder's Lane. Crossing what was then the "high road to Dedham" (now Centre Street, U.S. Route 1), the stream traversed "Gore's Meadow," a property mentioned in the "Ancient Transcript" of 1654, the oldest record of Roxbury landholding. In 1883, an agreement was reached

57. The Fairbanks House, located at 511 East Street in Dedham, Massachusetts, was built in 1636 by Jonathan Fairbanks, and it is purportedly the oldest wooden structure in the United States. Eight succeeding generations of Fairbankses lived in their ancestral home until, in this century, it became a family-owned museum open to the public. The original house was of salt-box design—a shape so named for its resemblance to the kitchen salt boxes used by the colonists—and it faced south to capture the sun's heat during winter; the long sloping roof of the salt-box faced north, or into the prevailing wind. This house, as did most seventeenth-century houses, turned its back to the cold. The lean-to, which was added not long after the main structure was completed, contains two rooms and continues the roof line almost to the ground. Additions such as this one added extra space and also served as an additional buttress against the winter wind. On the rear wall of the original dwelling in the lean-to attic, seventeenth-century cedar clapboards are still in place. This photograph, which shows the rear elevation and the rambling roof line, was taken around 1900, when the house was completely surrounded by giant old American elms.

between the city of Boston and Harvard University that made the construction of roads, fences, benches, and other amenities the city's responsibility and the care and curation of the plantings the Arboretum's and, in 1890, city workers built Meadow Road, neatly dividing Gore's Meadow in two. The *Tilia* (basswood or linden) collection occupies the drier half, while the former swampland on the other side is now a wetland meadow. The Arborway, completed in 1895, dammed and defined the swamp's eastern edge, and Goldsmith Brook disappeared into a culvert to become a subterranean stream. For the next 30 years, with more than half the holding capacity of this wetland lost through road construction, and with the "drainage improvements" attempted by the city not complete, water ponded here for most of the year. Except along the edge, its boggy, peaty soil has foiled attempts to establish a permanent collection of woody plants. Still very wet, and appearing unchanged from the early days of the Arboretum, it is only in the fall, when its surface is dry and firm enough to support heavy machinery, that this part of the Arboretum can be mowed. It is mowed on a two-year cycle; the biennial mowing keeps volunteer tree and shrub seedlings in check, and a herbaceous flora rich in many wetland species covers the area.

"Wood Hard As Iron"

Until "bog iron" (the deposits of iron oxides found in the sediment of freshwater ponds, swamps, and marshes of southeastern New England) had been discovered, and until furnaces and foundries had been built, colonists advised potential emigrants that success—perhaps even survival—depended on arriving in America equipped with iron tools. A broadax and felling ax were essential, but so were hoes, shovels, spades, and saws. Whenever possible, and often out of necessity, implements made of wood replaced costly and scarce iron tools. Wooden shovels, sometimes tipped with an iron edge, worked well in winter; the snow slid off the wood. Plowshares could be made from the black tupelo (*Nyssa sylvatica*), because its wood is light and moderately strong and has an interlocking grain that resists wear and withstands shock. Trees of this genus once grew in all temperate regions of the world, but only those native to the New World and southeastern Asia survived the Pleistocene glaciations. The colonists picked up the name tupelo for this new tree from the Creek Indian words *ito,* "tree," and *opilwa,* "swamp." Tupelos grow in moist bottom land and swamps. Linnaeus chose *Nyssa,* the name of a water

58. Entitled "A winter morning shoveling out," this illustration by Winslow Homer, which appeared in the magazine *Every Saturday* on 14 January 1871, lends credence to the generational refrain that when father (or grandfather, or even great-grandfather) was young, the snowfalls were deeper, the winters were colder, the summers were hotter . . . and, most probably, the task of shoveling out after a storm was much more difficult.

59. A specimen of *Nyssa sylvatica* growing at Green Harbor, a coastal village that is part of the town of Marshfield, Massachusetts. The spreading, flat-topped crown of this tree is typical of most tupelos. The pendulous lower branches, which can often almost touch the ground, are also typical of this species. So too are its twiggy branches, which are often the first characteristic of this tree that catches the eye. According to the author of an unsigned article published in *Garden and Forest* in 1893, who was obviously a champion of tupelos, "it is always individual, always picturesque, and if planted for ornament in any situation, low or high, it invariably gives pleasure. In form it is always attractive."

nymph in classical mythology, to acknowledge this trait, but these trees actually fare better and live longer when they grow adjacent to, not in, a wetland habitat. *N. sylvatica* has other common names; black gum and sour gum refer to the color and taste of the fruits, and southerners also use the name pepperidge.

The black tupelo is polygamodioecious, which means that male and female flowers are borne on separate trees but that perfect flowers—those that contain both male and female parts—appear on each tree as well. In spring, these greenish flowers are easy to overlook, but the bril-

liant scarlet to ruby-red color of the leaves of black tupelo in the fall more than makes up for the tree's lack of floral display.

A slow-growing understory tree, often found sharing the black tupelo's wet domain, has wood that made another fine substitute for plowshares. This small tree, with its thin, smooth, bluish-gray bark stretching taut over curiously sinewed trunk and limbs, looked familiar to the colonists. The European hornbeam (*Carpinus betulus*) has multiple trunks, similar flowers and fruits, and extraordinarily dense wood as hard as the bony

60. The tupelo's leathery leaves are smooth-edged and alternate, and they cluster together at the ends of its twiggy branchlets. In spring, its greenish flowers are easy to overlook. In fall, however, the brilliant scarlet to ruby-red color of tupelo leaves more than makes up for the tree's lack of floral display. The pigment anthocyanin is primarily responsible for the tupelo's fall color. Anthocyanin is found in the cell sap, and, for most of the growing season, the bright green of the chlorophyll in the leaves (which turns energy from the sun into carbohydrates) masks the red of the anthocyanin. In the fall, once the leaves stop producing chlorophyll, the bright red is revealed.

61. These greatly enlarged drawings illustrate a staminate or "male" flower (*left*, × 14) and three carpellate or "female" flowers (*right*, × 10.5) of the black tupelo (*Nyssa sylvatica*), also known as the black gum or sour gum. Several staminate flowers are clustered together at the end of a long pedicel to form the male inflorescence, while the corresponding female inflorescence consists of three or four flowers, as shown here. Individual trees usually produce flowers of only one type.

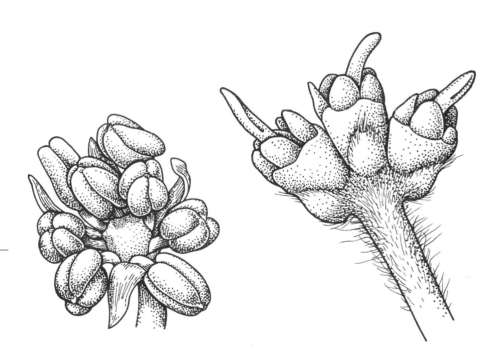

62. Perhaps the most striking aspect of the American hornbeam (*Carpinus caroliniana*) is the sinewy look of its trunk and branches. The tree's exceptionally smooth bark appears to be wrapped around taut, powerful muscles and tendons that spiral and ripple their way from the bottom of the trunk up and through its many branches.

antler of a deer. Describing the new tree in his *New England's Prospect,* William Wood declared that "the Horne-bound tree is a tough kind of Wood, that requires so much paines in riving as is almost incredible." Some called the native tree, *C. caroliniana,* hornbeam after the European species. Farmers christened it ironwood, carved it into mallet heads, and fitted pieces of its trunk and branches to their plows and their short-handled tools. The common name blue beech is an appropriate one for the American species, because they do look like diminutive bluish-barked beech trees.

Appropriately sited in a shallow depression bisected by a spring-fed stream, the Arboretum's *Carpinus* collection displays the broad range of shapes that members of this genus can assume. Not only are there specimens that have dense, rounded, and regular crowns that look as if they have been meticulously pruned into shape, there are also trees whose contorted, angular, and irregular limbs seem to defy the tools of any pruner. Viewed from above or from Valley Road, the varied habits of these small, dense-limbed trees are apparent.

"Torches of Pine"

In dark, small-windowed Colonial homes, the roaring fireplace brightened the room by day, and it often produced the only light available at night. Had domestic animals been abundant, the typical melted beef-suet or mutton-suet candles that the guildmakers produced in England would have been made. Tallow was scarce, however, and the inventive and resourceful settlers turned to materials ranging from extremely combustible meadow rushes soaked in lard to fish oil burned in shallow, wrought-iron holders, called Betty lamps, to illuminate their homes. These lamps sputtered, smoked, and smelled unpleasant. A new method of lighting discovered by the colonists consisted of burning the resin-rich wood of a conifer that grew on the sandy coastal plains and ridges and in the sand barrens of river valleys. *Pinus rigida* earned the names candlewood and torch pine from the Europeans after they had observed how easily the Indians produced a bright flame by igniting several slivers of wood cut from its "fat" heartwood. The colonists referred to these sputtering torches that dripped pitch as "splint lights."

Whether growing in sterile seaside sands, where they are frequently bathed by salt spray, or rooted on exposed, windswept rocky hilltops, the torch or pitch pine thrives under adverse conditions. Easily blown over when young,

a pitch pine eventually develops a root system that is substantial and deep enough to anchor it and to allow the tree to grow on an extremely dry site. Trees not more than four inches in diameter can have roots that penetrate to a depth of more than nine feet. Forest fires in these dry, windy habitats are devastating; however, not only do pitch pines survive, they often come to dominate the landscape after a fire. In New England, only *Pinus rigida* and the rarer *P. banksiana,* the jack pine—a tree of the Boreal Forest—are members of a group of conifers known as fire pines. These trees can withstand fire because they have evolved several specialized characteristics. All fire pines are pioneer trees—trees able to tolerate growing in full sun. Some have a high percentage of cones that remain closed until heat generated by fire melts the resin that glues the tips of their scales together, thereby releasing their seeds. These seeds remain viable inside the cone for many years, and they have the ability to germinate on soil totally lacking a humus component. The term "serotinous," which means late-developing, describes the habit of bearing closed cones that contain viable seeds for many years. Jack pines retain their tightly closed cones for so long that they often become embedded in the wood of the tree's branches and can completely disappear as the branches thicken. Pitch pine's special adaptations include a thick, protective bark, some cones that remain closed, and the ability—unusual among conifers—to sprout from dormant buds on the main stem or at the base of the trunk if the tree is burned or cut.

In New England, wherever the soil is exceptionally sandy, it is likely that pitch pines will be found. One of the few trees that can grow at the ocean's edge, flourish in salt marshes, and inhabit slowly moving sand dunes, *Pinus rigida* abounds on Cape Cod. Stunted oaks (black, red, scarlet, and white), along with the smaller post oak (*Quercus stellata*) and the Cape's ubiquitous scrub oak (*Q. ilicifolia*), are the common deciduous trees, but rising slightly above their crowns are the branches of the pitch pine, the true indicator of this sand-plain community. Usually reaching heights of less than fifty feet under the best of growing conditions, at thirty feet these trees overtop the Cape's stunted forest canopy or form pure stands of low pine woods. Whether described as being New England's most grotesque or most picturesque pine, a stand of *P. rigida* growing on a sandy hillside evokes an image of an untamed landscape.

Pitch pines seldom grow straight; they twist this way and that. Their bark is remarkably rough and scaly, its color a very dark reddish gray-brown. Sparse, irregularly

63. This photograph of a transverse section of the trunk of a jack pine (*Pinus banksiana*) was taken in 1978 by Alfred J. Fordham, the Arnold Arboretum's plant propagator for more than thirty years. He collected this specimen from a fast growing, approximately nine-year-old tree in the Arboretum's nursery to illustrate an article he was writing, with Richard Warren, on fire pines. A synopsis of Mr. Fordham's observations on how this occurred in this specimen follows: "Cones of *Pinus banksiana* often appear in multiples of two and three. This illustration shows one of a pair that continued to grow and evidence of one that failed six years previously. In this instance, the cone that failed was probably destroyed by a squirrel seeking seeds. Both cones originated at the tip of a shoot that was about one-quarter inch in diameter. As the trunk increased in girth during the first four years, the surviving cone became embedded, the wood that was formed during the fifth annual growth increment surrounded the cone, and this process continued each year until only the tip of the cone remained visible."

spaced limbs droop downward. Many of them are dead and devoid of any foliage, but they are still covered with old, open, weathered gray or blackened cones. The stiff, twisted needles grow at the ends of stout, short twigs. Each fascicle, or bundle, has three of these three- to five-inch-long yellowish-green needles. These dense clusters of needles festoon the live branches and also form tufts of foliage along the trunks. A multitude of cones with sharp, curved spines at the end of the scales also cling closely to the branches. A few of these cones mature, shed their seeds, and then fall off; most, however, remain firmly attached to the branches long after their seeds have been dispersed.

"Pitch—the Juice of the Pine"

It was *Pinus rigida*'s imperfection as a source of illumination that proved to be a clue to its most marketable asset—its abundance of pitchy tar. In the scramble to find and develop commodities for trade, the production of naval stores—pitch, tar, rosin, and turpentine—flourished on the sand plains of the New England colonies, the home of *P. rigida*. As early as 1628, residents of Plymouth requested that "men skylfull in making of pitch" be sent from England. Boiling pine tar made pitch, but extracting pine tar could be accomplished only by burning trees. To extract tar, a kiln is constructed that is much the same as that of a charcoal burner—that is, a furnace that greatly restricts the amount of air reaching the fire. The process requires that a pile of pitch pine be burned in the kiln as slowly as possible, often for two weeks or more, while an encircling ditch traps the liquid product as it oozes outward. The simple process of "boxing" or "milking" a tree—chopping away a section of the lower trunk, followed by chipping a channel in the bark—produced rosin, another salable commodity. Apparently, this process appealed to almost everyone who possessed a hatchet. Although the life span of trees treated this way was shortened, a farmer could add to his yearly income by "boxing" a stand of pine for several seasons.

As the production and trade of naval stores increased, whole forests of pitch pines vanished from coastal regions and from the outskirts of river-valley towns. When

Quercus alba. *1. pinnatifida.*
2. repanda.

Plate 9. This drawing of the white oak (*Quercus alba*) is reproduced from *Geschichte der Amerikanischen Eichen,* the German translation of André Michaux's *Histoire des Chênes de l'Amerique.* Michaux held the oaks in highest esteem. His studies led him to conclude, in his *Histoire des Chênes,* that "the oak family comprehends a great number of species which are not known; and the greater part of those which grow in America appear under such diversified forms when they are young, that we cannot be certain what they are until they have arrived at mature age, or have got their full growth." However, after planting and cultivating in his nursery many of the New World oaks that he had encountered in his travels, Michaux was confident enough to go on to state that "after two years, I had the satisfaction to recognize all the varieties which had perplexed me so much when I traversed the woods."

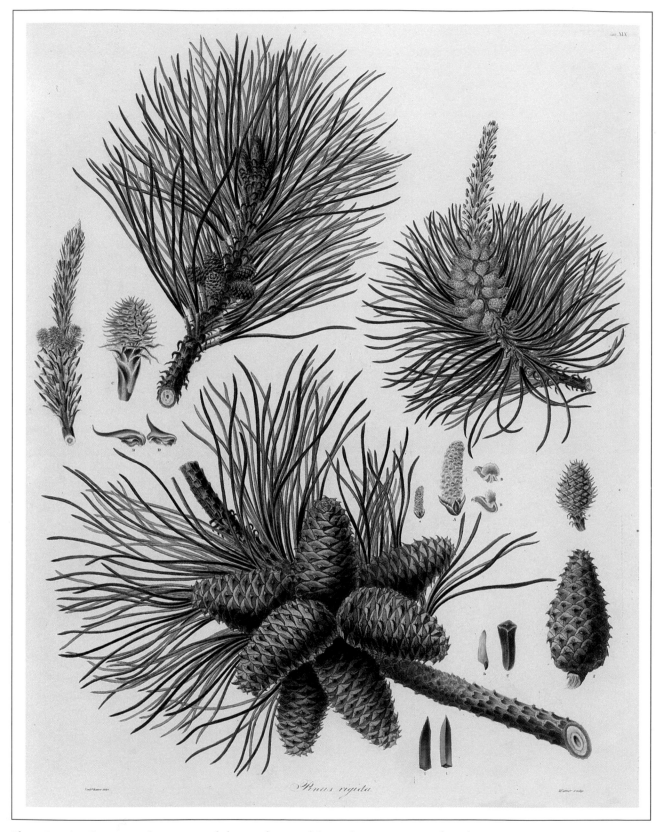

Pinus rigida

Plate 10.   This illustration shows a typical cluster of cones of the pitch pine (*Pinus rigida*), whose unopened scales will often remain closed until fire causes them to release their seeds. Although generally overlooked as an ornamental, because it is not well suited for providing shade or for use as a street tree, this pine's ability to prosper on poor soil, coupled with its unique, craggy habit, and thick, flaky, dark-red bark, should make it a candidate not only for reforestation of sand dunes and waste places but also as a specimen tree for parks and gardens.

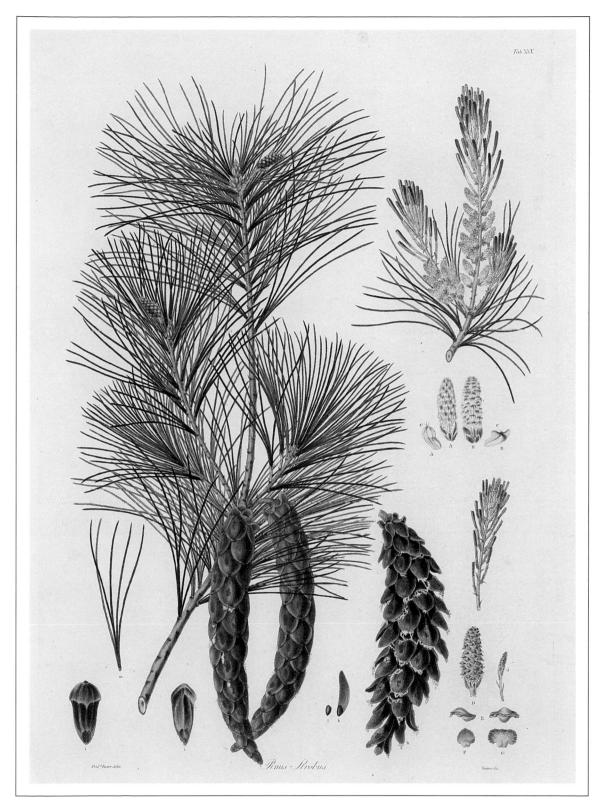

Plate 11.   This description of the habitat of the white pine (*Pinus strobus*), taken from Lambert's *Description of the Genus Pinus,* calls to mind the formidable task of felling these pines that North America's first loggers faced when they harvested the massive mast trees for the British navy: "The vallies, the crevices of the mountains, and banks of rivers, are the conservatories, as it were, to which the rains and melted snows in the spring carry down the fattest parts of the soil of the higher lands. In these spots, which are sometimes pretty elevated, the natural plantations of *P. Strobus* are seen growing to a height and thickness, not exceeded by any other of the tribe; indeed, few come near to it in these particulars. It is certain that among full-grown trees, on the best ground, there are some two hundred feet in height, and four or five in diameter at the lower end of the trunk."

Tab XXXIX

Pinus pendula.

Plate 12. Although the tamarack or American larch (*Larix laricina*) seems during winter to be the most dismal tree in the forest, in spring, the combination of blood-red buds, golden-yellow stamens, light green needles, rose-colored scales, and vivid magenta cones transforms the tamarack into the most colorful conifer of the New England woods.

Pinus canadensis.

Plate 13. Historically, the genus to which the hemlocks belong has been overburdened by botanical names. This explanation of the evolution of the present binomial for the eastern hemlock, *Tsuga canadensis,* was published in *Bulletin Number 3* of The Hemlock Arboretum at "Far Country" in 1933. "In the beginning of scientific botanical practice the [eastern] hemlock was included with the pines. It was labeled *Pinus Canadensis* by Linnaeus in 1763. Michaux, the French botanist, in 1796 grouped it with the firs and named it *Abies Canadensis,* while later scientists included it with the spruces and called it *Picea Canadensis.* It was the celebrated Austrian botanist Stephen Ladislaus Endlicher who, in 1847, used the name *Tsuga,* which is the Japanese name for the hemlock, as a section in his genus *Pinus.* Later [in 1855], Elie Abel Carriere, a famous French botanist, classified all the hemlocks into a separate . . . group under the generic name *Tsuga.* Thus this important section of our North American conifers bears a Japanese name, given by an Austrian, confirmed by a Frenchman, and now accepted by scientists generally."

Plate 14 (*top*). Of all the trees and shrubs native to New England and eastern North America, the flowering dogwood (*Cornus florida*) ranks both among the most ornamental and among the most adaptable to a wide range of growing conditions. This illustration, as well as the illustration of white ash (*below*), was drawn by Mark Catesby, an English naturalist who made two trips to the English colonies in North America during the eighteenth century with the express purpose of exploring for botanical and zoological novelties.

Plate 14 (*bottom*). Prominently displayed in this drawing by Mark Catesby is the infructescence of the white ash (*Fraxinus americana*). Each fruit included in this structure is technically a samara, a fruit type characterized by a prominent wing that allows the fruit to be dispersed by the wind. The samara fruit type is also characteristic of maples and elms. Catesby based himself at his sister's home in Williamsburg, Virginia, while he traveled extensively throughout what is now the southeastern United States, gathering specimens and recording his observations in his notebooks. Catesby made accurate, if somewhat primitive, drawings of the plants and animals he encountered. These were eventually published (between 1731 and 1743) in his *The Natural History of Carolina, Florida and the Bahama Islands*.

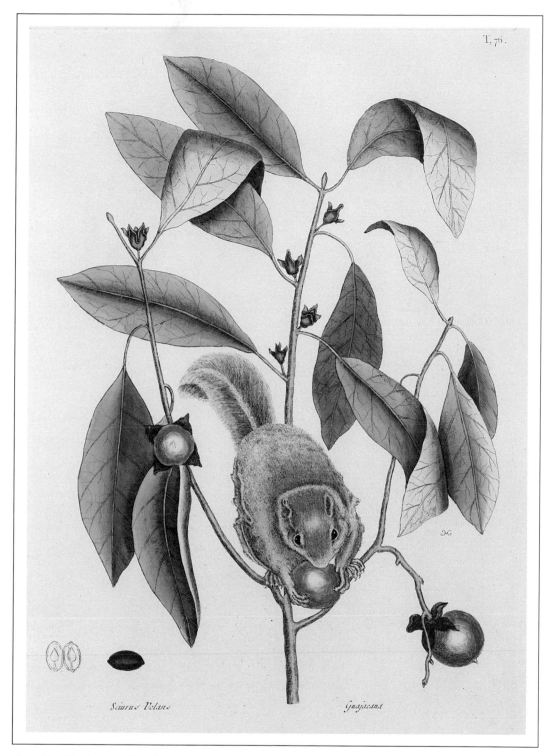

Scirus Volane   Guajacana

Plate 15.   The binomial for the common persimmon is *Diospyros virginiana*. the generic name, *Diospyros*, means "fruit of Zeus." Unfortunately for most New Englanders, few of whom are acquainted with this tree, and fewer of whom have any traditional knowledge of the nature of its fruits, the first taste of persimmon is usually a mouth-puckering experience not likely to be repeated with any haste. Persimmon fruits are deceptive; they taste best when they look their worst. Initially green, these odd-looking fruits first turn amber and then a pumpkin orange. But color alone is not the determining factor: an unripe persimmon, regardless of its color, is horribly astringent. Persimmons do not reach their sweet ripeness (some people describe this state as "dead ripe") until after a frost has wrinkled their skin, turned their pulp mushy, and made them look a bit like half-rotten, orange tomatoes. The flying squirrel that Catesby depicted here is not the only night creature that feasts on persimmon fruits: In the southern states, a common name for this tree is possumwood.

Tab. 48.

Liriodendron tulipifera
Virginischer Tulpenbaum.

Plate 16. This illustration, taken from *Osterreichs Allgemeine Baumzucht,* written by the Austrian botanist Franz Schmidt, depicts the tuliplike flowers of the tulip tree (*Liriodendron tulipifera*). As a teacher of botany and forestry, Schmidt was more likely interested in the value of this species as a timber tree than in the ornamental qualities of its unusual flowers. The wood of the tulip tree was favored during Colonial times because it was easily worked with hand tools. Today, because its wood is extremely versatile and can be used for a wide variety of products, yellow poplar (as it is known in the lumber trade) is one of the most important commercial hardwood species in the United States.

64. The cone of a two-year-old pitch pine (*Pinus rigida*) is about the size and shape of a goose egg, and, with each of its scales armed with a sharp prickle, the cone somewhat resembles a squat, woody pineapple. At maturity, at the end of the second season (after their scales have opened and shed their seeds), the shape of the cone changes dramatically. Some cones, however, do not open at maturity but remain closed until a fire, or cutting, triggers the opening of their scales. Trees may bear fertile cones when they are only eight years old, or perhaps even younger. Although pitch pines produce an abundance of seeds beginning at an early age, seedlings are extremely intolerant of shade and will not grow in the shade of the parent tree. It is easy to understand how the common name torch pine was applied to this tree. According to Francis Higginson of Salem, commenting (in his *New England Plantations*) on its abundance and value, "... our Pine-Trees that are the most plentifull of all wood, doth allow us plentie of Candles, which are very usefull in a House; and they are such Candles as the Indians commonly use, having no other, and they are nothing else but the wood of the Pine-Tree cloven in two little slices something thin, which are so full of the moysture of the Turpentine and Pitch, that they burne as cleere as a Torch."

66. This illustration, taken from
Andreas zum Forst-wesen . . . , a German
forestry manual by Johann Andreas
Cramer published in 1766, shows a
furnace, or open-air pit, made for extracting pine tar. The chief difference between
the construction of a charcoal kiln and
that of a tar-pit is the presence of a dike,
or berm, around the circumference of the
tar pit, which catches the liquid tar. The
plant material seen in the the cutaway
(or perhaps unfinished) portion of the
furnace is the other critical difference:
Because of the high resin content in their
wood, conifers, rather than hardwoods,
are burned in the production of tar.

65. An open-air pit charcoal kiln in the process of being constructed in western Massachusetts at the beginning of the nineteenth century. Billets of wood three to five feet long and two to six inches in diameter were stacked around kindling in a circular, conical pile, approximately twenty feet in diameter, until there was as much as 35 cords of wood in the pile. Openings were left at the base to provide a draft, and a central shaft or chimney, called a "pigpen," was left open to carry off the smoke. In this photograph, the wood is in the process of being covered, first (to a depth of three to five inches) with grass, leaves, moss, branches, or needles, then with earth, and finally with large sheets of sod, or "floats." Before the charcoal can be harvested from such a kiln, it must be kept burning slowly from ten to fourteen days. It is important to control the intake of air and to guard against flames bursting out, because *partial* combustion is the key to producing charcoal. During charring, constant supervision is needed to guard against air leaks or "explosions." If the earthern blanket burns through, it must be plugged immediately with short pieces of green wood and covered with fresh floats and earth. Hardwoods, such as beech, birch, maple, hickory, and oak, make the best charcoal. But many charcoal burners used wood of all shapes and sizes, including trees too small for other uses, and often stripped the nearby forest of all its growing trees.

67. Henri Louis Duhamel du Monceau described the art of collecting pitch in *Traite des Arbres et Arbustes qui se cultivent en France en pleine terre,* published in Paris in 1755. He wrote of how the peasants lifted strips of bark four fingers wide, from as high as they could reach down to two feet above the ground, all around the trunk of the tree. They returned two or three years later with hooks to scrape off the resin that had formed in the grooves, and they carried the resin to furnaces in cone-shaped baskets made from the bark of the *cormier,* or service tree. There they transferred the resin into cone-shaped copper kettles, each with a half-inch hole at the bottom, and placed them in an airtight furnace, which was fired slowly. The liquid pitch, which was sold as "greasy pitch" or "thick pitch," ran out through a pipe that exited the furnace at the rear, where it was caught in wooden barrels. Further refinement of the residue that remained in the kettles produced either dry (or black) rosin or lamp black.

rampant cutting of these trees occurred near the ocean, dunes became unstable, and drifting sand threatened harbors, homes, and pathways. Less than thirty years after the founding of Plymouth, rigid restrictions governing the cutting and the use of pitch pine had been established. By 1702, the town fathers forbade the taking of any pine from Plymouth's beaches. A wealth of pines grew on the sandy plains along rivers, and the rivers themselves provided an easy means for transporting forest products. Although families were allowed to continue gathering wood for lighting and fuel, the taking of candlewood for making tar was prohibited within six miles of the Connecticut River. Massachusetts enacted conservation measures in 1715 to protect both the pine trees and the land. No one, without a license, could "cut, carry off, bark or box any pine tree. . . ." Violation of the law carried a fine of twenty-five shillings for each tree harmed. Caught between the need to generate revenues and the desire to conserve resources, the fledgling government levied excise taxes, established fixed prices, and imposed controls on the quality and the quantity of naval stores. This New England industry flamed as brightly and burned out as quickly as a knot of pitch pine. By the first quarter of the eighteenth century, the pine belt in the Carolinas and Georgia—a region with an abundance of yellow and loblolly pine—would claim the lead in the production of these commodities. Thus, North Carolina came to be known as the Tar Heel State and its citizens as "tarheelers."

By Early Candlelight

For lighting the home, New England's sand-plain flora yielded an even more aromatic and cleaner-burning plant product. Sharing the ability of the pitch pine to grow in pure sand, the northern bayberry (*Myrica pensylvanica*) was abundantly distributed along the coast when the colonists arrived. The native Americans made medicinal tea from its aromatic leaves and bark and knew how to obtain wax from its "berries," but it was the new settlers who first turned the fatty coating on its berrylike nutlets into candles. Burning with a steady, blue flame and emitting a pleasant, delicate odor, bayberry wax was considered by the colonists to be far superior to splint lights, pine knots, Betty lamps, and candles made from animal tallow.

In autumn, after the bayberries had ripened, the thrifty housewife turned pounds and pounds of berries into a few, precious, straight, green candles. (Between five

thousand and ten thousand berries were needed to make a single two-ounce candle.)

Forming low, dense mounds on seaside dunes, the many-branched, angular plants, when laden with small berries, whose color is unlike that of any other northern plant, were easy to find. Its hard, nutlike seeds are embedded in a waxy substance speckled with grayish or bluish granules. These fruits, about a quarter of an inch in diameter, are borne by female plants, and they appear in conspicuous clusters on short spikes along the branches and at the base of the twigs of the preceding year's growth.

Most of the species in the bayberry family (Myricaceae) are evergreen. Unlike the southern species, *Myrica cerifera*, which it closely resembles, the northern bayberry is deciduous. A wise woman waited to gather the berries until several light frosts had brought the growing season to an end and the bayberry's green, shiny leaves had fallen. Stripping the berries earlier than 10 September was outlawed in Connecticut beginning in 1724. Berry gatherers apparently ignored this legislation, however, and illegally collected berries before the authorized date.

As they picked, the women and children noticed that their hands grew smooth as they acquired a thin film of wax from the berries. Inventive housewives saved some of the berries that they collected, and they filled cloth bags with them in order to grease the bottoms of their heavy flatirons.

For candlemaking, the twigs and other debris that came home in the berry pails were removed, and the cleaned berries were placed in large cauldrons, covered with water, and heated and simmered for hours. A greenish, oily liquid floated to the top and solidified as it cooled. Repeated several times, this part of the process included straining the liquid through cloth to remove any impurities. Finally, a clear, solid cake of olive-green wax resulted. The blue-green water that remained was put to good use: homemakers used it to dye their home-spun cloth.

Patience and a steady hand came next. Dipping a wick twenty-five times or more into the remelted wax made a thin, tapered candle. Allowing each layer of wax to harden before the candle was dipped again meant that this process could take at least half an hour. Dipping several wicks at once saved time; only the size of the pot governed the number of candles that could be produced. Revolving candle stands that enabled the woman to dip several wicks at once decreased the time required; and tinsmiths made metal molds into which the heated wax

68. *Myrica pensylvanica* is a shrubby plant that usually grows to a height of three to eight feet, but, in some situations, it can become a leggy shrub of fifteen feet or so. A typical plant usually assumes a dense, rounded, conical shape, but in places where the plants are exposed to constant winds, such as the seashore, they form a matted ground cover about twelve to fifteen inches high. *M. pensylvanica* is a pioneer species that can colonize sandy, sterile dunes, soil-poor abandoned fields, and disturbed waste places, and it is a perfect plant for use in dune stabilization. Bayberries are nonleguminous, nitrogen-fixing plants that have soil-enriching nodules on their rootlets, similar to those of beans and clover. Their wax is not a true wax but a vegetable tallow made up of stearin, palmitin, myristin, and glycerides. While ordinary white candles are sometimes coated with bayberry wax to give the olive-green color and scent of bayberry, most of the "bayberry" candles sold today are made of a chemically scented, synthetic wax or are made from the wax of one or more species of shrubs from Central America and South America that are somewhat related to the North American bayberries.

69. The rocky upland area of the Arnold Arboretum that is now bounded on the north by Centre Street was described as pasture in 1764, when the seventeen-acre parcel was sold to a farmer by the name of John Morey. It is likely that the land remained relatively open until the present sparse woods became established. In this area, known now as the Arboretum's "Central Woods," the native trees that have seeded themselves include white, red, and black oaks (*Quercus alba*, *Q. rubra*, and *Q. velutina*), the bear oak (*Q. ilicifolia*), pitch pines and white pines (*Pinus strobus* and *P. rigida*), and the eastern redcedar (*Juniperus virginiana*). The ground cover that carpets the area is the lowbush blueberry (*Vaccinium angustifolium*), a species of blueberry that often grows in dry, open woods or barrens in sandy, gravely, or rocky soil. Its presence is indicative of the poor pasture land with which farmers like John Morey had to contend. This small section of the Arboretum is reflective of many places in New England where the soil is light and sandy and where, once the forest is cut, lowbush blueberries often invade and become so dense and matlike that trees have a difficult time reestablishing themselves. The leaf litter that is caught in the blueberry's twiggy stems also makes these dry areas susceptible to fire. Periodic burns kill most of the few seedling trees that do manage to become established, but they also favor not only the blueberries, which spread by underground stoloniferous roots that respond vigorously to fire, but pitch pines (fire triggers the release of seeds from their cones) and oaks (which are able to regenerate from stump sprouts).

could be poured, which eliminated the laborious dipping process altogether. It is no wonder that these highly prized and brittle candles, the finest light source available, were carefully stored in long, narrow boxes specifically made for holding candles.

Not only were bayberry candles a useful domestic product that was saved for use on special occasions, they also became articles of trade in the colonies, and they were probably the first objects manufactured by women to be exported from New England. The English held these candles in highest regard, and they even tried to grow bayberries themselves. The French also hoped to establish bayberry plantations. However, neither the French nor the English succeeded in bringing *Myrica pensylvanica* into cultivation on a large enough scale to support a candlemaking industry.

The Arnold Arboretum can claim no sandy beaches or seaside dunes within its boundaries, but pitch pines and bayberries do prosper on the dry, gravelly knolls and rocky slopes of this cultivated, urban forest. At the side of Valley Road, a low, rounded but elongated outcrop of Roxbury puddingstone—polished smooth by glaciers—marks the beginning of Conifer Path, along which both species can be found growing. After a short incline, Conifer Path levels off and begins to meander through pines, spruces, tamaracks, and firs. To the north, on the uphill side, a prominent ridge of puddingstone forms a natural divide between the Arboretum's collections of coniferous and deciduous trees. Few exotic species have been planted amid the sparse woodland trees that grow on thin soil that barely covers the underlying bedrock. Most of the trees on the high ground and along the ridge are species native to central New England woods. The view downhill, south into the conifers, is strikingly different. Species of cone-bearing trees from all the north-temperate regions of the world now grow side by side in this location. The view is obstructed in many places by evergreen branches that reach the ground and form the walls of multitextured outdoor rooms. The difference in the two views is most noticeable in winter, but it is most beautiful in fall, when the cool, soothing shades of the green valley contrast sharply with the upland's fiery hues. A group of pitch pines started from seed collected in 1883 grows to the left of the path where the first glimpse of Hemlock Hill Road can be seen through the conifers. Other native fire pines grow on the knoll, and a specimen of *Pinus banksiana*, jack pine, stands nearby. Its small lopsided cones remain tightly sealed, waiting to be released by the heat of a fire, and its needles, less than an inch and a half long, are among the smallest of all North American pines. On the other side of the path, almost directly across from this grove of pines, a group of bayberries, *Myrica pensylvanica*, surround a small outcrop of puddingstone.

Inside the typical colonial dwelling, in the principal room—called either the hall, after the great halls of English houses, the "fier room" (a Yorkshire term), or the great room or kitchen—a huge fieldstone or catted chimney stack dominated one wall. At its base, logs blazed in a fireplace that may have been as much as five feet high, three feet deep, and nine feet wide. A necessity, not an amenity, a "fireplaced livingroom" (in the parlance of contemporary real estate agents) was the core of the house and the center of family life. It was the woman's workroom, and she tended the fire even through the heat of summer; beside it or on it, she prepared the family's meals, and its smoke kept the swarms of insects away.

At first, like almost every tool needed for work outdoors, much of the kitchen equipment was carved, whittled, or turned from wood. Large metal pots brought from England hung suspended over the fire from trammels and chains attached to wooden lug poles, and even early "gridirons" were fashioned from green wood rather than iron. The lug poles tended to char and burn through, pitching the contents of pots into the fire. Burnt wooden gridirons caused less trouble: as soon as the gridiron's wood dried sufficiently to allow it to ignite, a new one was whittled to take its place. In the performance of their many everyday chores, women chopped, churned, pounded, mashed, and ground meats, vegetables, grains, dairy products, and herbs with "treen," small wooden objects fashioned into useful domestic tools—the wooden predecessors of our plastic kitchen gadgets. Usually, these one-piece objects were produced by a cooper or a turner, but, when winter storms buffeted the house and little could be done outdoors, many farmers occupied their time by making homemade woodenware.

Metal utensils replaced wooden ones as soon as they could be had, but, until the family could afford the luxury of ceramic or pewter plates, the sound of wood on wood accompanied dinner conversation. Boiled meats, vegetables, and stews went from iron pots, via wooden ladles, to wooden trays, platters, and bowls, from which they were eaten with wooden spoons. A single wooden tankard, passed from hand to hand, or wooden noggins (small mugs with handles, which were shared by dining partners), held the family's liquid refreshment, often cider, ale, or beer. Commonly, two or more family members, sitting beside a long, narrow trestle table made from

70. Ledges and outcrops of a conglomerate rock, or puddingstone, made up of large pebbles, cobbles, and rounded or angular rocks and boulders that are held, or seem to float (like raisins in a pudding) in a matrix of fine-grained material, come to the surface at many places in the Arnold Arboretum. There is a relatively high ledge of conglomerate outcrop that runs north to south at the edge of the Central Woods upland, and it forms a natural divide between the Arboretum's main conifer collection and most of the groups of deciduous trees. This photograph of the conifer collection was taken from atop the ledge that separates the two collections. A rounded silhouette, the crest of Peters Hill (which is one of the many drumlins formed by glacial movement in the Boston Basin), can be seen in the background on the right-hand side of the photograph.

71. Many puddingstone outcrops at the Arboretum, locally called Roxbury puddingstone, are notable because they may be the only outcrops of tillite of Late Precambrian age in New England. Known by geologists as Squantum tillite, this puddingstone is approximately 600 million years old. The surface of the outcrop in this photograph, close by Valley Road and the entrance to Conifer Path, shows how the action of the ice in the last glacial age smoothed the surface of this older formation as it passed over with its load of rocky debris. The striations in the outcrop clearly show the direction of the glacier's movement as it crossed the land on its way toward the Atlantic Ocean.

72. Probably because of their fragility and the fact that the first colonists were unlikely to include them among their personal possessions, few ceramic pieces were transported to the New World during the Colonial period. Beverages were drunk from common containers, such as pewter tankards, leather jacks, or mugs, noggins, or tankards made from wood, such as the tankard shown here, which is from the Pilgrim Society's collection in Plymouth, Massachusetts. Colonial beverages included beers and ales made from whatever was available, including corn, pumpkins, nettles, potatoes, and apples (in the middle colonies, they made beer from persimmons); cider, both hard and sweet; and wines and brandies made from wild or cultivated fruits and berries.

one or two planks of wood, shared small, round, wooden trays called trenchers. Often carved from maple burls, these wooden dishes had a shallow depression and served as both plate and bowl.

Sugar maples abound in New England; they grow in each of the six New England states. A long-lived, beautifully shaped tree, it is the sugar maple, along with the native birches and the American beech, that dominate northern New England's hardwood forest. The leaves of all maples grow opposite one another, and those of the sugar maple are dark green and large—from three to six inches in width. They are greater in width than in length, and they are usually five-lobed (but three-lobed leaves are common). A primary vein runs the length of each lobe, terminating in a sharp point, and each lobe has other sharp teeth along its margin. On the leaves of red maple and silver maple, the sinuses (the clefts or spaces between the lobes) are sharp and angled; on the leaves of sugar maple, the sinuses are rounded.

The twigs of sugar maple are a shiny reddish-brown, and they are covered with light-colored specialized cells called lenticels. Lenticels are openings or pores in the bark that allow for the interchange of gases between the outside environment and the interior of the twig, stem, or trunk. These cells often protrude through the bark and are most noticeable when the bark is smooth. In some trees, these cells are evident only on the newest growth, and they disappear as the bark becomes older; in other trees, they persist. While sugar maples have these lenticels on their twigs, the trunk bark on young trees is a smooth, pale grayish brown. On mature trees, the bark is dark gray and deeply furrowed. At a quick glance, an old sugar maple can sometimes be mistaken for a shagbark hickory (*Carya ovata*). As sugar maples age, one side of each of the bark's long vertical plates may curve outward, somewhat like the bark of the hickory, which lifts away from the trunk at the top and bottom.

In late April or early May, after the silver maples and

73. Wooden bowls and plates came in every shape and size imaginable: a basinet was a small wooden bowl; a becker, a small wooden dish; a losset, a wooden trencher; a maeser, a wooden drinking bowl. This well-worn wooden bowl, also from the Pilgrim Society's collections, was carved from a maple burl. Maple wood is either "hard" or "soft," depending upon the species. Wood of the red or swamp maple (*Acer rubrum*) and the silver maple (*A. saccharinum*) is not as dense and compact, and therefore not as well suited to the making of woodenware, or "treen," as that of the sugar or rock maple (*A. saccharum*). The wood of sugar maple imparts no taste, polishes to a smooth, rock-hard finish, and resists abrasion. These attributes make it a perfect material for holding or preparing food. Hollowed-out burls, the knobby, tumorlike growths that sometimes protrude from tree trunks and limbs, made excellent bowls—called knotware, once they were carved or turned. A burl often develops when dormant bud shoots go awry because of infestation by pests or a disease of some sort in the tree. The result is an extremely hard, fine-figured piece of wood that is difficult to work but that, because of its convoluted grain, shrinks little and is unlikely to split or crack.

74. Photographed on 13 October 1923 by Ernest Henry Wilson, this sugar maple dwarfs his wife, Helen, who had surely been asked to stand beside the tree to provide scale. Although he is most famous for his exploration of China and for the Asiatic plants that were introduced into cultivation through his efforts, E. H. "Chinese" Wilson also traveled extensively throughout New England, documenting, through his photographs, the native flora. The Wilsons were undoubtedly taking advantage of a beautiful fall day to enjoy the scenery along the Mohawk Trail when they spotted this grand sugar maple in Charlemont, Massachusetts, and stopped to record it on film. A project of the Massachusetts Highway Commission that was completed in 1912, The Mohawk Trail—part of Massachusetts Route 2 that wends over the Hoosac Range on its way from Greenfield to North Adams—was so named because, in many places, it touches or crosses a Native American trail that ran westward to the Hudson River Valley and then on to the Great Lakes region. Along the Mohawk Trail, the Massachusetts State Forest Commission preserves the land on both sides of the Cold River and Manning Brook and along parts of the roadway to protect the trees and slopes in the river valleys and to maintain scenic vistas.

75. Wooden buckets do not heat up in the sunlight and cause the maple sap to ferment, but galvanized sap buckets, like those shown in the photograph, are lighter than wooden ones, easier to carry and store, and also easier to keep clean. They do not leak like wooden ones, which were often painted (unfortunately, with paint that contained lead) to seal the wood and to prevent leakage. The sugar content of an individual tree's sap is of vital importance in the maple-syrup business because less energy and labor go into removing water from sap with a high ratio of sugar to water. The percentage of sugar varies from tree to tree, but, by using a hand-held device called a refractometer to test the sap, the genetically sweeter tree can be identified for tapping. "Jones Rule of 86" states that, if you divide the sugar content of the sap by 86, you can determine how much sap it will take to make a gallon of syrup.

Labels within image: using sight-level · Surveyor's tape · mainline · tension grip · non-maple tree used as a support · Storage tank

76. Pipeline made of plastic tubing is fast replacing the galvanized sap bucket. Its predecessor, the staved and hooped wooden sap bucket, with its single protruding handle with a hole, along with spiles, shoulder yokes, and large staved tubs for storage—all wooden accoutrements for the work of sugaring—have already become relics of the past. But pipelines are not an entirely new invention: closed piping systems of tinned metal were recorded in the late eighteenth century, and, more than fifty years ago, galvanized steel pipes zigzagged their way downhill from maple to maple in some Vermont sugar bushes.

the red maples have flowered and just as the leaves of the sugar maple are beginning to unfold, long, thin, thread-like stalks bearing clusters of greenish-yellow flowers can be seen in the sugar maples. Occasionally, a sugar maple will bear only male or female flowers, but usually both can be found in different clusters in the same tree. The sugar maple's winged fruit—a double samara comprising two "keys" joined at the center—does not ripen until fall. Although there are two carpels, only one contains a viable seed.

The Native American's technique of collecting sap had much in common with the way Europeans boxed conifers. With deft cuts from their razor-sharp hatchets, they sliced large sections of bark away from the tree and allowed the sap to run freely into birch-bark containers. Unfortunately, once in the hands of growing numbers of settlers unwilling—and unwise enough—to limit the number of trees "boxed" year after year, this method

proved to be as hard on sugar maples as the naval-stores industry had been on pitch pines. The open wounds that resulted attracted insects and hastened decay, and usually the boxed trees died within a few years. Fortunately, innovations were soon made that allowed for an annual harvest of sap without harming the tree. A hole bored with an auger replaced the open wound, hollowed out wooden rods (spiles) captured and directed the trickle of sap, and the Native American's folded and sewn birch-bark containers gave way to birch or pine pails.

The sap of sugar maples averages only 2 to 3 percent sugar, which necessitates harvesting 35 to 50 gallons of sap to make a gallon of maple syrup (or about 8 pounds of maple sugar). The Native Americans reduced the liquid to sugar by casting red-hot stones into hollowed out logs filled with sap, then removing, reheating, and casting them in again. The emigrant from Europe, armed with his precious few metal pots, did not have to contend with

77. A Michelin Man look-alike, draped with plastic pipe, setting off with a portable auger to install a pipeline in his sugar bush. Although he certainly appears to be heavily laden at this point, once his pipeline is in place—and as long as the line runs downhill—gravity will do the work of moving the sap from the tree to the storage point. It takes less time to gather sap by pipeline than it does to gather it in buckets, and the time spent sugaring can be spent in boiling down the sap rather than in slogging through snow to collect it. Using tubing, one person can handle 3000 taps, but only a third as many taps can be handled by a person using buckets. At the sugar house—the other end of the line—new machines employed by bulk processors of syrup include ultraviolet treatment systems for killing microorganisms that can spoil sap within thirty hours, if it is not boiled down within that time, and a device called a reverse osmosis machine, which uses external pressure to push fluids of higher concentration across a membrane. This speeds up the process of reduction by separating the water from the sap more quickly.

flammable cooking containers; the Native Americans, once introduced to iron pots, quickly adopted them in place of heated stones. Metal spiles and pails superseded wooden ones and today plastic pipe often takes the place of both. Even with new methods and materials, however, New England's capricious spring weather continues to dictate the maple-sugaring season.

Sap moves up through the tree in a series of water-conducting vessels in the xylem. Optimum conditions for the greatest movement of sap develop when nighttime temperatures dip well below freezing and daytime highs reach 40–50 degrees Fahrenheit. When this occurs, the watery sap that is moving through the tree gets an added boost. As the temperature changes, pressure fluctuates within the gas-filled tissue surrounding these vessels or tubes. Warming increases the internal pressure, and the vessels compress and move the sap up through the tree more quickly.

The formation of the annual xylem increments produces the distinct rings that can be counted to determine a tree's age. In the heartwood—the older, darker-colored tissue—these vessels no longer function, and the wood becomes primarily a structural support. Maples are diffuse-porous species—that is, the xylem vessels formed during the early part of the growing season are similar in size to those formed during summer, but there is a greater proportion of sapwood to heartwood. In ring-porous species, such as oaks and elms, the sapwood is restricted to the outermost growth rings.

"The King's Broad Arrow"

With such forest commodities as "Pitch, Tar, and Rozin" available from the New England colonies (specific amounts of each had to be supplied to the Royal Navy on a yearly basis, and all such goods became "enumerated articles" that had to be transported to England before being shipped to any other port), wood-poor England could relieve her long and tenuous dependence on supplies of naval stores from the Baltic countries.

But England's unbridled determination to secure trees of mast size and length from her colonies met with more resistance than she could have anticipated. In the eyes of the Crown, the tall, straight, supple trunks of the magnificent pines that soared above the forest canopy represented perfect mast material with which to outfit the ships of the line. For more than eight hundred years, English mastmakers had relied on the Baltic pine or

78. Mr. Theodore P. Bacheller, cabinet maker, once kept his tricorn, or cocked hat, in this triangular wooden hat box. Measuring sixteen inches on a side and six inches high, the box was painted maroon, probably to simulate the grain of mahogany or cherry, more expensive woods than the white pine from which the box was constructed. The lid is hinged, and, although "1771" is inscribed on the lid, the inside is lined with newspaper dating from September 1770.

"Riga fir" (*Pinus sylvestris*) for straight, elastic, and durable timbers. The Dutch Wars of the seventeenth century threatened supplies from the Baltic coast, but ship masts could be procured from a new source over which the Crown had control. A report of "notable high timber trees, masts for ships of four hundred tons" and living specimens of these pines, the tallest species of conifer in eastern North America, reached England as early as 1604. Secured in the hold of the *Archangel*, a ship commanded by George Weymouth, were timbers and seedlings of pines taken from the banks of a river in Maine. The plants prospered in English soil in the garden of a distant cousin of the captain, and *Pinus strobus*, the white pine, became known as the Weymouth Pine throughout England.

The first cargo of these giant trees, destined for the dockyards of English shipbuilders, left Portsmouth, New Hampshire, in 1634. By the middle of the 1600s, specially built bargelike mast ships that could carry one hundred "single stick" white pine masts at one time traveled regularly across the Atlantic; only fur rivaled their value as an export. In order to force the colonies to export mast timbers, England enacted a series of unpopular laws between 1691 and 1729 that came to be known as the King's Broad Arrow Policy. Being directed at a tree the colonists had come to value for their own purposes, these laws, which empowered England to commandeer the biggest and best white pines, were scorned, ignored, or circumvented.

These same stately conifers could just as well mast the ships of New England and provide the young country with strong, lightweight materials for building houses. White pine timber made sturdy planks and clear, wide boards for houses, barns, and outbuildings, for chests of drawers, shelving, tables, and chairs, for boxes for storing spices, salt, candles, and even three-cornered hats. The white pine became the softwood equivalent of the valuable white oak. These two trees so symbolized the growth and strength of a new nation that their images would be chosen by John Hull (an artisan and merchant, and the Bay Colony's first mintmaster) to grace the earliest coins made in North America.

Laws governing the ownership and use of any white pine standing on land not granted to a private individual may have been on England's books, but miles of ocean and acres of forests, as well as self-serving agents and wily colonists, made them almost impossible to enforce. Cunning colonial woodsmen practiced every deception to harvest the valuable trees without detection. Because all white pines more than 24 inches in diameter (measured 12 inches from the ground) belonged to the King, it was almost impossible to find pine boards in New England houses whose width exceeded 23 inches.

In New Hampshire, when deputies to the Surveyor of

79. On 27 May 1652, Massachusetts authorities ordered the establishment of the first mint in the Colonies. John Hull of Boston was chosen to be the first mintmaster, and he presided over a mint house erected on his property that was ordered to be made of wood, sixteen feet square and ten feet high. While the first coin he issued simply bore the letters "NE" (for New England) on one side and the denomination in Roman numerals on the other, each of the next three coins bore the emblem of a tree. The second coins struck had the image of a willow; the third, an oak. The pine appeared on the last and largest issue, which dated roughly from 1667 to 1682. When they were first made, the coins were known as Boston shillings or Bay shillings. Today, all three are referred to as "tree coins," or more often as "pine tree coins" or "pine tree shillings." While John Hull grew quite rich as mintmaster—he was accorded fifteen pence for every twenty shillings he minted—a presumably apocryphal story that appears in almost every history of early American coinage describes how his son-in-law, Samuel Sewell, came to have a sizable portion of John Hull's profits. As the story goes, when John Hull's daughter married Samuel Sewell, Hull gave Sewell her weight in shillings as a dowry. Apparently, Miss Hull was not a dainty maiden: It is said that Sewell thereby acquired the sum of 30,000 shillings.

the King's Woods began marking white pines with the dreaded three-stroke symbol of the arrow and restrictions on logging these trees began to be stringently enforced, the colonists struck back. On 14 April 1772, after government officials fined a local man for cutting what by British law were the King's pines, a skirmish broke out between the angry citizens of a small village and two regiments of soldiers. Today a monument attesting to "one of the first acts against the laws of England" stands in the town of Weare, New Hampshire, the site of the uprising. Occurring just two years after the Boston Massacre and only a year before the Boston Tea Party, the "Pine Tree Riot" proved to be another portent of things to come. In 1775, Colonial troops marched into battle at Bunker Hill under a flag that bore a likeness of the white pine. News of the battle and the last cargo of masts the King's men had cut in the Colonies reached England at almost the same time.

White pines can be found growing naturally from Newfoundland to Manitoba, as far south as northern Georgia, and west to Minnesota and Wisconsin. In New England, they grow in every county from southwestern Connecticut to northeastern Maine, but the forested areas in which white pines are most prevalent border the sea from Nova Scotia south into northeastern Massachusetts and inland to the Connecticut and Hudson river valleys. In 1623, in southeastern Maine, where this great belt of pines begins its inland sweep, the waters of the York River set New England's first sawmill waterwheel in motion, and the New World's lumber industry was innaugurated. Maine's rivers and streams provided waterpower and her forests provided timber. Temporary fishing stations became settlements as Europeans harnessed the travel routes of the Native Americans by building dams and waterwheels. Mills sprang up beside almost every navigable waterway, and even small streams, flooded by the seasonal surge of spring run-off, had temporary mills erected on their banks. These new mills, with their water-powered, mechanical upright sash or gate saws, replaced the laborious and time-consuming hand riving and hewing and the slightly more efficient pit saw or whipsaw. Using one water-driven saw, a father and son could mill 2000 feet of inch-thick pine boards in a day. Within four decades, Maine's river valleys rang with the rasping sound of sharp metal teeth ripping through wood in more than a hundred sawmills.

In southern New England, tall groves of white pines punctuate the landscape of deciduous woods. Preferring a deep, moist soil of loamy sand, these blue-green islands of white pine are the perfect foil for the blood-red spring

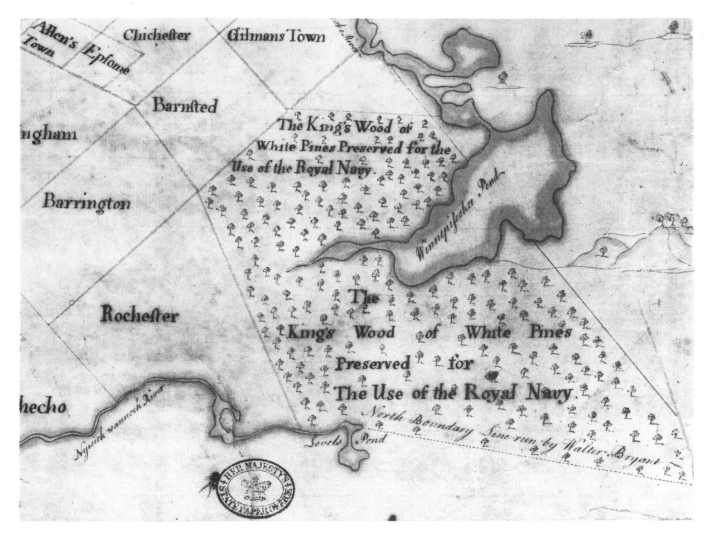

80. Residents of the area around Laconia, New Hampshire, on the shores of Lake Winnipesaukee may be surprised to find that their homes are situated on land that was once held by the Crown as "The King's Wood of White Pine Preserved for the Use of the Royal Navy."

81. This plaque, set in a grindstone, is on the site of Aaron Quimby's Inn in Weare, New Hampshire. When Governor John Wentworth was appointed "Surveyor of the King's Woods" in 1771, his deputies found more than 250 pine logs in a sawmill yard in Weare that, according to British law, belonged to the King. After arresting Ebenezer Mudget, who had brought the logs to the mill, Benjamin Whiting, the sheriff of the county, and his deputy, Mr. Quigley, retired to Aaron Quimby's Inn for the evening. At dawn, a group of about twenty local townsmen disarmed and beat both men and ran them out of town. Two regiments of soldiers, armed with guns and swords, marched on the town but were able to find and jail only one man. On hearing of the jailing, the other participants turned themselves in and were indicted. In a court presided over by Judge Mesheck Weare, who gave his name to the town, they were fined a small amount and set free.

1772   1928
SITE   OF
PINE TREE TAVERN
WHERE TOOK PLACE APRIL 14, 1772
THE PINE TREE RIOT
ONE OF THE FIRST ACTS AGAINST
THE LAWS OF ENGLAND
ERECTED BY TOWN OF WEARE

82. Photographed in the town of West Ossipee, New Hampshire, in 1926, this white pine (*Pinus strobus*) stood one hundred ten feet tall and had a girth of fourteen feet. The length of its trunk falls just short of the length of the mainmast of a warship ship in the Royal Navy. A first-rate ship of the line carried twenty guns and had a smooth, sixteen-sided, perfectly straight mainmast that measured forty inches in diameter, was one hundred twenty feet long, and weighed as much as eighteen tons.

83. In this application of the pit-sawing method at Plimoth Plantation, the pitman, who pulls down on the blade, need not, obviously, be actually standing in a pit. The pulley in mechanized saws that performs this function is still referred to as the pitman.

growth and brilliant fall color of the red maples (*Acer rubrum*). When white pines are growing close together, their lower limbs die from lack of light. Sometimes the trees are free and clear of branches almost to the crown, but, most often, broken, lifeless limbs protrude from the trunks like short, irregular spokes of a rimless wheel. The white pine's top branches lengthen and curve upward; facing away from prevailing winds, their configuration can be read like an ancient, stationary weather vane.

Pines have slender, needlelike leaves. Those of the white pine are two and one-half to five inches long. Soft and flexible, they are grouped in fascicles of five. Compressed into a tight bundle when first formed, these evergreen leaves emerge from coverings suggestive of the sheaths that protect the feathers of a bird. The needles are not round but triangular in cross section; when the needles are rolled between finger and thumb, the ridges become obvious to the touch. On bright, sunlit

days, the needles fan out and look feathery, but, if the weather turns cold, each fascicle draws tight to bring its bundle of needles together.

As with all pines, the flowering of a white pine is a modest event. No showy petals or swarms of bees herald the occasion. In the gymnosperms, or cone-bearing woody plants, virtually everything that signifies a typical flower is absent. Not only is there no perianth (the sepals and petals), there are no calyx, stamens, or pistils. Pollination in the angiosperms, the flowering plants, occurs when pollen is transferred from the anther to the stigma; gymnosperm pollen is transferred from the staminate strobili (the male cones) to the ovulate strobili (the female cones). Pines are monoecious: both male and female cones occur on the same plant.

In spring, a fine, yellowish-orange dust appears, as if by magic, on car hoods, windshields, lawn furniture, and decks: it is the abundant pollen being shed from the white pine's small, yellow male cones. Grouped in clusters at the base of new twigs on lower branches, these staminate strobili persist only long enough to send clouds of pollen grains swirling through the air. Late in June, the ground at the base of most conifers, including white pines, is littered with what appears to be thousands of Rice Krispies. These are male cones, their pollen sacs spent and empty.

It is the female cones of conifers that become the much admired and sought after components of wreaths, swags, and centerpieces. The female strobili are also small at first, but, within days of being pollinated, they begin to grow. The scales of the female inflorescence become the scales of the cone. In the first summer, these purplish cones will attain a length of about an inch. During the following summer, they will become twice as wide and grow at least six inches longer. The heat of summer dries the tissue on the outside of the scales, the tips bend outward, and, by September, the cones open wide enough to release their seeds. Female cones are borne on the highest branches. The height is advantageous; seeds carried by the wind from these lofty perches will sail far. A violent summer storm will often blow down immature female cones during their second year of growth. Although your hands will get sticky, take the opportunity to observe the interior of these soft, green cones before they have had time to mature. Cut from end to end, and excepting the paired seeds, which remain ivory-colored and look like two beads of tapioca, the interior of the cone quickly discolors and darkens and the layers of scales become obvious. Peel one off to see the impression of the seed's wings upon the scale. With two winged seeds to a scale, each female white pine cone contains an average of seventy viable seeds. Once every three to five years, white pines will have an exceptional year for cone production, and on each tree as many as 400 female cones will bear at least 28,000 seeds. Some seeds will sail distances exceeding 700 feet, land in hospitable surroundings, germinate, and become new plants, but the majority will become food for a wide assortment of wildlife.

"In Their Own Boats upon the Sea"

In Maine, during the winter of 1607–08, near the mouth of the Sagadahoc River (the Kennebec), the carpenters of the Popham Colony framed houses, a church, a storehouse, and New England's first ship, a "pretty Pynnace" of thirty tons that they christened *Virginia*. The colony did not survive another winter, and the next New England vessel would not be constructed until a shipwright settled at the Plymouth Colony in 1624. Although fishermen plied the coast in shallops (even the Pilgrim's ailing ship's carpenter had managed to build two of these stoutly constructed open work boats) and Governor Winthrop's thirty-ton bark *The Blessing of the Bay* sailed out of the Mystic River on 4 July 1631, it would be more than a century before thriving shipyards took over the Boston and Salem waterfronts and the North River's shoreline. By 1700, the Massachusetts Bay towns of Salem and Scituate rivaled Boston, the leader in shipbuilding. Shipyards dotted the coast of Narragansett Bay. Both Newport and Portsmouth had begun launching ships by the 1650s. Connecticut had a number of settlements building small vessels, but its chief port, New London, led in the construction of larger ships.

It was northeast of Massachusetts Bay, where forested rivers ran down to the sea, that lumbering and shipbuilding grew hand in hand. Colonial settlement areas that offered the possibility of self-sustaining, year-round habitation were limited to the lowlands along Maine's southern coast. The rest of Maine's shoreline, perhaps the most ragged and irregular in the world, offered rich fishing grounds and deep coves and harbors. Captain John Smith had correctly appraised the potential of this landscape in 1614: "From Penobscot to Sagadahoc this coast is all mountainous, and isles of huge rocks, but overgrown with all sorts of excellent woods for building houses, boats, barks, and ships."

With pine for mainmasts, other trees would provide the raw material needed by the skilled carvers, joiners, boatbuilders, and sparmakers who fitted out the ship. But shipbuilders faced even greater difficulties than did colonial carpenters: Poorly made houses simply sagged, but poorly made ships sank. Consequently, master shipbuilders were hard pressed to learn what kinds of trees should be used and what types should be shunned.

Plank was the skin of a vessel, and timbers were the ribs or frame that supported the skin. Shipwrights favored the straight and close-grained trunks of black, red, and white spruce for topmast timbers and beams. White pine, Atlantic white-cedar, and white oak, steamed and curved into place, all made good plank. Often a piece of water-seasoned elm was used for the false keel, and sometimes the sugar maple provided timbers for keel and frame, but "compass" (curved) white oak wood was the shipbuilders first choice. Short-handled mauls and wooden mallets drove wooden dowels—tree nails or trunnels—through borings in plank and beam. Above the water line, treenails of seasoned white oak soaked in tar held timbers and planks together. However, as early as

84. In England, treenails (or "trunnels") were usually made out of carefully seasoned oak. Colonial shipbuilders used oak at first, but, by the 1630s, most employed dowels made of locust wood (*Robinia pseudoacacia*). The treenails shown in this photograph have been driven through the plank and frame of a ship's hull being repaired at the Maritime Museum Apprentice Shop in Bath, Maine, and have been sawn off flush at both ends. When metal fastenings are used, weeping and condensation often causes the wood to rot around the metal. Not only are these wooden dowels not subject to rust, they will swell tight and become an intergral part of the hull once the vessel is launched. Fishing boats were usually treenailed because they were exposed to so much salt that metal fastenings would have corroded away. To protect such a boat from rot, the space between the planking and the inner sheathing of the hull was filled with rock salt, and salt was also kept in the hold to keep the catch from spoiling. One disadvantage of treenails is that, because the grain in the dowels does not swell in the same direction as the grain in the planking, an indentation appears wherever a treenail has been set.

the 1630s, the discovery that the wood from a tree imported from the southern colonies was even harder and more resistant to decay than oak made locust (*Robinia pseudoacacia*) the wood of choice for treenails intended for use below the water line. The shipcarver made figureheads, nameboards, and scrollwork out of solid or joined blocks of oak and elm, but he preferred to work with the soft, orange-colored wood they called "pumpkin pine." Pumpkin pine is a common name for white pines whose wood has an orange cast. Lumbermen claim that

the wood of white pines that grow in deep fertile soil—often in sheltered valleys—not only has this unusual coloration but is easier to carve. Ship painters ground their own pigments, made their own varnish and shellac from the gum of conifers, or sometimes, in place of paint, applied only a liberal coat of pine oil to protect the wood.

The master shipbuilder, working from a scale model carved from pine and cedar, sometimes built full-scale pine templates of the ship's timbers and beams and then searched the forest for elms, maples, or oaks that matched

85. The lengths to which British ship-builders went in order to procure suitable timbers to frame their ships is evident in these two figures that illustrate how to train young trees to grow into the required shape and how to recognize the necessary timber forms in standing trees.

86. A floating mat, or quaking bog, in a protected cove on Upper Richardson Lake in Maine. This cove probably had its origin in a kettlehole left by the glacier. Unlike a marsh that develops through sedimentation and basin filling, a quaking bog evolves over a period of centuries as a mat of vegetation floats on the water and accumulates organic matter from the surface down, rather than from the bottom up. Leatherleaf (*Chamaedaphne calyculata*) is the primary woody species in floating mats in northern New England. A shrubby member of the heath family (Ericaceae), it invades still water and pond shores. As this profusely branching shrub begins to spread out over open water, the increasing weight of its leathery textured leaves begins to depress the older branches below the surface of the water, and new branches are stimulated to grow above the water line. After a while, enough litter accumulates on the heath bog to support colonization by other plants. Sphagnum moss, sedges, pitcher plants, sundews, and other plants of the heath family follow until scattered individuals of black spruce (*Picea mariana*) and larch (*Larix laricina*) establish themselves. In this photograph, almost all of the conifers growing out of the tangled mat of leatherleaf are larches.

the templates' curves. (In England, they actually trained trees, like oversized bonsai, into the typical shapes needed for framing timbers). Some shipyards employed a local farmer to deliver logs, others contracted with a timber merchant to supply sawn and seasoned timber and plank. Conveniently for the industry, the belief that exposure to the salt air toughened the wood of living trees was widely accepted, and suitable trees growing within a few miles of the coast were quickly extirpated. During the six or more months that passed between the laying or "stretching" of the keel to the construction of the launching cradle, the master shipbuilder oversaw the work of a succession of sawyers, joiners, caulkers, plankers, painters, riggers, mastmakers, glaziers, sailmakers, coopers, tanners, and ropemakers whose special skills put the ship together.

For the making of "ship's knees," the naturally grown crooks that joined, strengthened, and unified the vessel, the hard, spiral-grained wood of the roots of the tamarack or hackmatack (*Larix laricina*) could not be surpassed.

Both tamarack and hackmatack are Indians names. The colonists adopted these and added larch to the list. Like the roots of the black spruce, its companion on boggy

87. Except for their soft green color, immature larch cones are reminiscent of rosebuds, or at least of radishes cut by a skillful culinary artisan to resemble a rosebud.

ground, the tough, stringy roots of the tamarack were also fashioned by the Indians into twine. The Native Americans knew that, unlike other the needles of other conifers, tamarack needles would turn a golden orange and drop from the tree in response to the cooler, shorter days of autumn. Because there were no conifers that shed their leaves in the British Isles, transplanted Englishmen must have found the change from green to golden foliage perplexing. During the winter, the bare branches could mean only that the trees had died. For almost half of the year, tamaracks look desolate. It is a wonder that the colonists returned to tamarack swamps after seeing acres of these skeletal trees in winter. With every tree a mass of drooping branchlets covered with lumpy, needleless spurs and deteriorating cones, tamarack bogs and swamps appeared to be devoid of life.

In spring, small bright-red female and yellow male strobili appear, and the trees begin to look very much alive. Unlike pine cones, tamarack cones mature and shed their seeds in just one season. After the small cones (each made up of less than twenty scales) shed their seeds, they darken and then, like the cones of the pitch pine, persist for many years. Lacy, inch-long, flattened, light-green needles, which stay soft and flexible throughout the growing season, emerge soon after the cones. In the thin spring sunlight, the ethereal tamarack seems to shimmer against the darker, stiffer foliage of spruce and fir.

Tamaracks are most abundant in the cool swamps and sphagnum bogs of northern Maine, New Hampshire, and Vermont, but, as this species' southern limits reach into Pennsylvania and Maryland, there are also suitable habitats for *Larix laricina* in Massachusetts, Connecticut, and Rhode Island. In most areas of New England, tamaracks become moderately tall (thirty to seventy feet high), have long, clear boles, and bear sparse and irregular limbs that are almost horizontal. These trees are much smaller near the northern limits of their range. Truly a cold-climate tree, the tamarack grows farther north than any eastern American conifer, and lilliputian forests of this species, as dense as 13,000 trees per acre, can be found carpeting muskegs above the Arctic Circle. In northern Quebec, foresters have counted the growth rings of tamaracks with trunks less than two inches in diameter and found them to be three-quarters of a century old.

Tamarack wood does not warp, shrink, crack, or split to any great degree, and it is both light in weight and durable. A lateral root and a section of the lower part of a tamarack trunk form a "knee," a natural curve so necessary in building a wooden ship. Such roots had to be harvested when the soil could be worked. After a killing frost, but before the cold worked its way into the soil, men shouldered broadax and adz and went in search of knees. Knees cut in the fall could season in place over winter and be dragged from the forest before the snow left the ground. Standing knees were used above deck, hanging knees supported the deck from below, and lodging knees tied the beams to the hull. Treenails driven through tamarack knees to secure the beam ends did little damage, and if treenails were employed, they stayed fast once hammered into place. The wood also seasoned quickly, and knots remained firmly wedged in the timber long after a plank had lost its moisture.

In the Name of Liberty

On the eve of the Revolution, the country's population mirrored the range of the Atlantic white-cedar. Two and one-half million people lived in towns, villages, and farms that dotted a ribbonlike band, less than 200 miles wide at its broadest, that ran the length of the coast from Maine to Florida.

In New England, home to 400,000 of these colonialists, forest no longer blanketed the land; its edge had been unraveled. With land often parceled out in tracts of 36 square miles, growth had been measured, deliberate, and phenomenal; trees had been turned into houses and barns, and into the meetinghouse spires that rose above the treetops in 566 towns. Rhode Island, Connecticut, and much of Massachusetts could be counted as "settled"; in place of forest, cleared, thin-soiled, rocky fields supported farms. New communities could be found beside the rivers that ran north into southern New Hampshire, the wilderness that would become Vermont, and the spruce forests of Massachusetts—the land that would be called Maine.

In Boston, the country's third largest city, open-air markets, where everything in the way of goods and services could be bartered or purchased, had become popular gathering places. One such market took place in the "neighborhood of the elm trees" that grew in Garret Bourne's yard at the corner of Essex Street and Orange Street (which, after the revolution, was renamed Washington Street).

During the summer of 1765, this market, like many others, had rung with angry words. The Sugar Act had been in effect for almost a year and a half, and in less than three months the Stamp Act, passed by Parliament on 22 March, would take effect. On 14 August, the group of men that gathered in the shade of the elms to escape

88. This rough-cut hackmatack knee, part of the root and the trunk split in two, is being seasoned at Maritime Museum Apprentice Shop in Bath, Maine. Eventually this knee will be finish-cut and used in the construction of a ship. Depending on their position or function, knees are known by different names. A standing knee stands on its own foot above the beam it supports; a hanging knee supports a beam from underneath, with its foot overhead; and lodging knees and bosom knees are used between two upright beams, with the foot being lodged against the beam.

(Drawn and Engraved by A. Bowen, for the History of Boston.)

LIBERTY TREE, 1774,

CORNER OF ESSEX AND ORANGE STREETS.

The world should never forget the spot where once stood Liberty Tree, so famous in your annals.—*La Fayette in Boston.*

89. This illustration of the famous elms that stood in Garret Bourne's yard (quite likely highly idealized) appeared in *Bowen's Boston Newsletter and City Record* in 1826.

the hot summer sun had come not to buy or sell but to protest British interference in Colonial trade.

Calling themselves the Sons of Liberty, they hanged the newly appointed stamp officer, Andrew Oliver, in effigy from the largest elm. Four months later, the Sons of Liberty demanded that Oliver stand beneath the same tree and take an oath renouncing his appointment. The image of this elm, which had been dubbed the Liberty Tree, began to appear in political cartoons as a symbol of Boston's resistance to British rule. A plaque attached to Garret Bourne's elm bore the inscription "This tree was planted in 1646, and pruned by the Sons of Liberty,

February 14, 1766." From Newport to New York, people planted or dedicated other trees in the name of liberty.

Nine years later, and less than four miles away in Cambridge, another patriotic tradition cast in the shade of an elm took root. Cantabrigians maintain that, on 3 July 1775, under an elm (commemorated by a plaque by vote of the City Aldermen in 1864 for "the Revolutionary event and date that rendered said Tree historical") that grew at the edge of the Cambridge Common, George Washington, astride a steed, amid gaily uniformed troops, and accompanied by great fanfare, drew his saber and took command of the Continental Army.

90. Samuel F. Batchelder took umbrage with illustrations, such as this quaint scene, depicting the venerable Washington Elm in Cambridge, Massachusetts. In October 1923, when (in his words) "'the Washington Elm' fell (or more accurately was accidentally pulled over by workmen trying to remove a dead branch)," he set out to debunk the myth. The result was a long letter, submitted to the *Cambridge Tribune*, that was published in December. On the one hundred fiftieth anniversary of Washington's assuming command of the Continental Army, Batchelder reprinted the letter (with some additions) at his own expense. His letter had become a booklet of thirty-six pages entitled "The Washington Elm Tradition: 'Under This Tree Washington First Took Command of the American Army.' Is It True? The Evidence Collected and Considered," by Samuel F. Batchelder. With caustic wit and precise and impeccable logic, Batchelder argued each of his points. He referenced diary and journal entries (apparently, none of the soldiers who kept diaries made note of the event); he analyzed Washington's personality (he was, in Batchelder's estimation, "notoriously modest—so modest that when he was nominated by the Continental Congress he immediately left the hall," and he was not inclined "to flourish his sword and prance up and down"); he made note of the condition of the weather (it was raining); and he documented the actual date on which Washington assumed command (Washington had arrived in Cambridge on July 2, and would not have waited a day before taking command). Although Batchelder readily admits that Washington "probably did do something, active or passive, beneath His elm," most likely it was simply taking shelter from the rain on his way into town. He contends that the actual assumption of command, most likely as simple an action as Washington reading his commission and receiving the headquarters documents, took place on the evening of 2 July, at General Ward's headquarters in the Hasting House (on the site of the present Malkin Athletic Center on Dunster Street.

CHAPTER THREE

Trees in the Marketplace and in the Garden

Enterprise and Industry

When soldiers and militiamen laid their muskets aside and returned to their fields after the Revolutionary War, the average New England farm covered about one hundred acres. Two-thirds of each farmstead was open land: pastures, mowing fields, tillage, and orchards. The valuable woodlot, a source of fuel, tools, building materials, and spending money, shared the remaining acreage with uncultivated swamps and marshes. With much of New England's coastline settled and developed, and with two-thirds of the central and southern parts cleared and under cultivation, many an enterprising Yankee migrated west beyond the Berkshires of Massachusetts and Connecticut to central New York or on to the Western Reserve (the 3.5-million-acre tract of land in northeastern Ohio that Connecticut had retained after ceding to the federal government, in 1786, the rest of the western lands it had claimed as a part of its territory). For others, the frontier lay in the upland interior regions of New England itself, and ambitious new communities quickly multiplied on rocky northern hills and along the narrow alluvial plains of fingerlike river valleys that ran through the mountains. Within fifty years, the population of Maine tripled, and census takers counted twice as many people homesteading in Vermont and New Hampshire.

At the beginning of the nineteenth century, sizable sections of the northern forest of New Hampshire and Vermont had fallen under the pioneer farmers' axes, and the forests of Maine were about to become the country's leading producer of lumber. In southern New England, cleared land far exceeded forest. According to the Reverend Jared Eliot, author of *Essays upon Field Husbandry*, despite "planting their Pastureland with Buttonwood, and Locust Trees" to shade their herds and fuel their fireplaces, Rhode Islanders had, as early as 1738, consumed almost all the trees available for firewood. As the number of farms and dwellings across southern New England multiplied and farmhouses with six rooms or more and numerous outbuildings replaced the modest one- or two-room house, consumption of wood increased. Although burning wood in huge fireplaces was an inefficient method of providing heat, fuel had appeared at first to be limitless. But, with the average family going through twenty cords in a year and those with more fireplaces consuming at least twice as much wood in the same time, firewood cut from forests near rapidly expanding coastal cities and towns and quickly growing river settlements did indeed have a limit. From the middle of the seventeenth century onward, shortages similar to those experienced in London a hundred years earlier had become commonplace in New York, Philadelphia, and Boston. The city's poor had little choice about what fuel to burn, but, until the Revolutionary War cut off supplies, some wealthy Bostonians gave up burning wood hauled in from the distant countryside by sled, or transported down the coast by schooner, and depended instead on shiploads of coal imported from England.

The woodmonger's escalating prices dashed the illusion of cheap, limitless fuel, and articles about the misuse of economically valuable species and the importance of preserving the nation's forests began to appear in the popular press and in the earliest of the country's scholarly publications. Moreover, the American practice of cutting down every tree within sight had long been of concern to European naturalists. Traveling to America in 1748 at the expense of the Sweden's Royal Academy of Science, Peter Kalm, a botanist and disciple of Linnaeus, noted in the journal he kept of his three-year journey that "we can hardly be more hostile toward our woods in Sweden and Finland than they are here; their eyes are fixed on the present gain, and they are blind to the future." Now, with the Revolution over and independence established, a new wave of foreign social critics and reporters swept through the country, eager to appraise the experiment that had established the new republic. Among their ranks were botanists and foresters, who set forth to review the nation's "endless" resources. Their observations echoed Kalm's earlier projections. Johann David Schoepf, court physician to the Margrave of Brandenburg, had been a surgeon of Hessian troops in the English service during the Revolution, and he remained in America after the war to tour the country and to study medicinal plants. Schoepf listed as many as four hundred North American species in his *Materia Medica Americana Potissimum Regni Vegetablis*, a book that he hoped "rendered sufficient service to America to be pardoned for my assistance in combating her." Schoepf wrote that "North America owns a rich indigenous *materia medica* in her plants and can find all she needs, apart from a few East Indian spices and plants, on her own soil," but his assessment of the nation's forests was much less optimistic. In a two-volume work entitled *Reise durch einige der mittleren und südlichen Vereinigten Nordamerikanischen Staaten, nach Ost-Florida und den Bahama-Inseln, unternommen in den Jahren 1783 und 1784*, published in 1788, one year after his *Materia Medica*, Schoepf predicted that, because there was "no sovereign right over forests and game, [and] no forest service," the onerous responsibility of insuring that future generations could hope to have "a bit of wood over which to hang a teakettle" would rest precariously on the shoulders of the nation's landholders, who were farmers rather than foresters. Most Americans remained unaware of the German doctor's misgivings until *Travels in the Confederation*, an English translation of his book, appeared in 1911.

A most authoritative and compelling argument that the abuse of forest resources should be curbed reached America early in the nineteenth century in two pioneer taxonomic studies undertaken by a father and son, who were keenly aware of the grave consequences that a nation could suffer through the loss of its trees. In 1785, André Michaux, as botanist to King Louis XVI of France, had been dispatched across the Atlantic to determine which trees, especially oaks, could be used to revegetate his nation's denuded land. Accompanying him as an apprentice naturalist on his botanical exploration of America was his fifteen-year-old son, François André. The elder Michaux discovered and named many new American species, and father and son together gathered seeds and established two nurseries, one in New Jersey and a larger one in South Carolina, where many of their plants could be grown before being shipped home. André fulfilled his mission by collecting thousands of plants for

91. Pehr [Peter] Kalm (1716-1779), one of Linnaeus's most brilliant and most energetic students, for whom he named the genus *Kalmia*. When *Species Plantarum* was published in 1753, Linnaeus cited Kalm as the source of ninety species, two-thirds of them new. Already an accomplished veteran of botanical expeditions in Finland (his homeland) and Russia, Kalm spent three years in North America making his way through Delaware, Pennsylvania, New York, and parts of eastern Canada. The vivid descriptions of colonial life that he recorded in his journal indicate that Kalm was as perceptive an observer of social and economic conditions as he was a keen-eyed collector of plants. In *En Resa til Norra America*, which was published between the years 1753 and 1761 (an English translation was published ten years later as *Travels in North America*), Kalm foretold the American revolution: "For the English colonies in this part of the world have increased so much in their number of inhabitants, and in their riches that they almost vie with Old England. . . . in the space of thirty years [they] would be able to form a state by themselves, entirely independent."

the garden and forests of France, and his explorations also led to the publication, in 1801, of the first accurate study of New World oaks. Two years later, the elder Michaux fell ill, but he lived long enough to see his study of North American plants published. In March of 1803, when François André Michaux wrote, "I now exhibit my father's flora, gathered up from the author's unfinished manuscript," the first comprehensive systematic treatment of the plants of North America, *Flora Boreali-Americana*, joined the world's botanical literature. Within ten years, the son would complete his own monumental work, the first manual of North American trees.

On forays into the wilderness on foot and by horseback, stagecoach, and canoe, and even by way of a "new

92. During his travels, François André Michaux made note of the different species of wood used for fuel and of the growing scarcity of fuel wood in the new nation's cities and large towns. Cost, too, had become an issue: the prices commanded in 1806–1807 had, by his estimate, doubled within twenty-five years. He also took issue with the unregulated manner in which the fuel-wood supply was handled. "The large towns are furnished with fuel by individuals who are subject to none of the regulations adopted in Europe. In our cities every wood-merchant is abliged to have a certain quantity of fuel in his yard at the entrance of winter, and effectual measures are taken to render the price independent of the variations in the seasons. In the United States the markets are supplied from day to day with wood exposed to sale as soon as it is felled; hence, when the navigation of the rivers is suddenly arrested by frost, the supply is cut off; the price once rose, on such an occasion, at New York, to 40 dollars a cord."

means of navigation"—joining Robert Fulton on the maiden voyage of his steamboat in 1807—François André Michaux continued his father's investigations into what he chose to call America's "botanical geography." François André not only hobnobbed with the young republic's cognoscente, he queried cabinetmakers, ship-builders, and carpenters as well as tanners and basketmakers about their uses of wood. Throughout his travels, he observed the loss of acre upon acre of forest and recorded not only that wood was becoming "extreme-ly dear" near the cities but also that "for a space of 600 miles from Philadelphia to a distance beyond Boston, [he] did not see a single stock of the white pine large enough for the mast of a vessel of 600 tons." In August 1807, after surveying Boston shipyards and being feted at a party held on Deer Island in Boston Harbor, Michaux proceeded to botanize his way across New England. In Maine, he acquired several quart-sized containers full of the minuscule seed of white and yellow birches (*Betula papyrifera* and *B. alleghaniensis*). He gathered the winged samaras of elms and maples from trees growing in New Hampshire and Vermont and cut two- to three-inch sections of hemlock, spruce, and Atlantic white-cedar to add to his collection of woods of native species, probably the first such assemblage of American woods.

Michaux's *Histoire des Arbres Forestiers de l'Amérique Septentrionale, Considérés Principalement sous les Rapports de Leur Usage dans les Arts et de Leur Introduction dans le Commerce* stood for more than half a century after its publication (between the years 1810 and 1813) as the most comprehensive study of the eastern North American forest. His insatiable curiosity about American customs and trades provided as precise a review of "what wood is employed in the different parts of the United States in all branches of industry" as the subtitle of his book promised.

An acute observer, Michaux's comments on chair-making—specifically, the manufacture of the distinctive Windsor chair—reveal his typical penchant for detail. Imported from England during the first quarter of the eighteenth century, the Windsor chair evolved into many different variations, as chairmakers along the Atlantic seaboard experimented with its design and with the types of wood used in its construction. Michaux wrote that, in Maine, "at Hallowell, Portland, Portsmouth, etc., the seat is of Basswood, the lower frame of Sugar Maple, and the bows and rods which compose the back, of White Ash." When the same type of chair was made "at New York, Philadelphia, Baltimore, and Richmond, the seat is of Tulip Tree, the legs of Red-flowering Maple, the rods of

93. *Betula alleghaniensis* was known until the 1950s as *B. lutea,* the name Michaux chose for this species because of its yellowish bark. The color of the lustrous bark, which peels back into papery-thin yellow curls, is most prominent when the tree is young. The conspicuous, long, horizontal markings on the trunk are called lenticels.

B. alleghaniensis often grows in association with two other birches, the paper or canoe birch (*B. papyrifera*) and the sweet birch (*B. lenta*). These three birches often grow in the company of two small maples—the striped maple, or moosewood (*Acer pensylvanicum*), and the mountain maple (*A. spicatum*). The large, goose-foot-shaped leaves of the striped maple can be seen in the lower left corner of the photograph.

94. The seeds of the yellow birch ripen in late July and August and persist until fall. When the fruiting bodies (the mature form of the female flower clusters) begin to disintegrate during the cold days of October, these heart- and fleur-de-lis-shaped fruit parts are scattered by the wind. The heart-shaped structures are achenes, winged, one-seeded fruits; the fleurs-de-lis are three-lobed hairy bracts, the modified leaves of the infructescence to which the fruits are attached. Yellow birch trees begin producing seeds when they reach about forty years of age. During a good seed year, a stand of yellow birches can disperse seeds in excess of one million per acre.

the back, of Shell-bark Hickory, and the bow of White Oak." Local craftsmen and merchants must not have been pleased to read that, "at Boston, chairs of this sort are made wholly of White Pine, except the bow, which is of White Oak: they are light and cheap, but easily broken and of little value."

In the introduction to *The North American Sylva; or a Description of the Forest Trees of the United States, Canada, and Nova Scotia, Considered Particularly with Respect to Their Uses in the Arts and Their Introduction into Commerce* (as the manual became known in its English translation, just four years after the first French edition), Michaux forewarned Americans of the need to manage their forests or face economic reversals, and he urged the government to make conservation a priority.

A generation would pass before Americans would act on Michaux's advice. Indeed, one year before his first

visit, the last legislative attempt to manage the region's forest resources had been enacted by the Massachusetts government. This act, passed in 1784, levied a $100 fine for cutting white pines on public lands. Unfortunately, by 1793, in an effort to recover financially from the Revolutionary War, Massachusetts had allowed 3.5 million acres of public nonagricultural lands—the vast forest of conifers destined to become the state of Maine in 1820—to pass, by lottery, into private hands.

England's Industrial Revolution arose, in part, because of efforts to develop substitutes for scarce wood. In America, the exploitation of wood, both as a raw material and as a component in innovative machine technology, became the catalyst that propelled the nation into the industrial era. Trees and waterpower stimulated the mechanization and industrialization that changed lives and altered landscapes. For close to a decade—from 1807, with the passage of the Embargo Act (which kept American ships docked in American ports), until 1815, when the Treaty of Ghent resolved the War of 1812—Americans had been, once again, unable to obtain English goods. These critical years stimulated the production of domestic commodities. Following the Revolution, many families had remained independent and self-sufficient; for the most part, both production and consumption of necessities took place at home on the farm. Equipped with woodworking tools, chimney forge, spinning wheel, loom, and dyepot, each farm was virtually a self-contained family factory. The men made and repaired tools, utensils, and furnishings; whittled hickory brooms, wooden pegs, bolts, hinges, and latches; tanned leather; and hand-forged tacks and nails. In addition to their other household tasks, women carded, spun, bleached, and dyed the wool and linen that they transformed into the family's clothes; wove garters, staylaces, hatbands, and suspenders; and, in spare moments, knitted mittens, shawls, stockings, and hats.

For most New Englanders, however, the era of the homespun and the handmade had passed, and the time of the one-man village shop and the itinerant artisan was evolving into an age of factories and machines. Wherever waterpower, river transportation, or good roads existed, industries based on the use of wood and tree products proliferated, and small manufacturing centers began to appear in the larger cities and as satellite villages of prosperous agrarian towns. Although in many cases these manufactories simply sheltered a process of piecework and hand labor taking place under one roof, chair and clock factories, carriage shops, dyehouses, and tanneries —as well as the more mechanized power-driven carding,

95. In England, during the eighteenth century, fashionable cabinetmakers, such as Thomas Chippendale and George Hepplewhite, produced standard designs for all types of domestic furnishings, including chairs. Because a chair's proportions have great bearing upon its comfort, Chippendale and Hepplewhite published the exact dimensions of their padded, turned, or joined chairs in their pattern books. These books were intended to serve as catalogues of their wares, but they also became guides with which skilled craftsmen could reproduce the latest in stylish designs. The Windsor chair, however, did not appear in pattern books, because this unpadded, all-wood chair was not the product of urban cabinetmakers but was designed and developed by rural craftsmen. Windsor chairs made in England were usually made from the wood of European beech (*Fagus sylvatica*), which is both strong and fairly hard. When the Windsor chair made its way to the American colonies in the 1730s, it usually became a three-wood piece, with the wood of a different species chosen for each of the chair's three elements—seat, legs and spindles, and back. A comfortable, stylish, and inexpensive chair that was both durable and easy to produce, the Windsor became a huge success. Probate inventories from Concord, Massachusetts, establish 1788 as the year that this type of chair first appeared in Concord. Fifty years later, nearly half the Concord households inventoried had at least one Windsor chair.

96.   As late as 1894, excursionists wishing to behold a view of the White Mountains, Mount Ascutney, Camels Hump, and Killington Peak from the summit of Mount Mansfield, Vermont, had the dubious pleasure of being transported across this corduroy bridge. Through the graphic illustrations by Harry Fenn that appeared in *Picturesque America Or, the Land We Live In*, which was edited by William Cullen Bryant, armchair travellers could enjoy the scenery "and the glimpses downward, through entanglements of trees into the deep ravines" while forgoing the ascent on a "road [that] passes over terraced solid rock, and . . . jolts over the crazy scaffolding of a corduroy bridge that spans a chasm in the mountain-side." There was yet another advantage to viewing the mountaintop prospect vicariously: the text that accompanied this illustration stated that "Mr. Fenn was three days on the summit of Mansfield, during all which time a dense, gray vapor enveloped all the facial features of that grand profile, and veiled the surrounding scene as completely as the curtain at the play shuts from view the splendors behind it."

fulling, and cotton mills—began to appear where once only sawmill and gristmill had stood.

As vital as wood and waterpower were to the growth of manufacturing, economic success hinged on the construction of good, all-season roads and dependable bridges. Surveyors, navigating by compass and measuring distance by lengths of chain, blazed trees to mark the courses of the public roads, toll roads, and turnpikes that eventually linked interior towns with the coast. As they made their way up and over mountains and passed through muddy swamps, the axmen that followed the blazes turned the saplings and tree trunks that stood in their way into temporary bridges and narrow-track roads. "Corduroy" roads (roads made of logs eight to ten inches in diameter laid side by side across a boggy stretch of ground) might have been named for a soft, ribbed cotton fabric, but these byways rode like the hard ridges of a washboard, and the bone-rattling, teeth-clattering early bridges were no smoother—they were simply raised corduroy roads. At the beginning of the nineteenth century, as hand hewn planks replaced tree trunks and truss bridges covered over like barns and designed to span broad rivers evolved, a new breed of engineer, the builder of covered bridges, utilized wood cut from the rich assortment of species that grew along rivers and streams. Cold, damp, north sides of deep gorges harbored northern hardwoods and conifers well south of their normal range, and the wood of trees typically restricted to more moderate climates became a part of bridges built on the rolling flood plains of the Connecticut, Housatonic, and Hoosic river valleys.

In a typical covered bridge, whose roof and side walls were intended to protect the bridge itself and not the traffic passing through, thick planks of red oak (*Quercus rubra*) or black oak (*Q. velutina*) were often used for flooring. White oak (*Q. alba*) was typically used for beams, trusses, and kingposts; ash (*Fraxinus americana* or *F. pennsylvanica*) was typically used for lattice; and chestnut (*Castanea dentata*) was used for sills. The creamy-white wood of the tulip tree (*Liriodendron tulipifera*) made wide, clear planking, and strong timbers could be cut from either the red elm (*Ulmus rubra*) or the American elm (*U. americana*). Conifers—white pine, eastern redcedar, and Atlantic white-cedar—provided wall planking and roof shingles. In Vermont, a bridge spanning the Ottauquechee River that was built with stringers of pine (*Pinus*), braces of beech (*Fagus grandifolia*), and posts of red elm (*Ulmus rubra*) that were capped with spruce (*Picea*) used the qualities of locally occurring species to their best advantage. Unfortunately,

no matter how well constructed they were, such bridges were not invulnerable. The great slabs of ice that careened down the rivers when the temperature rose and ice-out began on the lakes and rivers, the subsequent spring floods that followed in the ice's wake, and summer downpours could, in the wink of an eye, sweep away bridges, covered or not. Debates on bridge financing, repair, reconstruction, and design were almost an annual occurrence at town-meeting time.

Not only wooden bridges but corduroy roads and roads made of planks also wore out or rotted away. Regardless of the higher costs of maintenance, farmers considered roads made of planks a boon and a vast improvement over corduroy roads. With plank roads, the mud seasons of spring and fall did not take such a toll on wagonloads and backbones when traveling to church, to visit neighbors, or to conduct business in town. Usually, only one side of the road was paved with wood, and, in deference to the farmers' incoming carts, that side had the right of way; it was the right-hand side that led into town that sported the thick, eight-foot-long planks laid at right angles to the road. However, after five years of bearing shod hooves and heavy wagonloads through the summer's drying heat and the winter's soaking rains and snows, very little of the wooden planking remained.

Many varieties of wood went into plank roads, but, when the settlers felled hemlocks (*Tsuga canadensis*), they found the wood hard, coarse, splintery, and difficult to work. With so many other superior species available, hemlock was not considered to be a significant or valuable lumber tree; almost by default, this graceful conifer became one of the woods most commonly used as paving material.

The eastern hemlock (*Tsuga canadensis*) grows slowly and lives to a great age—centuries, in fact. The record age for a hemlock is 988 years. In their natural range, hemlocks are often found scattered through deciduous upland forests or completely covering the northern slopes of ridges and the steep banks of narrow river gorges. In New England, in the northeastern portion of their range, they become one of the dominant forest trees.

In a dry, open field or burned-over area, a hemlock seedling would be scorched by the sun. If young hemlocks are to survive, they must grow in cool, moist soil and the protective shade cast by a forest canopy. Here, the amount of light that filters down to the forest floor is sufficient for hemlock seedlings to maintain growth at a slow but steady pace. Their roots are shallow, and the trees can subsist on thin soil; in fact, as long as there is enough moisture, hemlocks can take root and grow in mossy rock crevices or on fallen logs. Eventually, these conifers begin to shade their own roots and those of neighboring plants that compete for moisture and nutrients. When the established forest trees that sheltered the emerging hemlocks reach old age and begin to die, or are blown down by winds, the hemlocks in the understory are in their prime. Taking advantage of additional space and increased light, their growth rate accelerates; scientists use the term "released" to refer to this phenomenon. With time, hemlocks outlive, shade out, and overtop their neighbors.

At the Arnold Arboretum, Hemlock Hill is typical of the habitat where these graceful conifers flourish. Records of ownership of this parcel of land date to around 1640, and there is evidence that the Arboretum's hill of hemlocks, which borders Bussey Street, has been logged and thinned but never subjected to clear-cutting. Natural events ranging from decay to hurricane winds brought down the ancient trees; yet today, on Hemlock Hill, trees that predate the signing of our country's Constitution still grow; and these are the descendants of generations of hemlocks that originally formed part of the primeval forest that covered New England.

Foresters once assumed that hemlocks occupying the understory were all young trees. By counting growth rings, however, it has been shown that many are equal in age with nearby hemlocks that are three and four times larger in girth. The difference in size between the "mature" trees and those thought to be younger depends on the amount of sunlight and space each received. Evidence of accelerated growth rate and changing position within the forest canopy can be revealed by examining the growth rings on the stump of a large, old hemlock. The

rings toward the center are usually narrow and numerous, reflecting the years when little sunlight reached the tree and only a small increment was added to the tree's circumference each growing season. Hemlocks exposed to minimal sunlight continued to grow in these small increments. When more sunlight became available, a sudden corresponding widening in the annual rings occurred as growth increased. Once the tree reached extreme old age, the rings at the outer edge of the cross section narrowed again, reflecting the natural slowdown of growth that comes with age.

The fine texture of the hemlock's foliage, combined with its slender, curving branches, give an elegant appearance to well-grown specimens of this tree. Unlike those of many other conifers, the hemlock's uppermost growing tip, its leader, is not rigid but pliant. The flexibility of the terminal shoot adapts it for survival in the understory for the simple reason that the leader tends to yield rather than to break under the onslaught of snow or falling limbs. During each growing season, the leader slowly straightens, as more wood cells are produced on the underside of the shoot than on the upper surface. This asymmetrical growth results in a gradual erection of the shoot tip. The growth that changes the direction of the curvature—referred to as "compression wood" in conifers—is usually darker than, and differs structurally from, normal wood. The presence of compression wood has significant ramifications for the economic importance of hemlock lumber. Unwanted splits, which follow the concentric growth rings, appear when hemlock wood is cut and dried. These "shakes"—in the language of lumber dealers—occur where cells along the margin between two growth rings, or within one, break. This defect is

97. More graceful than pines, less stiff and less formal than spruces and firs, hemlocks were considered by Andrew Jackson Downing, America's preeminent landscape gardener, to be the most picturesque and most beautiful of all the evergreen trees in the world. The contrast between the hemlocks' large, straight trunks and their slender, pendulous branches certainly makes this conifer one of the most decorative trees of the New England woods. This photograph, taken by T. E. Marr at the turn of the century, depicts the timeless quality of the quiet surround that is still evident today within the confines of the rocky slopes and ridge crest of Hemlock Hill. Although the hurricane of 1938 inflicted great damage upon many of the older trees that appear in Marr's photograph, their demise made possible the "release" of numerous younger hemlocks in the understory that, by now, have matured into equally impressive specimens. More than half a century has passed since the 1938 hurricane, and a contemporary view of this same path, which runs midslope along the hill and then descends to follow the course of Bussey Brook, looks strikingly similar to Marr's 1903 portrait of Hemlock Hill, which remains one of the most beautiful aspects of the Arnold Arboretum.

98. Hemlock foliage is soft and feathery rather than needlelike. The fine-textured leaves are a very dark and shiny green on the upper surface, while the undersides have a silvery-whitish cast caused by two white lines that parallel the midrib of each leaf. In contrast to the dark color of the older foliage, the dense new growth at the ends of the branch tips is a bright yellow-green. This attractive two-toned effect lasts only for a few weeks during spring, until the soft, new needles darken and take on the same polished shine as the older ones. Donald Culross Peattie—botanist, naturalist, and author of *A Natural History of Trees of Eastern and Central North America*—captured the delicate spirit of hemlock boughs by describing their sound: "When the wind lifts up the Hemlock's voice, it is no roaring like the Pines, no keening like the Spruce's. The Hemlock whistles softly to itself."

99. A young tree, growing undisturbed, adds growth rings, or annual rings, in a fairly concentric pattern, as the core of about twenty rings in the upper portion of this cross section of the trunk of a red spruce (*Picea rubens*) indicates. However, when something interferes with the tree's ability to grow straight—a heavy limb falls on it, or a severe windstorm blows it sideways—a conifer reacts by adding compression wood on the underside, or leaning side, of the trunk. With the addition of each annual ring, abnormally narrow on the upper side and exceptionally wide below, the tree develops a curve that slowly rights the trunk again. In broadleaf trees, such wood, called tension wood, forms along the *upper* side of the affected tree trunk, whence it exerts a pull on the trunk to straighten it.

thought to occur because differential shrinking occurs between compression wood and normal wood; compression wood has a higher moisture content and thus dries more slowly.

Tanner, Tailor, and Shoemaker

In the colonies, the process by which green or raw hides were converted into stable and pliable leather had changed little since ancient Egyptian times. When an animal skin is soaked in a water extract of bark, the astringent and antiseptic vegetable tannins from the bark combine with the animal proteins to render the hide resistant to moisture, changing temperatures, and bacterial decay.

Initially, almost every farmer tanned his own hides. Later, as demand increased for the wide array of objects that were made of leather, farmers began to rely on the services of a tanner, and an open-air tannery became as common a fixture as a gristmill in nearly every town and village. In addition to belts, vests, breeches, jackets, jerkins, and aprons, people needed strong, flexible material for harnesses, saddlery, ships' rigging, bellows, pails, and other indispensable items, such as shoes and boots. In early tanneries—small one- or two-man operations, like the one established in Lynn, Massachusetts, in 1629—strips of tree bark were ground by hand into small chips, which were then soaked in water to leach out the tannic acid. This solution was used to cure the hides that the local populace turned into simple clothes and crudely made footwear. During the winter months and in other periods of inclement weather, many farm families of Lynn and the surrounding countryside supplemented their income by cobbling leather in "ten footers," the small wooden outbuildings where they kept the tools of their second trade. As a result, well into the twentieth century—long after local sources of tanbark and animal skins had disappeared—Lynn remained the center of the country's shoe industry.

By 1800, each New England village supported at least one busy shoemaker or cordwainer—from *cordovan* (after the Spanish city of Córdoba), a popular European leather made from horsehide and tanned with sumac—and, in the larger cities, only house joiners and carpenters exceeded in number the artisans who cobbled shoes. The boots and shoes that these artisans fashioned on wooden lasts were perfectly straight, and each one of a pair could be worn on either foot. Crooked shoes—lefts and rights—did not appear until the middle of the nineteenth century.

Europeans used oak and sumac to tan skins, and, when they started making leather in the New World, at first they sought New World species of the same genera. Among all the new species of oaks the colonists encountered, the bark of one cured leather best. This species, *Quercus velutina*, became known as the tanbark oak, or, because in comparison with other mature oaks its outer bark was the darkest, the black oak. Its Latin specific epithet *velutina*, "velvety," is derived from the fact that its emerging, bright red leaves have long, silky, silvery-white hairs on the upper surface and a short, dense, velvety matting (or tomentum) of white hairs on the underside. The upper surfaces of the leaves lose the long, threadlike hairs and turn a dark, shining green, but the undersides retain some of the velvet. These scurfy, or flaky, patches of down, which usually occur in the axils of veins where they join the midrib, help to distinguish *Q. velutina* from *Q. rubra*, the red oak, and *Q. coccinia*, the scarlet oak, both of which have similarly shaped leaves.

Quercus velutina reaches its northern limit in the light, dry soils of the Champlain Valley of Vermont and New York. Skirting the northern and mountainous regions of New Hampshire, black oaks appear again in the coastal areas of southern Maine. Along with the red oak, *Q. rubra*, *Q. velutina* dominates the hardwood forest of southern New England.

Two other names for this species, yellow oak and dyers oak, came into common use because another valuable product could be obtained from its bark. The chemical compounds that color the thick inner bark of *Quercus velutina* a bright orange yellow made a potent dye. Named quercitron in 1784, it turned wool, linen, and cotton such intense shades of yellow that black-oak bark became a commercial product exported from the colonies to the dyehouses of England. Synthetic replacements for plant dyes, discovered by chance in England in 1856 and perfected through the development of aniline dyes by German chemists in the early years of the twentieth century, supplanted the once thriving trade in natural plant dyes. During World War I, one indication that the United States lagged far behind in the organic chemical industry was that the demand for khaki-colored cloth outstripped American production of synthetic dyes, and thousands of cords of black-oak bark had to be harvested in order to dye cloth for the military.

Tanning even the lightest of animal hides took several weeks; the time required for tanning a heavy skin often exceeded a year. Because all leather made with black-oak bark assumed a yellow hue, tanners had to incorporate into their already lengthy process the additional step of

100. Until the American Revolution, tanning was a cottage industry, but, as the demand for leather grew during the industrial revolution and the westward expansion, tanning itself became mechanized. During the middle 1800s, the massive cogwheels and upright and horizontal shafts used to transmit power in mills were being replaced by new machines that were driven by belts. Leather was needed to make the belts that now drove the nation's factories, and more leather was needed for the harnesses and traces that connected horses to combines, plows, and wagons. In response to the growing market for leather goods, manufactories such as the Page Belting Company of Concord, New Hampshire, moved the process of tanning leather (which had formerly been carried on outdoors, and then only during the summer) indoors, thereby making tanning a mechanized, year-round operation. By the 1880s, water-powered machines, such as bark mills, had replaced the heavy millstones that old-fashioned "one-horse" tanneries rolled around on edge to grind up the bark. The bark mill figured in this illustration of the interior of the Page Belting Company was capable of grinding up three cords (or 384 cubic feet) of bark in one hour, a vast improvement over the tedious and time-consuming millstone method.

101. The abundant occurrence of the black oak (*Quercus velutina*) in eastern Massachusetts is reflected by the large number of naturally occurring specimens that populate the Arnold Arboretum's grounds. The mature black oak that grows at the junction of Meadow Road and Bussey Hill Road exemplifies the characteristics of this species. The black oak is seldom planted for ornamental purposes; even in youth, it is a rugged-looking tree. As it matures, it acquires a craggy habit—a short, massive trunk, heavy limbs, and twiggy branches. These attributes, coupled with the rough, thick, black bark that the tree develops as it ages, are typical of old black oaks. This noble tree probably predates the Arboretum's existence, and it is considered to be part of its "spontaneous" flora. However, the young black oak planted close beside it in 1990 grew from an acorn collected by an Arboretum staff member in Burleson, Texas, in 1986.

leaching away the yellow dye. Within a short time, the colonial tanner had substituted eastern hemlock for black oak. *Tsuga canadensis,* a tree whose bark imparted no unwanted coloration yet contained higher concentrations of tannins than most other plants, became the most common source of tanbark in the New World.

An early report of the Native American's use of hemlock—which John Josselyn described in *New England Rarities Discovered*—told of how they "break and heal their swelling and sores with it." Later observations seemed to indicate that hemlocks are rarely injured by insects, bacteria, and fungi, which led to the inclusion of hemlock resin, known as *"Pix Canadensis,* Hemlock pitch, Hemlock gum, or Canada pitch," in the first American pharmacopoeia published in 1810. Boiled in

water, fresh buds and sections of wood and bark taken from around knots made the tincture of Canada pitch used in medical plasters. Apparently, it was reasoned that, if hemlock bark could safeguard the tree from insects and diseases, an external application of Canada pitch would do as well for human skin. By the beginning of the nineteenth century, however, hemlock had become such an indispensable material in the tanning industry that its medicinal use became minor.

By 1810, there were more than 4000 tanneries nationwide, the majority of which were based in the Northeast. Surprisingly, within the next thirty years, the number of tanneries in New England doubled. Because it took roughly a cord (128 cubic feet) of hemlock bark and 120 gallons of water to tan ten hides, and because the

102. The region of the Catskill Mountains of New York led the nation in the production of tanned leather from 1820 to the 1880s. Although the hemlock tanning industry reached its peak in Maine in the 1880s and had all but disappeared by the first quarter of the twentieth century, the industry continued well into this century in Pennsylvania. By the 1930s, however, hemlock bark, most of which was then being harvested and processed in Pennsylvania, supplied only 18 percent of the domestic tannins. This woodsman, peeling hemlock bark from logs, practiced his craft for the Pennsylvania logging company W. W. Bowman & Sons in 1939. In 1931, when hemlock became the state tree of Pennsylvania, it was cited not only as "the tree most typical of the forests of Pennsylvania" but also acknowledged as the tree that provided the Commonwealth with "its bark to found a mighty industry."

bark weighed six times the weight of the hides, tanneries sprang up wherever hemlocks grew and water was available to drive bark-crushing mills and to provide liquid for the "ooze" or bark infusion.

During the "barking" season, which traditionally lasted from the first full moon in May until the last full moon of August, the cambium—a layer only one cell thick between wood and bark—was soft, allowing the bark to be slipped easily from the trunks. A team of men skilled in this special task worked the woods harvesting bark. Using hatchets, axes, or saws, the "ringer and splitter" cleared a ring of bark from around the base of the trunk before the "chopper" felled the tree and the "knotter" trimmed its branches. Then the "ringer and splitter"

returned to split the bark so the "spudder" could remove it. Leaving the stripped logs to rot, or perhaps to be turned into planks for paving roads, the four-man crew could produce one-half to three-quarters of a cord of hemlock bark a day. After laying the four-foot lengths out to dry in order to prevent mold and extreme curling, they "ranked" or stacked the bark in cords until winter, when teamsters arrived, driving sleds pulled by horses or oxen, to haul the bark to the mill.

At the height of the tanning industry in the Northeast, raw hides shipped from as far away as South America arrived in New York's Catskill Mountains to be processed into leather. The source of tannin was not inexhaustible, and by the end of the nineteenth century, at about the same time that hemlock lumber had finally achieved some commercial value, New England's supply of hemlock lumber was almost depleted. In the meantime, the principal source of hides shifted westward; the wood of a South American tree, the quebracho (*Schinopsis lorentzii*), from Paraguay, Uruguay, and Argentina, became a more economical tanning agent; and local tanneries began closing down.

Handles, Cradles, and Baskets

Every farmer—whether his fields ran along ridges, sloped down to the rich bottom land adjoining a river, or lay flat and abutted a salt marsh—had to have a plow, a harrow, and a cart to plant, cultivate, and harvest his crops. An array of hand tools, each designed for a specific chore, met his additional needs. Farmers learned by experience that their long, wooden-handled tools—pitchfork and rake (whose tines and teeth were, at first, also made of wood), hoe, long-handled shovel, and scythe—had to be shaped from wood that seasoned quickly and splintered rarely. It was essential that the wood be strong and tough for its weight and remain flexible. The springy wood of white ash (*Fraxinus americana*) had furnished the best material for snowshoes for Native Americans and the European explorers, hunters, and trappers; now it satisfied the farmer's need for tools.

For harvesting grain, farmers employed the ancient, short-handled, hook-bladed sickle. The heavier, more modern, crooked, long-handled scythe was used to cut grass and hay. The serpentine design of the snath—which is the name Anglo-Saxon hay farmers bestowed on the scythe's sinuous handle—allowed the reaper, gripping it by two short, protruding handholds, to swing its long, curved cutting blade in wide arcs. There was no better

103. *The Veteran in a New Field* was painted in 1865 by Winslow Homer, a descendent of Captain John Homer, a shipmaster who had settled in Boston in the seventeenth century. Winslow Homer was born in Boston in 1836, and he moved with his family to Cambridge, Massachusetts, in 1842. Basically self-taught, he became an apprentice to John H. Bufford, a lithographer and publisher of prints, after responding to this ad: "Boy wanted; apply to Bufford Lithographer. Must have a taste for drawing." In America, the new advances in science and technology influenced painters such as Winslow Homer to reject idealism and to illustrate themes of work and manual labor. In *American Painting of the Nineteenth Century: Realism, Idealism, and the American Experience*, Barbara Novak describes Homer's work between 1862 and 1881 as having "further transformed the art of genre from reportorial narrative into a kind of monumental contemporary history painting." Homer later abandoned his early matter-of-fact realism in his studies of country life. His dominant themes became the forest and the sea, and he began to depict man's struggle with natural forces. In 1883, Homer moved to Prouts Neck, Maine, where he painted dramatic seascapes of rocks, wind, water, and light, and where he remained until his death in 1910.

American wood than white ash, steamed and bent into a pattern, with which to make a snath. By attaching a wooden framework of slender, pointed tines cut from the natural crooks of an ash tree, an inventive New Englander devised a cradle that made it possible to use the scythe to harvest grain. Once equipped with a cradle, a scythe became a tool that could cut, catch, and bunch together enough stalks to make a sheaf. A skilled cradler using a perfectly balanced cradle could harvest four acres of grain during a typical fourteen-hour workday.

When industrial development shifted the production of many traditionally homemade articles into the factory, and nineteenth century farmers had the option to buy ready-made hand tools, white ash became a factory wood. As mechanization slowly replaced hand labor on the farm, enormous quantities of ash went into the manufacture of new implements. Beginning in the 1830s, the invention of such machines as the reaper created an increased demand for ash wood. Ash whiffletrees, singletrees, eveners, and yokes bound oxen or horse to reaper, harrow, harvester, and thrasher. Ash, in the form of felloes (the curved pieces of wood that make up wheel-rims), tongues, shafts, trees, and axles, became even more integral to the production and assembly of the new machines than it had been in the construction of the humble handcart or oxcart.

104. An illustration of the Vaughan's cradle from *Maine Farmer*, volume 5. Named after its inventor, Charles Vaughan of Hallowell, Maine, it was also known as the Scotch bow or Scotch cradle. One contributor to *Maine Farmer*, possibly Vaughan himself, lauded this new cradle as being "much lighter, more easily made and kept in repair, than the common clumsy cradle, which is burdensome for a man to bear on his shoulder, and which to swing all day requires great strength and effort."

105. The farmer in this photograph could well be Winslow Homer's veteran, his work made easier by the use of a cradle scythe. However, as skillful as the man may be and as useful as the scythe has become, the photograph, unlike Homer's painting, conveys none of the reaper's grace, nor does it give a sense of the space and quiet that surrounds his solitary labor.

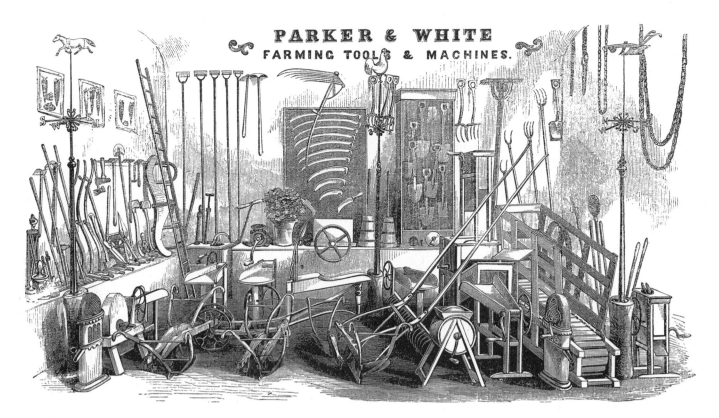

PARKER & WHITE
FARMING TOOLS & MACHINES.

106. Before 1800, the state of Connecticut, the city of New Haven, the town of Hallowell, Maine, and Middlesex County, Massachusetts, had all formed societies devoted to promoting agriculture. In 1811, when Elkanah Watson of Pittsfield, Massachusetts, organized the Berkshire Agricultural Society to sponsor either an annual cattle show or an agricultural fair, he was pioneering a way to reach the working farmer. This display of shovels, spades, rakes, forks, flails, hoes, billhooks, snaths, scythe blades, Scotch cradles, mattocks, butter churns, yokes, seed drills, plows, and other miscellaneous farm equipment was on display at a fair held in Boston in 1853. By this time, large farm machines, such as threshers, reapers, and harvesters, were being made farther west. But New England manufacturers, inspired by an economy of materials and Yankee thrift as well as their ability to combine lightness and grace with strength, retained the lead in the production of hand tools. Companies in Massachusetts manufactured more of these articles than those in any other two states combined.

107. Although the old triangular harrow, or "A" harrow, was still used on fields obstructed with stumps or rocks, a new invention, "the two-horse hinged harrow," proved more economical on cleared land. The whiffletree (or whippletree) is the pivoted swinging bar to which the traces of a harness are attached and by which a wagon—or, in this case, a hinged harrow—is drawn.

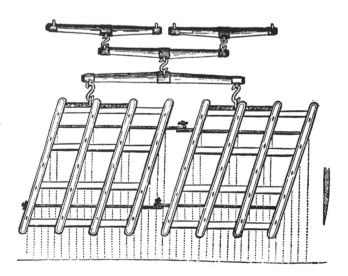

108. Guided by the premise that the plant collections of the Arnold Arboretum should be laid out following a taxonomic scheme in which related genera are grouped by family, Frederick Law Olmsted found the hillside above Bussey Hill Road an appropriate site for the Oleaceae, a family that includes not only large ash trees but lilacs and forsythia as well. Although two showy ornamental shrubs and an economically important forest tree may appear unrelated to the untrained eye, taxonomists assign these three genera—*Forsythia, Syringa,* and *Fraxinus* (among others) to the Oleaceae, or olive family, because of the similar construction of their flowers and other vegetative characteristics. New Englanders may find the origins of the two shrubs more surprising than their botanical relationship. Neither the forsythia nor the lilac is a native plant. The yellow, bell-shaped flowers that announce the timid beginnings of a New England spring adorn shrubs that were introduced from Japan, China, and Korea. The fragrant, purple blossoms of the lilac that proclaim that our winter is truly over trace their ancestors to southwestern Asia.

There are at least sixteen different species of ash native to North America, but the New England forest harbors the three that have been most important commercially. In addition to *Fraxinus americana,* the white ash—a tree that prefers rich, well-drained land and that occurs in almost every New England county—both *F. pennsylvanica,* the green ash, and *F. nigra,* the black ash, grow on more poorly drained soils. Of the three, *F. americana* is the tallest—reaching seventy to eighty feet in height—and the most abundant. But even though its natural range extends from Cape Breton Island west to eastern Minnesota and south to eastern Texas and northern Florida, it is not the most widely distributed. Although rarely found at higher elevations, *F. pennsylvanica,* the green ash, is the most widespread of the three, growing as far west as Alberta, Canada. *F. nigra,* which varies in height from thirty to seventy feet, is slightly smaller than either the white ash or the green ash, and it has a more limited range. A wetland species that extends into Labrador, well beyond the range of any other ash, the black ash is native to southeastern Canada and the northern parts of the eastern United States.

All ashes—save the aptly named *Fraxinus anomala* or single-leaf ash, which grows along streams in the dry chaparral country of the Southwest—have opposite, pinnately compound leaves that consist of an odd number of leaflets. Depending on the species, or sometimes even the individual tree, each leaf may have anywhere from three to eleven of these leaflets set in pairs with a solitary leaflet at the tip. The shape of the leaflets and the way in which they are attached to the central, or common, leaf stalk can help to identify New England's three species. Leaflets of white ash are the most rounded and have long stalks (petiolules) that connect the blade of each leaflet to the midrib of the compound leaf. Leaflets of green ash are more lance-shaped, often finely toothed at the margins, and have short petiolules. Leaflets of black ash have a more wedge-shaped base, their margins are toothed, and they lack individual stalks. Described as sessile, the leaflets attach directly to the midrib.

After ash leaves have turned shades of yellow and purple, then chocolate brown, they drop from the tree, but conspicuous clusters of the thin, paddlelike winged fruits called samaras remain to rustle against one another. Sometimes called "keys" because they resemble the metal keys once used to open medieval locks, the samaras of each species differ slightly. Those of black ash are notched at the top and clearly surround the seed capsule. While it is easy to distinguish the junction between the seed and the wing in the keys of the white ash, it is very difficult to tell where the seed capsule ends and the wing begins in the keys of the green ash.

Remaining bare-limbed and somber late into spring, ashes are among the last of the native trees to leaf out. The swiftness with which the large compound leaves finally appear depends upon the pores, or vessels, in the springwood being sizable enough to transport vast quantities of sap quickly. By comparison, the summerwood of *Fraxinus* is hard and dense. So similar is the wood of *F. americana* and *F. pennsylvanica* that lumber from both is often marketed today under the name "white ash." Black ash, which is just as long-grained but neither as strong nor as hard, has its own special qualities. A shorter growing season for this most northern ash restricts the amount of wood that is added to the girth of individual trees each year by the alternating bands of ring porous springwood and denser summerwood. The springwood of black ash has pores that are the largest of any ash,

making the summerwood easy to distinguish from the earlier growth. These easily separated, narrow growth rings, which reduce the value of the black ash as a lumber tree, enable the woodworker to turn its pliable wood into smooth, flexible splints. If a farmer had to make a basket or a barrel hoop, or needed to weave a seat for a chair, he looked in wet woods, along stream beds, and at the borders of swamps for this small, slender ash. Its soft bark, with corky ridges that are easily removed by rubbing, helped to identify the tree. Sawing a log into short sections or billets, then quartering each billet, then slicing each section in fourths again, produced "sticks" about one and one-half inches thick. The sticks were squared off with a drawknife and then pounded with the butt end of an axhead or maul until the wood split into splints one-eighth inch thick. The splints were then soaked in water and made ready for the weaver.

The Native Americans of Maine and Canada's Maritime Provinces turned basket weaving into a commercial venture by supplying farmers and rural settlers with strong, functional splint baskets. Black-ash baskets woven in Aroostook County continued to be associated with the potato harvest until modern mechanical methods all but replaced the slow, back-breaking work of digging the edible tubers by hand.

The Spinning Frame

Supple leather and agricultural implements were but a fraction of the goods being turned out by the entrepreneurs of New England. A new type of mill, one that housed machines born of English technology, began to spin southern-grown cotton into yarn.

To power their machines, the cotton mills, like all New England mills, relied on dams, raceways, and gates to impound and divert the energy of New England's rivers. Some cotton manufacturers simply utilized existing structures, replacing grinding stones and saws with spinning frames. However, workers toiling in these new mills needed better lighting; the heavier machinery required stronger, deeper foundations, and the machines needed to be positioned in line with the gears and shafts driven by the waterwheel, their source of power. These requirements fostered the construction of mills designed specifically for the textile industry. After locating a suitable site and obtaining "water rights" or a "mill privilege"—the authority to control part or all of the water power along a river or stream—the prospective manufacturer set out to erect a dam. The best time to begin this work came when

109. President Andrew Jackson called Samuel Slater (1768–1835) "the father of American manufactures." Slater's original carding machine, made almost entirely of wood, is now housed in the National Musem of American History, which is a part of the Smithsonian Institution.

Only two years earlier, on 20 December 1790, using "an old fulling mill water wheel" to generate power, William Almy, Smith Brown, and Samuel Slater had set the frames and cards of the country's first cotton mill in motion. Pieces of maple, chestnut, oak, birch, and pine had become the bobbins, pulleys, spindles, and frame of a small, but soon to be celebrated, twenty-four spindle cotton-spinning machine. Within the year, sixty-seven feet of oak for spindle rails alone went into their next, even larger, waterframe, for wood was the principal material of these new drawing, roving, carding, and spinning machines, which processed the raw cotton into parallel fibers first, then stretched them finer and finer, and lastly twisted them into finished yarn, all by means of waterpower.

William Almy and his cousin Smith Brown had been set up in the textile-manufacturing business by Almy's father-in-law, Moses Brown. In preparation for the venture, Moses, a prosperous Providence merchant, purchased all the new, Arkwright-type cotton-spinning machines he could find and had them installed in a narrow, wood-frame clothier's shop that stood on the west bank of the river just below the Pawtucket Falls. The machines, poor copies based on the Arkwright style, sat idle until Moses Brown hired Samuel Slater, an immigrant English master miller, to modify their design. After Slater came aboard, Almy and Brown's machines began producing yarn, and for two years the firm milled cotton in the cramped confines of the clothier's shop. In 1793, Slater joined the partnership and moved the machines upstream into a new mill, which would be known by his name.

Built with what had become traditional American techniques, the Slater Mill became the model for most of the textile mills constructed during the industry's infancy. Framed in the same manner as a New England barn and covered by clapboards, the modest wooden structure resembled a meetinghouse more than a mill. Set perpendicular to the river as a grist mill would be, its undershot wooden waterwheel was of the simplest and least costly design. Fashioned out of white pine, the wheel's shaft and short projecting arms quickly acquired the coat of green algae that millers believed insulated and protected the wheel from the constant force of the water. Outside the mill, white-pine planking directed the course of the millrace; inside the 29-by-43-foot building, white-pine planking covered the floor. Also inside, a large wooden wheel connected to the hand-hewn waterwheel shaft moved the wooden gears, pulleys, rollers, and cylinders of the perpetual carding engine and the cotton-spinning frames.

river levels were at their lowest, and the men who labored knee-, waist-, and even chest-deep in the Blackstone River during the summer of 1792 must have appreciated being warmed by a hot August sun. Like other mill dams that would be built during the same summer, and for many summers to come, the one built on the Blackstone for the firm of Almy, Brown & Slater would be constructed almost entirely of wood. According to a description of the dam published in the records of the Superior Court of Bristol County, Massachusetts, "fifty ox-cart loads of hewed timber, four thousand feet of two inch plank, and one thousand weight of wrought iron" went into its framework and downstream planking (the apron of wood that helped control erosion). At least twice that amount would be consumed in planking the upstream side and building the flume, gates, waterwheel, and mill. Designed to bow slightly to its downstream side, this dam would stand six to seven feet tall and stretch two hundred feet across the river's channel. At the time, it was one of the largest, if not simply the largest, dam in America. Set at a bend in the river within sight of the busy Post Road—originally an Indian pathway known to early settlers as the old Pequot Trail and today as U.S. Route 1— this dam would harness the energy of the Blackstone just before it plunged over the Pawtucket Falls.

110. The Slater Mill Historic Site, a National Historic Landmark, is now occupied as a museum by the Old Slater Mill Association. Rhode Island, one of nineteenth-century America's most important industrial states, maintains a justifiable claim as the birthplace of the American factory system. From its origins at the Slater Mill in Pawtucket, the textile industry fanned out to dominate Rhode Island's river valleys. Cotton milling, as well as woolen and worsted mills, flourished along the Blackstone River in the nineteenth and early twentieth centuries and transformed an agrarian landscape into a series of mill buildings, dams, power canals, and mill villages. The Slater Mill Historic Site includes the Wilkinson Mill, built in 1810–1811, which was both a textile mill and a machine shop. It is now a National Historic Mechanical Engineering Landmark. Oziele Wilkinson, his son David, and the Wilkinson Mill were critical components in the development of textile technology, steam-power generation, and the machine-tool industry.

By 1809, New England had twenty-one cotton mills clustered along the streams and rivers of Rhode Island, eastern Connecticut, and southern Massachusetts. One year later, the first census of manufacturing listed 238 mills, and in the next five years 135,000 spindles had begun spinning yarn in the 169 mills that stood within a thirty-mile radius of the city of Providence alone. To keep pace with the yarn being produced by their spinning machines, mill owners employed thousands of weavers. Men, women, and children toiled either at home on family looms using machine-made yarns "put out" by the mills or worked in quasi-industrial "weave shops" on looms owned by the manufacturers. Slater ran his first cotton mill with nine children, all between the ages of seven and twelve, but he depended on more than 600 handweavers, some of whom lived sixty miles away, to turn his yarn into cloth.

Because of the unsuitable climate, New England farmers could not hope to raise cotton, but they did grow flax to weave into linen. And where the land proved to be more suitable for grazing than tillage, flocks of small, hardy sheep had provided wool for home consumption since Colonial times. The first mills that turned out coarse woolen yarn by using the new water-driven textile machinery were built in 1794, in Newbury and Pittsfield, Massachusetts, centers of sheep raising. This "domestick industrie," as it was then commonly known, attracted the attention of a number of Boston businessmen. Benjamin Bussey, part of whose estate eventually became the setting for the Arnold Arboretum, was one such Boston businessman. He amassed a considerable fortune and numerous parcels of land in the woolen industry.

As was true of many of the new manufacturers, Benjamin Bussey's career in the textile industry came after earlier mercantile successes. His first trade was that of silversmith. According to a brief summary of his life that Bussey composed in his later years, he had been born in that part of Stoughton, Massachusetts, that is now known as Canton. He had soldiered in the Revolutionary War, and then he returned to Massachusetts and settled in Dedham. In the spring of 1778, he recorded how he set about learning to make "tankards . . . spurs and spoons" from his first partner, a skilled Prussian silversmith. His connection with the former Hessian soldier ended within three years, but Bussey continued to prosper. After ten years of trading in gold, silver, and furs (which he conducted "almost wholly [as] a cash bus. and seldom gave or took Cr."), Bussey bought a home in Boston, opened a store, and worked "as I'd in Dedham, day and night." Bussey "did a large bus: owned several ships,— engaged in many kinds of merc. adventures" and, within fifteen years, had accumulated a substantial fortune. In 1806, Benjamin Bussey acquired the first of a series of properties that would eventually result in holdings of almost three hundred acres of farmland in Roxbury and embarked upon two new careers: those of manufacturer and farmer. Bussey established the Dedham Woolen Mills and built a "mansion" at "Woodland Hill," his Roxbury farm, in 1815, where he devoted his

attenn to agricultural pursuits here & manufactg at Dedham. I bel. ye greatest impts in ye woolen manuufacs have been made in my facs. -vis in ye use of power looms, spring, &c. — I was among ye 1st to introduce merino sheep here: I've felt a great desire to promote ye cause of agriculture & manufacs & trust that I shall be considd hereafter to 've been useful frd as well as well wisher.

On 30 July 1835, Bussey affirmed his wish by willing "Woodland Hill" to the President and Fellows of Harvard College to be used as a "Seminary" for "instruction in practical agriculture, in useful and ornamental gardening, in botany, and in such other branches of natural science, as may tend to promote a knowledge of practical agriculture." His bequest came at a time when New England was experiencing an agricultural as well as an industrial revolution.

By the early 1800s, a number of organizations had been founded to promote the study of natural history, the arts, agriculture, and manufacturing. Agriculture was but one of many interests for most of the participants in these "learned societies"; few members actually tilled the soil at all, and few of these societies' publications or lectures reached the eyes or the ears of the average farmer. Farmers in the Northeast—many of whom still checked the phase of the moon before sowing seeds or harvesting crops—were more apt to be introduced to new methods, crops, and livestock through cattle shows and agricultural fairs. They could also glean advice, usually sound if sometimes impractical, from such publications as *The Ploughboy* and *The Cultivator* (both issued from Albany, New York), the *Genessee Farmer* (from Rochester), or *The New England Farmer* (a journal based in Boston that began publication in 1822). The opening of the Erie Canal in 1825 not only enabled farmers in the interior to move their products eastward more easily, it also established a route for the increasing numbers of New Englanders who were migrating westward. Although more than 70 percent of New England's forests had been cleared for farming by 1830, more flour and corn were being imported from other sections of the country than were being produced in New England. The small stony fields and sandy soils suited to hand labor could not keep pace with new farms on the rich, fertile soil of the Ohio River valley.

New England's industrialization created an expanding urban market. Many a farmer in Vermont or in the Berkshire Hills of Connecticut and Massachusetts gave up cultivating grain and turned to raising vegetables and other market crops, sheep, and cattle. In order to make their land more productive, "gentlemen farmers" such as Benjamin Bussey became the leading proponents of "scientific farming." A member of the Massachusetts Society for Promoting Agriculture, which had been founded in 1792, Bussey experimented with new varieties of fruits and vegetables suited for local conditions and imported European breeding stock, such as the fine-wooled Merino sheep from Spain, to better his herds. By endowing a school where agricultural investigations could be carried out and the results disseminated to farmers, Bussey anticipated, by more than a quarter of a century, the Land-Grant College Act (the Morrill Act) of 1862. Congress, through the Morrill Act, established 69 land-grant colleges designed to promote agricultural and technical education. In 1869, after the life estates of Bussey's heirs had expired and all the legacies and annuities had been paid and secured, Harvard began organizing the Bussey Institution, the school of agriculture and horticulture for which its benefactor had provided. Initial appointments to the staff of the Bussey Institution included instructors of farming and entomology and professors of agricultural chemistry, horticulture, and applied zoology. In 1872, an additional position was created: On 19 June, Charles Sprague Sargent joined the staff of the Bussey Institution as the first Director of the newly formed Arnold Arboretum.

Power Looms and Flowering Dogwoods

The spinning machine initiated the textile revolution; newly mechanized looms, such as those that Benjamin Bussey had installed in his Dedham mills, had propelled the industry into a factory system. Weaving became mechanized in America in 1814, when another Bostonian, Francis Cabot Lowell, built the nation's first truly successful water-powered loom along the Charles River in Waltham, Massachusetts. Basing his design on machines that he had surreptitiously studied during a two-year visit to England, Lowell constructed his "new and wonderful" machine almost entirely out of wood. Lowell's corporation, the Boston Manufacturing Company, was the first to use waterpower in all aspects of the making of cloth—from the raw material to the finished fabric—and was the first company in either England or America to accomplish this feat under one roof. When the Waltham plant exceeded the Charles River's power capacity, the company moved their operation twenty miles north. Described in 1868 (in the *Illustrated History*

of Lowell, by Charles Cowley) as being "a magnificent and truly National Establishment," the company's new mills were built of brick, not wood. The larger of Lowell's mills was six stories tall, 150 feet long, and 40 feet wide. This mill, with its power looms and economically superior integrated factory system, set standards for design, scale, and building materials for the textile mills that would be built during the next three decades. As power looms displaced those run by hand, and as the mill city superseded the sleepy mill village, bricks, mortar, and iron all but replaced wood in the textile industry. Between 1820 and 1831, cotton mills increased in value by $2.5 million; and the value of woolen products rose from less than $1 million to more than $11 million during the same period. However, in the complex process of weaving cloth, one simple wooden device remained unchanged: the fast-flying bullet-shaped shuttle. As a source of raw material for shuttles, one American tree became the industry's favorite. From the northern beginnings of the American Industrial Revolution until long after most textile manufacturers moved their operations south and left New England's mills standing silent, the wood of the flowering dogwood remained an essential part of the weaving industry.

Woven products combine two components: when the warp threads (those that lie lengthwise) cross the weft threads (those that lie widthwise), they form a weave. The terms "shedding," "picking," and "beating in" define the three basic motions that repeat as the the warp and weft threads are manipulated by the loom. Each time the heddles, which hold the warp, separate to open a "shed," the shuttle, its bobbin unwinding, passes through and lays down a "pick" or line of weft. The reed "beats" the pick snugly against the previously inserted one, and the sequence is repeated again. By the time that Francis Cabot Lowell had opened his "new and elegant establishment at Waltham," heddles, once made of cord or leather, and reeds, originally made of natural reeds, were both made of wire, but, for another 150 years, no better material than wood would be found for making shuttles.

The first shipment of logs of flowering dogwood (*Cornus florida*) and common persimmon (*Diospyros virginiana*) bound for England left Virginia in 1865. After their arrival, the logs were cut, seasoned, and turned into shuttles for England's textile mills. Up until midcentury, shuttles made of common boxwood (*Buxus sempervirens*) imported from India and eastern Asia had been the mainstay of the industry, but, as the amount of lumber needed for shuttles rose in proportion to the number of looms in operation in the northeastern United

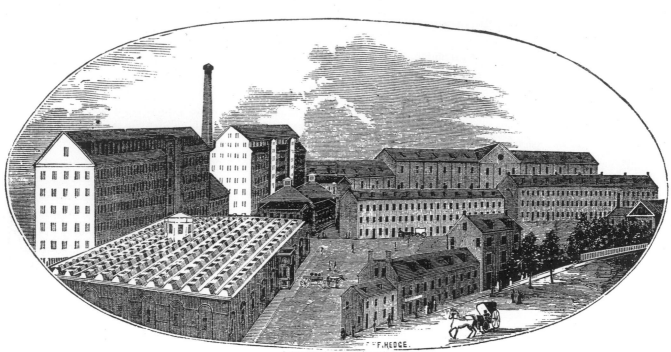

LOWELL CO. MILLS.

111. The Lowell Company Mills, as found in Charles Cowley's *The Illustrated History of Lowell*, revised edition, 1868. Kirk Boott, an English-trained Bostonian, was the manager of the Lowell Mills. The Boott Mills were built along the Merrimack River and Eastern Canal in 1836. Five years later, Lowell was home to ten major textile corporations weaving cloth in more than 40 mill buildings. By 1896, the 10,000 women and 7,000 men that worked the 877,000 spindles and 25,000 looms housed in these mills produced 6.5 million yards of cotton cloth per week. The Boott Mills, which were erected around an open courtyard designed for the pleasure and recreation of the mill workers, continued operating up until 1954 and are now part of the Lowell National Historical Park. In June 1992, the Boott Mills Building, the first major National Park Service Museum on industrial history, was opened to the public as the Boott Cotton Mills Museum.

States and in England, the two new American trees became popular substitutes for boxwood. By the third quarter of the nineteenth century, the use of dogwood and persimmon had increased markedly; during those years, a new use for the smooth, durable wood of the exotic boxwood had been found. A roller-skating craze swept thousands of people off their feet and onto wheels made of boxwood.

Legend credits a Dutchman, frustrated by not being able to skate year-round, with the invention of the roller skate in the early 1700s. For the next hundred years, skates on rollers remained a curiosity relegated to the company of other whimsical creations. After 1800, however, European ballet and opera directors found that the graceful moves of ice skaters could be mimicked, indoors on stage, by putting their troupes in shoes with wheels. How gracefully these dancers and singers performed on

skates is debatable. The earliest skates consisted of a single line of wheels that were all but impossible to steer left or right.

In 1863, James Leonard Plimpton, a machinist and inventor from Medfield, Massachusetts, perfected a skate that could move in a curved line, or "edge." Plimpton's skates had two parallel pairs of boxwood wheels, one pair under the ball of the foot and the other under the heel. His design incorporated a set of rubber springs that allowed the skater to change direction while keeping all four wheels in contact with the floor.

More than a hundred other inventors tried to duplicate Plimpton's innovative skate, creating a new market for boxwood and another for vulcanized rubber to be made into springs. Plimpton sued and eventually won (in 1876) a settlement on what he considered infringements on his patent, but by then the cost of boxwood had risen from

112. Shuttles, with their sharp, metal-tipped ends, flew back and forth carrying the weft across the warp. When the shuttle passed in one direction through the warp, all of the odd-numbered threads were lifted; as the shuttle returned, the even-numbered threads were raised.

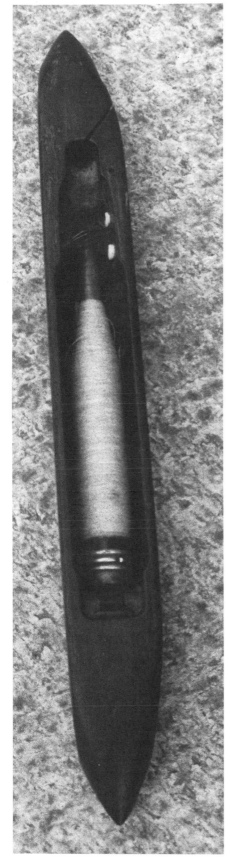

thirty dollars to one hundred dollars per ton. Even the extremely hard wood of boxwood eventually wore out, and skate manufacturers switched to using steel for roller skate wheels; but, by the time sufficient amounts of boxwood were again available for shuttles, textile mills had sucessfully switched to the wood of dogwood and persimmon.

The wood of flowering dogwood, *Cornus florida*, and common persimmon, *Diospyros virginiana*, are similar in texture, firmness, and weight; both are hard, heavy, tough, close-grained, and resistant to abrasion. But, when textile manufacturers realized that the longer a dogwood shuttle was in use the smoother its satiny wood became, dogwood became their first choice and persimmon fell into second place. Smoothness had topped the list of criteria used to determine a wood's acceptability for shuttles soon after John Kay, an English carpet weaver, invented a mechanized shuttle in 1733. Prior to Kay's invention, almost any hardwood made a satisfactory shuttle; handweavers simply passed the small, oblong piece of wood that held the bobbin from one hand to the other. Being a weaver of carpets, Kay had to station a worker on each side of his large, oversized looms; one worker would toss the shuttle across the loom to the other, who would catch it and toss it back. Apparently, clumsy workers were his inspiration. Besides having to employ two people to do the work of one, Kay was concerned that uncaught shuttles often dropped onto the warp threads, damaging the fabric and stopping the loom. Kay devised a driver attachment, controlled by a cord, that propelled the shuttle from one side to the other; but now, because the shuttle remained in contact with the warp threads as it shot back and forth, a shuttle made from a wood that checked, split, or had rough edges was worse than useless. Kay's invention, aptly called the flying shuttle, had been the first step in the automation of weaving.

The first American mill to produce flying shuttles began operating in Lowell, Massachusetts, in about 1875. Like its English counterparts, the Lowell mill acquired dogwood and persimmon logs from the forests of Vir-

113. James Leonard Plimpton, born in Medfield, Massachusetts in 1828, was a young man with a clear idea of what he wanted to do with his life. Plimpton left his family's farm at age sixteen to serve as an apprentice at a small, local machine shop. A year later, he was working at a larger shop in Claremont, New Hampshire, where he was promoted to foreman and had fifty men working under his direction before he turned eighteen. By the age of twenty-one, James, with his brother Henry, had established a machine-building business in Westfield, Massachusetts. Eventually, the Plimpton brothers began designing, decorating, and manufacturing fine furniture, and, in 1862, they opened a second office in New York City, which James oversaw. After enjoying a winter of ice skating in Central Park, James was determined to continue skating year-round. Not one to waste time, he managed to invent, patent, and promote his roller skate in one year. He also organized the New York Roller Skating Association in 1863, and began touting roller skating to the "educated and refined class." He later built, at a cost of more than one hundred thousand dollars, an indoor rink in New York City in a building aptly named the Plimpton Building.

THE PLYMPTON SKATE.

The Plympton Skate is too well known to need any extended description, having been used in rinks for nearly twenty years. We are now prepared to offer this skate to the trade and to rinks at a price corresponding with other skates on the market.

Sizes from 7 1-2 to 11 1-2.   **Price, per pair, $3.00.**

Price List of Parts.

Ebonized Foot Boards	per pair,	$0 40
Heel Straps	"	35
Toe "	"	25
Heel Bands	each	7
Trucks	"	20
Hangers	"	20
Steel Axles	"	10
Turkey Boxwood Wheels	"	5
Cotters	per 100,	35
Large Screws	each,	3
Rubbers	per doz.,	35
Double Rivet Buckles	per gross,	1 50

PLIMPTON'S ROLLER SKATE
As advertised in *Spalding's Manual of Roller Skating,*
1884

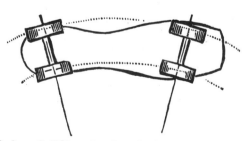

The principle of Plimpton's skate as illustrated in *The Champion Skate Book*, c. 1879

ginia. Flowering dogwood grows from extreme south-western Maine southward into northern Florida. Even in the center of its commercial range, which is in the southern Mississippi River valley and the southern Appalachian Mountain region, seldom is this tree found growing in pure stands. Often a woodcutter had to scour ten or fifteen acres of forest in order to find enough flowering dogwoods from which to harvest a cord of wood. Although not rare in eastern Massachusetts, this small understory tree appears with greater frequency in the Connecticut River valley and in Rhode Island and Connecticut. By comparison, the common persimmon is primarily a southern species that hardly makes its way farther north than Long Island, New York, whose climate is moderate for the latitude. It is one of a small group of trees, which includes the American holly (*Ilex opaca*), the sweetbay (*Magnolia virginia*), and the swamp cotton-wood (*Populus heterophylla*) that reach their northern limits along southern New England's coastline. Unlike the American holly, which is fairly common and seems to be slowly extending its range northward and farther in-

land, the sweetbay, the common persimmon, and the swamp cottonwood occur naturally in only one or two locations in New England. The cottonwood is found in Connecticut only in one coastal county in Connecticut. The persimmon has been reported growing along the Rhode Island coast, and, in 1846, a grove of about one hundred twenty-five small trees was identified growing within one hundred feet of the ocean at Lighthouse Point in New Haven. In the South, however, common persimmon (as its name suggests) is a common pioneer tree that invades old fields, roadsides, and fencerows. Common persimmon (*Diospyros virginiana*) is a member of the ebony family (Ebenaceae) whose close relatives include the true ebony, *D. ebenum*, from Sri Lanka. *D. texana*, the black persimmon, which occurs in Texas and Mexico, is the only other member of this family found in the United States.

By 1926, ninety percent of the harvest of flowering dogwood went into shuttles. Most were manufactured in Massachusetts and Rhode Island, and more than half were exported to Germany, France, and the United

114. A member of a genus that consists primarily of tropical trees, the common persimmon (*Diospyros virginiana*) is the only temperate American species that occurs naturally in New England or that can be cultivated there successfully. This specimen, which is located in the Arnold Arboretum near Rehder Pond, is an exceptionally striking tree. Typical of all mature persimmon trees, its bark is deeply furrowed, dark gray to nearly black, and broken into prominent, small, almost square plates. The texture of its corky bark is enhanced by the form and habit of the tree. With its short, angular branches and its fine, crooked twigs, it cannot quite be labeled a graceful tree, yet the manner in which it contorts itself suggests a wiry dancer performing in an avant-garde ballet. In summer, persimmons have large, four- to six-inch-long, oval, deep green leaves arranged alternately along their branches. Their white, bell-shaped flowers appear in June and are quite attractive, although small and easily overlooked.

Kingdom. In 1942, demand for military cloth and war-use textiles increased the need for shuttles to the point that the country no longer had adequate reserve supplies, and the U.S. Department of Agriculture issued a plea to farmers and woodlot owners to harvest their flowering dogwoods. The notice stated that, although many substitutes had been tried, no wood had been found that possessed the same qualities, and it urged them to contact block mills or buyers to arrange for the sale of trees of marketable size.

Three years later, a footnote to a U.S. Department of Agriculture publication stated that "shuttles are indispensable to the cotton, woolen and silk mills of the country," yet, except for artisans using hand looms and a few specialty weavers creating one-of-a-kind fabrics on older wooden power looms, only shuttleless looms produce woven fabrics today. Plastic shuttles finally replaced wooden ones after the close of World War II, but the use of plastic in this aspect of weaving did not last long. The new shuttleless looms were designed, and, within a generation, New England mills that continued to use the old machines were deemed antiquated and were soon surpassed by their southern competitors.

Connecticut Yankees' Clocks

An ingenious mechanic from Connecticut capitalized on the scientific and tehnological methods spawned by the industrial era to make a luxury item affordable. Few clocks and even fewer clockmakers had arrived in the Colonies before 1700. Clocks were prohibitively expensive: only the very wealthy could afford to import even the most simple, unsophisticated clock made in England or Europe. Until the number of clocks—and the number of potential customers—grew large enough to attract skilled clockmakers, those who could add this costly item to the household inventory relied on blacksmiths, silversmiths, or gunsmiths to keep their timepieces running. By the beginning of the eighteenth century, both Boston and Philadelphia—home to merchant princes and government officials—were populated by the type of clientele that could entice clockmakers finally to cross the Atlantic.

Traditionally, making and maintaining each of the three main parts of a clock—the metal movement, the wooden case, and the metal appurtenances—required separate sets of skills. A clockmaker (in the strict sense) dealt only with the time-keeping mechanism—forging, hammering, and casting brass and iron into arbors, pillars, plates, and wheels. The work of building the case, which held the movement, and the job of fabricating the appurtenances, such as the dial or clock face, the winding key, the weights, and the pendulum, fell to cabinet joiners, engravers, dial-painters, and other craftsmen. Trained in Europe, early New England clockmakers continued this practice by securing cases built by local cabinetmakers and obtaining rough-metal and finished appurtenances from Boston merchants who, in turn, imported both the rough-metal and the finished items from England.

The clock's internal movements may have been made out of metal parts imported from abroad, but, for the most part, New England's cabinetmakers fashioned the elegant cases that housed them from native woods. Often the wood from one tree furnished the material for an entire case. Plentiful and easily worked, white pine (*Pinus strobus*) was an early favorite. Its light brown, close-

115. One of the most famous of Connecticut clockmakers, Eli Terry (1772–1852) made this tall clock, which is now part of the Mabel Brady Garvan Collection at the Yale University Art Gallery. The plain cherry case is crowned with a pagoda-shaped pediment and pierced fretwork, a design that shows a Chinese influence. The simple but elegant case houses a twenty-four-hour movement made almost entirely of wood. The plates are oak, and the train wheels are cherry. It has maple pillars, a cherry centerpost, main arbors of hickory, and other arbors and pinions of birch. Only the bell, winding cords, escape wheel, and striker are made of metal. Although Eli Terry's clocks were inexpensive, they were destined for the home market only; they could not be exported because the wooden works warped at sea. By 1840, brass works could be factory-made, and the export market skyrocketed. In three years, one Connecticut manufacturer exported more than forty thousand clocks. The use of interchangeable parts, simpler manufacturing processes, and, eventually, metal-cutting machinery caused the price of clocks to drop dramatically. By 1855, mass-produced clocks with metal works were selling for seventy-five cents apiece.

grained wood accepted paint well, and paint was the least costly, most commonly available, and quickest finish to apply. In Connecticut, the light-colored sapwood of the tulip tree (*Liriodendron tulipifera*), which can be several inches thick, or a combination of the creamy white or pale brown sapwood and the yellowish-brown heartwood of basswood (*Tilia americana*) were made into cases that could be painted or varnished, or even left unfinished.

Many of the native-born clockmakers worked with conventional materials in fabricating the works of their clocks. Others, especially those who practiced their craft in rural areas, broke with tradition. Taught by Europeans, they learned the metalworking methods, then Americanized clockmaking by adapting techniques used by millwrights and wheelwrights to work in the medium they had most plentifully at hand and knew best how to work—wood. With hand saws and hand-cranked clockmakers' engines, they cut fragile, if sometimes irregular, gear teeth into disks of wood sawed from the trunks or branches of cherry and apple trees. The delicate arbors and pinions that drove the gears came from thin spindles of the hard-grained wood of mountain laurel (*Kalmia latifolia*) and hickory (*Carya* species). Oak plates—parallel pieces of wood separated by maple pillars—held clock movements. And, for clock faces, rather than engraving metal or white-enameled metal dials, they glued painted paper dials to dial plates made of wood, or they painted designs or numerals directly on the wooden dial plate itself.

In 1801, with his patent for a water-driven "engine" for cutting wooden cogwheels in hand and a plan for making standardized parts in mind, Eli Terry set about to transform a former gristmill, located on the Naugatuck River in northwestern Connecticut, into the nation's first clock factory. By substituting wood for expensive metal works and by mass-producing wooden movements, thus reducing the cost from approximately twenty-five dollars to four, Terry succeeded in putting the ownership of a clock within the reach of many Americans. Using the energy produced by a waterwheel to drive belts and pulleys connected to woodturning devices, saws, and drills at his "Ireland" factory, Terry successfully turned the slow, costly, handcrafted method of finishing one clock at a time into a mass-production system that would turn out more than four thousand wooden clock movements within three years.

. . . and Connecticut Yankees' Chairs

Considering the rapidity with which machine-made articles began to overtake those made in shops or by hand, it would seem that there was hardly a craftsman in New England who did not dream of inventing a better tool or a more efficient machine. Prior to 1825, furniture joiners who made plain, simple chairs often sold their products in pieces. Yankee peddlers took wagons filled with bundles of chair parts through the countryside, or customers needing to replace a piece, or to construct a brand-new chair, could buy chair parts from their local general store.

Most villages had one or more stores where "European goods" (such as glassware, crockery, powder, and shot) and "India goods" (salt, rum, molasses, spices, and sugar) could be bartered for or purchased. These stores carried few ready-made chairs but instead stocked a much larger assortment of ready-to-assemble components: rungs, slats, seats, and legs. Lambert Hitchcock, a journeyman woodworker at the shop of cabinetmaker Silas Cheney of Litchfield, Connecticut, decided that machines shafted and belted to waterpower had unlimited applications in

116. After Lambert Hitchcock died in 1852, the factory in Hitchcocksville changed hands, eventually becoming known as the Phoenix Company, formed for "the purpose of carrying on the manufacture of chairs and other furniture of which wood is a component part. Also for manufacturing of planes, rules and other joiner's tools." The next manufacturer to occupy the building was a maker of ivory-tipped wood pocket rulers. After 1901, when the ruler-maker closed his shop, various small businesses engaged in woodturning and ladder-making remained as tenants until the building was closed and boarded up during the depression. In 1946, John T. Kenney and Richard E. Coombs formed the Hitchcock Chair Company, restored the factory, and began reproducing the chairs and furniture that had once made "Hitchcocksville" famous. Today, every piece of furniture produced in the Hitchcock Collection is marked with the same stenciled signature trademark (including the curious reversed Ns that appear on many early pieces) that Lambert Hitchcock had used to identify his famous chairs and cabinets.

The following is a representation of the principal part of the village of Hitchcocksville, in Barkhamsted; it is situated on the west branch of the Farmington river, near the corner of four towns, Hartland, Colebrook, Winchester and Barkhamsted. The village contains upwards of 20 dwelling houses, 1 chair factory, 2 mercantile stores and an Episcopal church, which was founded July 4th, 1829, and called the Union church. Part of the chair factory is seen on the left, and the church

West view of Hitchcocksville, Barkhamsted.

on the right of the engraving. The village was commenced about fifteen years since: it is 20 miles from Litchfield, and 26 from Hartford. There are superior water privileges for extensive manufactories in the immediate vicinity. A little more than a mile south of this place, a few of the last remnants of the Narragansett Indians have a location; they came here about the year 1779, and purchased about 200 or more acres of land. Their houses, or rather cabins, are along side of the road: there are about 20 souls that make their constant residence here, though at times they number as many as 30 persons.

117. This early combination wood treadle lathe and saw table, which is now part of the Hitchcock Chair Company Collection, was found in a barn near Riverton, Connecticut, and is believed to have produced some of the first chair parts made by Lambert Hitchcock. An inventory of the Hitchcock estate, which included the tools and machinery at his factory, listed (in addition to a variety of saws, hand tools, and lathes) "1 double tenanting machine, 1 dove tailing machine, 1 squaring up mortising machine, and 1 cramping machine."

chairmaking. He put the skills he had learned creating fine furniture in the Sheraton and Hepplewhite styles, using hand- and foot-powered saws and other common carpenter's tools, into making chair parts with the new woodturning, boring, and planing machines.

When Hitchcock sited his woodturning "works" in a shed attached to a lumber mill on the Farmington River at "the forks-of-the-river," he secured the necessary materials for his "manufactorie"—pine and hardwood lumber (especially the wood of maples, birches, and tulip treess, the right species for making inexpensive, durable chairs)—and, for his production machinery, the necessary power from the mill's waterwheel. In the same manner in which the success of Eli Terry's "Ireland" clock factory converted, for a time, the hamlet of Plymouth, Connecticut, into the bustling town of Terryville, the village of Barkhamsted, Connecticut (where Hitchcock had set up shop), became known as Hitchcocksville, as the chair manufacturer parlayed a small shop for making chair parts into a venture that, in its heyday, employed more than one hundred workers.

During the thirty-eight consecutive years that the factory in Hitchcocksville operated, its inventory of woodworking devices expanded to include a wide array of newly specialized machinery for making wooden furni-

ture. Added to the hum and slap of leather drive belts and the screech and whine of whipsaws and circular saws came the whir of machines boring holes for dowels and the clatter of mechanized cutting and milling machines. "Mortisers," which cut the square openings for mortise-and-tenon joints, and "double tenanting machines," which were capable of forming tenons at both ends of a board simultaneously, contributed their own unique sounds to the din that emanated from the factory.

Hitchcock's shop turned out 15,000 "fancy" chairs per year, and, eventually, his line of furniture expanded to include fashionable bureaus, bedsteads, and tables. Men sawed, turned, sanded, and assembled the parts while women and children stenciled and painted decorative patterns on finished pieces in a room isolated from the sawdust-filled air of the main shop. By daubing fine-grained, multicolored bronze powders onto a foundation coat of paint that was not quite dry, the women created the baskets of flowers and the bowls of apples, peaches, and plums, as well as the bunches of grapes and the golden pineapple fruits, that graced the faces of bureau drawers and the backs of chairs. Their skill was not limited simply to producing a cornucopia of fruit or a florist's display. Through a process called "graining," Hitchcock tables and bureaus made of pine or tulip tree became what would someday be cherished family heirlooms and coveted museum pieces. Graining consists of painting the wood with a base color—Hitchcock's artists used red or black—then overlaying another coat of paint that is removed, in part, with a comb, a sponge, or a lump of soft putty before it dries. In this manner, Hitchcock workers produced wood-grain patterns that imitated the handsome configurations of the high-priced native walnut, maple, and cherry, the rare and even more costly imported mahogany and rosewood, and even some species that existed solely in the artist's imagination.

The wood of the tulip tree takes paint well. In fact, because it is fine-grained and contains no resin, it accepts paint even better than its coniferous counterpart, white pine. Attractive too was the price that furniture manufacturers and cabinetmakers paid for tulip tree stock. It was, in André Michaux's words, "very cheap, being sold at half the price of the Black Walnut, Wild Cherry and Curled Maple."

The genus *Liriodendron* (in which there are only two species, *L. tulipifera*, of North America and *L. chinensis*, which was discovered in China in 1875) is in the family Magnoliaceae. Eastern Massachusetts lies outside of the native range of the tulip tree, and, although the Arnold Arboretum's century-old trees have grown tall and have gained an impressive size, they can convey only a mere hint of the stature that tulip trees can attain at the heart of their native range. The finest stands of tulip trees occur in the fertile soils of the Ohio River valley, where massive trees often reach heights close to two hundred feet and have trunks with a girth of twelve feet, and cathedral-like forests of huge tulip trees are found on the slopes of the Appalachian Mountains in Tennessee and North Carolina. In New England, tulip trees occur in southwestern Vermont, western Massachusetts, and in Connecticut and parts of Rhode Island. Their range extends westward beyond the Mississippi River into Illinois and southward into the northern part of Florida.

In 1754, Linnaeus combined the Greek words *leiron*, "lily," and *dendron*, "tree," for the generic name and used *tulipifera*, "tulip bearing"—the earliest generic name ever applied to this species—as the specific epithet for the North American tree. *Liriodendron tulipifera*, like many trees that have a large range and are widely used commercially, has had a host of common names. Tulip tree, a shortened, English version of Linnaeus' binomial, celebrates the fact that these trees, with their greenish-yellow flowers, which have a crescent-shaped blotch of bright orange at the base of each of their petals, look indeed as if tulips had forsaken their earthly confines and

118. A mortising machine of this design was patented on 8 June 1807. The simplicity of its design, coupled with its functionality, made it a classic example of American machine ingenuity. This particular machine, a copy of the patent model, was made for display at the World Columbian Exposition of 1893.

119. This group of tulip trees, photographed at the Arnold Arboretum during a January snowstorm, displays many of the characteristics that make this species easy to identify, even in winter. The snow accentuates the deeply furrowed bark, straight trunks, and large primary branches that, at the lower part of the tree, are often horizontal or pendulous. The branches that are closer to the top of the crown grow upright. Young trees grow rapidly; under optimum conditions (deep, rich, moist, well-drained soil), a tulip tree can reach a height of one hundred feet and have a trunk five feet in diameter. Because of their majestic appearance and quick growth, tulip trees, along with American elms, were planted throughout the colonies as "trees of liberty." In 1976, in celebration of the nation's bicentennial, the Arnold Arboretum distributed tulip trees to cities and towns throughout Massachusetts.

120. Tulip tree flowers are usually borne high on the tree, partly hidden by foliage, and so are often overlooked. If seen from below, which is most often the case, tulip tree flowers do resemble tulips. However, this impression lasts only until one has the opportunity to look inside the flower. The flowers open in June to reveal a large pointed pistil surrounded by as many as thirty-six stamens. These central flower parts are characteristic of the magnolia family, and, although the proportions between the sepals and the petals are different, tulip tree flowers look very much like those of the large, native *Magnolia acuminata,* commonly known as the cucumber tree. The conelike fruits ripen in September or October after developing from the fertilized pistils. The fruit spreads open as it dries, allowing the winged seeds to fall, leaving a starlike outer ring and a slim, candlelike stalk to decorate the tree throughout the winter.

121. The pit saw, a two-man hand-operated saw, and the mill saw, a single-bladed saw that slid up and down in a groved frame, powered by a waterwheel, were the forerunners of the many-bladed gang saw. Gang saws, such as this one, produce plain-sawn or slash-grained lumber and are capable of sawing a whole tree into planks in a single pass.

had reappeared on the limbs of a tree. Early settlers of the southeastern United States dubbed the trees canoe-wood, because there the Native Americans felled and hollowed out their huge trunks to make dugout canoes. Because of the shape of their many-seeded and cucumberlike fruit, the name cucumber tree (a name shared with the largest and hardiest of the native magnolias, *Magnolia acuminata,* for exactly the same reasons) was equally appropriate. People in New England and New York appreciated the light color of the long, smooth planks they could rive from these trees, and they called them white wood. Old wife's shirt tree and saddle-wood, two of the more obscure common names, apparently referred to the rather unique shape of the tree's four-lobed leaves,

while the names popple, yellow poplar, white poplar, blue poplar, tulip poplar, and hickory poplar suggest that, like the true poplars, their large three- to eight-inch-long leaves can be set in motion by the slightest breeze. This detail presumably had caught the attention of John Tradescant, who, during the middle of the seventeenth century, had journeyed to America to acquire plants for the museum of natural objects—a cabinet of curiosities open to the public, the first of its kind—that his father, John Tradescant the Elder, was assembling in England. In 1656, after the death of his father, the son named this tree *Populus alba Virginiana Tradescanti*—Tradescant's white Virginia poplar—in a catalogue of the trees that he had collected.

Unfortunately, although *Liriodendron tulipifera* is not at all related to the poplars, the name poplar—specifically yellow poplar, which refers to the color of its heartwood—is the common name that many people, and virtually all lumbermen, use today to identify this tree.

When painted, the wood of the tulip tree acquired a smooth, satiny finish, and, when decorative carving was called for, the wood could be cut "like cheese." When boxes and chests of all sizes and shapes held the family's possessions, a decorated piece usually held the items that the family most treasured. Geometric designs laid out with a compass and then chipped out with a chisel adorned many such household repositories. Whether it was only one part or panel or the whole piece that was carved, chipped out, or painted, craftsmen fashioned tiny boxes that held pills, ornate boxes that protected Bibles, and large, legless chests that stored bedding and clothes from the workable wood of the tulip tree. In Connecticut, cabinetmakers often made chests of a combination of pine or oak and tulip tree. They built the frame and the side and back panels with the other woods, reserving the front panel, which they then would embellish with a design, for the easily worked tulip tree wood. Floral designs that incorporated leaf-laden vines sporting a miscellany of flowers were popular decorations for chests and wardrobes, but a simple carved or painted tulip blossom was also a common motif.

Once machines that were capable of producing lathe-turned woodenware were invented, bowls, scoops, spoons, and other small round utensils could be produced for the mass market. Maple, boxwood, and lignum vitae, all hard and close-grained, were the primary woods used for machine-made woodenware, but tulip trees provided an inexpensive, light-colored, clear, odorless, and tasteless wood for the production of an assortment of common articles.

Cabinetmakers and manufacturers of fine furniture often chose to play the color, figure, and grain of different woods against one another. The true mark of a master joiner lay not only in the precision with which he cut or drilled dovetail or mortise-and-tenon joints—a finished piece often concealed these skills—but in his ability to expose the hidden beauty in the structure of the wood. Depending on the species, lumber cut from logs by one of two different methods either enhanced the qualities of the grain—the direction, size, and arrangement of the wood's fiber—or intensified the appearance of the figure—the patterns displayed by annual growth rings, rays, knots, and deviations from common grains. Were it not for the craftsman's knowledge of these internal patterns, the wood's most attractive elements might remain undiscovered.

When planks are cut by running a saw the length of a log without changing the log's orientation, the saw cuts tangentially through the annual growth rings, producing what is called plain-sawn lumber in hardwoods and flat-grained or slash-grained lumber in softwoods. Only on the center plank, which is aligned directly across the pith—the small, soft core at the center of the trunk—will the growth rings appear as straight lines. On the rest of the planks, as the saw moves away from the center to the outer edge with each cut, the growth rings form ellipses and parabolas on the cut surface, which make striking designs, especially when the rings are irregular in width and outline. Trees with large pores and distinct annual rings, such as oak, ash, hickory, and chestnut, are described as having open-grained wood. Conversely, close-grained wood contains small, closely spaced pores and inconspicuous rings.

Quartersawing of hardwood, or edge-grain or vertical-grain sawing of softwood, unmasks the wood's rays, the ribbonlike strips of cells that radiate out from the center of the tree. Quartersawing takes longer, produces more waste, and requires that the log be turned as each quarter section is cut so that the saw is oblique to the rays and passes radially through the growth rings. When species such as butternut (*Juglans cinera*) are quartersawn, the rays form a three-dimensional figure that looks like bands or waves of flecks crossing, on a different plane, the stripes made by the annual rings. Combining both

122. An early quartersawing machine. Either plain-sawn or quartersawn lumber works well for many purposes, and there are advantages and disadvantages to each method. Because logs that are quartersawn are not cut tangentially through the growth rings, the planks cut in this way are less apt to twist and cup, to shrink and swell in width, even if they are not seasoned correctly. Quartersawn lumber wears more evenly and, for the wood of many species, holds paint better. Plain-sawn lumber shrinks and swells less in thickness, and if shakes and pitch pockets are present in the tree, these imperfections will extend through fewer boards. Plain-sawn lumber may cost less because it is easier to obtain; but, today, a computer-run sawing machine is capable of obtaining the greatest amount of marketable lumber from each trunk by combining and adjusting the various ways in which it is able to cut it.

123. This black walnut was photo-graphed early in this century in Ulster County, New York. Most of the black walnuts that remain today are trees isolated in a forest of other species. In New England, most black walnuts that survive are those that have been planted or preserved. Many of these trees, being open-grown, like this one, have short trunks and large alternate and spreading branches. Walnut wood, routinely used in construction up until World War I, is so valuable today that it is used mainly for face veneers; almost any piece of furniture found to be made of solid walnut is considered to be an expensive antique. Typically, black walnut logs are purchased by American or foreign veneer manufacturers and cut into the thinnest veneers possible. Tall, straight trees that are in good condition and have little or no decay have become so scarce—black walnut trees have actually been cut down and stolen from private property—that they command exorbitant prices. In 1977, the Veneer Corporation of North Carolina bid on the purchase of eighteen walnut trees; for eighty thousand dollars, they acquired five veneer logs, each about sixty feet long, with diameters ranging from twenty-seven to thirty-eight inches, which were thinly sliced and shipped to Germany to be made into fine veneered furniture. The smaller logs were sold to gunstock manufacturers.

plane-sawn and quartersawn lumber from the same species can achieve the effect of having used different kinds of wood.

   With the rich variety of species that make up the east-ern forest to choose from, seldom did carpenters use the most expensive woods for the parts of furniture that did not show. The wood of pines and of deciduous trees con-sidered to be of lesser quality, such as chestnut, elm, tulip tree, and basswood, were relegated to the interior of the piece—to drawer interiors and other hidden structural elements. However, when a master craftsman wanted to make the surface of a piece of furniture seem to shimmer,

he often turned to the hard and heavy wood of the sugar maple (*Acer saccharum*). With luck, he would select a tree whose wood contained the distinct grain and unusual figure called "birds-eye" or the fine "fiddleback" waves that sometime appear in the grain when maple is quarter-sawn. *Prunus serotina,* the black cherry, was another favorite, and furniture joiners built clock cases, tables, headboards, and chests that glowed with the luster of this tree's dark reddish-brown heartwood. For their finest pieces, furniture joiners sought the beautiful and rich, deep chocolate-brown heartwood of black walnut (*Juglans nigra*). In plain-sawn pieces of walnut, they often uncovered a mottled pattern that was especially prized.

The first settlers told of black walnuts that stood more than one hundred fifty feet tall. Some had straight trunks whose diameters exceeded six feet, and some of these impressive boles remained clear of branches for fully half their length. Black walnuts are sensitive to soil conditions and intolerant of shade and root competition, and the tallest of these majestic trees were discovered growing in clearings, rooted in the deep, loose, well-drained alluvial soils that are found on lower north- and east-facing slopes, stream terraces, and flood plains. The center of the range of the black walnut falls west of the Allegheny Mountains. This tree is seldom found in pure stands, more commonly being mixed with other hardwoods, such as ash, cherry, basswood, and tulip tree.

The Virginia colony shipped walnut wood to England beginning in 1610, and, by the middle of the eighteenth century, Peter Kalm reported that "the joiners say that among the trees of this country they use chiefly the black walnut, the wild cherry and the curled maple. Of the black walnut (*Juglans nigra*) there is yet sufficient quan-

124. A serpentine split-rail fence borders a farm in the Adirondack Mountains of northern New York. Covering more than 3.2 million acres, the Adirondack State Park is the largest land preserve in America. However, in 1884, when this photograph was taken for the Forest Commission of New York, battle lines were being drawn between those wishing to exploit the natural resources of the area and those wishing to conserve the wilderness. Charles Sprague Sargent, a proponent of "scientific forestry," headed the commission, which was charged with recommending a system of preservation for the region. In the process of documenting the condition of the nation's forests for the Tenth Census Report, Sargent had witnessed the devastation that unscrupulous lumbering practices could cause, and he believed that lumber men had already logged the Adirondacks too extensively, leaving preservation as the only option. A bill that incorporated some of the commission's findings was eventually passed by the state legislature, and a unique land preserve, in which more than 60 percent of the land is owned by private citizens, was created.

tity, but careless people are trying to destroy it, and some peasants even use it for fuel." Although black walnuts were highly regarded for their nutritious and delicious nuts—farmers commonly planted rows of them to complement their orchards of fruit trees—and as attractive as the tree was to the furniture maker, the wood's hardness made difficult work for the inexperienced carpenter. Because black walnut proved to be very durable when in contact with the soil—posts made of walnut reputedly lasted more than a quarter of a century—and the wood split easily and burned with a hot flame, *Juglans nigra* became a prime source of wood for split-rail fences and for woodpiles.

Walnuts and Gunstocks

Black walnut was never an abundant tree in the New England woods, and its natural distribution in the region was severly reduced by the small-arms industry, whose growth intensified the demand for the wood, which was already prized for making fires, furniture, and fences.

The handicraft of gunsmithing, often a sideline of blacksmiths who forged agricultural implements, predated and coexisted with the small-arms industry—the factory production of muskets, rifles, and revolvers. In gunsmithing, unlike many other trades, the evolution from handicraft to industry depended on the availability of a high concentration of skilled workers and a source of high-grade iron. By the middle of the eighteenth century, the majority of New England's gunmakers worked in the vicinity of the Connecticut River, where iron could be obtained from western Massachusetts and Connecticut and from eastern New York. The industry took hold in Worcester, Massachusetts, and in Middleton, Hartford, and Springfield, the latter three being towns in the Connecticut River valley where independent gunsmiths prospered.

In 1795, the fledgling government of the United States commissioned its second national armory. Sited on the Connecticut River at Springfield, Massachusetts, a mecca for skilled gunmakers, the armory's location made it accessible to barges, yet far enough upriver to be safe from enemy attack. The local gunsmiths and arms makers used black cherry, red maple, curly sugar maple, dogwood, and lesser quantities of birch for gunstocks, but government agents of the armory refused to use any wood other than black walnut for the stocks of military weapons.

In order to meet the Springfield Armory's rigorous standards (according to a pamphlet on the subject issued by the federal government), black walnut timber had to be seasoned for a minimum of three years and to be "of a firm, tough kind free of sap and knots," harvested from "open grown trees . . . in winter when the sap was down and the damage from worms less." Because lucrative contracts were let on a three-year cycle, and because government inspectors constantly checked the condition of the wood, lumber dealers acquiesced to the government's wishes. High-quality walnut reached Springfield well seasoned, rough-sawn, and ready for finishing. However, within five years of the armory's establishment, lumber for gunstocks began arriving from the forests of Pennsylvania and Maryland, because suitable walnut trees no longer existed within easy reach of the Connecticut River. In twenty years, the quest for raw material forced dealers to look westward, and, subsequently, contractors from as far away as Marietta and Huron, Ohio, became the most dependable sources for lumber for the Springfield Armory.

After water-driven machines capable of rolling, forging, grinding, boring, turning, and polishing metal parts became common in the arms industry, inventing a machine capable of turning the irregular shape of the wooden stock proved to be the last obstacle in the standardization of parts. Inadvertently, while attempting to design a machine capable of turning both the cylindrical and octagonal shapes needed to make rifle barrels, Thomas Blanchard of Millbury, Massachusetts, solved the problem. He invented a woodturning machine, which he successfully patented in 1820, that automated the stockmaking operations that had formerly been done by hand. His invention not only enabled the industry to standardize gunstocks, which ensured the interchangeability of parts in the manufacture of arms, but became the forerunner of woodturning machines that made shoe lasts, wheel spokes, tackle blocks, and other irregularly shaped wooden items.

The black walnuts that grow beside the Arnold Arboretum's Valley Road constitute one of the first of the major tree groups to be planted. This road was the first in the Arboretum constructed by the city of Boston, and its completion in 1884 enabled Charles Sprague Sargent to begin the realization of his plans for planting the Arboretum. On Valley Road, the single black walnut set slightly apart from a group of five others of its kind is one of Sargent's original plantings. This group of black walnut trees displays the typical small, open, rounded crowns and the straight, branchless trunks that forest-

125. This Blanchard lathe, complete with a walnut gunstock, is part of the Smithsonian Institution's collections in Washington, D.C. An equally impressive collection of hand and machine tools designed and manufactured in New England can be seen in Windsor, Vermont. In 1964, when the curator of mechanical engineering at the Smithsonian Institution, Edwin Battison, realized that the historic Robbins & Lawrence Armory, located in his boyhood home of Windsor, was about to be torn down, he moved to have the building listed on the National Register of Historic Places and to establish a nonprofit corporation to oversee the development of a national museum of tools. Today, the armory is listed as a National Historic Landmark Building, and exhibits of the American Precision Museum feature "Yankee Ingenuity," the "American System" of manufacturing, and energy development. Edwin Battison, now the director of the museum, oversees a unique collection of machines that have been selected to demonstrate the evolution of industrial America. Among the many items on display is a Blanchard grinder, a twentieth-century adaptation of Blanchard's original lathe, an early woodturning lathe that was used in the manufacture of spinning wheels, yarn reels, and Windsor chairs, and an engine lathe made in 1825 for the Crown & Eagle textile mills in North Uxbridge, Massachusetts, that includes features covered by the 1798 Wilkinson patent.

126. During the summer, the pinnately compound leaves of these large walnut trees, which are one to two feet long, cast a dappled shade on the grass pathway that leads to the Arboretum's oak collection. In 1884, Jackson Thornton Dawson, the Arnold Arboretum's first plant propagator, collected the seeds from a tree at Harvard's Botanic Garden in Cambridge, from which the Arboretum's grove of walnuts grew. Now, just a few years into their second century, these three black walnuts, which constitute half of the Arboretum's walnut grove, are just beginning to mature. The lifetime of a black walnut tree can exceed two and a half centuries. According to the National Register of Big Trees, the largest black walnut in the country, which has a height of 132 feet and a circumference of 22 feet, grows in Humboldt County, California, which is roughly 1500 miles beyond its natural range. In New England, the largest black walnuts range in height from 65 feet, with a circumference of 9 feet (Plympton, Massachusetts), to 100 feet, with a circumference of 10 feet (in Lincoln Woods, Rhode Island). With the average height of the Arboretum's trees being 65 feet, and the tallest being closer to 75 feet, these black walnuts are certainly in contention for the distinction of being some of the largest in the state and the region.

127. The staminate (or pollen-bearing) flowers of the black walnut, *Juglans nigra*, appear in May in two- to four-inch-long tassels on the previous year's growth. The inconspicuous carpellate (or female) flowers appear in groups of two to five at the ends of new-growth twigs.

grown trees develop. The grove, with its accompanying specimen tree, is one of the Arboretum's best remaining examples of Sargent's early scheme to exhibit trees growing in a forestlike environment.

Plant Hunting in the New England Woods

By the middle of the nineteenth century, many European trees and shrubs—to say nothing of European weeds—had become familiar components of the New England landscape. In *New England's Rarities Discovered*, published less than fifty years after the colonists took hoe and ax to the native flora, John Josselyn listed twenty-one "naturalized weeds, the plants as have sprung up since the English planted and kept cattle." The common lilac (*Syringa vulgaris*) and the snowball (*Virburnum opulus*) guarded the dooryards of New England, and, by 1784 or thereabout, European lindens (*Tilia* spp.) and horsechestnuts (*Aesculus hippocastanum*) shaded the lanes and commons. The China trade had provided evidence of a rich new source of horticultural treasures in the Orient. By the first quarter of the nineteenth century, many Asian species had found their way into American gardens through the agency of British and European nurserymen. In addition to the economic value of native trees, New Englanders were by now also discovering the ornamental resources of their native flora. Josselyn had been the first to enumerate the plants of this vicinity. Manasseh Cutler, of Ipswich, Massachusetts, gave an "account of some of the vegetable Productions naturally growing in this part of America, botanically arranged," in the first volume of the *Memoirs of the American Academy of Arts and Sciences* in 1785, and, in 1814, Dr. Jacob Bigelow's *Florula*

Bostoniensis ("little flora of Boston") brought the record up to date. Identifying and collecting plants, as well as other natural curiosities, became the rage. Hunting for plants promoted healthful exercise and enticed ladies, as well as gentlemen, to make their way through mountain meadows, overgrown thickets, and quaking bogs. An activity formerly undertaken only by stalwart naturalists, botanizing became a fashionable pastime.

Native trees and shrubs, initially sought for the qualities of their wood or for their value as medicine, began to be planted as specimen plants on large estates and in small gardens. Many aspiring horticulturists and plant collectors became familiar with the riches of the native flora through Dr. Bigelow's book. Beginning in 1812, Bigelow offered a course of popular lectures on botany at Harvard's Botanic Garden, and, "finding that a considerable taste had sprung up among my pupils for the study of plants, I began to collect materials for a description of the native plants of Boston and its vicinity." Dedicated to the Massachusetts Society for Promoting Agriculture, *Florula Bostoniensis* went through three editions. The last edition, published in 1824, was expanded in scope and almost doubled in size; for more than a quarter century, it was, for professional and amateur alike, a treasured guide to the flora of New England.

It was through Bigelow's flora that the public was first alerted to the presence of a stand of *Magnolia virginiana*, the sweetbay magnolia, situated far beyond its normal range. "The only species of this superb genus, that has been found native in our climate. . . . It grows plentifully in a sheltered swamp at Gloucester, twenty-five miles from Boston, which is perhaps its northern boundary." A Boston judge, the Honorable Theophilus Parsons, making his way from Manchester to Gloucester on the "old Salem Road," is credited with first sighting the trees in 1806. Unsure of their identity, Parson dashed off a note containing a description of the trees and their location to the Reverend Manasseh Cutler, and he showed the flowers he had collected to his colleague Judge John Davis of Boston. Cutler and Davis both recognized the plant as being the sweetbay magnolia, and word quickly spread through their circle of friends. Over the next eighty years, virtually every amateur naturalist in the area and scores of professional botanists made pilgrimages to the site. By the middle of the 1800s, the residents of this area of Gloucester, Massachusetts, were so taken by the distinction of having a highly prized southern tree discovered in their midst that they changed the name of their section of the Cape Ann peninsula, Kettle Cove, to Magnolia. Once the ornamental attributes of *Magnolia virginiana* had become well known, no serious gardener in the region could do without it. However, so many unscrupulous collectors dug up plants and sold them that botanists feared that this most northern outpost of the species would be wiped out. Not only were the plants themselves being uprooted, but boys, and even some thoughtless adults, carelessly stripped whole branches from the trees and carried off the sweet smelling flowers to hawk in the markets of nearby Salem and even as far away as Boston. In 1889, John George Jack, the dendrologist at the Arnold Arboretum, wrote a piece for the horticultural journal *Garden and Forest* on the status of the plants. He advised fellow botanists and naturalists that, if they wished to observe the magnolias in their natural habitat, they should act with some haste, and, if the "explorer would find the swamp magnolia in its best condition, he must make his excursion about the first week in July, and be prepared for a rough tramp. Bogs, springs, rocks, thickets and fallen branches and trees may beset the way." Jack feared that this disjunct population had been so decimated that "the day would soon come when the *Magnolia* could only be classed in the New England flora as one of the indigenous plants of the past." That same year, the owner of the swamp estab-

128. Published in 1860, the *History of the Town of Gloucester, Cape Ann, Including the Town of Rockport,* by John H. Babson, notes the presences of a botanical rarity: "The botany of Cape Ann is rich in the possession of a rare plant called the *Magnolia glauca,* whose only native place in Massachusetts is a swamp in the westerly part of town." The *Map of Gloucester, Cape Ann, Showing the Roads, Harbors, Rivers, Coves, Islands and Ledges from an Actual Survey and Observations by John Mason, 1831,* shows "The Old Path to Salem" that passes between "The Highlands & Pitch Pine Shrubs" and "Norman's Woe" along the coast and the area of "Woodland & Swamps" on the inland side. The 1886 U.S. Geological Survey map, "Gloucester Sheet," shows that this area had since been named Magnolia and that its site had since been named Magnolia Point. Following suit, the Gloucester Branch of the Boston and Maine Railroad named the local stop Magnolia Station.

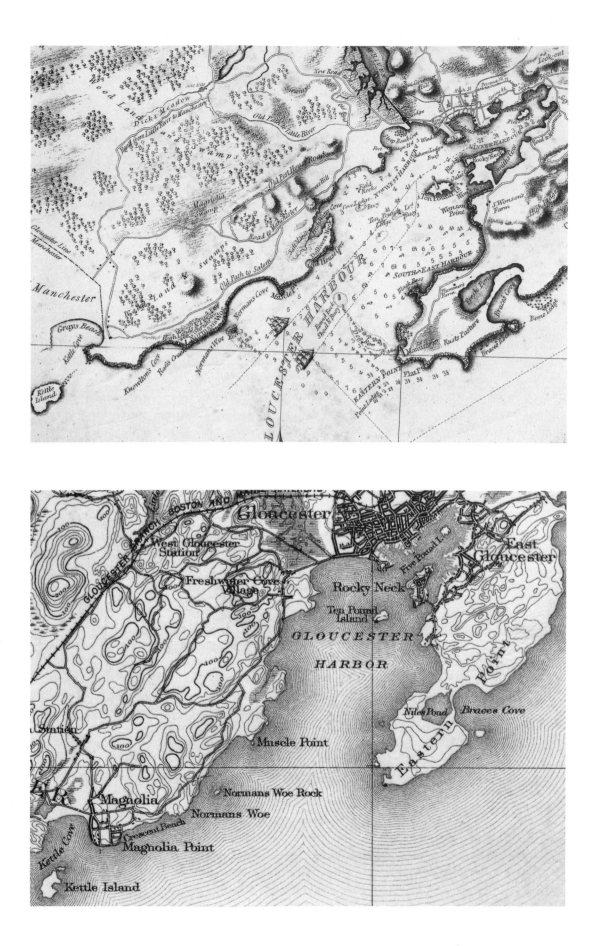

lished a trust fund to manage the land, which he had named Ravenswood Park. Unfortunately, this did nothing to deter vandalism, and, by 1916, another Arboretum staff member, C. E. Faxon, would report that "only two little plants a few feet high had escaped the Magnolia hunters."

Dr. Bigelow also referenced a second relatively rare plant of New England's wetlands. He first found the rosebay rhododendron (*Rhododendron maximum*) in a swamp in Medfield, Massachusetts, and later discovered a red-flowered variety of that species growing "abundantly on the banks of the Charles River, a dozen or fifteen miles from Boston." He reported his find in 1820 in the third volume of his *American Medical Botany, Being a Collection of the Native Medicinal Plants of the United States*. Like *Magnolia virginiana*, the rosebay rhododendron inhabits cool, shady woods. Appearing in New England only in scattered locations, this shrub's most northerly station is believed to be a swampy area near Safford Pond, in Somerset County, Maine.

Dr. Bigelow found the rosebay rhododendron much more appealing as a horticultural subject than as a medicinal one. He wrote in his *Florula Bostoniensis* that "we have no shrub that surpasses the Rhododendron in elegance," while admitting in his later work that he was "induced to examine the Rhododendron . . . on account of [its] reputation . . . of being poisonous." He dutifully ate a leaf—a fairly large one. He found it unpalatable, but he suffered no ill effects. Species of *Rhododendron*, along with other members of the the heath family (Ericaceae), are today known to contain andromedotoxin, a potentially dangerous poison. However, Bigelow's conclusion that,

"if it have any narcotic powers, they will probably be developed only by an extraordinary dose, which few persons will likely put to the test," appears to be true, for there are no substantiated human poisonings attributed to the rosebay rhododendron.

Rhododendron maximum becomes abundant in the hills of Pennsylvania, and it grows in profusion in the mountains of the Carolinas and Tennessee. It is likely that Bigelow first became aquainted with the rosebay rhododendron while studying botany under the noted surgeon Benjamin Smith Barton at the University of Pennsylvania. Professor Barton's *Elements of Botany* had been illustrated by his friend William Bartram, author of *Travels through North & South Carolina, Georgia, East & West Florida* and son of America's first native-born naturalist, John Bartram. As King's Botanist in North America during the reign of George III, John Bartram established a garden of native plants at his home that his sons, John Bartram, Jr. and William Bartram, continued to nurture after their father's death. Professor Barton used the Bartrams' famous garden for his classes, and he often led his students into the countryside to see plants in their natural state. Bigelow saw the rosebay rhododendron growing at its best, and his description reflects his admiration for the plant:

The scenery of the American forest is distinguished not less by the greatness of its natural features . . . than it is by its magnificent clothing of its wild shrubs and trees, the uncommon beauty of which, gives to rough and inaccessible spots a richness, that cultivation can hardly imitate. The Kalmia . . . and the Rhododendron

129. This photograph of *Rhododendron maximum* was taken by the Arnold Arboretum's plant explorer, Ernest Henry Wilson, at Borderland, the estate of Oakes and Blanche Ames in North Easton, Massachusetts, on 8 July 1924. Drawn to the North Easton location early in the nineteenth century because of its potential for waterpower, Oakes Ames's great-grandfather Oliver Ames founded the Ames Shovel Works. In 1835, the Ames Works made fewer than five hundred shovels per day, but, in 1855, after the addition of twenty-six trip hammers powered by a steam engine and thirty-seven water wheels, the company was making twenty-four hundred shovels daily. On the eve of the Civil War, the business was valued at four million dollars, and in 1879, at the height of production, three out of every five shovels sold in the world were made in North Easton. After the death of Charles Sprague Sargent in 1927, Oakes Ames—a close family friend of the Sargents, an orchidologist, a professor of economic botany at Harvard, and Curator of the Botanical Museum—became "Supervisor" of the Arnold Arboretum. Borderland is now a Massachusetts State Park. The native rhododendrons that Dr. Bigelow cited in his book constitute one of the few remaining stands of native rhododendrons in the state, and they are now known as the Medfield Rhododendrons Reservation, one hundred ninety-six acres in Medfield, open to the public under the aegis of the Massachusetts Trustees of Reservations.

130. By October, the handsome clusters
of *Cornus florida* fruits have ripened.
Often they persist throughout winter, as
do the flower buds, which begin to form
in the summer. The color of the flower
buds—a pearly or silver gray—fits their
turbanlike appearance and makes a pleasing contrast with the bright red color of
the fruits.

... which are reared with care and difficulty as
ornaments of European gardens and pleasure grounds,
can be seen in perfection no where but in the uncultivated recesses of our own continent.

Not everyone could enjoy the luxury of this pespec-
tive. Settlers in the southern Appalachian Mountains
would find little comfort in Bigelow's glowing account of
the landscape of gorgeous flowers that *R. maximum*

presented in early summer. Southern farmers called these
thickets of rhododendrons, which could encompass
hundreds of acres and were all but impassable,
"rhododendron hells."

In addition to the rhododendron and the magnolia, the
Florula Bostoniensis included a third "white-flowered"
native woody plant that became a favorite of gardeners.
Cornus florida, the flowering dogwood, was, in Bigelow's
estimation, "the most splendid of its genus [and] one of

the chief ornaments of our forests." When one sees this tree in flower along the borders of natural woods or against a backdrop of evergreens, it is easy to understand how its value as an ornamental tree could equal its usefulness to the textile industry.

In spring, these small understory trees are covered with large, handsome, white bracts, which surround the small clusters of the minute yellowish-green true flowers. The flowers begin to form during the previous summer. Throughout the fall and winter, they remain enclosed and protected by four light-brown or grayish involucral scales. During winter, the flower buds are conspicuous. Looking like little Turkish caps or turbans the size of a pea, they stand up from the ends of the branchlets on stout, reddish, quarter-inch penduncles. In spring, the penduncle, or stalk, lengthens to an inch or an inch and a half, and the buds' protective scales, the bracts, begin to unfold, enlarge, and turn white. Some trees have pinkish-white bracts, and occasionally a tree will sport bracts of a deeper pink hue. Flowering dogwoods can reach forty feet in height, but in New England they usually grow to be less than twenty-five feet tall. An understory tree that needs only about one-third the amount of light that other trees require, *Cornus florida* flowers well in shade or in sun, but it forms a more compact shape with a flat-topped crown when growing in the open. With wide-spreading horizontal limbs that are delicately aligned tier upon tier, a mature flowering dogwood tree can often become as wide as it is high. Dogwood leaves are from two to five inches long, have wavy margins, and grow opposite one another. The fall color of this small tree's leaves and berries make the dogwood as handsome a tree during this season as it is in spring. By October, the upper surfaces of the leaves have turned from a dark green to a shiny rose, scarlet, or violet. Providing an ideal foil for these deeper hues, the undersides of the leaves remain as pale and whitish as they were throughout the growing season. By midsummer, several berrylike drupes, each containing two very hard notched stones that enclose the seeds, have developed. By fall, these oval drupes are a brilliant red, and they then become a source of food for migrating flocks of birds.

Like most contemporary scientifically arranged gardens, the Arnold Arboretum was laid out following a taxonomic or classification scheme developed by two British botanists, George Bentham and Joseph Dalton Hooker. The magnolia family (Magnoliaceae) is an ancient group of plants, and, because of the construction of magnolia flowers and fruits, it is considered to be, in an evolutionary sense, among the most simple and primitive

131. May Theilgaard Watts, naturalist emeritus at the Morton Arboretum in Lisle, Illinois, recorded her thoughts on holding "an authentic floral antique"—a magnolia flower—in *Reading the Landscape of America*: "First things, beginnings, have fascination, and to anyone familiar with botanical literature, here was a first—the flower at the base of the 'family tree' of flowers; the first tree in the book of Sargent's fourteen-volume *North American Silva*; the first family described in Pool's *Flowers and Flowering Plants*; the first family discussed in Arnold's *Paleobotany* in the chapter Ancient Flowering Plants; the flower named for Pierre Magnol (1638–1715), professor of botany at Montpellier, who was the first to indicate the natural families of plants."

families of plants. Because they occur at the beginning of the Bentham and Hooker classification scheme, the magnolias in the Arboretum's collection are growing in the area adjacent to Hunnewell Building, where they are among the first plants that visitors encounter upon entering the Arboretum's grounds.

The two- to three-inch ivory flowers of the sweetbay magnolia are the smallest of any American magnolia, but

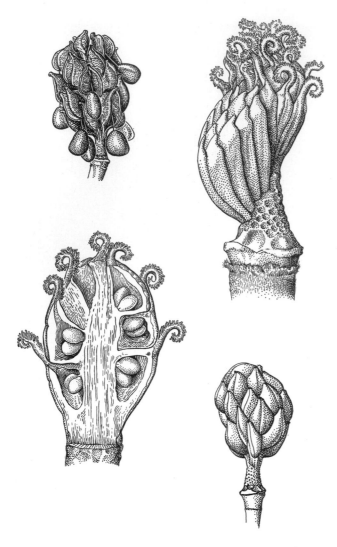

they are the most exquisite and the most fragrant. Visitors who return to the Arboretum during fall find that the fruits of *Magnolia virginiana* are as attractive as their flowers. By midsummer, the upright, cone-shaped, compound fruits are about two inches long and bright green. By summer's end, the color has changed to a yellowish pink. At maturity, the numerous one-celled vessels thst make up the fleshy fruit open to expose bright, coral-red, berrylike seeds, which slowly emerge and then hang suspended from slender, almost invisible threads.

During the fall of 1980, Peter Del Tredici, who was then the Arboretum's assistant plant propagator, visited Ravenswood Park and collected seed from the remaining trees. Seedlings grown from these seeds were replanted at the Gloucester swamp in 1982, and young plants grown from this seed lot also joined the magnolia collection at the Arnold Arboretum. These young plants of *Magnolia virginiana* can be seen along Willow Path across from the Arboretum's Hunnewell Building.

Flowering dogwoods used in woodland plantings exemplify an important component of Olmsted's "naturalistic" gardening style. Rather than restricting *Cornus florida* only to their place in the botanical sequence, they were planted throughout the grounds. When the dogwoods flower, the Arboretum seems to sparkle. The multitude of brilliant white bracts serves to unify the various collections like a lacework motif.

132. These carefully executed botanical drawings show the morphology of the reproductive organs of the sweet-bay magnolia flower (*upper right, lower left*) as well as mature and immature fruit aggregates. At the time of flowering, a large number of pollen-producing stamens subtend the elongated axis of the flower, which is studded with female structures, the carpels, each of which terminates in a recurved stigma (*upper right*). In longitudinal section (*lower left*), it can be seen that each carpel contains two ovules. These will develop into seeds, if pollination and fertilization are successful. A developing fruit aggregate, comprising numerous spirally arranged carpels, is shown at lower right, while, in the aggregate shown at the upper left, the fully mature carpels have dehisced, exposing the one or two seeds that have developed in each.

Growing Plants for Pleasure

As more people had the leisure and the means to develop their gardens, interest in horticulture gained momentum. With many new and exotic varieties of produce available from seed houses, the vegetable garden supplemented, rather than supplied, the basics, which now could be purchased at the market. For the middle class, cultivating a kitchen garden acquired the status of a luxury in which, with the aid of mass-produced, light-weight gardening tools, even the daintiest of ladies could indulge.

The founding of the Massachusetts Horticultural Society in 1829 and of the Worcester County Horticultural Society in 1842 brought fruit, vegetable, and flower expositions, modeled after the popular fairs that were being run by agricultural societies, to farmer and horticulturist alike. Purchases of fruit-tree stock, ornamental plants, and flower and vegetable seeds could be made from enterprising nurserymen, and their catalogues described what appeared to be endless lists of new

133. Frederick Law Olmsted planned the design of the Arnold Arboretum around existing stands of trees and the natural topography of the site. The "hanging hill of hemlocks" was one prominent feature of the future Arboretum that Olmsted admired. He selected this "ancient grove" as one of the three exceptional vistas that would be lost to the citizens of the city if the Arboretum were not incorporated into Boston's park system. Although most of the groups of trees are arranged according to the Bentham and Hooker classification system, Olmsted wisely chose to disregard the dictates of taxonomy when siting many of the shrubs. He enhanced the beauty of the hemlock grove and created one of the Arboretum's most stunning landscapes when he removed the rhododendrons and kalmias, members of the heath family, Ericaceae, from their position in the botanical sequence and placed them along the foot of Hemlock Hill. This photograph, by T. E. Marr, was taken in the early 1900s, soon after the shrub plantings were begun. During the last days of winter, when mist rises from the snow that remains deep along Hemlock Hill Road, visitors today enter a landscape that is as somber and enchanted as the confines of a mountain gorge. By setting the dark, leathery evergreen leaves of the rhododendrons and kalmias against the feathery evergreen boughs of the hemlocks, Olmsted produced a striking monochromatic composition of shape and texture.

varieties and species. In 1802, in Enfield, Connecticut, a community of the religious sect popularly known as the Shakers put up for sale the first packaged garden seeds sold in America. Reknowned for their economy and craftsmanship, the Shakers were also admired for their elegant labor-saving devices. (Counted among their many inventions are the first metal pens and flat brooms, a machine for turning broom handles, one for paring, coring, and quartering apples, a pea sheller, cut nails, and the common wooden clothespin.) But the Shakers had based the foundations of their economic industry on tilling the soil. To keep intact their reputation for producing flawless goods, the Shaker deacons and gardeners vowed never to purchase "seeds of the world" and mix them with their own. At the beginning of the nineteenth century, the packaged seeds that they offered for sale had the reputation of being the best available.

In Massachusetts, early seedsmen and nurseries with whom farmers and gardeners could trade included B. K. Bliss & Son in Springfield, Joseph Breck in Pepperell, John Kenrick and his son William Kenrick in Brighton and Newton, and the brothers Charles Mason Hovey and Phineas Brown Hovey in Cambridge.

The Hoveys opened their nursery in 1832, and two years later they launched the first successful periodical in the United States devoted almost exclusively to horticulture. Fashioned after the popular British monthly *Gardener's Magazine*, edited and published by John Cladius Loudon, the Hoveys' magazine first appeared under the title *The American Gardener's Magazine, and Register of Useful Discoveries and Improvements in Horticulture and Rural Affairs.* After two years, its name was changed to *The Magazine of Horticulture, Botany, and All Useful Discoveries and Improvements in Rural*

134. The cool shades of green that prevail throughout most of the year at the base of Hemlock Hill are interrupted by a burst of color in spring when the ericaceous shrubs blossom. This photograph of Hemlock Hill Road, also by T. E. Marr, was taken in the 1920s, by which time the young shrub plantings in the previous photograph had matured into magnificent specimens.

Affairs and Charles Mason Hovey became its sole editor, a position he held until the magazine ceased publication in 1868.

By spending the sum of three dollars per year, Hovey's subscribers could acquire information about topics as diverse as a "notice of a fine and showy species of cow-parsnip (*Heracleum Wilhelseii*)" to the "employment of ornamental trees and shrubs in North America . . . as regards their effect in the formation of parks and pleasure grounds. . . ." The second article, written by the doyen of

American landscape gardening, Andrew Jackson Downing, preceded by ten years his own debut, in 1846, as editor of *The Horticulturist* and *Journal of Rural Art and Rural Taste*. The publisher of the agricultural journal *The Cultivator*, Luther Tucker, had recognized that farmers were not the only people eager for information about growing plants. Tucker invited Downing to edit *The Horticulturist* and, seven years later, merged *The Cultivator* with a new weekly, *The Country Gentleman*. Like Charles Mason Hovey, Downing was a nurseryman. His

135. Charles Mason Hovey (1810–1887), nurseryman, horticulturist, writer, and editor. Liberty Hyde Bailey considered Hovey's *Magazine of Horticulture* to be "a record of the budding stage of New World horticulture." This portrait of Hovey, executed by William Sharp, appears as the frontispiece to the first volume of his book *The Fruits of America.* In 1840, Hovey's nursery occupied what had been 40 acres of woodland on Cambridge Street. Today, Cambridge City Hospital occupies much of the nursery site.

136. Andrew Jackson Downing (1815–1852) spent his life in the Hudson River valley. In *A Treatise on the Theory and Practice of Landscape Gardening, Adapted to North America; with a View to the Improvement of Country Residences,* Downing extols the beauty of the estates and the river valley. "There is no part of the Union where the taste in Landscape Gardening is so far advanced, as on the middle portion of the Hudson. The natural scenery is of the finest character, and places but a mile or two apart often possess, from the constantly varying forms of the water, shores, and distant hill, widely different kinds of home landscape and distant views." Raphael Hoyle, an English landscape painter who had immigrated to America in the 1820s and who worked both in New York City and in Newburgh, taught Downing the elements of landscape composition.

career began in 1834, when he joined his older brother Charles at the nursery that their father had founded in 1801 in Newburgh, New York, on the northern flank of the Hudson River highlands. Charles left the family business in 1839 to pursue his interest in pomology, the science of fruit growing, and Andrew became the sole owner of the nursery. The prosperity of the Downing Nursery kept pace with its owner's reputation, and Downing continued to grow plants at Newburgh until his untimely death in 1852.

137 (*following pages*). After Thomas Cole's death in 1848, Asher B. Durand assumed the mantle of dean of the Hudson River school. In his attention to the smallest detail in nature, he led younger artists to a naturalism that characterized American landscape painting in the 1850s and 1860s. These two paintings by Durand, *Kaaterskill Cove* (p. 166) and *Dover Plain* (p. 167), reflect the sublime beauty of the Hudson River valley.

Trees in the Marketplace and in the Garden

Downing's innovative ideas on landscaping and Hovey's horticultural expertise on growing plants insured the success of their publications. For six years, the two men carried on a friendly rivalry, often trading barbs in the editorial columns of their respective magazines. Both editors called on a wide range of gardening experts to contribute news on cultural techniques and on economically and ornamentally useful plants. Among their circle of friends was a young man, Frederick Law Olmsted, who published a piece on Liverpool's Bickenhead Park in the May 1851 issue of *The Horticulturist*, and Downing's patron and Charles Sprague Sargent's cousin, Henry Winthrop Sargent, often contributed articles on English gardens and comments on conifers to Hovey's *Magazine of Horticulture*.

"Original communications" in Hovey's *Magazine of Horticulture* usually focused on the practical aspects of growing flowers, fruits, and vegetables, and its editor included a section in each issue entitled "Calls at Gardens and Nurseries." During the years that he edited *The Horticulturist*, Andrew Jackson Downing emphasized the "artistical combination of the beautiful in nature and art" rather than the cultivation of individual plants. In Downing's words, "Landscape Gardening differs from gardening in its common sense, in embracing the whole scene immediately about a country house . . . not through plots of fruit trees, and beds of choice flowers . . . but by collecting and combining beautiful forms in trees, surfaces of ground, buildings, and walks, in the landscape surrounding us."

The introductory issue of *The Horticulturist* came out five years after Downing had published the first edition of his most significant work, *A Treatise on the Theory and Practice of Landscape Gardening*. Written when Downing was only twenty-four years old, his treatise contained directions for arranging plantations and for laying out grounds, walks, and roads; descriptions of the finest hardy deciduous and evergreen trees; the use of water in landscape design; and the use of architectural, rustic, and floral embellishments.

At the same time in which Downing was adapting the principles of the natural or English landscape gardening style of Henry Repton and John Claudius Loundon to North America, writers and artists were discovering the wild and romantic landscape of the Hudson River valley. While Downing created designs for country estates that embodied the aesthetic principles of the "sublime" and the "picturesque" along the Hudson River's shoreline, its mountains, cliffs, rocks, and trees challenged painters to capture this landscape on canvas. Downing's *Theory and Practice of Landscape Gardening* could have been written as a guide to trees, shrubs, and vines for the artists of the Hudson River school. Americans had begun to embrace a less hostile view of nature. This new appreciation began with European notions of romanticism that had crossed the Atlantic in poetry, painting, and literature; the wilderness no longer howled, and, having been tamed, it had become a national asset.

By the middle of the nineteenth century, New Bedford, Massachusetts, was the wealthiest city of its size in America. Unlike the Hudson River's idealized landscape of tranquil hills overhung with vines and forest trees, New Bedford's waterfront, viewed from the waters of Buzzards Bay, bustled with stevedores and sailors and with merchants making their way to the counting rooms in their warehouses. The city's prosperity could be measured by the number of large estates that overlooked the harbor, and the gardens of the merchants' stately mansions had caught the attention of the horticultural world.

Charles Mason Hovey visited this coastal city in southeastern Massachusetts on one of his regular garden-hunting excursions in the fall of 1840, and a record of his impressions appeared in the October issue of *The Horticulturist*. It is likely that Hovey had heard about the great number "of well laid out and well tilled gardens" that he praised in his article from his friend John Quincy Adams, a fellow member of the Massachusetts Horticultural Society. The former president and his son, Charles Francis Adams, had "walked out and around the town with Mr. Arnold and admired the fine Palace Houses of the Citizens" in 1835. In Hovey's estimation, for a town with "so many residences which evinced such excellent taste in the laying out of the grounds," Mr. Arnold had the most ornamental garden that he had ever seen. The editor described how the "broad sweeping carriageway . . . fine lawn . . . elegant groups of trees . . . winding walks . . . shady bowers . . . and umbrageous retreats . . . convey to those who have not a good conception of the modern or English style of gardening, a better idea of what this style consists in, than they could learn by reading a hundred descriptions of the same." Andrew Jackson Downing concurred with Hovey's appraisal. In the second edition of his *Theory and Practice of Landscape Gardening*, Downing singled out Arnold's garden from all the many beautiful residential gardens in the environs of New Bedford. He declared that "there is scarcely a place in New England, where the pleasure grounds are so full of variety, and in such perfect order and keeping as this charming spot."

138. The home of James and Sara Arnold was located on Country Street in New Bedford, Massachusetts. Greatly altered architecturally, the former Arnold residence is now home to the Wamsutta Club.

In Herman Melville's novel *Moby-Dick*, which was published in 1851, the narrator, Ishmael, alludes to the way in which New Bedford's monetary and horticultural wealth had been amassed. The city's "brave houses and flowery gardens came from the Atlantic, Pacific, and Indian Oceans. One and all, they were harpooned and dragged up hither from the bottom of the sea." New Bedford began its long, illustrious career as a whaling town in 1765, when Joseph Rotch (a Nantucket merchant) built wharves and warehouses along the frontage of its harbor. Rotch was perceived as "a man of great activity and shrewdness in business, his manner quicke and vivacious," and, after Rotch arrived, according to a local history, "houses and shops multiplied, highways were opened, wharves were built, and the riverfront became the center of an active business." The firm of Joseph Rotch and Sons laid the keel of the firm's first ship, the *Dartmouth*, under a grove of buttonwood trees, in 1767. Joseph's son Francis would be the managing owner of the *Dartmouth* when she sailed into Boston six years later, her holds filled with her most infamous cargo—bales of tea that would end up in the harbor, tossed there by the "Boston Indians." Joseph Rotch had made a wise choice

when, in expanding his business, he moved its operations from Nantucket, home port to the New England whale fishery, to the mainland at New Bedford. The great lobe of ice that had stalled, melted, and created the moraine that became the Cape Cod towns of Bourne and Falmouth, as well as the nearby Elizabeth Islands, had also made Buzzards Bay, a wide, deep, and sheltered bay with a coastline of many deep, V-shaped inlets. Shielded from the open sea, the harbor at New Bedford was deep enough to accommodate the large ships that would soon come to dominate the industry. Before long, most of New England's whaling fleet sailed from New Bedford and the smaller ports that dotted the inlets along the western coast of Buzzards Bay. By 1820, the industry had fully recovered from the Revolution and the effects of the War of 1812, and New Bedford had clearly surpassed Nantucket in the number of whaling ships that set out from their wharves. The city could now justly claim to to be the whaling capital of the world.

In 1821, James Arnold moved to New Bedford from Providence, Rhode Island. He entered the firm of William Rotch, Jr., and, in short order, married his employer's daughter, Sarah. Her family's long history of whaling and

139. James Arnold's eulogist, the Reverend William J. Potter, spoke of him as a man who had "possessed a strong physical constitution, full to overflowing with vitality, capable of great labor and great endurance. . . . [and] having the large practical understanding, which, combined with an untiring energy and strong will, gave him excellent administrative ability, and made him a most successful merchant. . . ." As a prosperous merchant, Arnold had successfully invested his whale-oil fortune in real estate, railroads, and a saltworks, and he had also directed his administrative abilities toward civic-minded and charitable pursuits. Not only was he a founding member of the New Bedford Horticultural Society, and its president for many years, but in 1812 he helped found the Friends Academy, and he served on the board of that institution until his death in 1868. He was a member of the Dialectic Society (and reputedly a very capable speaker), the president of the Port Society, and a director of the Bedford Commercial Bank. From 1844 to 1851, Arnold also advised Governor George N. Briggs as member of his council.

boat building was equaled by their penchant for building mansions. Now, as a young merchant prince of the New Bedford whaling trade, James adopted the family custom. Country Street ran along the crest of a hill that paralleled the bay, and the new Arnold residence sat at its highest point. The two-story brick structure commanded a fine view of the harbor and the wharves owned by James and his parents-in-law. Bounded by Cottage Street to the rear and by Arnold Street and Union Street to the east and west, the Arnolds' land was approximately eleven acres in extent, which gave them ample room to lay out their garden. At the rear of the house, inside an eleven-foot-high stone wall, were two graperies, a greenhouse, a parterre with borders of boxwood, a fruit garden with trellises for peaches, a gardener's cottage covered by climbing roses, and a grotto.

James Arnold marched in step with the leading horticulturists of the day. The Massachusetts Horticultural Society made him an Honorary Member in 1839, an honor the society bestowed on very few plantsmen. Arnold entered the fruits his garden produced in the Society's expositions, and he competed with—and at times bested—professional nurserymen. His 'Black Hamburg' grapes won prizes, and the sweet, lucious peaches he grew on specially designed trellises were the envy of pomologists. In 1847, Arnold and several of his gardening colleagues founded the New Bedford Horticultural Society, and the members then elected Arnold the society's first president. The pleasure Arnold derived from his advocation he shared with others: Arnold's gardens were open not only to former presidents and venerated horticulturists but to the public as well. A Sunday afternoon perambulation through the Arnold estate was a New Bedford custom. Maypoles festooned with flowers complemented the lawn on May Day, and, throughout the warm summer months, couples found the secluded, rustic benches set in the dense grove of native and exotic trees to their liking.

James Arnold's life had just passed the half-century mark in 1835, when the golden age of American whaling began. In 1845, New Bedford was riding on the crest of the wave. In that year alone, ten thousand seamen landed 158,000 barrels of sperm oil, almost double that amount of whale oil, and roughly three million pounds of whalebone. At the northern end of the city, where the Acushnet River flowed into the harbor, New Bedford's first cotton mill, the Wamsutta Mill, was being built. It is likely that Arnold attended the festivities that heralded its opening in 1847, for it was the first textile mill in America whose spindles and looms would be driven by steam power. Arnold may have questioned the wisdom of local businessmen for investing in such a venture, but he soon had business problems of his own. The discovery of gold in California in 1849 created immediate havoc within the whaling trade: entire crews often jumped ship upon reaching California, and sometimes even their captains went with them. But the black gold that would come from hills much closer to home would prove to have much more devastating consequences on the whaling industry. Arnold may have given the news of the successful drilling of petroleum in Titusville, Pennsylvania, in August of 1859 little more than passing notice. He, like most northern businessmen, was more concerned with the economic uncertainties brought on by the increasing hostilities between the North and the South. Had Arnold read the editorials published in the *Charleston Courier* that debated the question of seccession, he would have had something to add to the question, "Whence come your axes, hoes, scythes . . . Yes, even your plows, harrows, rakes, ax and auger handles . . . your furniture, carpets, calicos, and muslins? . . ." Yes, whence comes the whale oil that lights your lamps?

For more than a decade, the nation had girded itself for a civil war that seemed inevitable. Between the vast plantations of the Gulf States and the mill cities of the Northeast stood an issue that could not be resolved. During the antebellum years, cotton exports constituted more than sixty percent of trade; the economy of the United States floated on a white sea of cotton picked by four million black hands. The mechanization of cotton production, from separating the fibers from the seed to processing the fibers into fabric, had exacerbated the political, social, and economic differences that divided the country. In the South, the cotton gin had elevated cotton to king; the loom had been the kingpin of the factory system in the North. As the "crop value per slave" rose from $15 in 1800 to $125 in 1860, the use of slave labor grew more indispensable to the Southern plantation system and more despicable to Northern abolitionists.

The firing on Fort Sumter on 12 April 1861 plunged the country into four years of bloody war. The battles that raged across Southern cornfields and farmlands fueled Northern industries. The average Union soldier was better equipped, better clothed, and better shod than his Southern cousin. While Confederate soldiers used the green hulls of *Juglans cinerea* to dye their homespun fabric butternut brown, women and children in Northern woolen mills wove enough dark blue woolen fabric to make one and one-half million blankets and an equal number of dark blue woolen uniforms for each year that the fighting dragged on. In Massachusetts, the boot and shoe industry had teetered on the brink of full-scale industrialization, and the war pushed it over the edge. Each year, as the Union Army crisscrossed the South, its soldiers marched through three million pairs of shoes. The making of shoes and boots consumed eighty percent of the leather that tanneries produced, and hemlock bark was gathered and used in record amounts that did not diminish until the end of the century. In addition, a growing proportion of the leather produced went into the making of industrial drive belts. The old wooden cog gears that transmitted power from the main shaft of a mill could not transmit power at the high speed that many of the war industries required. Leather belts eliminated almost all gearing, and small mills were able to switch from making articles of peace to producing articles of war.

James Arnold accumulated considerable wealth, which he and Sarah administered with charity. His death in 1868 at the age of eighty-seven left New Bedford bereft of one of its leading citizens and benefactors. His largess continued after his death; he committed a portion of his estate to benefit the poor of his city. Arnold also entrusted three friends who shared his interest in plants with one and one-quarter twenty-fourths of his estate to "be by them applied for the promotion of Agricultural or Horticultural improvements, or other Philosophical, or Philanthropic purposes." As trustees of Arnold's bequest, George Barrell Emerson (his brother-in-law and the author of a report on the trees and shrubs growing naturally in the forests of Massachusetts), John J. Dixwell (an educator and amateur horticulturist), and Francis C. Parker negotiated with Harvard University to create, on land left to the University by Benjamin Bussey, a garden of trees, shrubs, and vines to be called the Arnold Arboretum, a fitting memorial to a man whose "garden, freely open to strangers as to friends to the day of his death, was a place of public interest and resort."

CHAPTER FOUR

The New Yankee Forest

From Rags to Phoenix Trees

Newspapers brought the tragic events of the Civil War into Northern parlors and onto Southern verandas. Staccato dots and dashes transmitted over telegraph lines sped vivid accounts of defeats and victories to the daily newspapers, and engravings in the illustrated weeklies froze the horror of front-line combat in detailed, if sometimes romanticized, drawings. Reports of the fighting increased circulation, but, as the war continued, newspapers ran the risk of running out of newsprint. The paper that the presses consumed was made from cotton and linen rags, and these were in short supply.

The scarcity of rags had plagued American paper producers since the Colonial era. With most of the printed material generated by the colonists consisting of legal forms and government documents, printers and papermakers (who were often one in the same) found a brisk market for the meager amounts of paper that they could produce in the seats of Colonial government. But, because nearly all paper was imported, it was costly, and delivery was irregular. To increase domestic paper production, rag drives sponsored by publishers and newspapers became commonplace.

In 1728, the General Court of the Province of the Massachusetts Bay Colony issued the first charter for a paper mill in New England. The court granted monopoly protection for ten years if the mill, built on the banks of the Neponset River in Milton, could produce 250 reams of paper within fifteen months. To procure enough rags to insure the survival of the mill, its owners regularly sent a cart through the streets of Boston to collect scraps of cotton and linen cloth. The *Boston Newsletter*, the city's first newspaper and most likely one of the mill's best customers, encouraged contributions by publishing this jingle in 1769:

Rags are as beauties, which concealed lie,
But when in paper how it charms the eye;

Pray save your rags, new beauties to discover,
For paper, truly, everyone's a lover.
By the pen and the press such knowledge is displayed,
As wouldn't exist if paper was not made.

Apparently, most housewives preferred to recycle the families' meager amount of old clothing for their own household needs; rag merchants continued to obtain almost all of their rags from abroad. Until the beginning of the nineteenth century, most rags were imported from Russia and the Scandinavian countries. By midcentury, they often came from the Middle East, and, by the end of the Civil War, with many American cotton mills shut down, India, China, and Japan had become the leading suppliers.

With the advent of local textile manufacturing, New England captured the lead in American papermaking. Paper mills set up to take advantage of the waste from the textile industry soon joined the textile mills constructed alongside Yankee rivers. But cotton mill waste and ends supplied these new mills only a fraction of the raw material that they needed.

Soaring prices forced papermakers to search for viable substitutes for rags and, before long, scientists had developed an economical process of manufacturing paper from wood. In Germany, there had been an ambitious precedent. One hundred years earlier, Dr. Jacob Christian Schaeffer had not only succeeded in making paper from wood but had gone on to make paper out of potatoes, corn husks, wheat straw, and more than eighty other kinds of plants. Experiments on both sides of the Atlantic using lye to dissolve wood fiber eventually led to the establishment, in 1866, of the American Wood Paper Company in Philadelphia. The company used a tree whose wood was known to be "light, soft, and destitute of strength." Until its emergence as a source of paper pulp, it was a tree whose wood was considered to be "of no utility." It was poplar—harvested from the outskirts of Philadelphia, sawed into half-inch disks, cooked in caustic soda for six hours, and thereby reduced to pulp. After the pulp was drained, washed, and bleached, the papermakers added to the solution small amounts of paper pulp made from straw. The result was a paper that was eighty percent wood.

Of the thirteen poplars native to North America, it is likely that trembling aspen, *Populus tremuloides*, and bigtooth aspen, *P. grandidentata*, were the first species to be used in making paper. Their wood is virtually identical, and, like all poplar wood, it is classified as a "soft hardwood." In addition to these two poplars, three other species of *Populus* can be found in New England. The balsam poplar, *P. balsamifera*, is the most northern hardwood tree in North America. Valued today as an important component in the northern "pulpwood" forest, balsam poplar grows in Maine and in northern Vermont and New Hampshire in association with black, white, and red spruces (*Picea mariana*, *P. glauca*, and *P. rubens*) and the paper birch (*Betula papyrifera*). Balsam poplar does, however, range south along rivers into Massachusetts, Connecticut, and Rhode Island.

Of the six New England states, Connecticut may be the only one that plays host to all five species of poplar. Although balsam poplars are few and far between in the Connecticut woodlands, *Populus heterophylla*, the swamp cottonwood, is an even rarer find. This southern species grows along the Coastal Plain from northern Florida to southern Connecticut. Distribution maps indicate its presence in New England by a small, shaded area in Connecticut's most southwestern corner. *P. deltoides*, the eastern cottonwood, whose leaves are shaped like the the three-sided Greek letter *delta*, grows from the southern Atlantic coast to the eastern edge of the Rocky Mountains. A tree that is more at home on the plains and in the prairie states, it skirts mountainous regions, preferring river valleys and coastal lowlands. In the East, *P. deltoides* is absent from the Appalachian highlands. Although not common in New England, the eastern cottonwood can usually be found growing in the moist soil that occurs along rivers and streams.

Of New England's most widely distributed poplars, one produces leaves with large teeth along their margins. This characteristic led André Michaux to select the Latin word meaning "large-toothed" to identify the species. *Populus grandidentata*, commonly called the bigtooth aspen, grows from sea level to altitudes of about three thousand feet. The bigtooth aspen is a coarse-looking tree with deeply fissured brown bark on its trunk and smoother

yellowish-green bark on its limbs. It is a medium-sized tree that is common throughout northeastern North America.

The fifth New England species looked familiar to tree-conscious Europeans. Because it shares many taxonomic characteristics with a poplar that grows throughout their homelands, it was assumed at first that *Populus tremula*, the Old World species, also inhabited the forests of North America. The flowers of both species are similar, and both have leaves that are approximately the same size and shape. Their leaves are broad and rounded to heart-shaped at the base, and the margins of the leaves have small, fine teeth; both trees also have long, slender stalks—or petioles—that connect the leaf blades to the twigs. The flatness and thinness of these petioles where they connect with the leaf allow the leaf blades to flutter and rustle in the slightest breeze. While classifying and naming New World poplars in 1803, André Michaux identified the American species as being distinct, but he acknowledged the similarities between the two by naming the American tree *Populus tremuloides*, from the Latin *tremulus*, "to tremble," and the Greek suffix *-oides*, "looking like"—in other words, "like *Populus tremula*." *P. tremuloides* grows across North America from the Atlantic coast to the Pacific. It can be found from sea level to 10,000 feet, growing as often in deep, moist, loamy sands as on shallow, rocky soils or clay. Not only does *P. tremuloides* have the widest range and the most tremulous leaves of the American poplars, but it qualifies as the most widely distributed tree in North America. Only one other deciduous tree in the world has a larger distribution—its closely related Eurasian counterpart, *P. tremula*. *P. tremuloides* is a slender, graceful tree with bark that may be smooth, pale, and grayish-green to white in youthful trees, but it becomes darker with age. Its bark is marked by crescent-shaped scars and rough bands that encircle the trunk. To New Englanders, it is known as poplar, popple, or trembling aspen. Westerners also consider its fluttering leaves to be a unique characteristic, and, appropriately, they know it as quaking aspen.

Most plants reproduce by sexual means through the production of seed. By contrast, the trembling aspen most often clones itself by reproducing vegetatively. As a group, poplars are dioecious, with male and female flowers produced on separate trees. Individual trees of *P. tremuloides* flower very early in spring, usually in March or April, and their seeds are mature and ready to be dispersed at about the same time that their leaves begin to unfold. Female trees produce prodigious numbers of lightweight seeds—a pound can contain two to

140. Male and female poplar flowers, consisting of long catkins, are borne on different trees. The flowers usually appear well before the leaves and are pollinated by the wind. With female catkins that can become four to five inches long, the balsam poplar (*Populus balsamifera*) has the longest catkins of all species. Balsam poplar is a fast-growing, relatively short-lived pioneer tree that is intolerant of shade and acts as a "nurse" to other trees. In northern New England, this is the tree that provides the shade for spruce to become established. Eventually, like many pioneer trees, balsam poplars are overtaken and crowded out by the very trees that they sheltered. Eventually, the spruce overtops the poplars in the forest canopy, and the forest floor becomes too shady for the germination and survival of poplar seeds. The common name balsam was derived from the sticky, clear, and very aromatic gum that coats the winter buds. This gum was once regularly sought after as the principal ingredient an a pleasant smelling salve or ointment.

three million—but, although each small, pear-shaped seed has a great feathery tuft of hairs that allow the seed to float in the air and to be blown for miles by the wind, very few, if any, will come to rest in an area that can provide the optimal environmental conditions that the seedlings need to survive. The seeds remain viable for a very short time—two to four weeks—and they must come in contact with a well-watered mineral soil in order to germinate. Those that come to rest on ground heavily littered with leaves, or in areas where their microscopic root hairs are unable to penetrate the surface of the soil, will fail to survive. The brief viability of the seeds and the sensitivity of the seedlings to fluctuations in the amount of water result in a very low rate of survival. Moreover, the seedlings require full sunlight for optimal growth.

The rare seedling that does survive its first year usually becomes an ortet, the solitary parent of a potentially limitless number of genetically identical plants. A clone consists of an ortet and a group of individual stems or trees called ramets that arise vegetatively from the single individual of seedling origin. A successful seedling allows the tree to gain a foothold in a new area, and, once the initial plant becomes established, a *Populus tremuloides* clone is likely to proliferate through an extensive root system. During its first year of growth, the seedling becomes a sapling that can attain a height of four feet. Its taproot usually penetrates only to a depth of six inches or so, but its lateral roots normally extend about three feet from its base. During the following growing season, the sapling is apt to grow more slowly, but its lateral roots double in length and—more importantly—they develop sucker shoots. Over the next two or three years, sinker roots grow downward from these lateral roots and the suckers, the ramets, form new trees. Each one of these new trees sends out its own series of lateral and sinker roots, and, as the number of trees proliferates, an increasingly larger network of "individuals" expands outward from the parent plant. Eventually, a grove of poplars surrounds the individual from which the colony arose. A fire severe enough to destroy the above-ground growth will actually stimulate the root system to produce more suckers and create a denser stand. Like the legendary Phoenix, the clone will rise in youthful freshness from its own ashes.

The trembling aspen is only one of many plants that reproduce vegetatively. Because vegetative propagation in nature most often takes place underground, it is a method that largely goes unnoticed. Suckers that sprout from the fleshy roots of the sassafras (*Sassafras albidum*) also initiate succeeding generations of genetically identical trees, and the black spruce (*Picea mariana*) uses a similar strategy—layering—to reproduce itself. Violets, starflowers, false lily-of-the-valley, and wild sarsaparilla are just a few of our native herbaceous woodland plants that also reproduce primarily through clonal growth.

The poplar collection at the Arnold Arboretum occupies an area that is often overlooked by visitors. The pop-lars have been planted in, and at the edge of, a deep, bowl-like depression at the foot of the western side of Peters Hill. The toe of the slope is bounded by the commuter railroad line and South Street, and the Arboretum's Peters Hill Road follows along the bowl's upper rim. The combination of roads and railroad virtually isolates this small neck of land from the rest of Peters Hill. Because of their siting, the poplars—which are rarely, if ever, known for ornamental attributes—have to compete for attention with one of the Arboretum's most spectacular floral displays. The main body of the *Malus* collec-

141. This excavation of a poplar clone has exposed the intricate network of lateral and sinker roots that connect the original seedling, the ortet, and the subsequent new trees, the ramets. Because plant clones are very successful in nature—not only do poplars proliferate this way, but many of our most troublesome agricultural weeds also grow and spread from underground roots, rhizomes, or buds—ecologists are studying the implications of clonal growth on natural selection and gene flow, as well as the ecological advantages such as the acquisition of territory and survival that may be enhanced by these complex systems.

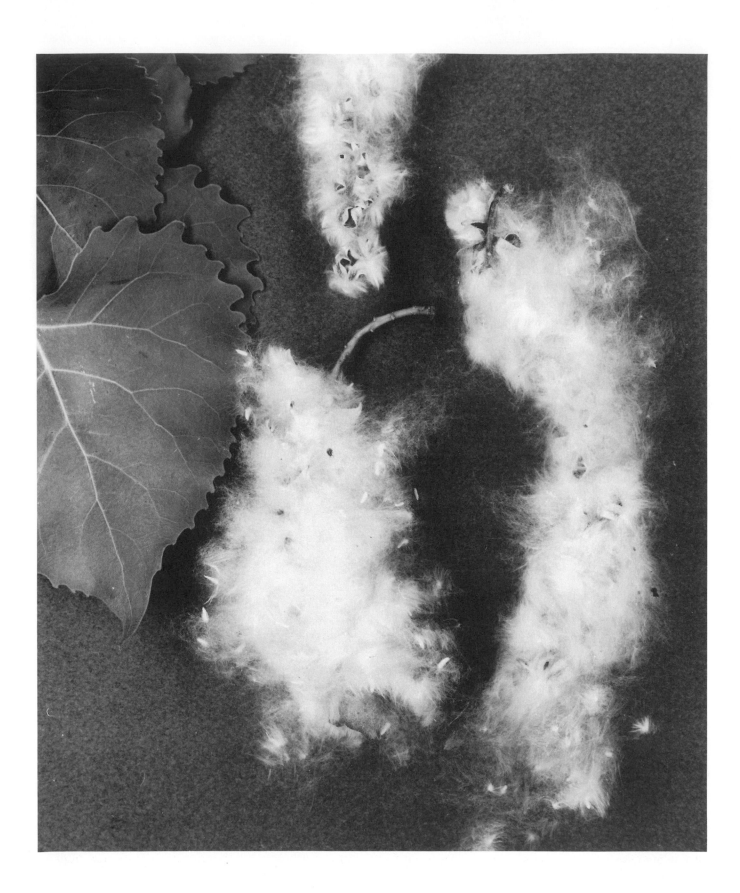

142. *Populus deltoides*, the eastern cottonwood, is the largest of the poplars that grow in New England. It is a stately river-bottom tree that can be found growing along the shoreline of Lake Champlain, and on the banks of the Hoosac, Housatonic, Farmington, and Connecticut rivers and their tributaries, as well as in other riverine locations. The eastern cottonwood commonly grows to between fifty and seventy-five feet, although it can attain a height of one hundred feet or more. It is a short-trunked tree with massive, sometimes pendulous limbs. On mature trees, its ashy-gray bark is thick with conspicuous parallel furrows. On young trees, the bark is smooth, thin, and a yellow green. This poplar's most prominent feature is apparent in the spring, when the sky in the vicinity of these trees can become filled by the large masses of white, cottony, downlike dispersal hairs that transport this species' minute seeds through the air.

---

tion, the Arboretum's prized ornamental crabapples, cascades down and sweeps around the western side of Peters Hill, just upland from the poplars. In May, when the flowering crabapples blanket Peters Hill with swatches of bright white, dark rose, and innumerable shades of pink, the green fluttering leaves of *Populus tremuloides* are no match for the visitor's attention. But a visit at this time of year to the trembling aspen will reward the viewer with the sight of beautiful four-inch-long fruiting aments, which are the slender, flexible catkins that harbor the tree's finely tufted seeds. Many of the poplars in the Arboretum's collection are young, recently planted specimens. However, there is a grand old stand of eastern cottonwoods (*P. deltoides*) that should not be overlooked. Visitors entering Peters Hill by way of Poplar Gate pass through an allée of red oaks planted along a straight stretch of Peters Hill Road. Turning left, or clockwise, at the end of the allée, as the road begins its circuit of Peters Hill, brings visitors to a stand of eight enormous eastern cottonwoods planted on the left-hand side of the road. In August 1895, and a little more than a year later, in September 1896, John George Jack, an Arboretum staff member and plant explorer, collected fifteen seedlings of this species in Châteauguay, Quebec, and brought them back to Boston to be planted on what was then a newly acquired portion of the Arboretum, called Peters Hill.

Unfortunately for the American Wood Paper Company, although poplars respond to logging in the same way they do to fire, at least twenty-five years would pass before the sprouts would again reach harvestable size. In Pennsylvania, demand for the wood outstripped the local supply, and the same situation existed in southern New England. But the handful of small paper mills that had been established in northern New England suddenly held an advantage; many operated in areas where poplar was very plentiful.

At first, farmers, not lumbermen, delivered the wood —cut and debarked—to the paper mills. But when this handy local supply of pulpwood diminished, the price of poplar soared, and paper mills began to adopt the logging methods and strategies earlier employed by the lumber barons who had cut the region's white pine. Agents hired loggers to harvest the poplar that grew farther north, beyond the outskirts of the farming communities, in the "big woods" of Maine.

From Timber to Pulpwood

Poplar remained the preferred wood for papermaking until the midle of the 1880s. During the latter part of the century, however, not only was poplar being cut, but the logging of spruce, which papermakers found could also be easily turned into pulp, was increasing steadily. The spruces, too, had a reputation for producing an inferior wood, but, with the growth of commercial paper production on a large scale—the combined daily capacity of Maine's twenty-five pulp mills exceeded three hundred tons—and with a "pulp craze" about to seize the state of Maine, the time was ripe for paper corporations to buy land from the lumbermen and harvest these new paper-producing trees.

When spruce logs came crashing down the Kennebec River, they signaled the end of an era; for the previous two hundred years, loggers had sought out and felled white pine. It had been New England's largest, most valuable, and most accessible timber tree, but, with the noble "mast trees" gone and with much of the white pine forest cut, the peak years of Maine's pine-lumber industry had passed, and an exodus of loggers and lumber barons began. They migrated to the unexploited pineries of the Great Lakes region, to Michigan's Upper Peninsula, the

143. The red spruce (*Picea rubens*), the white spruce (*P. glauca*), and the balsam fir (*Abies balsamea*) are the predominant species in the northeastern spruce–fir forest. The black spruce (*P. mariana*) is a minor component of this forest type, which occupies eleven million acres in New England and New York. Although the black spruce plays a minor role, it is a remarkably adaptive species that can thrive in barren, windswept areas above the tree line. In these open, exposed situations, the black spruce forms dense prostrate mats that spread by layering; their roots, called adventitious roots, develop from the branches. In more typical situations, spruce and fir are both spirelike trees that have regular tiers of whorled branches and aromatic leaves. From a distance, differentiating the spruces from one another and from firs can be difficult, although the balsam fir has the most compact, narrow, spirelike silhouette. However, it is easy to tell spruce and fir trees apart by examining their cones and needles. The cones of all three species of spruce that grow in New England hang downward on the branches; balsam fir cones are held upright. Spruce needles are usually four-sided, and, when they are bruised, the scent is quite different from the Christmasy aroma that fills the air when the flattened, not squarish, fir needles are bruised or crushed. The odors of polecat and skunk are often invoked to describe the smell of white spruce; red spruce needles smell like orange rinds; and the needles of the black spruce have a medicinal menthol smell. The undersides of fir needles also have two whitish lines that are not present on spruce needles.

Tab: 121.

Rhododendron maximum.
Virginisches Rhododendron.

L. Herr. sculp:

Plate 17. The rosebay rhododendron, or so-called white laurel (*Rhododendron maximum*) is native to a wide area of eastern North America and ranges northward into Nova Scotia and Ontario. It is most common and best developed, however, in the mountains of the southeastern United States. Unlike the majority of *Rhododendron* species and the multitude of hybrids and cultivars available in the nursery trade that are cultivated on a wide scale in New England, which flower in late May or early June, the rosebay, refreshingly, flowers in late June and early July.

T.39.

Magnolia Lauri folio, Subtus albicans.
The Sweet Flowring Bay.

Coccothraustes cæruleus.
The blew Grofbeak.

Plate 18.   Despite the fact that this drawing of the sweetbay (*Magnolia virginiana*) illustrates both the creamy white, fragrant flowers and the egg-shaped fruit aggregates with their red seeds suspended on thin threads, these two structures do not occur on the same plant simultaneously. In New England, these small, usually shrubby trees flower during June, and the fruit aggregates develop from late summer to early fall. It is surprising that this species, which is most frequently associated with the flora of the southeastern United States, reaches its northernmost natural distribution in Ravenswood Park in the coastal village of Magnolia, Massachusetts, roughly thirty miles northeast of Boston.

Plate 19. The red spruce (*Picea rubens*), illustrated here, and the balsam fir (*Abies balsamea*) are so often found growing together in the higher elevations of the Allegheny Mountains that the southern woodsmen called both species by the name balsam. They dubbed the spruce the "he-balsam" and the fir the "she-balsam." It is interesting to note that, although these two conifers are companions in the wild, their life expectancies differ greatly: the red spruce can live for as long as three hundred years, while the balsam fir seldom lives longer than eighty years. In the White Mountains of New England, these are the two conifers that persist at higher elevations, becoming gradually smaller in stature until they reach the timberline on the highest mountain tops.

Tab. 8.

a

c

b

d

Acer Saccharinum
Zucker = Ahorn.

Plate 20.   The exquisite illustration captures the coloring of the opposite, simple leaves of the silver maple (*Acer saccharinum*), which are pale green above and a silvery-white on the underside. Also detailed are the five prominent veins that radiate out from the base and extend to the tips of the teeth along the margin of the leaf. The greenish-yellow flowers open before the leaves, usually during the first warm days of late winter or early spring. The fruits are large paired samaras with widely spread wings. Although the fruits ripen in April or May and the seeds are capable of germinating at once, usually only one samara in each pair contains a viable seed. The silver maple is perhaps the tallest of all the maples. The huge silver maple that grows at the edge of the meadow along Meadow Road in the Arnold Arboretum ranks as the tallest tree in the Arboretum, and it can provide visitors with a yardstick against which the height of other trees in the collection can be measured. Now more than one hundred years old—the seed from which it was grown was received in 1881—this giant towers one hundred ten feet above the alluvial soil in which it grows.

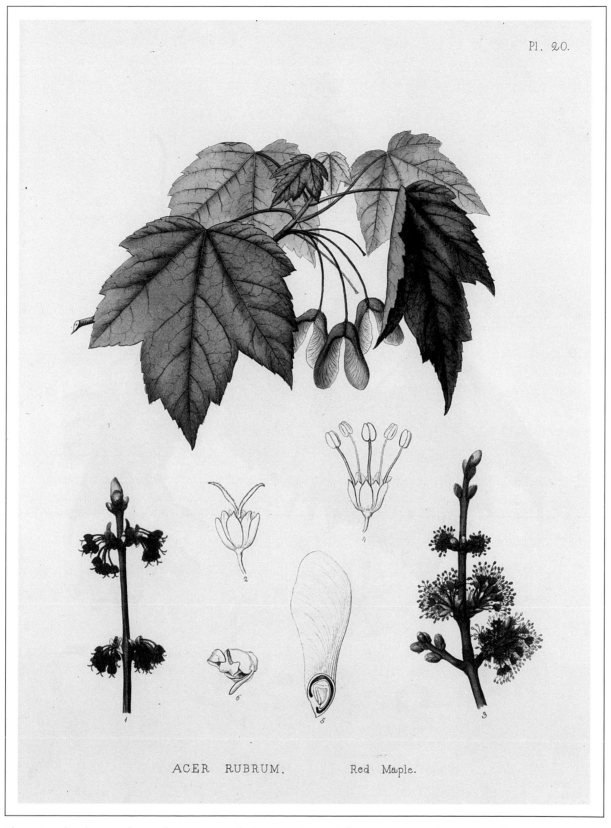

Pl. 20.

ACER RUBRUM. Red Maple.

Plate 21. This drawing depicts fruits (commonly known as "keys") and typical leaves of the red maple (*Acer rubrum*), a species that is extremely common in New England and one that enlivens the landscape with its brilliant fall color. The red maple is a variable species, however, and not all individuals produce the bright crimson fall coloration that is typical of the species and that is responsible, in part, for its specific epithet, *rubrum.* In some individuals, the leaves turn a dark burgundy; in others, the leaves assume a clear butter yellow before falling to the ground as the season advances.

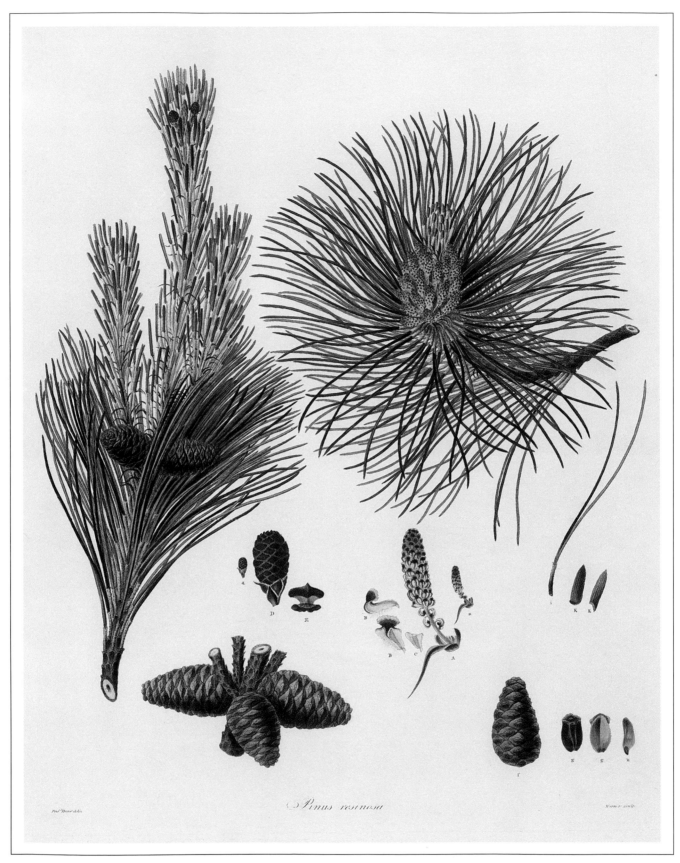

Pinus resinosa

Plate 22. The dark, shiny leaves, or needles, of the red pine (*Pinus resinosa*) are slender, flexible, and very soft, and they range in length from four to six inches. They grow two to a bundle, have sharply pointed tips, and are flattened on one side and rounded on the other.

Plate 23.   Although the witch hazel (*Hamamelis virginiana*) ranges widely in the deciduous forests of eastern North America, it is, perhaps, one of New England's most overlooked ornamental plants. Well-known as a fall-flowering shrub among horticulturists and widely available from nurseries, it is not a plant that is commonly encountered at local garden centers. Another species of the genus that often escapes the attention of home gardeners, *Hamamelis vernalis*, occurs primarily in the Ozark Mountains of the south-central United States. As its specific epithet indicates, *H. vernalis* flowers in the spring, from January to April. The addition of these two species to a garden landscape will extend its flowering season most satisfactorily

Plate 24 (*top*). The fruit of the black cherry (*Prunus serotina*), which grows in the wild in much of the eastern United States, has a sweetish, astringent, somewhat bitter taste. However, people assume that, because "wild cherry" cough drops taste sweet, and because they associate that sweet taste with the fruit of cultivated cherries, the lozenges that provide them with soothing relief from coughs and sore throats are made from the fruits of the wild or black cherry. It is the inner bark of *Prunus serotina*, however, not the fruit, that is used as an ingredient in cough medicines, in which it functions primarily as a flavoring agent.

Plate 24 (*bottom*). Taken from Michaux's *The North American Sylva*, this plate depicts the conelike fruit of the yellow birch (*Betula alleghaniensis*) and its oval, double-toothed leaves (that is, leaves ringed all around the margin with teeth of two sizes).

144 (*preceding page*). Although a Vermonter by the name of Mathew Lyon had made paper from a combination of basswood (*Tilia americana*) bark and rags as early as 1794, it was not until the middle of the nineteenth century that three different methods of making pulpwood were developed into commercially feasible processes. The soda method, the first to gain a foothold in America (in 1855), was perfected by Hugh Burgess of England and Morris Kean of Philadelphia. In Germany, Heinrich Voelter developed the groundwood process, in which pieces of wood were forced against a grindstone while a stream of water washed away the resulting ground-up fibers. By 1876, there were at least thirty American paper mills using the wood of poplar, spruce, and pine, as well as basswood and birch, in this process. The third method, the sulfite process, developed in Sweden, was adopted by another Pennsylvanian, Benjamin Tilghman. Lime and sulfurous acid rendered the cellular part of wood into fiber that could then be turned into pulp. In 1882, Providence, Rhode Island, was the site of the first successful paper mill that used the sulfite process. In both the soda and the sulfite processes, the logs were split and sent through a chipper. The chips were then screened to remove sawdust, dirt, and knots before being subjected to the appropriate chemicals.

145. Mechanization was slow to come to the logging industry. Trees were felled with axes until the end of the 1890s. From the turn of the century until about 1915, the raker-tooth crosscut saw was used almost exclusively. It was replaced by the one-man bucksaw, which, in turn, was replaced, in the 1950s, by the power-driven chain saw.

146. An island of trees surrounded by a lake covered with pulpwood. Environmental concerns had halted pulpwood log drives by the 1970s.

new source of virgin white pine. But the discovery that the spruces excelled in the length and strength of their wood fiber, which could easily be reduced into pulp, tipped the scales from pine to spruce in New England's logging industry.

The heart of the region's greatest stand of spruce is found where the climate is cold, the lakes are large and deep, and the topography is rough and mountainous. Spruces thrive on the high land whose streams feed the headwaters of rivers or flow into lakes with such names as Androscoggin, Magalloway, Cupsuptic, Kennebec, Penobscot, Chesuncook, and Kennebago—the chains of wild northern waters once known for their long-log

drives and still renowned for their fly fishing and land-locked salmon. There, deep in New England's north woods, one can see acre upon acre of blue-green foliage and smell the distinctive "polecat" odor of what lumbermen call the cat or skunk spruce (*Picea glauca*). More commonly known as the white spruce, it is a transcontinental species of the northern coniferous forest with a range that stretches across Canada from Newfoundland to Alaska. It is one of Canada's most widely distributed trees, and, being a major source of pulpwood and lumber, it is also one of Canada's most important economic species. Stands of white spruce are common in northernmost Vermont and New Hampshire and north of

147. The Hurricane of 1938 blew down so many white pines in northern New England that long-log river drives, which had been displaced by drives of four-foot pulpwood logs, were necessary once again to move the downed trees out of the forest while the wood was still sound and merchantable. This photograph shows men using peaveys to help boom the long logs across a lake in Maine known as Pond-in-the-River. Situated on the Rapid River, which flows between the Richardson Lakes in Maine and Lake Umbagog in Maine and New Hampshire, this lake and its surround provided the setting for books written by Louise Dickenson Rich in the 1930s. Her books told of her life as the wife of a Maine guide and contained colorful stories about meeting the independent characters who had made the Maine woods and logging their life. In *We Took to the Woods,* Ms. Dickenson described this last long-log drive, complete with the Boston newspaper photographers, flown in especially for the occasion, who were determined to capture on film the ideal "photogenic" woodsmen. It is very likely that Ms. Dickenson was on hand when this photograph, which accompanied the article on the drive published in the *Boston Globe,* was taken.

Casco Bay in Maine. This species also crosses the Canadian border into the United States in northern Minnesota and Wisconsin, central Michigan, and northeastern New York. The distribution of the black spruce, *P. mariana,* which is also transcontinental, is slightly smaller, but it follows closely that of the white spruce. Black spruce can grow a bit farther south in the eastern part of its range, and it appears not only in New England but also in isolated sites in southern New York and Pennsylvania. Black spruces inhabit the floating mats of sedges, mosses, and shrubs that form at the edges of small ponds. It is often the tree species that pioneers the slow evolution that transforms the north country's cold, acidic, tea-colored ponds into sphagnum bogs. Red spruce, *P. rubens,* is restricted to the East. In Canada, it is a major component of the Acadian Forest Region. It is absent from Rhode Island, but it occurs in the other five New England states. Scattered groves of red spruce also grow along the high ridges of the Appalachian Mountains southward into North Carolina. The characteristics of white, black, and red spruce wood are similar. All three woods are straight-grained, light in weight and color, odorless, tasteless, and, for conifers, low in resin content. Only in northeastern North America do the ranges of these three pulpwood species overlap.

Spruce and the Budworm

The twentieth century ushered in a new era in logging and papermaking. In 1899, the raker-tooth crosscut saw largely replaced the axe, and two of New England's paper mills destined to become giants—International Paper and Great Northern—had just been established. Before the advent of World War I, paper companies as a group had become the largest industrial landholder in New England.

In 1912, the annual cut of pulpwood first outstripped that of saw logs, but, over great expanses of the north woods, the provenance of the pulpwood logs, the forests were dying. The devastation was caused by a serious outbreak of the spruce budworm (the larval stage of the moth *Choristoneura fumiferana*) that had begun in 1909. Such outbreaks—which could, depending on their severity and length, leave the trees either dead or with their growth greatly retarded—appeared to recur in cycles. During a typical outbreak, the larvae emerged early in the spring and fed first on the tender new buds of the staminate flowers, then on the vegetative buds, and finally, by midsummer, they consumed the foliage of the developing shoots. A severe outbreak that lasted for at least three years usually killed the tops of the trees. After five years, many trees died, and, if the outbreak continued for another three years, it was unlikely that any infested tree would survive.

A history of the onset, length, and severity of an infestation can be read, in part, by studying the patterns that are formed by a tree's annual growth rings. When American and Canadian government entomologists traveled through the spruce forests in the 1890s collecting insect specimens, they observed growth rings in the stumps of trees that had been harvested and sought out information from the local inhabitants about earlier forest conditions. Farmers and loggers recalled stories they had heard of how a "worm" had riddled the north woods during the years preceding the War of 1812. One investigator was told the story of a farmer finding all the spruce trees dead on Harpswell Neck and Orrs Island, Maine, in 1807. For six weeks, the farmer used the spruce firewood to boil sea water to obtain salt, a provision that had been embargoed by England. Another lumberman recounted how his father often spoke of an insect that had caused the death of every spruce tree west of the Penobscot River in 1818.

The American and Canadian entomologists concluded that the first major outbreak of spruce budworm that they could chronicle with certainty came during the first two decades of the nineteenth century, and their field observations indicated that a second outbreak of the budworm began in 1870 and lasted for at least ten years. With many stands of spruce dead and others stag-headed and stunted, many lumbermen at that time had made the best of a bad situation and had simply felled the the dead and damaged trees. During the 1880 season, the currents of the Androscoggin, Kennebec, and Penobscot rivers carried more than 3 billion board feet of spruce, compared with only 200 million board feet of white pine.

While its common name implies that the spruce budworm targets species in the genus *Picea,* the balsam fir (*Abies balsamea*) is actually its preferred host. The budworm flourishes in mature and overly mature stands of balsam fir, feeding on spruce, as well as larch, hemlock, and pine, to a much lesser degree. It was a matter of economics and timing that wed the budworm's name to the spruce. When an 1909 outbreak galvanized government entomologists on both sides of the border to conduct investigations, the injury to spruce was the chief concern of lumbermen. At that time, balsam fir was considered a weed tree; its value as a pulpwood species would not be discovered for several years. Only then could the magnitude of loss that the pulpwood industry could sustain in a severe infestation of spruce budworm

148. The dark band of conifers in this photograph is one of the three stands of red spruce (*Picea rubens*) that grow on Mount Greylock in the area known as "The Hopper." The trees in these stands range in height from sixty to eighty feet and have diameters, at breast height, of from twelve to thirty inches. Estimates of their ages indicate that this part of the mountain has been undisturbed for at least one hundred fifty to one hundred eighty years. Although these trees are growing in extremely shallow soils and on steep topography that ranges from 60 percent to 100 percent slope, the trees are extremely healthy and spruce regeneration is very dense. Known as the Mt. Greylock Old Growth Spruce, these trees have been recognized by the United States Department of the Interior as being a significant example of our nation's natural heritage worthy of the status of a National Natural Landmark. In 1977, the rugged topography of the steep-walled, semicircular "Hopper" itself was formally designated by the Society of American Foresters as a Unique Natural Area.

149. In lumbering, log marks served the same function that cattle brands did in ranching. Log marks, not unlike cattle brands, were originally made up either of a combination of letters or a combination of letters and symbols cut or branded into the bark to ensure that, although the logs would be intermingled with those belonging to other companies during the long log drives that ended at the mill, each individual log would be credited to its proper owner. Before a log drive ended, men from each logging camp, stationed at sorting booms upstream from the mills, used the marks to identify their own particular logs, which they then rafted together and sent along downstream to the appropriate mills.

be appreciated, and only after the relation between the spruce budworm and balsam fir was understood could forest-management practices for containing the outbreaks begin to be formulated.

The discovery, in 1920, that hardwoods could also be used to make paper was driven, in part, by the damage wrought by the spruce budworm. Trees that survived the 1909 outbreak would not reach merchantable size until the 1950s. This predicament would set the course for New England's pulp and papermaking industry for the rest of the century. Making paper from hardwood species is more difficult and more expensive than production from softwoods or such diffuse-porous hardwoods as poplar or basswood, but the short hardwood fibers, while lacking strength, make a well-closed, smooth-surfaced paper. Technological advances in the last fifty years in the hardwood-pulping process, coupled with New England's stands of fine hardwoods, have enabled the region's papermakers to lead the nation in the production of specialty papers.

In Massachusetts, on the slopes of Mount Greylock, the state's highest mountain, where trees of the Northern Boreal and Hardwood Forests meet and mix with the Southern Hardwood Forest species, there are red spruce trees that have persisted for generations. Many of them grow in the Boreal Forest that covers the mountain's highest elevations. However, three distinct stands of un-

disturbed old-growth red spruce lie within an area that is populated by Northern Hardwood Forest trees, such as paper birch and yellow birch (*Betula papyrifera* and *B. lutea*) and sugar maple (*Acer saccharum*). This location, directly below Overlook Trail on the mountain's steepest slope, probably made these red spruce trees inaccessible to loggers. The old-growth red spruce trees are concentrated in a twenty-acre area located in "The Hopper," a steep-walled, semicircular valley that is shaped by two saddles that connect Mount Prospect, Mount Williams, and Stoney Ridge with the main Greylock ridge. The slopes of these mountains appear to meet at their bases, forming a hollow that suggests the shape of a huge grain hopper.

No other stand of red spruce exists in southern New England, and northern New England—which lies at the heart of this species' range—today has only a few areas of equal or larger size that contain red spruce trees that are as healthy or as vigorous. Once only natural causes and events (such as growth cycles, drought, fire, and hurricanes), combined with lumbering practices, influenced the status of red spruce. Now new factors that are not yet well understood have entered the equation. Unfortunately, it appears that air pollution and acid rain have plagued northern New England's red spruce stands, causing many of them to suffer a heavy and accelerating mortality rate during the last two decades.

150. Because of its durability, the American chestnut (*Castanea dentata*) was one of the species best suited for making railroad ties. Approximately 2500 ties were required to lay a mile of track, but each year, in order to maintain one mile of existing track, an additional five hundred new ties were needed. By 1890, the United States Forest Service estimated that the railroads were replacing seventy million ties annually and adding an additional nineteen million for new construction. Surprisingly, it could take as much as seventy-five feet of standing timber to produce a single eight-foot tie. In Connecticut, in 1909, the railroads were purchasing these heavy seven-foot by nine-inch chestnut ties for approximately seventy-two cents apiece.

Ties, Sleepers, and Keys—All of Wood

At the same time the pulp and paper companies were constructing mills, dams, conveyors, sluiceways, and gates and perfecting the art of driving logs on rivers, they were also building railroads. In this undertaking, however, they were not alone. All over the nation, men were laying down an ever-expanding web of wood and steel that would, in a span of fifty years, link cities with hamlets, raw material with factories, and products with consumers.

The construction of two short "roads" in 1826 inaugurated America's age of locomotion. Three of the initial twelve miles of railroad track carried granite from a quarry in Quincy; the remaining nine miles transported Pennsylvania coal from its source in a mine. The coal, which was used to stoke furnaces, disappeared, but the cargo that the Massachusetts Granite Railway carried became the building blocks of the Bunker Hill Monument, Boston's most familiar and prominent memorial to the Revolutionary War. From modest beginnings—both railroads depended upon a combination of gravity and horsepower to move their loads—grew a system that, by the nation's centennial in 1876, consisted of nearly eighty thousand miles of track.

Only a few railroads used wooden rails before switching to metal, but initially almost everything else—from wood-fired boilers to wooden trestle bridges, and the wooden "keys" that held track and ties together—came from the forests through which the railroads ran. Although replacing wood-burners with coal-fed steam engines reduced the annual consumption of fuel wood from an estimated high of 6.5 million cords at the start of the Civil War to 2 million during the 1880s, by the end of the century, their insatiable need for wood made it obvious that, as an industry, the railroads had surpassed agriculture as the greatest consumer of the forest.

The forested East, unlike the treeless prairie region, could keep pace with the industry's requirements. But the railroads, in turn, opened up areas for logging that had theretofore been inaccessible and fueled fears that the eastern forests would soon be depleted. Enormous numbers of trees did fall under the onslaught of the railroads, and waste was tremendous. Merchantable high-grade timber was funneled into railroad use rather than into other domestic industries, as trees that had not been harvested by lumbermen now fell under the farmer's ax to be sold to the railroad.

In 1890, 445,000 acres of timber went into ties alone and, if all other wood products used by the railroads were counted, between twenty and twenty-five percent of the annual forest production was consumed by what had become the nation's biggest business. The amount of wood that went into railroad ties served as a bellwether of the industry; the types of wood turned into ties pointed out its waste.

The preferred wood for ties was white oak (*Quercus alba*), the perennial building favorite. All other woods were measured against it for strength and durability. In reality, however, from the time the first ties were laid, the railroads purchased almost any sound wood they could, which usually meant the local native species that grew along each railroad's right-of-way. In New England, hemlock, cedar, and most of the native oaks were used, but the hardwood that most often measured up to the white oak's reputation for excellence was the American chestnut (*Castanea dentata*). While not quite as hard as white oak, the wood of the American chestnut was durable, stood up well to moisture, and was slightly more elastic and lighter in weight. In fact, when made into poles, its elasticity and lighter weight made chestnut preferable to oak.

The American chestnut was prevalent and a mainstay of the eastern forest. A tall, straight tree whose trunk diameter could exceed six feet, *Castanea dentata* reached its greatest height in the Appalachian Mountains, where it often grew in pure stands high on the ridges. Even on the thin, impoverished hillside soils of southern New England, where they grew in mixed stands with hickory, oak, and maple, chestnut trees often exceeded a height of eighty feet and were one of the most rapidly growing of New England's trees. Once cut, chestnut sprouted again from its roots. Soon, three to six harvestable coppice sprouts replaced the original tree. Chestnut trees also provided a type of tannin especially useful in processing heavy leathers, and the large quantity of edible nuts that they produced made them a valuable food resource for the farmer's family and fodder for the family's swine.

Chestnut served many a New Englander's needs for a wood that could withstand rough conditions over a long time. The farmer favored chestnut for the construction of barns and outbuildings, with roofs, shingles, siding, and beams all from the same tree. It had finer uses, too; chestnut wood was made into interior paneling and trim, and furniture, from cradles to desks, was commonly constructed of chestnut with an oak veneer. Its abundance and its ability to sprout—one of its most noted characteristics—coupled with its rapid growth, versatile wood, and bountiful nuts, made *Castanea dentata* one of New England's most valuable hardwood trees.

But it was with the great expansion of the railroads

151. In 1846, George B. Emerson published an assessment he had made of the woody flora of the state of Massachusetts for the Zoological and Botanical Survey that Governor Everett had commissioned in 1837. In his *Report on the Trees and Shrubs Growing Naturally in the Forests of Massachusetts,* Emerson enumerated the trees and shrubs growing in the Commonwealth. He also located and measured many of the outstanding specimens of each species and added liberal doses of his own opinion as to the value and merit of each tree. He championed the American chestnut, which he knew by the botanical name *Castanea vesca* var. *Americana,* as being both an exceptionally beautiful and an economically important tree. Emerson felt that old pasture chestnuts, such as the one illustrated here in a photograph taken in Ware, Massachusetts, should be spared as, in his opinion, "An old chestnut throws out arms almost as strong as the oak, and its foliage forms as beautiful a mass and a thicker shade. The chestnut flourishes on rocky hills, where there is no great depth of soil, on a surface difficult of tillage, and fit for pasture or forest. Of the many acres of this description in various parts of the state, especially in the middle counties, it is to be hoped that a portion will be spared to this valuable and rapidly growing tree."

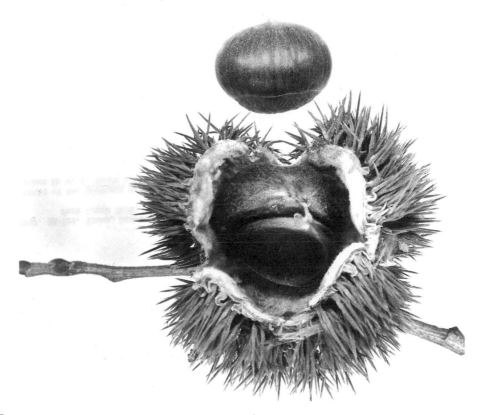

152. Chestnut trees bloom in late summer, long after most other trees have blossomed. The first flowers that appear are the showy, cream-colored catkins of the staminate (or pollen-bearing) male flowers. Slightly later appear the less noticeable nut-producing (or carpellate) flowers, which consist of small, spikelike green scales. Although chestnut trees are monoecious, with both sexes appearing on the same tree, cross-pollination, facilitated by the wind rather than by insects, seems to be necessary in order for viable seed to be produced. Sometimes only one of the carpellate flowers will be fertilized and produce a prickly bur, but often two or three will mature into edible nuts. By the middle of August, the sharp-spined burs have reached full size, and at maturity the spiny husks, having changed in color from green to brown, will split open to expose the enclosed bright, shiny brown, sweet-tasting nuts.

153. The American chestnut was primarily a tree of the southern Appalachians, and its loss, through the blight, was an economic blow to the region. In 1937, A. W. Brooks published a paper on *Castanea dentata* in *The Journal of the Southern Appalachian Botanical Club* and, in recognition of of the chestnut's demise, the genus name *Castanea* was added to the journal's title. Today, the journal continues to be published under the name *Castanea*. In his article, Brooks described the taxonomic and economic aspects of the tree and also recounted his memories of its sentimental and social attributes. "In central West Virginia, where the writer lived on a farm the woodlands of which were well stocked with chestnut, it was the good practice of farmers to leave groups of scattered trees in certain fields as chestnut groves. These were the delightful resorts of young and old when October frosts had opened the burs and showered the nuts to the ground. . . . The choicest of the nuts were gathered and eaten fresh, roasted or boiled, or were hoarded for winter consumption. In some sections country boys and girls sold enough nuts to buy their winter clothes and school books." Winslow Homer's illustration, entitled "Chestnutting," was published on 29 October 1870 in *Every Saturday* and shows a well organized system of gathering chestnuts.

that chestnut wood was put to its greatest use. Trains rode rails laid on chestnut ties that ran over trestles constructed of chestnut piles; chestnut telegraph poles followed alongside the fencing that hung on chestnut posts. The railroads consumed such an abundance of chestnut wood (8 million ties were purchased in 1908 alone) that, although the chestnut cut in Connecticut in 1909 amounted to more than 46 percent of the lumber cut in the state—double the amount of all softwoods and nearly more than all other hardwoods combined—the

Forest Service reported that Connecticut's "cabinet manufactures and others using finishing lumber find it well nigh impossible to obtain seasoned and well-graded stock of sufficient length for their needs and are compelled to import their chestnut, often from distant points." Connecticut farmers and small woodlot owners preferred to sell their chestnut stock to the railroads, which provided a market that was not only stable but seemingly insatiable.

Almost half a century before, Henry David Thoreau

154. During the early 1900s, hundreds of millions of bushels of chestnuts were produced on hundreds of thousands of acres in the eastern United States. Almost all of the nuts were gathered from the wild, with few coming from commercial chestnut orchards. While many were sold in country stores or on the street, the rest went by rail into the produce houses of the cities, where, at the beginning of the season, chestnuts sold for as much as three dollars a bushel. Only a small percentage of chestnuts were sold in American markets; American chestnuts were considered to be so superior in taste to those of the European and Asiatic species that most of the nuts were exported. Today, however, the reverse is true. Because of the blight, chestnuts sold in stores or purchased already roasted from street-corner venders, such as this one the Boston Common, are the nuts of exotic species, which have been imported from the other chestnut growing regions of the world.

had been fearful of the loss of the chestnut to the railroads. Upon finding a "cluster of little chestnuts six inches high" in an oak and pine wood, Thoreau penned this passage in his journal for 17 October 1860: "It is well known that the chestnut timber of this vicinity has rapidly disappeared within fifteen years, having been used for railroad sleepers, for rails, and for planks, so that there is danger that this part of our forest will become extinct."

The American chestnut would withstand the demands the railroads made for its timber, but Thoreau's premonition of its extinction would almost come to pass.

Ornament and Improvement: Street and Shade Trees

New Englanders had expended countless hours, axes, and saw blades—and even many precious lives—removing trees, one by one, from the forest they wished to turn

155. In winter, the solitary fruits of the American plane tree or sycamore (*Platanus occidentalis*) distinguish it from the hybrid London plane tree (*Platanus × acerifolia*), which of the two is the more widely planted street tree. While the buttonball fruits of these two trees are virtually impossible to tell apart when detached, those of the London plane tree are always borne in pairs.

into fields. By 1850, cleared land had reached its greatest extent in Rhode Island. The victory of plough over forest came in Connecticut a decade later, and, by 1870, farmers could claim the same achievement in Massachusetts. Not since the era of glacial retreat had the underlying land forms of southern New England been so exposed. Nor had the upland interior country of northern New England been spared its trees. From their pastures and fields, hill-country farmers in Vermont, New Hampshire, and Maine had a clear view down into the valleys, with the clusters of houses that made up the towns, and could see, rising up on distant hills, a patchwork of small, irregularly shaped clearings that mirrored their own. In all, 23 million acres, slightly more than half of New England's land mass, had been cleared of its virgin forest.

At the same time that New England's agricultural industry was reaching its zenith, the industrial revolution and the coming of the railroads had given rise to the growth of many of its towns. In 1840, less than one-fifth of the population lived in towns; forty years later, more than two million people—slightly more than half of all New Englanders—resided in towns with populations of 2,500 or more. By the 1880s, many of these towns had a prosperous and well-tended appearance, owing, to a great degree, to the preceding generations of public-spirited individuals who, contrary to the prevailing convention of their farmer "cousins," had planted trees.

The early popularity of the American elm (*Ulmus americana*) and other native species—such as the American sycamore or buttonwood (*Platanus occiden-*

talis) and the silver maple (*Acer saccharinum*)—as street trees can be explained, in part, by an agricultural tradition, European in origin, that equated the presence of certain trees with the quality or "sweetness" of the soil. European settlers staked agricultural claim to New England's river-valley meadowlands; homesites were clustered in nearby villages on higher ground above the reach of the waters of the annual spring flood, which yearly added to the fertility of the low-lying fields. The vase-shaped silhouette of the elm, the bone-white crowns of the buttonwood, and the trailing branches of the silver maple indicated deep, fertile, relatively rock-free alluvial soil. Like other fast-growing bottom-land species, these trees thrive in spite of alternating periods of flood and drought—circumstances as demanding as those that street trees must endure—and the presence of these trees came to indicate not only fertile soil but abundant harvests and prosperous villages.

The American sycamore (*Platanus occidentalis*) possesses a strikingly attractive element found on no other native tree. Between the clay-colored, yellow-brown, ridged bark at its base and its smooth, gray, almost whitewashed upper branches is a unique piebald trunk whose massive size exceeds that of any other eastern hardwood. Along its gray, elephantine bole and huge limbs, the bark flakes off in irregular plates to expose a patchwork of mottled buff or greenish-tinged inner bark. *Platanus* is from the Greek *platys*, "broad," and refers to the width of the leaves; *occidentalis* is Latin for "western," from *occidere*, "to set," as with the sun. Sycamore leaves look very much like those of some maples, but, unlike those of maples, which grow opposite one another, these leaves are placed alternately along the twig, where each leaf stalk completely encircles the bud of next year's growth. The three species of *Platanus* native to the United States share the common names buttonwood and buttonball because of their spherical fruits. During spring, these small, inconspicuous male and female flowers appear in tight clusters on separate stalks that are produced near the tips of the branches. After pollination, each female flower in the cluster produces a small, dry, one-seeded fruit called an achene. The seeds, which have a number of stiff brownish hairs attached to their base, are packed tightly together in dense, spherical heads that are reminiscent of an old-fashioned leather button. The fruits persist throughout winter and well into spring, making each tree look as if decorated by someone who has carefully assigned a "bauble" to the end of each of its branch tips. The buttonballs disintegrate slowly, and, as each seed separates from the cluster, the hairs aid in the seed's dispersal.

Known also as the plane tree, and in the past as the whitewood, the eastern American species of *Platanus* grows from the Atlantic coast westward to the edge of the Great Plains. The climate of Massachusetts, Connecticut, and Rhode Island, and of scattered parts of coastal Maine, suits the American sycamore, and, through its propensity to thrive along watercourses, its range extends northward into Vermont's Champlain and Hoosic valleys and along the Connecticut River as far north as Hartford, Vermont.

Because of their age and size, the most impressive trees of the genus *Platanus* that grow in the Arnold Arboretum are three specimens of *P. × acerifolia*, the London plane tree. The origins of this hybrid are unclear, but it is believed that a natural cross between *P. occidentalis* and *P. orientalis* (the Old World species) that occurred in England around 1670 produced the tree now known as the London plane tree. *P. × acerifolia* is hardier and more tolerant of urban conditions than either of its parents, and it is the most extensively planted of the three. Our native species, *P. occidentalis*, can usually be distinguished from the London plane tree by the number of "buttonballs" that dangle from the ends of each of the branches. The American species has solitary fruits; those of the London plane tree come in pairs. The Arnold Arboretum's *Platanus* collection is located just inside the Centre Street Gate at the beginning of Valley Road. Three young *P. occidentalis* that complement the Arboretum's grand, century-old trees and insure that a new generation of buttonwoods will mature at the Arboretum during the next hundred years have been planted across from the main collection of *Platanus* at the edge of Bussey Hill Road.

By the middle of the nineteenth century, not only were individuals planting trees but "improvement societies" had been sprouting up in towns and villages even faster than the saplings that their members planted. Tree-lined streets and well-shaded greens exemplified modern civic ideals and provided esthetic, sanitary, and economic values. It was during this time that the nation's horticulturists first turned their attention to street and shade trees. To their observations and remarks on the qualities that made good street trees they added those that made good citizens, and they urged their readers to go beyond the boundaries of their properties and ornament their villages. After all, as Andrew Jackson Downing pointed out, were not the sylvan and charming streets and greens of many an old New England town but a reflection of the character, intelligence, and civic-mindedness of their early inhabitants? If any of his readers doubted that

156. With industrialization and urbanization having changed the face of the New England landscape by the last quarter of the nineteenth century, Americans wholeheartedly embraced not only the social, civic, and aesthetic values associated with the planting of trees, but their screening and softening virtues as well. The care and planting of trees along roadways and on city streets was being addressed in popular publications. The advent of Arbor Day in 1872, made tree planting festivals, such as this one held in Hingham, Massachusetts, annual events. The refreshments offered at the end of the day reflect this town's seaside location on Boston's south shore.

GRAND
Tree Planting Festival!

A Grand Tree Planting Festival will take place under the auspices of the

HINGHAM AGRICULTURRAL & HORTICULTURAL SOCIETY,

On their Grounds,

On WEDNESDAY, May 1st, 1878.

Members and friends of the Society are invited to meet on the Grounds any time during the day, prepared to furnish and plant one or more trees. A Committee will be in attendance to designate locations.

Clam Chowder and Coffee

Will be served at 4 o'clock P. M., to which all contributors are invited.

Per Order of the Committee of Arrangements.

HINGHAM, MAY 23, 1878.

Journal Press, Hingham.

worn-out, stubbly, deforested, and overgrazed pieces of land could be improved by the addition of trees and the lapse of a hundred years or more, they needed only to heed Downing's advice and "set out on a pilgrimage to such places as Northampton, Springfield, New Haven, Pittsfield, Stockbridge, Woodbury and the like."

In Woodstock, Vermont, the villagers had struggled for some time to improve the barren look of the town center. Their early efforts had failed; the trees they set out on the common "were slightly protected and did not last long." Finally, in 1830, "a subscription was raised, a meeting was held, a committee was appointed, and each boy in town acquired the task of taking care of a portion of the newly planted Green." The Committee achieved its goal:

the trees thrived and the green gained a white rail fence (replaced in 1878 with one made of iron); the barrenness of the prospect had been greatly improved. In New Hampshire, members of the Dartmouth Ornamental Tree Planting Society set out maples and elms in the spring of 1844, and, in the fall of that year, in Keene, at the town meeting, a motion "to see if the Town will permit the Forest Tree Society to fence and ornament with trees a small central portion of the commons" was voted on and approved.

Town and village improvement societies did not hold a monopoly on the crusade to plant trees. Prompted by the pall of smoke and grime that industrialization inflicted on urban life, a city-beautification movement also sprang

157. This humble cottage is dwarfed by a hundred-year-old silver maple. Belonging to a species that long ago fell out of favor as a street tree, this magnificent specimen belies the admonition, written, presumably, by Charles Sprague Sargent in an editorial published in *Garden and Forest* in 1891, that "It is this rapidity of growth that has made the Silver Maple a favorite with people who are in a hurry to obtain immediate effects and do not care to look too far ahead." It was not, however, the ornamental qualities of this maple that Sargent objected to, but, rather that, although silver maples did well on dry upland sites for their first fifty years or so, they would not thrive in these situations.

into being. Large public projects—guided by such men as Frederick Law Olmsted, engaged in a new discipline that he had christened "landscape architecture"—began civilizing cities by reintroducing nature through the addition of trees, open spaces, and quiet surroundings. In cities, not only did trees have to thrive in spite of being "surrounded by smoke and dust, beset by bruises and accidents, and having pavement covering their roots" but they also had to meet the horticultural fashion of the day. During the prosperity that followed the end of the Civil War, many of New England's existing street trees were threatened by the rapid expansion of the cities, and measures were taken not only to maintain these trees but to add new ones along the newly widened roadways. The

resurgence in national pride that came after the war also sparked a renewed interest in the native flora, and many of the exotic trees that had been in fashion fell out of favor, as horticulturists championed the planting of native species.

"Stateliness and symmetry, large and abundant foliage, healthiness, cleanliness," and, most important, the ability to "transplant easily, grow rapidly, and be patient under difficulties" were qualities considered to be de rigueur at the time. The silver maple, a favorite of earlier generations and a rapid grower, appeared to meet these requirements. As Andrew Jackson Downing had observed in a essay on street trees, "rapid growth is an argument too powerful to be resisted, especially in a community

158. In Charles Sprague Sargent's opinion, the silver maple "is one of the largest and most beautiful trees in a genus peculiar for the beauty of its species [but] is a valuable tree in ornamental planting only when it can be placed in deep, rich, and moist meadow-land or by the banks or streams or lakes." Obviously, when he sited this tree at the edge of the wetland beside Meadow Road, Sargent had his own advice in mind and chose an appropriate location. Planted in 1881 and now, at approximately 110 feet in height, the tallest tree in the Arnold Arboretum, this magnificent silver maple has attained the the classic proportions and grace that great age and perfect growing conditions can bestow on this species.

where there exists an active rivalry as to who shall produce the greatest results in the shortest time." Although the criteria for selecting a street tree today differ from those of the last century, people were as impressed with instant results then as they are now.

Silver maples (*Acer saccharinum*) often grow several feet in their first year, and, at maturity, they become the tallest of our maples. The bole, or trunk, of a silver maple usually supports several large ascending limbs of equal or nearly equal size that begin to branch out from the trunk a short distance from the ground. These large limbs often remain clear of major branches until they reach nearly to the top of the tree, where smaller branches divide at wide angles to form a broad, full crown. Secondary branches curve down, sweeping up again at their ends. This almost weeping form, with the branch tips turning up, is so characteristic that this maple can often be identified from some distance by its shape alone.

The silver in this tree's common name refers to the color of its deeply lobed, sharp-pointed, and sharp-toothed leaves; they are pale green on the upper side and distinctly silvery white beneath. In fall, the leaves turn a pale, almost translucent yellow. The yellow-green flowers of *Acer saccharinum* appear late in the winter at the first hint of spring, just ahead of the flowers of the red maple, *A. rubrum*. Like those of the elm, the flowers of the silver maple are inconspicuous. And, also like those of the elm, the female flowers of the silver maple mature into winged fruits in a very short time. The seeds of both species germinate quickly, and their seedlings become well established by the fall. If the trees of swamp and bottom land flowered later and their seeds did not ripen until fall and germinate until the following spring, it is likely that they would be unable to germinate or survive on flooded bottom land.

Residents of the prairie and plains states were also persuaded to plant trees. In January 1872, J. Sterling Morton, the Governor of Nebraska and a proponent of tree planting on a large scale, introduced to the state's legislature the concept of setting aside one day each year for citizens to plant trees. His constituency took up the idea with a vengeance and reportedly set out more than a million saplings as windbreaks and in shelterbelt plantations that spring during the nation's first "Arbor Day."

Prompted by "the desire to ward off the rigorous winds of northwestern prairies, and to supply fuel as well," the crusade to modify a harsh environment swept across Nebraska's treeless plains and into surrounding states. Eventually, each state in the Union adopted legislation that decreed an annual Arbor Day. In 1948, a National Arbor Day Committee established a date—the last Friday of April—on which the event would take place nationwide. While Nebraskans could righteously claim to have planted an estimated 700,000 acres of trees within fifty years, what had begun as a movement to turn the great American prairie into a well-wooded land did not succeed.

Arbor Day itself, however, was a huge success, because the concept had gained support from another sector. The idea of a day devoted to planting trees had the enthusiastic backing of the nation's schoolteachers, who were concerned that city-bred children knew nothing of wild nature. Within a few years of its inception, the celebration of Arbor Day became a well-established annual event and one of the highlights of the school calendar year. Elaborate ceremonies, complete with marches, songs, poems, and readings, accompanied the actual tree planting, which usually took place on school grounds.

In 1894, as part of an Arbor Day celebration, Rhode Island schoolchildren voted for their favorite tree from a slate of ten. A total of 16,776 ballots were cast, and the maple garnered 5750 votes. (The elm was a close second, with 5260.) The state school superintendent's report for the following year declared the contest a success, as "a good deal of interest in the subject was aroused, and the comparative merits and demerits of the various trees were discussed most voraciously on all sides." Seventy years later, when the Rhode Island Federation of State

Arbor Day Manual.

AN AID IN

Preparing Programs

FOR

Arbor Day Exercises.

CONTAINING

Choice Selections on Trees, Forests, Flowers, and Kindred Subjects; Arbor Day Music, Specimen Programs, etc.

EDITED AND COMPILED BY

CHARLES R. SKINNER, A.M.

SUPERINTENDENT OF PUBLIC INSTRUCTION, STATE OF NEW YORK

SECOND EDITION

SYRACUSE, N. Y.
C. W. BARDEEN, PUBLISHER
1896

159. At first, the idea of a setting aside a day for planting trees was popularized by agricultural associations and town committees, but, by about 1882, only ten years after its inception, Arbor Day became a school festival. Arbor Day manuals, such as this one, published by the school superintendent of New York, helped students and teachers celebrate the day. Each state's publication contained programs that included appropriate activities and instructions on what trees to plant and how and where to plant them.

Garden Clubs supported legislation to have the children's choice made official, they carried the selection a step further and specified the *red* maple. Official legislation was passed and approved on 1 March 1964, in time for the Arbor Day celebration that year. The red maple complements nicely the state bird, another sturdy and dependable native, a laying chicken bred in the state and named the Rhode Island Red.

Acer rubrum has been cultivated as an ornamental tree since the mid-1600s, when one of America's English explorers carried it home to be grown in a garden near London. This species can prosper in almost any type of soil on land that can be wet or dry. True to another one of its common names, swamp maple, *A. rubrum* is a denizen of pond edges, stream banks, and especially poorly drained areas, where it grows in stands so dense that it is hard to find another type of tree. The most common tree in eastern North America, the red maple has the widest north-to-south range of any eastern tree species, and it is familiar to almost anyone living east of the 100th meridian.

The name *rubrum* means red or ruddy, and this color is truly an aid to the tree's identification during each season of the year. Late in March or early in April, when most trees are still in their winter dormancy, red maple trees begin to flower. At a distance, male flowers look almost orange because of their bright yellow stamens, while the female flowers are crimson. A red maple will usually have either male or female flowers, but sometimes both will appear on different branches of the same tree. On early spring mornings, low, boggy areas can seem bathed in a red mist—the effect of great masses of maple flowers. As the flowers fade and drop their petals—after a spring rain, sidewalks and streets beneath them can be covered with maple flowers—the winged fruits begin to develop from the carpellate flowers. These are the lightest of all maple fruits, and they hang in clusters on long reddish stalks. While still immature, the bright pink to red fruits stand out among the new, light green leaves of spring. At maturity, the fruits redden in pleasing contrast to the leaves, which by then have darkened to a deep emerald green.

It is not unusual to find a red maple beginning to develop its autumn color by the end of September. Pigments that have been in the leaves all summer are now unmasked in response to the change in temperature and the length of day. Shorter warm days and longer cool nights stop the cells in the leaves from manufacturing food. This food-manufacturing process has been taking place all summer in the cells that contain chlorophyll, and

160. Elaborate Arbor Day ceremonies, complete with marches, poems, readings, and singing, such as the one illustrated here, accompanied the actual planting, which usually took place on school grounds. However, it was with this support from the schools that the scope of Arbor Day eventually transcended both the schoolyard and the common and became the vehicle by which citizens became educated about the importance of forestry and the planting of seedling trees.

now the chlorophyll, which is a green pigment, breaks down, allowing the other colors—yellow, orange and red—to become visible. At this time of year, many red maples look as if they have burst into flame.

In winter, the twigs at the ends of the branches are crimson, and they are studded with small brown spots called lenticels. These twigs, the tree's newest growth, were green at first, but they will remain crimson all winter. The younger branches are a smooth, silvery gray; young trees are almost entirely silver. As the trees age, the bark on the bigger, older branches becomes dark and rough. The trunks of older trees are darker still, with the bark broken into furrows or ridges.

Red and silver maples are among the 120 species of *Acer* that grow in the Arboretum's maple collection. Good examples of both of these species, along with other wetland trees and shrubs, can also be found alongside Willow Path and Maple Path. Willow Path follows the

161. Open-grown red maples (*Acer rubrum*) form a symmetrical shape that makes them desirable both as street or shade trees and as a specimen tree on the front lawn. This classic red maple was photographed in Mattapan, Massachusetts, by Ernest Henry Wilson in November 1924. Although Wilson introduced many outstanding exotic ornamental trees into American gardens, when asked by Richardson Wright, the editor of *House & Garden*, to list his ten favorite trees, his first choice was the native red maple.

sliver of high ground between the meadow and the Arborway, while Maple Path lies between Meadow Road and the meadow itself.

In the Arboretum during August of each year, when the summer doldrums have settled in and have stilled the leaves on all the trees, there is a maple that quickens to the coming season. *Acer rubrum* 'Schlesingeri,' a cultivar of the red maple that Charles Sprague Sargent discovered growing in a neighbor's yard in Brookline in the 1880s, is the Arboretum's flagship tree of fall. The tree, whose early fall color Sargent thought unusual enough to justify naming the tree in honor of his neighbor, has grown across from the Visitor Center, just inside the main entrance at the beginning of Willow Path, since 1888. A hint of red can often be seen in its leaves by Labor Day, and, by the middle of September, this tree alone among all the Arboretum's late summer greenery has caught fire with a deep vibrant red that signals an end to the growing season and provides a preview of New England's arboreal passage into fall.

Two vines have clambered up its trunk and bedecked its limbs. Purpleleaf wintercreeper, *Euonymus fortunei* 'Colorata,' also known under the cultivar name *Euonymus fortunei* 'Purple-leaf,' is one of the hardiest of the broadleaf evergreens in the genus. This vine uses rootlike holdfasts to cling to walls, tree trunks, or any other surfaces with which it comes in contact. In the fall, its pale pink capsules split open to expose bright orange berries, and its leaves turn a dark purplish red above and a lighter shade of this same hue on their undersides. These purple-colored leaves become most apparent after the second vine, which is deciduous, has lost its leaves. Although *Parthenocissus tricuspidata* is native to Asia, it has so successfully attached itself to the city's buildings and walls that the common name Boston ivy has become just as well affixed to this exotic vine. In the summer, this tenacious climber has bright green leaves. In the fall, about a month after the "Schlesinger maple" has turned color, the leaves of the Boston ivy turn yellow, gold, and scarlet in pleasing contrast with the still-green leaves of the euonymus and the bright red leaves of the maple.

The name *rubra*, another form of the Latin word for red, denotes a species of oak that rivals the red maple as a companion of sidewalks and roadways. *Quercus rubra*, a tree intolerant of wet soils and the most northern of our oaks, is New England's upland counterpart of the red maple, but the northern red oak displays its red in more subdued and subtle ways. In summer, only in the midribs of its dull green leaves can a reddish tint be found. In fall, the red oak's leaves turn a russet hue and its large,

162. Unlike their darker hues of summer, the springtime colors of oak leaves are pastel grays, pinks, and soft shades of red. The northern red oak (*Quercus rubra*) flowers when its unfurling leaves are about half grown. At this stage, the leaves are a pinkish color and are covered with downy, silky, pale hairs on the upper surface and thick, dense, wooly white hairs on their underside. The male and female flowers are in separate catkins. The small, pink-budded, male (or staminate) flowers are arranged in slender drooping catkins that are four to five inches long and appear in clusters near the tips of the previous year's branchlets. The female (or carpellate) catkin is a tiny, often solitary, few-flowered spike that emerges from the point at which the petiole of a new leaf is attached to the twig from which it grew.

163. Better knowledge of how trees grow has led to changes in the way trees are planted since this detailed illustration of the process was published in 1932. The original instructions have been amended to include the more recent discoveries:

1. A tarp or, better still, a wheelbarrow, to hold soil removed from the planting hole, makes the job easier.

2. It is best to work the soil a considerable distance beyond where the tree will be planted. The hole need not be straight-walled or deep-walled; a hole shaped like a satellite dish is recommended. The hole should be large enough to accommodate the roots without crowding. Twice the width of the root ball is sufficient; three times the width is better.

3. Be sure the hole drains freely; break up hardpan subsoil, if present—good drainage is essential.

4. Reasonably good soil will not have to be amended. Some studies even indicate that trees do best in soil that has not been amended.

5. Do not plant too deeply, because this can cause root problems. Plant the tree at the same depth at which it grew in the nursery. In clay soil, a slight mounding of the soil is acceptable.

6. If the tree is balled-and-burlapped, set it in the hole and then either untie and remove the burlap or pull it down to expose the root ball entirely. Otherwise, the burlap may girdle the roots. With a container-ized specimen, it is important to loosen the roots so that they may grow outward. Remove any broken or damaged pieces of root, making clean cuts, and then spread the roots naturally in the hole.

7. Replace the soil, working it carefully around and between the roots.

8. A tamping stick may be used to firm the soil around the roots. After the tree is planted, do not stomp down the soil around the tree; instead, press down gently with the palms of your hands.

9. Soak the tree until the whole root ball is thoroughly soaked; then keep the root system moist but not wet.

10. Conventional wisdom once called for extensive pruning; often, the top of the tree was cut back to make it conform to the size of the root ball. This can cause injury to the tree. Trim only broken, damaged, or diseased branches and those that cross or otherwise detract from the the tree's habit.

11. Do not prune back the central leader or stem, as this will result in undesirable forking. Avoid trees that have two or more leaders of equal size. If you are working with a tree with more than one leader, remove all but one.

12. Although large trees or those in exposed situations may need to be staked, it is best to stake as little as possible. An unstaked tree will develop a stronger root system. When staking can not be avoided, use webbing or flat strapping to protect the trunk.

13. Leave a cultivated area around the tree. This helps to prevent mowing injuries.

14. A mulch applied after planting will serve both practical and aesthetic purposes.

---

shallow-cupped acorns have only a slight reddish cast. During winter, its buds and twigs are a dull reddish brown. In spring, when their leaves unfold and their trailing tasslelike flowers begin to open, these massive trees assume the most gentle, soft-toned pink of spring. But neither flower nor leaf inspired Linnaeus to apply the binomial *Quercus rubra*. It is from the reddish color of its hard, heavy, coarse-grained wood that this tree takes its name.

Extensively planted in the early part of this century, the red oak, with its tall, sturdy bole, its stout spreading limbs, and its symmetrical, round-topped crown, was an attractive choice for shading broad avenues and parkways. In Boston, these long-lived, relatively fast growing oaks provide a sense of esthetic continuity in the chain of parkways that constitute Frederick Law Olmsted's "Emerald Necklace."

There is one native oak that is much more likely to be found along our roads than in our forests. The pin oak, *Quercus palustris*, has been one of the most frequently planted street trees in the eastern and central states. Unlike the red oak, which is one of New England's most common trees, the northern limit of the pin oak's range extends only into the southern and western parts of our region. Unlike most oaks, both the red oak and the pin oak transplant easily—a must for street trees—but they differ in their habitat. The shallow root system of the red oak allows it to thrive in the sparse, dry soil of ridge tops; the pin oak's shallow roots, which grow in the hydric (or moisture-saturated) soil above the water table, enable it

PROCESS *of* PLANTING   FINISHED PLANTING

to persist in a wetland environment. The pin oak is a flood-plain and bottom-land species that is able to survive the effects of standing water for weeks at a time. In New England, naturally occuring pin oaks are seldom found growing any distance from a watercourse. Their Latin name suits them well: *palustris* means "of marshes" or "marsh loving." Pin oaks differ from all other oaks in their habit. Whether they grow in the open or in forests, their trunks are straight and mastlike from root to crown, without forks, twists, turns, or diversions, and the branches that encircle their trunks are arranged in a curious semiformal and fanlike pattern. The uppermost branches ascend, those of the middle tier grow at right angles to the trunk, and the lowest ones droop downward. The branches have such a large number of short, pointed spurlike twigs that the common name "pin oak" is an eminently suitable name for this species. The leaves of the pin oak are similar to those of the red oak, but they look as if a designer had taken a pair of shears to the leaf of a red oak and, by snipping away and making deeper sinuses and sharper-toothed lobes with more gracefully tapered tips, turned the red oak leaf into a streamlined fashion statement.

A New Forest Type—Urban Forest

In the course of time, many of the civic-improvement groups concerned with planting trees succeeded in turning their program into public policy and so relinquished their authority to local governments. In New Hampshire, the Laws of 1858 authorized the mayor and aldermen of Portsmouth to "set out trees and shrubbery on public squares and highways at the expense of the city." Similar laws followed in each of the New England states, and, eventually, in Massachusetts, the Tree Warden Act of 1899 (the first such law in the nation) provided the mechanism by which every town and municipality in the Commonwealth could select an individual to be charged with responsibility for the planting, care, and protection of street trees. New Hampshire and Connecticut had their wardens in place by 1902. Initially, the wardens' duties included, but were not limited to, shielding their charges from horses' teeth (the wardens erected metal guards to encircle the trees), from fumes escaping from underground gas pipes (they learned the symptoms of carbon monoxide poisoning and did their best to detect leaks), and from defacement, the posting of bills, and unauthorized removal (they cited violators and collected fines).

The management of street trees changed dramatically within the next fifty years. The smoke pollution produced by the mills and factories in New England's booming industrial centers created only the first of many problems in the struggle to grow trees in cities. The urban centers themselves, linked together by railroads and trolley lines, overflowed their limits and spilled into neighboring towns. On city streets, horse-drawn trolleys—and, later, electric trolleys—carried everyone to and from home and work. As the number of multiple dwellings and the people they held increased along the trolley routes, streets were widened, lots were subdivided, and many venerable trees were taken down. Some well-to-do citizens used the railroads to flee the squalor and the crowded tenements of the older cities and what once had been "model" factory towns. They established themselves in more agreeable countryside surroundings, creating the new suburbs that grew up around railroad stations. Beautifying the stations and the railroad rights-of-way along these commuter train corridors became an enthusiasm among station masters, passenger agents, and even some townships and civic-improvement groups. Some stations and their surrounds were planned and planted by the leading architects and landscape architects of the day. Frederick Law Olmsted joined forces with his friend and Brookline neighbor Henry Hobson Richardson in designing the stations and landscapes of the "Newton Circuit" (now Riverside Line), the commuting line of the Boston & Albany Railroad that ran through one of Boston's wealthiest suburbs.

Although train and trolley lines dictated growth on a linear progression, clusters of these newly created suburban communities that were dispersed like beads along the transportation lines resulted in the beginnings of urban sprawl. After World War II, when automobile ownership had become common, a new generation of potential homeowners was no longer bound by the old linear mass-transportation routes. On the remaining rural farms and in the many pockets of "unimproved" land that had formerly been out of reach, developers staked out subdivisions made up of equal-sized parcels upon which a new crop, one of houses, would grow. The 1950s ushered in the era of the freeway, the interstate highway, and unprecedented urban growth.

Sometime during the middle of the twentieth century, the scale that measured land use in New England tipped once more. However, although the farm abandonment and subsequent reforeststation that began during the previous century had changed the look of the land, it was now not the balance between forest and farmland that

164. The northern red oaks (*Quercus rubra*) that line the Arborway between the rotary at the junction of routes 1 and 203 and Jamaica Pond as they looked in 1925, approximately a quarter of a century after their planting.

165. Also photographed in 1925, these pin oaks (*Quercus palustris*) are located in the Mattapan section of Boston along the Walk Hill Street entrance to what was then the Massachusetts State Hospital. Both of these species are in the red oak group and share certain botanical similarities, such as the length of time it takes for their acorns to mature (two years), and the presence on their leaves of bristle-tipped lobes, but the different habits of these oaks are readily apparent in these two photographs. The branching structure in the northern red oak, which is the fastest-growing oak that can be planted in northern areas, has already developed into the characteristic broad crown. The pin oak, also a fast-growing species, has a straight mastlike trunk with many slender branches that array themselves vertically along the trunk in a fanlike pattern.

shifted. By the midcentury point, for the first time in the region's history, less of its "improved" land supported working farms than sustained cities, subdivisions, shopping centers, and the black ribbons of asphalt that connected them all.

Regardless of whether they were planted by design or arrived on the scene by chance, a continuum of trees accompanied the evolution of the metropolis as it radiated outward from the city center to the edge of the hinterlands. Today, from the core of the city through the residential, suburban, and exurban zones, this woody vegetation not only provides a green canopy of shade and shelter that softens the hard edges of human structures but, in many situations, represents the last remnant of unspoiled nature.

City trees are found not only in vest-pocket parks, along median strips, or in foot-square sidewalk plots: they also push their way out of pavement cracks and they shade back alleys and loading docks. In residential areas and suburban zones, trees are planted along parkways, pampered in parks, and propped up with stakes in mall parking lots, but they are just as likely to appear unbidden beside a fence, a sign, or a utility pole. For commuters, they enliven the daily ride by clinging to the sides of railroad beds and riverbanks and by emerging beside freeways, on the slopes of road cuts, and in the no-man's-land of median strips and cloverleaves.

With the 1960s, the realization that these planted and volunteer woody plants constituted a forest unto itself, coupled with the recognition that this forest contributed

166. The characteristic silhouette of a silver maple (*Acer saccharinum*) growing in the alluvial soil of the Connecticut River floodplain. The structures in the background are tobacco barns, many of which were constructed entirely out of American chestnut wood. Although the Bay Colony outlawed the cultivation of tobacco in 1629, it was being raised throughout the Connecticut River valley in the late 1700s. When cigar factories were established in East Windsor and Suffield in 1810, Connecticut cigar-making changed from a household into a shop industry. Local shops first made plug and twist tobacco, but, in the 1830s, an unusually fine-textured and broad-leafed plant was introduced into the area. Through cultivation and selection, this variety became a highly regarded long-leaf plant especially well suited for the outer wrappers of cigars. Up until the first quarter of the twentieth century, when cigarette consumption increased substantially, this area was a center of production for fine cigar wrappers. More recently, the long-leaf market supplied the wrappers for Cuban-grown fillers. Cigar-wrapper tobacco is the most difficult type to grow; in order for the leaves to be blemish-free, the plants must be "shade-grown" under the added protection of cloth screening. The combination of the loss of trade with Cuba and the decrease in the use of all tobacco products has left only a few growers still cultivating cigar-wrapper tobacco along the Connecticut River. Less than thirty years ago, acre upon acre of white cloth netting surrounded these barns; many slender doors along their length allowed the air to pass through and cure the tobacco. Once the hallmark of the Connecticut River valley farmers, these stark, simple barns are rapidly becoming scarcer than roadside silver maples.

M-184

167.   In the late 1880s, when this photograph of the Sunderland buttonwood (*Platanus occidentalis*) was taken for Lorin L. Dame's book *Elms and Other Trees of Massachusetts,* the tree was already a venerable old giant. In 1919, in *The Historic Trees of Massachusetts,* James Raymond Simmons counted the Sunderland buttonwood, then with a girth of twenty feet and six inches, among the state's most impressive and well known trees. Most of the old native trees are long since gone : the Eliot, Grafton, and Avery oaks, the ancient Oaks at the Wayside Inn, the lindens at Plymouth Oak, and the Endicott pear, and certainly all of the elms that Dame and Simmons described, but the Sunderland buttonwood remains. Its girth is now twenty-three feet six inches, but the loss of one of its huge ascending limbs has dropped its height from one hundred ten feet to just over a hundred. The Sunderland buttonwood is not, however, the largest reigning buttonwood in New England; at ninety-three feet, the champion tree, in Simsbury, Connecticut, is not quite as tall, but it has a trunk circumference of more than twenty-five feet six inches.

to the "physiological, sociological, and economic well-being of urban society," begat a new branch of forestry, and a new type of forester emerged. Urban foresters have now joined the ranks of arborists, tree wardens, landscape contracters, and tree-, shrub-, and lawn-care firms that work within a forest that today covers more than 70 million acres.

Many of the trees set out in schoolyards and parks and along streets during the last quarter of the nineteenth century are now reaching maturity. Whether they grow on a town green or in an abandoned lot, the trees of the urban forest face unique and increasingly more complex growing conditions. In cities, these trees have become an integral part of our urban heritage. Although most elms are gone and few ancient buttonwoods or silver maples remain, many of New England's woodland species are well represented by venerable specimens that still shade our streets and make our cities and towns more pleasant and more habitable.

The red oaks that line Boston's Emerald Necklace are just beginning their second century. Although their life span can exceed more than two hundred years, many are already showing signs of decay. They have lost many of their massive branches, and the condition of their trunks bears silent witness to wounds inflicted by automobiles. These giant scars represent only the mechanical damage wrought by vehicles powered by internal combustion engines. Sulfur dioxide and ozone are the two most devastating air pollutants that urban trees face, and many species that historically have been used as street trees have been tested for their susceptibility or resistance to both. Red oaks (*Quercus rubra*) fall into the group of trees that are both tolerant of sulfur dioxide and resistant to damage by ozone. To increase the life span and the

health of city-grown trees, breeders will have to develop a cultivar of the red oak that will be able to tolerate levels of pollution that are higher than those the native species can abide.

Surprisingly, pin oaks (*Quercus palustris*) do remarkably well in cultivation when planted in dry soils, but research conducted by urban horticulturists indicates that they do not fare well in many soil types. Pin oaks also suffer from a disease similar to chestnut blight that can be carried from tree to tree on pruning tools. Although Thoreau thought that "the dry rustle of the withered Oak-leaves is the voice of the wood in winter," many people dislike the pin oak's tendency to retain its leaves long after the glossy, ruby red has faded to a dull, tiresome brown and all other vestiges of autumn have been swept away. Another drawback to the use of pin oaks as street trees is their many thickset, drooping lower limbs, which must be pruned often or removed entirely. Unfortunately, some municipalities perform this pruning too soon and end up with sapling pin oaks that look either like miscast deciduous Christmas trees or green equilateral triangles set atop slender brown poles.

The renewed popularity of the silver maple (*Acer saccharinum*) as a street tree was short-lived; before the nineteenth century had ended, it had fallen out of favor. Because fast-growing trees such as the silver maple often have brittle wood, a storm severe enough to damage many trees can make a very visible impact on a tree whose appearance in the landscape can easily be disfigured by the loss of just one large limb. The shape of an open-grown silver maple should be an asset, but, along roads accommodating much traffic, it can be a distraction, unless the tree is pruned severely. Although fine mature specimens still abound along what were once New

168. If a book on the famous trees of Massachusetts were written today, the much beloved, and stridently protected, London plane trees (*Platanus × acerifolia*) that line Memorial Drive in Cambridge would undoubtedly rank near the top of the list. This photograph, taken in the second decade of this century near the corner of Memorial Drive and Boylston Street (now John F. Kennedy Street), shows them as very young trees.

England's less-traveled byways, few silver maples have survived in cities, and very few, if any, are being planted today.

Not growing as quickly as the silver maple, yet producing greater growth increments each year than either the sugar maple or the Norway maple, the red maple and its many cultivars remain popular among urban planters because of their adaptability, habit, and attractive seasonal attributes. However, there can be problems with grafting

scions of red maple cultivars onto root stocks. Many grafts fail because of an incompatibility between scion and stock, and occasionally problems arise in maintaining the traits for which the cultivars were selected. Most cultivars of woody plants are propagated through cloning. Repropagating a plant vegetatively preserves its genotype: the genes of all subsequent plants are exactly the same as those of the parent. But vegetative repropagation sometimes goes awry. The wrong material is collected, or the material that is collected is from a vegetative sport (a genetic mutation) that does not carry all of the genes of the parent plant for which the cultivar was selected. In the case of plants that have been nursery grown for many years, at every repropagation there is the chance that these problems will occur, causing the loss of the original characteristics of the cultivar that were exceptional and that led to its selection and naming in the first place.

The horticulturist at the Arnold Arboretum discovered this to be the case in maple trees being sold as *Acer rubrum* 'Schlesingeri.' Because its strong fall color develops several weeks earlier than the average for the species, and because it retains its brightly colored leaves through most of the fall season, this cultivar has had a long career in the nursery trade. In order to guarantee that the Arboretum would have a new generation on site to replace its aging trees, several young individuals of *Acer rubrum* 'Schlesingeri' were purchased in the early 1980s. Unfortunately, it became apparent, after several years of observation, that these young trees did not have the exceptional fall color of the tree that the Arboretum introduced into cultivation more than a century before. To insure that *Acer rubrum* 'Schlesingeri' remains distinctive and true to form, propagation material, in the form of scion wood for grafting, has been taken from the Arboretum's original tree and has been reintroduced and made available to the nursery industry.

In a similar case, scientists at the National Arboretum in Washington, D.C., recently duplicated an event that occurred spontaneously more than three centuries ago. They intentionally crossed *Platanus occidentalis* and *Platanus orientalis* to reproduce the London plane tree (*Platanus × acerifolia*), which is much less susceptible to anthracnose (a disease that causes the loss of leaves in the spring) and to air pollution than either of its parents. Over the course of generations of repropagated plants, many London plane trees on the market no longer shared these two strong characterists that the original *Platanus × acerifolia* possessed. The National Arboretum has introduced two improved cultivars, 'Columbia' and 'Liberty,' from propagules of this "renewed" London plane tree.

The New Yankee Forest

While an urban forest developed as an expanding population made inroads on the outlying rural areas, the native forest reclaimed the land it had lost to farming and logging. Hidden beneath the wave of land clearing that crested in New England during the 1880s lay a powerful undertow. Toward the close of the nineteenth century, nearly two-thirds of New England's rural townships posted losses in population, which translated in the last decade of the century to more than seven thousand abandoned farms in Maine, Massachusetts, New Hampshire, and Vermont. Forsaking New England's fields for more fertile lands was not a new event. Many of New England's most adventurous sons and daughters had left for the level, relatively rock-free soil that stretched westward from the Allegheny Mountains as soon as that frontier had opened. The development of the principal railroad lines and the disruption caused by the Civil War only accelerated the pace with at which New Englanders packed up and departed from their ancestral homes.

By the end of the nineteenth century, regional railroad lines had snaked their way into virtually every nook and cranny of New England. Some farmers took advantage of the opportunity that the railroad network offered by turning away from subsistence farming and toward specialized market farms. From different regions in New England came dairy products, fresh poultry, potatoes, and onions, as well as apples, cranberries, strawberries, and fresh vegetables, which the railroads sped to the city markets.

While the virgin soils and expansive farmlands of the West enticed the young men, the lure of the city and lucrative factory employment appealed to their sisters. Even before the Civil War, scores of New England's young women had traded the isolation of the farm for the confined community of the boardinghouse, replacing long hours of back-breaking labor in caring for farm and family with less demanding (but nonetheless tediously repetitious) dawn-to-dusk shifts of operating machines. By the 1890s, at least one million women were working in textile mills and also in clothing, food processing, shoe, paper, and tobacco factories, as well as in other industries. But the growth of inland manufacturing centers along the very same railroad lines that carried agricultural produce from farm to market also enticed entire families to leave their farms. Soon the larger and more prosperous industrial cities beckoned to the children of these transplanted New Englanders, and most chose to go. In increasing numbers, people left the smaller, northern towns to work in the factories of southern New England, and Maine, New Hampshire, and Vermont steadily lost population to Massachusetts, Connecticut, and Rhode Island. By 1910, even with the influx of millions of immigrants from abroad, fully one-third of the people in the urban parts of New England were Americans of rural origin.

The farms that lay abandoned no longer rang with the sounds of the ax or the lowing of cattle; no longer heard was the scrape of the plough or the song of the scythe, yet not all was still. Within a year of the last planting of crops, pioneer native plants invaded empty pastures, fallow cornfields, and vacated vegetable plots. The first to arrive were annual plants, followed and supplanted in the next two to three years by perennial herbs, seedling shrubs, and sapling trees. This regrowth—secondary succession, the return of vegetation in areas disturbed by natural events, such as fire or hurricanes or by human intervention, as with logging or cultivation—follows nearly the same complex progression, but without the added constraints of time, climate, and distance, as the return of plants after the retreat of the continental glaciers. During the nineteenth century, the species poised to reclaim the land had not been pushed back great distances by glacial ice and modified climate; they grew in adjoining woodlots, in and at the edges of pastures, and intermixed in the native hedgerows.

On northern slopes where spruce had been extensively logged and fires had occurred, thickets of pin cherries (*Prunus pensylvanica*) and colonies of the quick-growing, short-lived, ubiquitous trembling aspen (*Populus tremuloides*) and its companion species, the taller, longer-lived bigtooth aspen (*P. grandidentata*) , established themselves. Where the soil held more moisture, a third poplar, the balsam poplar (*P. balsamifera*), appeared. In many areas, after ten to fifteen years, an understory of native conifers gradually seeded themselves and eventually overtook the deciduous trees to regain posession of the land.

Yellow and paper birches (*Betula alleghaniensis* and *B. papyrifera*) and red and mountain maples (*Acer rubrum* and *A. spicatum*) matured in even-aged stands in areas where the leaf litter and moss had been destroyed and the mineral soil was bare and exposed. Because farmland returning to forest in northern New England possessed a herbaceous layer that could provide cover for the germination and seedling stages of endemic conifers,

abandoned pastures and fields quickly supported stands of red spruce (*Picea rubens*), intermingled with balsam fir (*Abies balsamea*) and eastern arborvitae (*Thuja occidentalis*).

In central New England, where rural decline had begun as early as the 1830s, the white pine (*Pinus strobus*) became the pioneer tree most likely to reclaim the abandoned, well-tilled uplands from which farmers had removed all the endemic hardwoods. A strong September wind could blow the white pine's lightweight, airborne seeds for half a mile or more. In a year of heavy seed production, which usually occurs in cycles of five to seven years, it would take only one or two white pines of seed-bearing age growing adjacent to an abandoned field to reseed an entire area. The white pine's winged seeds came to rest amid the grasses, ferns, meadowsweets, goldenrods, blueberry bushes, and trailing blackberry vines that had already become well established. The pine seedlings, each little more than an erect, four- to six-inch stem topped with a tuft of needles, grew under this protective groundcover for two or three years. By the fourth year, they bore their first branches, their leading shoots overtopped the groundcover, and a dense forest of white pine seedlings appeared. These even-aged stands of "oldfield" white pines were such a phenomenon that parts of southern New Hampshire, most of eastern Massachusetts, and parts of northeastern Connecticut and Rhode Island (areas that were well south of this species' original range) were regarded by contemporary foresters as a "white pine region," and white pine was considered to be a widespread native. When these oldfield stands reached commercial maturity, the New England timber industry enjoyed a second surge of wealth from a harvest of white pine. During the first decade of the twentieth century, lumbermen cut more white pine in Massachusetts, in proportion to its area, than in any other state. Between 1890 and 1925, fifteen billion feet of pine lumber, 80 percent of which was harvested from abandoned Massachusetts farmland, was made into boxes and woodenware alone.

169. A second-growth forest of white pine (*Pinus strobus*) gains hold when the pine's winged seeds come to rest amid the leaf litter and the low vegetation that has already become well established in fallow fields and abandoned pastures. The pine seedlings grow under this protective groundcover for two or three years (*above*). By the fourth year, they begin to branch, their leading shoots overtop the groundcover, and a miniature forest of pine seedlings appears (*below*).

170. The New England farmer probably cut down more eastern redcedars (*Juniperus virginiana*) than any other tree and turned them into fence posts, and little more than the gullet of a bird stood between an eastern redcedar fence post and an eastern redcedar hedgerow. Birds feed voraciously on the bluish-black, fleshy, berrylike fruits, then transport the intact seeds to wherever they choose to perch. In this manner, clusters of eastern redcedar trees were planted unintentionally by cedar waxwings (a species that owes its common name to this tree), goldfinches, flickers, grosbeaks, and a host of other species. In addition to their fruits, this tree's dense foliage offers good protection for birds during winter and is a favorite nesting site for many of our songbirds. Unless they were constantly grubbed out by farmers, *J. virginiana* seedlings often gained a foothold in pastures even before the pastures were abandoned. As attractive as their berries are to birds, small mammals, and deer, only in desperation would cattle browse their prickly foliage; they much prefer to graze around eastern redcedar seedlings, leaving them to mature.

171. The wood of eastern redcedar (*Juniperus virginiana*) has a uniform, straight, fine, compact grain. The thin sapwood is almost white, while the color of the heartwood is a bright, rich red. The wood shrinks little, and its durability, coupled with its ease of working and its resistance to decay, made it a highly valued and sought-after commodity, both for export and for domestic use, since Colonial times. In New England, this conifer was quickly identified as the best source of wood for pails and for other objects that often came in contact with water. In the South, the early French colonists called this tree *baton rouge*, "red stick," because of its bright red color, and, supposedly, the capital of Louisiana derived its name from this tree.

These second-growth forests of white pine were transitory. As in the case of many pioneer trees, the white pines provided nursery conditions favorable for a succeeding generation of entirely different species. Young native hardwoods seeded themselves and grew under the protective canopy of the white pine.

Further south of the oldfield white pine region, different pioneer species made their appearance. Eastern redcedars (*Juniperus virginiana*) and their deciduous counterpart, gray birches (*Betula populifolia*), became the vagabond plants that reforested abandoned farmlands. The eastern redcedar, formal in its appearance, with its upright, narrow, pyramidal habit and its dense, tufted foliage, is undiscerning as to habitat and is apt to appear in the most unforgiving places. It was once the tree from which all lead pencils were made. It was also once used exclusively in the making of clothing chests. Charles Sprague Sargent wrote in *Garden and Forest*, in 1895, that "moths flee from the pungent odor, and that every good housekeeper knows the value of a red cedar chest or a closet lined with this wood." In 1922, cedrol camphor, the volatile oil in the wood of this medium-sized, sweet-scented tree, was actually proven to dispatch the larvae of certain moths from woolen cloth by research conducted by the United States Government Entomologist in Charge of Stored Product Insect Investigations.

THE FLURRY.

172. This illustration, which "represents that momentous and exciting scene—the 'flurry,'" was one of a series of six that accompanied an article on whaling written for *Ballou's Pictorial Drawing-Room Companion* in 1855. The flurry, according to the author, was when, almost spent, the whale "gaining the surface to breathe . . . flies over the wave with the rush of a flying-fish. The whale boat darts through the water in his wake, the waves rising up like walls of glass on either side. The whale boats are exceedingly light, and are clinker-built, that is, sharp at both ends, for it is sometimes necessary when the animal is in his 'flurry' to pull back from his reach with the speed of light."

This decay-resistant tree was put to other practical purposes, especially for items that came in contact with soil or water. Pails, buckets, and tubs, as well as sills—the bottom timbers in the frame of a house—and puncheons —logs halved and used in basements and under porches in building construction—and, of course, the inevitable railroad tie, were all fabricated from this durable wood. In early nineteenth-century Philadelphia, the barriers that separated sidewalk from roadway—where today you would find a granite curb—were made of ten-foot-long, eight-inch-diameter, eastern redcedar logs.

Shipbuilders used the very finest and largest eastern redcedar trees available for many above-deck structures on large ships, and the wood also went into the planking and the box (which held the coiled line) of whaleboats. In a era when things were built to last, these sturdy boats were considered expendable, almost disposable, and whaleboat makers built them quickly and cheaply because, in the planking of whaleboats, it was not eastern redcedar's durability that made it the best wood for the purpose. These small boats that gave chase to whales often became so battered that they were rendered unsafe

173. A gray birch (*Betula populifolia*) with its distinguishing black marks, each like an inverted V, that show the origins of its lateral branches. As shown by this gray birch, photographed in the Arnold Arboretum's *Betula* collection, the tree's grayish-white bark does not extend all the way to the ground. The base of the trunk is usually a dark gray that is almost black, and the bark is furrowed. As the tree matures, this furrowed portion extends farther up the trunk.

and unusable long before rot could set in. Eastern red-cedar wood was used for whaleboat planking because it is brittle; upon impact, it is more likely to puncture than to split. When a whale struck, the boat's crew could quickly plug the hole made in their cedar-clad boats rather than having to expend the much longer time needed even to make temporary repairs of the long splits created by comparable blows to other types of woods.

Pure stands of *Juniperus virginiana* commonly populate the waste places brought about by the construction of roads. Although the erect bearing and formal, trimmed-and-clipped silhouette of the eastern red-cedar conveys

the impression that their appearance beside highways has been planned, they arrive by chance, not design, and thrive unassisted and ignored in the poor and disturbed soils of these hot, shadeless places as pleasing ornaments of what might otherwise be wastelands.

While the invasion of a field by eastern redcedar can often be attributed to the chance flight and lighting of a bird, the establishment of the gray birch, *Betula populifolia,* usually depends on the capricious direction and variable velocity of the wind. Both male and female flowers of the gray birch occur on the same tree, and, although the birch flowers themselves are small and

174. The Latin name for the gray birch, *Betula populifolia*, can be roughly translated into English as "birch with poplarlike leaves." Its shiny-green, tapering triangular leaves, with their double-toothed margins, are very much like a smaller, daintier version of a compromise between of the leaves of the cottonwood (*Populus deltoides*) and those of the trembling aspen (*P. tremuloides*). All three trees have alternate leaves with flattened leafstalks, or petioles, and, while the the trembling aspen's leaves are a dull green and more roundish, and the cottonwood's leaves, although shiny-green, are larger, all three have leaves that the smallest breeze can set shivering.

unimposing, the beauty of birches in flower comes from the delicate appearance of their catkins, or aments, the structure within which the flowers are borne. The male catkins are formed in late summer; they mature during winter and develop in spring. The female catkins develop with the leaves and ripen in the fall. As the female catkins slowly disintegrate over the winter months, the wind catches the thin, chevronlike wings of the seeds and sends them in all directions. Even after the seeds have landed, it is not uncommon to see the wind send them winging again across the slick surface of snow-covered ground. These minute, nutletlike seeds are so light and can be blown so far from the parent tree that the source of the seed cannot easily be determined. It is no wonder that, when gray birches sprang up in abandoned fields or on land left barren after fire, farmers and woodsmen thought this tree somehow reproduced itself spontaneously without the medium of seed.

Because the gray birch prospers on sterile soils, even on the piles of spoil produced by mining and quarrying, this fast growing, short-lived tree has been called poverty birch and, due to its predilection to invade deserted agricultural land, it is also known as oldfield birch. Gray birch was once also called white birch, a name that is now more commonly used as a synonym for paper birch (*Betula papyrifera*). While the gray birch does have a white bark, it is not nearly as stunningly white, nor does it impart as chalky a whiteness to anything with which it comes in contact, as *B. papyrifera*. The inner surface of the bark of gray birch is yellowish-orange and, unlike that of the white birch, the bark of gray birch cannot be peeled off in thin layers. The bark also provides a distinction between the two species that is easy to discern. On gray birch trunks, a conspicuous, black, triangular, scarlike patch, like an inverted V, extends downward from each branch, or from beneath the place where a branch or bud once grew. These telltale hallmarks are absent from the trunks of white birches.

One remaining common name that is now seldom used identifies the characteristic leaf shape that the gray birch shares with another small, pioneer tree. Humphrey Marshall, a farmer-botanist and nurseryman, who wrote the first botanical treatise published in the United States, *The American Grove*, first described this American species. He chose the specific epithet *populifolia* to add to the genus name, because the leaves of this species resemble those of the poplars. Thus, the poplar-leaved birch has delicate, dark green triangular leaves with long, narrow tips and fine-toothed margins. Gray birches, like the trembling aspen, have long, flattened, slender petioles that

175. *Betula populifolia* is a small, short-lived tree that usually attains a height of twenty to thirty feet. Even growing in clumps of as many as ten stems, as they often do, each main stem is a continuous trunk that does not branch near the ground but continues up to the top of the crown. George B. Emerson commonly found this birch growing as a "companion of the pitch pine, in the poorest of sandy soils. But independently of its associations with sterility, which it is well entitled to, as it springs up and grows rapidly in spots deserted by every other deciduous tree [it] is valuable for the rapidity with which it grows on any kind of soil, or even without soil. It makes a pleasant border for the road—infinitely better than none."

cause the leaf blades to flutter in the slightest breeze. Although they are not nearly as aggressive or far-reaching as the sucker shoots of *Populus tremuloides*, nor do they figure as prominently in the self-propagation of the gray birch as they do in *P. tremuloides*, sucker shoots are also characteristic of this species. The gray birch commonly grows in clumps with four or five (or even as many as ten) separate stems, which often surround the remnant stem of the original tree.

Betula populifolia does not stand out in the gardener's quest for a white-barked ornamental tree. Although the multiple stems of this birch lend a picturesque quality to the landscape, the bark of seedling trees of this species, the smallest of New England's birches, is a golden yellow-brown. These slow-growing trees rarely attain their dusky grayish-white bark until their trunks are three or more inches in diameter.

At the Arnold Arboretum, eastern redcedars and gray birches are cultivated within the respective groupings that represent each genus, but seedlings of both are just as likely to be found beside one of the Arboretum's bordering stone walls or nestled in the lee of one of the

Arboretum's puddingstone outcrops. Despite the fact that, for more than a hundred years, the Arboretum's landscape has been developed from "worn out" farmlands to a designed and planted garden, these enterprising trees continue their advance over a piece of New England that was once claimed for pasture and fields.

These pioneer trees formed the vanguard of a forest that reclaimed nearly seven million acres of the region's farmland in less than fifty years. Nature had provided New England with a second (and, in some places, a third or fourth) generation of trees, but, through a combination of overexploitation, both of pulpwood and of the more valuable species of hardwoods, and occurences of serious outbreaks of injurious insects and diseases, the economic quality and quality of the regrown forest declined. Timber cruisers had once sought out only the larger, better timber trees for harvest, but, when more efficient log-ging methods and better means of transporting the timber were developed, the forests were cut more heavily. Although the amount of land producing timber in northern New England did not decline, inferior trees of diminished size gradually began to dominate the forest. Careless logging practices increased the accumulation of slash, causing numerous fires to sweep through the cutover land. The cycle of pioneer trees revegetating these burned and denuded lands recurred with greater frequency, producing smaller trees. Once the oldfield white pine was cut in southern New England, quick-growing "weed" trees appeared. The hardwoods that did emerge grew in thickets that produced only small trees, while the remaining hardwoods of good quality declined in vigor because of repeated harvesting from the same stump sprouts.

During the first decade of the twentieth century, each of the six New England states responded to the obvious decline in the economic quality of the timber and in the condition of their forests by appointing either state foresters or forest commissioners. These officials were charged with introducing legislation and establishing forestry policy, creating state forests and nurseries, and formulating fire-protection plans. Chief among their goals was providing education for farmers and owners of forest lands. Although the federal government had been churning out bulletins and circulars on research conducted by its Forestry Division since 1887, now each state's educational outreach programs often took the more immediate form of lectures presented at local Grange meetings and at farm clubs or exhibits mounted at agricultural fairs. Farmers standing hip-deep in pastures gone to pine or spruce were more amenable to receiving instruction on how to manage woodlands as a crop than were the region's lumbermen. The study of forestry was also developing in the nation's colleges as an adjunct to agricultural education, and most of the land-grant colleges included forestry courses in their curriculum by the end of the nineteenth century. During the first decade of the twentieth century, an awakening to the research and educational possibilities of forestry occurred to many of New England's college presidents, some of whom held under their aegis large forest tracts that had come to them as gifts or grants. Yale established a School of Forestry in 1901. The University of Vermont provided instruction in forestry, as did Maine, at Orono, in 1903. Harvard's Bussey Institution offered graduate courses in dendrology, silviculture, and forest management, and Harvard also conducted graduate courses at its 2000-acre forest in Petersham, Massachusetts, beginning in 1904. The formation of private forest associations was also on the upswing. The Society for the Protection of New Hampshire Forests and the Massachusetts Forestry

176. To some foresters, "a mature stand of red pine growing in a forest presents an appearance unexcelled by any other native conifer." This stand of red or Norway pine (*Pinus resinosa*) in southern Maine is a typical example of a planted and managed red pine forest. Forked or double-leader trees are very rare, and the trunks of the trees are almost cylindrical boles. There is very little ground cover, except in occasional openings where sunlight can penetrate the canopy. The ground cover that does exist consists chiefly of thin, scanty grasses. Because red pine is extremely intolerant of shade and is also apparently unable to reseed itself, even in grass cover, the forest floor is clear except for the small, bleached, and barkless limbs that have fallen from the trees. When grown in a plantation or in a thick natural stand, the red pine's sparse lower branches die quickly and drop off, leaving trees with trunks that are clean and clear of branches for easily two-thirds of their height. The combination of fewer branches and branches that are self-pruned before they have gained substantial size produces lumber with fewer knots, and the few knots that do occur seldom exceed an inch in diameter.

Association aggressively proposed and helped to implement education and conservation measures.

The creation of town forests, modeled somewhat in the European tradition, was the special bailiwick of the Massachusetts Forestry Association, which spurred their creation soon after the state enacted legislation that resulted in the Town Forest Act of 1913. The Town Forest established in 1914 by the citizens of Fitchburg—and planted and maintained, in part, by their school children, who spent a day each year setting out seedling trees— was the first in the nation. In 1923, the association, which advocated using land already in the hands of the towns, set as a goal the planting of fifty thousand young forest trees in ten town forests and offered, as an incentive, the free planting of five thousand trees to any city or town that would set aside one hundred acres for timber production. Cities as populous as Brookline, as well as Pioneer Valley farming communities, such as South Hadley and Conway, turned idle and neglected parcels of land into forests. All across the Commonwealth, from towns on the Atlantic coast to towns in the rural western reaches of the state, new forests grew up on cutover or burned-out areas, depleted pastures, and even on poorhouse farms.

Another incentive for reforestation was provided by the state's Conservation Department, which gave seedlings trees free of charge to the municipalities that had established Town Forests. At first, white pine seedlings constituted the majority of young forest trees that were provided or purchased for these new plantations, but, by the 1930s, seeds of two of Europe's most important timber trees, the Norway spruce (*Picea abies*) and the Scotch pine (*Pinus sylvestris*) were being imported and planted in forest nurseries along with seedlings of a native conifer, the red pine (*Pinus resinosa*).

Red pines were attractive plantation trees; they grew fast and straight, even in soils poorer than those the white pine required. Although the red pine grows from southern Canada and New England westward through New York and Pennsylvania and into Minnesota and the Great Lakes region, in New England it is tree that seldom occurs anywhere in great numbers. That it is extremely intolerant of shade and unable to establish itself on land that supports even a minimal amount of ground cover partially explains its scarcity. In forest openings where enough sunlight reaches the ground, a cover of moss, reindeer lichen, or lowbush blueberries can act as an impenetrable barrier to the growth of seeding red pines. Like the pitch pine, *Pinus rigida*, this conifer thrives on sterile, sandy soils. But, except for this predilection, and the fact that *P. rigida* is noted for its extremely resinous wood, while *P. resinosa* is not nearly as resinous (which can lead to confusion regarding the appropriateness of the specific epithet *resinosa* in the red pine's botanical name), the differences between these two species are straightforward. Pitch pines have rough, deeply furrowed, gray-black bark, and their three- to five-inch-long needles occur in bundles of three. Red pine needles come in pairs, not threes, and they are longer than those of the pitch pine by almost two inches. Red pine bark is a soft, almost burnished red-brown that reveals itself most prominently on the bark's flat plates, which are separated by shallow furrows. It is, however, in comparing the habit, the shape, and the growth pattern of these two conifers that the red pine is shown to be the far superior timber tree. Compared with the pitch pine's bole, the red pine's trunk is ramrod straight. Unlike the pitch pine, with its awkward, many-tiered branching pattern, red pines are thrifty trees that expend little effort on the growth of secondary limbs. When grown in a plantation or in a thick natural stand, their sparse, lower branches die quickly and drop off, leaving trees with trunks that are clean and clear of living branches for easily two-thirds of their height.

Red pine is frequently called Norway pine, a name that leads many people to assume that this species, along with the Norway spruce and the Scotch pine, is an exotic that was introduced from Europe into our forests, parks, and gardens. Lumbermen speculate that this common name refers not directly to the Scandinavian country but to a small town in Maine that was named for the country. *Pinus resinosa* became the Norway pine because, at one time, the forest around Norway, Maine, was noted for

177. When grown in the open, like these trees at the Arnold Arboretum, the quick-growing red pine assumes a broad pyramidal form that is both attractive and picturesque. When it is planted as a specimen tree, its reddish-barked trunk and its long, dark-green needles add to its ornamental appearance. On a late winter afternoon in the Arboretum's "pinetum," when all is white underfoot and a monochromatic band of green-needled trees separates the earth from the sky, the red-hued trunks of these pines catch and reflect the thin light just before the sun sets behind Hemlock Hill.

great numbers of this tree. The Italian botanist Luigi Castiglioni, who compiled a list of native American species in his *Viaggio negli Stati Uniti dell'America . . .* , in 1790, lent some nomenclatural status to the misnomer. *Pinus resinosa*, unlike most American pines, is very similar to a group of Old Word pines of which *P. sylvestris* is the best known. When Castiglioni called the New World pine *P. sylvestris Norvegica*, he believed that the European pine also grew in America. He chose the name *Norvegica* to identify it as being a form of *P. sylvestris* simply because "Norway" pine was what it was called by the people of Massachusetts (which then included Maine).

The zeal displayed in establishing forest plantations often faltered when it came to enacting a silvicultural management plan. Although the notion (proposed in 1923 by the state's forester) that, if Massachusetts towns established large town forests, they could, in the space of sixty to seventy years, reap enough income on a annual basis from the sale of timber to cover their expenses and thus eliminate the need for local taxes, seems fiscally quaint, given the size of town budgets today, it does not excuse the fact that most town forests have not been harvested by the citizens for whom they were planted. These overly mature specimens have achieved the dubious distinction and status of permanence. Aligned in rows, like an army battalion standing rigidly at attention, these forgotten trees bear silent witness to the fact that the planting of trees for commercial gain is more than a romantic undertaking. It can be accomplished in one lifetime, but it also requires that the forest be managed and that the product be harvested.

Assuming that there were considerable economic rewards to be had by pursuing a program of reforestation was merely the first mistake. Many municipalities used plantations consisting entirely of a single species to protect their watersheds. In southern New England, this management practice has come under close scrutiny. In the last twenty years, the Massachusetts Metropolitan District Commission, which oversees many of the state's watersheds and reservoirs, has been systematically eliminating its red pine plantations. By clear-cutting the red pine—the "reclamation of open fields," in the Commission's words—its foresters hope to establish a productive habitat of fields bordered by shrubs in place of these monocultural forests, which not only appear unnaturally devoid of life but are, in fact, able to provide little of substance to wildlife.

Red pines that grow intermingled with white pines (*Pinus strobus*) on the small bluff that overlooks Bussey Brook are among the Arboretum's oldest planted pines.

Seeds of red pine were collected from the cones of trees in New Hampshire's White Mountains by the Arboretum's plant propagator, Jackson Thornton Dawson, on 24 February 1879. Dawson planted the two dozen seedlings that he raised from this collection as a grove in "the pinetum," the Arboretum's conifer collection, in 1886. The seedlings fared well in the thin soil that covers the knoll; one-third of the original twenty-four seedlings have grown tall, with straight, clear trunks and well shaped crowns.

The forest had been the foundation of New England's vitality. By harvesting its products, the people of the region had progressed from a wooden to an industrial age. But this advance and the subsequent prosperity it provided had not been gained without exacting a heavy toll from what was potentially the region's most renewable resource. Mismanagement and exploitation, coupled with the lack of a meaningful commitment to conservation and the spread of endemic and exotic diseases, threaten the forest's future. By the end of the first quarter of the twentieth century, when scientifically trained foresters applied what they had learned in the study of forest mensuration—the measurement of forests and their raw timber products in terms of future and present growth, volume, and value—the prospect looked bleak at best. Some foresters even went so far as to predict that, as a crop, the future production of New England's forest should be considered a liability rather than an asset.

The Plight of the Chestnuts and Elms

The New World's forests, like the New World's native peoples, were susceptible to introduced diseases. Although the devastating effects of foreign diseases came swiftly to the tribes of the Northeast, three centuries would pass before foreign plant diseases became a recognizable threat to the forests that the Northeastern tribes once populated.

While exploration resulted in the discovery and exportation of many new ornamental and economic plants from the colonies, these same forest resources made large-scale importation of trees and tree products unnecessary during the country's early development. It was not until early in the twentieth century, when forest management, with its tree and nursery plantations and the reforestation of farmed lands (as well as commercial production of fruits and nuts) became widespread, that the tide began to turn. Exotic species of trees and shrubs (as well as native ones being reintroduced), along with any diseases they might harbor, began to enter the country on a regular basis. Importation practices were unsupervised, and, within a short time, destructive diseases had begun to take their toll on the forest.

One of the first introduced diseases to be identified was one that attacked the American chestnut. Called chestnut blight, the fungus *Cryphonectria parisitica* changed forever the composition of the Oak–Chestnut Forest. Later investigation found outbreaks of the disease in several isolated sites, but the first alarm was sounded in New York, where a number of dead and dying chestnut trees were discovered at the Bronx Zoological Park during the first decade of the twentieth century. The disease was devastating. In ten years, half of the American chestnut's range was decimated, and, within fifty years, almost every chestnut, from Maine south to Georgia and west to the Great Plains, was killed to the ground.

However, for three-quarters of a century, the American chestnut has persisted. The species survives not as a tree of magnificent size but as a leggy, shrubby tree that seldom reaches a height of thirty feet. Because the fungus is unable to enter the roots, the stumps continue to produce sprouts from the tree's root collar, the living tissue that exists just above ground level. The sprouts rarely attain the size of a mature tree or begin producing nuts before they are reinfected by the fungus and are once again killed to the ground.

The speed with which American chestnuts became infected and died caused an outpouring of financial support, as federal and state governments rallied to stop the blight. Between 1911 and 1913, Congress appropriated $165,000 to repel an invader that had been likened to a medieval plague. However, it soon became obvious that, with no clear understanding of the disease and no solution to its eradication in sight, emotion and frustration ran as high as financing. The first real progress in understanding the blight came with the discovery that, while Asian species of chestnut contracted the fungal disease, they were largely resistant to its effects. This corroborated the suspicion that the fungus had entered the United States on nursery stock of Asian chestnuts during the late 1800s. Controlling the disease through eradication had proved futile, and the possibility of crossing Asian with American species to obtain a disease-resistant hybrid became a viable alternative. For the next fifty years, researchers focused on breeding a tree that would have the resistance of the Asian species coupled with the vigor and form of the North American tree.

In New England, research on the blight continued unabated at the Connecticut Agricultural Experiment Station. Founded in New Haven in 1875, it was the first experiment station established in America, and the institution has maintained the longest tradition of chestnut tree research in the nation. Researchers at the station began working on a breeding program in 1929 with a collection of hybrid chestnuts grown on land in Hamden, Connecticut, known as the Sleeping Giant Chestnut Plantation. Although the search for a blight-resistant native chestnut was not abandoned, and various other techniques (including the use of radiation to produce a blight-resistant mutant) were also tried, breeding programs continued to be the most promising approach until published reports of an unusual observation in Italy reached the eyes of a scientist at the Experiment Station in New Haven.

By 1938, much to the consternation of Italian orchardists, the fungus *Cryphonectria parisitica* had taken up residence in chestnut groves in northern Italy. The European chestnut, *Castanea sativa,* was as susceptible to the fungus as the American species, and an epidemic, similar to the American one, swept through the chestnut-producing areas of Italy. In the 1950s, an Italian plant pathologist observed a curious phenomenon: infected chestnuts in his country appeared to be healing themselves. Initially, the pathologist's claims went unheeded, but, eventually, his persistence aroused the interest of a French mycologist who visited Italy, collected bark with abnormal cankers from the "self-healing" trees, and brought it back with him to his laboratory in France. By 1965, strains of the blight fungus had been isolated that were less virulent when introduced into the bark of chestnut trees. A new term, "hypovirulent" (which indicates a subnormal ability to cause disease), was coined for the strains that had been segregated.

The Connecticut Agricultural Experiment Station imported hypovirulent strains of *Cryphonectria parasitica* and began testing for blight control on seedlings grown in the Station's greenhouses. In 1978, the testing graduated from these "laboratory" conditions and entered New England woodlands. At two partially cleared forest areas in Connecticut, the cankers of sprouts of American chestnut were treated with the hypovirulent strains of *C. parasitica* at least once a year for four years. After nine years, abnormal cankers similar in appearance to those that had failed to kill chestnut trees in Italy had not only developed on the inoculated trees but were present on untreated sprouts more than two hundred feet away.

178. No naturally occurring native American chestnut, not even a stump encircled by sprouts, grows anywhere on the Arnold Arboretum's grounds. All of the Arboretum's American chestnuts were collected as seeds or seedling trees from other locations. Beginning in 1988, when the Arboretum began participating in the Connecticut Agricultural Experiment Station's program of inoculation, some of these American chestnuts have been treated with hypovirulent strains of *Cryphonectria parasitica*. Carrying out the Station's tradition of chestnut research, plant mycologist Sandra Anagnostakis inoculated six of the Arboretum's trees and has been monitoring their condition each year. In this photograph, Dr. Anagnostakis is treating all that remains of an American chestnut collected in Bar Harbor, Maine— a ring of stump shoots. Two of the larger shoots were inoculated, and one of the two seems to be respond ing to the treatment. Another younger tree was also treated. Collected in 1880 near Harvard, Massachusetts, this tree is planted close to the edge of Valley Road in the chestnut collection. Although it seems to be responding to the treatment, only time will tell if it will be able to resist the blight.

Naturally occurring, blight-curing strains of the fungus similar to those discovered in Italy have since been found in North America. Unfortunately, these American strains do not seem to spread as easily from tree to tree. This may be due to the difference in growing conditions: in Italy and France, the trees grow in dense orchard plantations, while the remnant stump sprouts of the American species often grow isolated from one another. It is also possible that the European hypovirulent strains have a vector that aids in their spread—a bird, a mammal, or an insect—whose counterpart is missing from the American forest. There is good indication that the "sleeping giant" of the eastern forest may some day be awakened and saved from extinction by a naturally occurring biological control that once only a poet could have imagined:

Will the blight end the chestnut?
The farmers rather guess not.
It keeps smoldering at the roots
And sending up new shoots
Till another parasite
Shall come to end the blight.

(Robert Frost, "Evil Tendencies Cancel," 1930)

One who spends time tramping through the the New England woods will be sure to come upon a persistent chestnut tree. Usually a ring of sprouts, some dead, others in the process of dying, arise from a decayed stump. Because both young chestnuts and young beeches have a pale smooth bark and leaves that look similar, they are easy to confuse, but telltale characteristics of bark, buds, and leaves distinguish the two trees. Unlike the beech, which remains smooth-limbed throughout its life, the chestnut develops ridges on its branches as it ages. In old age, the fissures that separate the broad, flat-topped, ridges become very deep. Both trees have prominent brown buds, but those of the beech are much longer (almost an inch) and lance-shaped. Chestnut buds are only about one-quarter inch long, and, although they, too, taper to a sharp point, they are broadest at the base. Chestnut leaves are leathery; beech leaves are thinner and paperlike. Like those of the beech, chestnut leaves are alternate on the twigs, but they are generally longer and thinner. Beech leaves are usually more oval shaped while chestnut leaves tend to taper more at both ends. The leaves of both have prominent, parallel veins and coarse teeth, but, on chestnut leaves, these veins extend beyond the teeth and form bristles that make the ends of the teeth look hook-shaped.

The devastation caused by the chestnut blight emphasized the need for a system of review and regulation for plant introduction into the United States. Congress passed the first National Plant Quarantine Act in 1912, slamming the door on unsupervised plant introduction. Unfortunately, this action was not taken soon enough, and it proved to be too easily breached.

From the same ancient and species-rich flora that was both the source of the chestnut-blight fungus and the home of blight-resistant trees came another pathogen that threatened yet another American species. Between 1925 and 1934, while Japanese and American chestnuts were being bred in plantations and plant explorers were collecting nuts from disease-resistant chestnuts in the Orient, a new fungus disease, whose provenance was eventually established as Asian, entered North America.

The route the new fungus followed and the mode of its travel differed from those of the chestnut blight. Outbreaks of the disease were first recorded in 1919 in the Netherlands, where subsequent research identified, described, and isolated the causal pathogen. Unfortunately, in this case, the messenger bore the onus of being forever associated with the message: *Ceratocystis ulmi* is today universally known as Dutch elm disease. Unlike the chestnut blight, which piggybacked on live nursery stock, spores of *Ceratocystis ulmi* and its initial vector, the European bark beetle *Scolytus multistriatus*, crossed the Atlantic embedded and well concealed in the inner bark of burl elm logs.

By 1930, when the disease was first sighted in this country, thousands of elms throughout Holland, Belgium, Germany, France, and England were already dead or dying. A chronology of the spread of the disease would later trace its dispersal to the entry into American ports of at least fifty-eight shipments of disease-riddled and beetle-infested logs. Ironically, the railroads sped the infected logs—destined for inland veneer mills and furniture factories—over rails that rode on ties made from wood harvested from dead chestnut trees.

Again, federal as well as state and local funds were committed to a scheme to stop an invasion. Battle lines were drawn, and a campaign was begun to identify and remove any infected elm within an area of 7500 square miles that encompassed parts of New York, New Jersey, and Connecticut. In 1934, with hopes of containing the disease when and if it appeared, the Massachusetts Forest and Park Association offered a lifetime membership in the Association as a prize to the first person to spot Dutch elm disease in the Commonwealth. Nineteen forty-one was the year that the prize would be claimed.

179.   In 1787, James Hillhouse—lawyer, state senator from Connecticut, and treasurer of Yale—
enhanced New Haven's already well-established tradition of tree planting by initiating a subscription to
ornament the city's green with elms. Hillhouse grew many of the elms at his own farm, carted the
saplings into town, and, after planting the trees, cared for them himself. His dedication rallied other
townspeople to plant trees on streets nearby, and visitors to New Haven could not help being inspired by
the soaring archways formed by the double rows of elms that encircled the green and the single rows that
had advanced along both sides of most central streets. Augustus L. Hillhouse apparently inherited his
father's fascination for trees; he translated François André Michaux's *Historie des Arbres Forestiers
de l'Amerique Septentrionale* into English. This photograph of the green reveals why New Haven was
dubbed "Elm City."

The remaining four New England states would continue unscathed only a decade longer. Maine's elms, escaping infestation until 1952, were the last to succumb. In the last sixty years, Dutch elm disease has spread from coast to coast, and estimates place losses at anywhere between 50 and 100 million trees. Not every elm has failed and fallen—in fact, the species still survives in the wild—but, because most individuals stricken by the disease were cultivated as ornamental landscape trees, the damage wrought by Dutch elm disease was much more apparent than the damage the blight inflicted on the Oak–Chestnut Forest.

If the chestnut blight cut to the heart of New England by decimating a major component of its forest, Dutch elm disease struck at its soul. Its victims had arched over quiet, narrow streets and lined bustling, broad boulevards. The towering vase-shaped silhouette of *Ulmus americana*, the American elm, stood as companion to farmstead, churchspire, and village green, and it cast its shade over dooryard, park, and pasture. The American elm typified the pastoral New England landscape; its loss amounted to a catastrophe.

An entire generation of New Englanders has now grown up deprived of urban and suburban landscapes defined and punctuated by the commanding presence of orderly rows of massive elms. Elms were so common, so regular in outline, and so pleasing in symmetry that most people easily recognized their distinctive shape and knew this species by name. Perhaps no other American tree inspired as much reverence. François Michaux called the American elm "the most magnificent vegetable of the temperate zone." For Thoreau, sighting their "magnificent domes" on the horizon suggested the presence of a village. But, to Thoreau, it was of "a secondary consideration whether there are human dwellings beneath them; these may have long since passed away. I find that into my idea of the village has entered more of the elm than of the human being." Referred to as noble, stately,

dignified, and gracious, elms were touted as our most aristocratic, picturesque, and courtly trees.

The American elm varies in form, but the typical elm has several large limbs that separate from a huge trunk at about thirty feet from the ground and continue to sweep upward and outward in broad and equal curves. The bark on the trunk and on large limbs is thick and dark gray, with ridges covered with flaky scales. The bark on old trees can thicken into shaggy, corky plates. Their greenish twigs, which are initially covered with down, eventually become a smooth, reddish brown. The elm's distinct leaves are easily identified. Sharp-pointed and doubly serrate, with large teeth and smaller teeth among them, like the teeth of a double-tooth saw, they have a lopsided heart shape (the two halves of the blade not meeting symmetrically at the base). The leaves emerge just before the small, brownish-red, inconspicuous flowers have fully matured into flat, oval, one-seeded, papery samaras.

Open-grown elms can attain heights of between one hundred and one hundred thirty feet, and the diameters of the trunks of these lofty specimens can be in excess of ten feet. An elm is considered to be mature at an age of one hundred fifty years. Attaining an age of two hundred years is not uncommon, and the lifetimes of many elms have easily spanned three centuries.

The wood of *Ulmus americana* is tough, fibrous, heavy, and strong. It withstands impact well and takes on a fine polish. Being hard to split and easy to bend, its wood found a ready niche in the barrel and furniture industries. Like the red oak, elm is a ring-porous species that produces wood well suited for slack-barrel staves. Because it steamed well and retained its shape after being bent, its wood could also be made into the hoops that hold barrels together. At the beginning of this century, more elm than any other wood, including red oak (*Quercus rubra*), went into the making of slack-barrel staves. When flour, sugar, butter, and cheese made their way by barrel from farm to table, American elm was the most

180. The American elms lining Boston's Commonwealth Avenue photographed as young trees in September 1898.

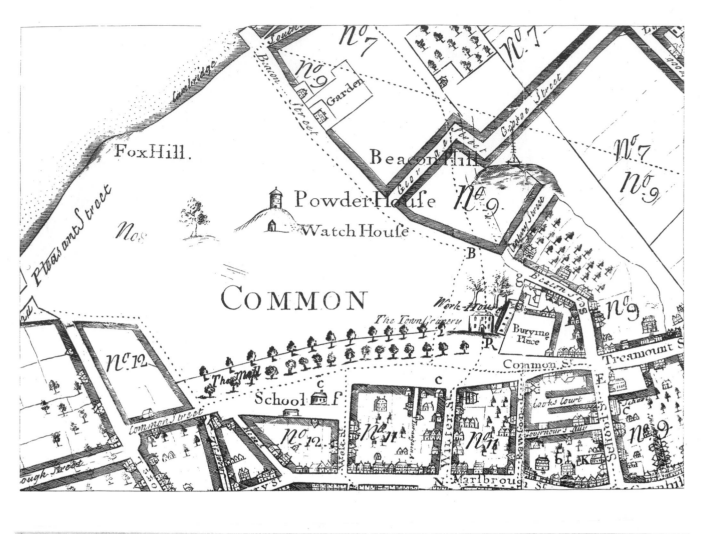

181. The Boston Common had been laid out in 1634 "for a trayning field . . . and for the feeding of cattell" on a fifty-acre parcel purchased from the Reverend William Blaxton for thirty pounds. Trampled by hooves and boots for almost one hundred years, this oddly shaped, irregular Common stood scruffy and barren, save for a powderhouse, a watchhouse, a burial ground, and three trees. In this 1722 map of the town of Boston, by Captain John Bonner, one of the trio of elms stood foursquare in the middle of the Common. This elm—whose crash to earth in 1882 inspired a funeral procession and numerous memorial poems and tributes—had been revered as a landmark since Colonial times. During 1728, at first one row of trees and then, in 1734, a second row, "with a fine footway between," adorned the Common's edge along Common (now Tremont) Street, and Bostonians could enjoy a stroll through the town's first mall. A second mall, created by another double row of elms, appeared in front of the Granary Burial Ground in 1756. In 1780, the patriot-planter, John Hancock, set out elms in front of his house, which faced the Common on Beacon Street, and, within twenty-five years, many of the stylish Lombardy poplars (*Populus nigra* 'Italica') and lime trees, both European trees, had taken root on the Common. By 1830, cows and sheep had been banished, the erection of buildings prohibited, and executions forbidden. The Tremont Street Mall, or Great Mall, which by now had three parallel rows of trees, had been renamed for Lafayette, in honor of the French general's visit, and new elms had joined those set out by John Hancock on Beacon Street. In 1823, Mayor Quincy ordered that the few surviving poplars along Park Street (they having proven to be both short-lived and, for the most part, unpopular) be replaced with elms, and he ordered work begun on the Charles Street Mall. With the completion of the plantings on Charles Street and the creation of the Boylston Street Mall in 1834, the Boston Common, like its counterpart in New Haven, was completely ringed with American elms.

---

182. Speculation on the age of the large elm that stood on the Boston Common led Dr. J. C. Warren, President of the Boston Society of Natural History, to "make an inquiry into the facts, and endeavor to ascertain the age of the tree" in 1855. Readily acknowledging that, while it was not the largest nor the tallest, and not even the oldest in New England, it was, by virtue of its prominent location, the most famous. The elm was indeed old, well known, and of considerable size. According to Warren, "It is known by the most ancient surviving inhabitants of Boston as THE GREAT TREE. Citizens, who were of advanced age in the youth of those who are now the oldest inhabitants, knew it equally as THE GREAT TREE." Although George Washington apparently never stood under it, nor did he ever take command of anything under it, the British Army encamped around it, and General Gage kept his troops from turning it into firewood. During the political riots of 1806, effigies were hung from it, and a small army, protecting Boston during the War of 1812, camped under it. In 1844, "the distinguished botanists, George B. Emerson, Esq. and Professor Asa Gray" measured it for Emerson's report and found the elm to be, at breast height, sixteen feet and one inch in circumference. In 1855, the tree was seventy-two feet tall and had a spread of more than a hundred feet. It also had a handsome iron fence, erected to protect it the year before, that bore this inscription: "This tree has been standing here for an unknown period. It is believed to have existed before the settlement of Boston, being full grown in 1722. Exhibited marks of old age in 1792 , and was nearly destroyed by a storm in 1832. Protected by an iron enclosure in 1854. J. V. C. Smith, Mayor."

---

sought-after tree on the market. In addition to its other characteristics, its wood imparted no taste or smell, and it also wore well in wet situations. Elm wood became the boxes, baskets, and crates that farmers filled with fruits, vegetables, and eggs. Moreover, the farmer's wife scrubbed clothes on elm washboards, set dishes to drain on elm drainboards, and stored perishables in ice boxes constructed of elm. In the barn, her husband favored elm for the floorboards of his stalls.

The Arnold Arboretum lost almost all its native elms to the Dutch elm disease. A good number of these specimens were "spontaneous" trees that predated the Arboretum's inception or dated from the late 1800s or early in this century. Today, the collection includes only two American elms, both young plants set out in 1990, but a number of *Ulmus americana* cultivars in the collection are being watched for resistance to the disease. A specimen of the cultivar 'Princeton,' now the largest elm at the Arboretum, remains hale and hardy, although all of the American elms that once surrounded it became infected, died, and were removed.

In the late 1960s, there was a resurgence of the epidemic, caused by a more virulent and destructive strain of *Ceratocystis ulmi*. When it became obvious that this far more pathogenic strain was present in the Arboretum's elm collection, the decision was made to try to save individual specimens through repropagation. A new strategy in siting both the repropagated plants and plants new to the collection was also adopted at this time. Rather than planting all of the elms of a new generation of elms in the same area, as has been done with most of the trees within each genus, new elm accessions would be planted out separately. This departure from the Arboretum's custom of growing the various species of a genus together to facilitate study and comparison was prompted by research that uncovered new information on how the disease spreads through root grafts. Once a tree has become infected and the fungus has spread, by

way of the xylem vessels, to all parts of the tree, Dutch elm disease can make its way to an adjacent elm by way of the tree's roots. Natural root grafts occur in many tree species; unfortunately, it is a common occurrence in elms. Root-to-root transmission explains how an apparently healthy elm growing in close proximity to an infected one, as is frequently true of elms planted in parks, along streets, or even in arboreta, can suddenly contract the disease.

The elms at the Arnold Arboretum grow on the north side of Bussey Hill above the lilac collection, a location from which visitors have a most commanding view of the city of Boston. This vista to the east toward the gold-domed State House on Beacon Hill—a view once punctuated only by spires and steeples that is now filled with concrete and glass—is one that Frederick Law Olmsted cited when lobbying to have the Arboretum included in the Boston Park System, his Emerald Necklace.

The middle of May, when elm seeds are mature, is a choice time to visit the Arboretum. Come on a windy day and watch elm seeds sail over the showy trusses of the lilacs and the sea of spring-green leaves. As one of New England's contemporary poets, David McCord, has observed, the wind can make the trees let go:

Along about then, the middle of May,
I say to myself: "any day . . . "
And I guess up there in the tall elm trees
The leaves say something like "Listen, breeze:
It's no good whispering stuff; just blow!
There's a skyful of seed here set to go."
And the breeze perks up
And the seeds fly loose—
Not hard like acorns, or cones like spruce—
But tiny saucers without a cup,
Till the air is full of their golden flutter
On street and sidewalk, lawn and gutter;
On windowsills, on doorsteps, mats;

183. In 1854, Mayor Smith had had the honor of protecting the famous elm; thirty-two year later, it fell upon Mayor Cobb's administration to preside over its demise. Mayor Cobb rose to the occasion and took the opportunity to furnish a number of individuals and institutions with fitting mementos of the tree, one of which is held in the Arnold Arboretum's archives. The inscription reads: "As the Great Elm on Boston Common, with an age in years outdating the settlement of the Town, was destined to fall, by wind and decay, during the time it was under my guardianship, as the Mayor of the City, I can do no less than give the attestation of my name to certify that this is a perfectly correct view of it, just before the fall, and that the surface on which the photograph is printed is a veneer from the wood of the veritable and venerable tree. March 31, 1876. Samuel C. Cobb, Mayor of Boston."

184. Towering over the family's classic New England farmstead, this formidable American elm (*Ulmus americana*) was photographed in Conway, New Hampshire, on 4 July 1930 by Ernest H. Wilson. With a trunk circumference in excess of 22 feet and limbs that reached more than 100 feet skyward, this massive specimen was then the largest elm in New England. Note, too, the elevation of the corn stalks—they appear to have attained the prescribed knee-high stature that the Independence Day rhyme decrees.

On coats and pants and skirts and hats;
On people, dogs; in shoes, in cars;
On roller-skates, on handlebars;
On everything and everywhere;
Pale flakes of gold with piles to spare.

(David McCord, from "Elm Seed Blizzard")

Botanicals: Medicine from the Vegetable Kingdom

Returning to the Arnold Arboretum on a cold, gray, November day—half a year after the seeds of the native elms have been dispersed—will reward observant hikers with a faint, clean scent reminicent of spring and the sight, not of flakes, but of "ribbons" of gold.

The witch-hazel tree is in full blossom on this magical hillside, while its broad yellow leaves are falling. Some bushes are completely bare of leaves, and leather-colored they strew the ground. It is an extremely interesting plant, October and November's child, and yet reminds me of the very earliest spring. Its blossoms smell like the spring. . . . its spray, so jointed and angular, is not to be mistaken for any other. I lie on my back with joy under its boughs. While its leaves fall its blossoms spring." [Henry David Thoreau, 9 October 1851]

While hiking in the woods, or walking through the Arboretum, make a point of looking for this plant in the fall, which is the witch hazel's best season. Look for a small tree or a large multibranched shrub with oval or egg-shaped leaves that have wavy or scalloped edges. Often, the fragrance of the yellow flowers, which appear in October and November, is sufficient to draw ones's attention to this unusual plant. However, because it has long been used as a natural astringent, witch hazel, *Hamamelis virginiana*, may be more familiar to most people as a bottle of liquid on a shelf in the medicine cabinet than as an understory species of the New England woodland.

Regardless of what they had heard about the animal, vegetable, and mineral riches of the New World, the colonists were, for the most part, doubtful that they could find and extract from the New England woodland the medicines they needed for the treatment of their Old World ills. They brought their medical insurance with them: seeds of medicinal garden herbs crossed the ocean safely stowed among the colonist's most valued possessions. But the notion, proposed by some British herbalists, that English bodies were best cured by English plants, ran counter to another popular notion, to which other contemporary scholars prescribed: wherever a particular disease arose, there too would be found a plant that could cure it.

Open-minded inquiry into the medicinal possibilities of New England's flora by trained herbalists, such as John Josselyn, produced not only a catalogue of the native plants, but a compendium of traditional Native American remedies that testified to the skill of the native healers. The native peoples of the Northeast used many plant substances to relieve their discomfort and aid in their healing. The properties of bark, roots, and leaves were exploited as anesthetics, emetics, styptics, antiseptics, astringents, cathartics, emollients, poultices, and salves. Native Americans contributed about one hundred seventy drugs that have been, or still are, like *Hamamelis virginiana*, officially recognized in the *Pharmacopeia of the United States of America* or in the *National Formulary*. In 1936, William T. Bradley, an instructor at the Massachusetts College of Pharmacy, accounted for fifty-six endemic New England species known to have been used by the native healers that were still being recognized officially. Thirty-three of the plants he listed were used for the same purposes in 1936 that the indigenous peoples had prescribed them for as much as three centuries earlier. Many of their remedies they extracted from woody plants, and, unlike the complicated nostrums and electuaries of the Europeans, which could contain upwards of eighty ingredients, the remedies of the Native Americans tended to rely on the use of a specific plant to treat a specific ailment. A representative sampling of

185. Until 1900, 80 percent of our medicines came from the vegetable kingdom. After a decline that lasted through the middle of the twentieth century, plants are again being eagerly sought and tested for their therapeutic properties. Television commercials and print-media advertising tout the use of natural ingredients in the products that compete for space on our drugstore and supermarket shelves. This selection of botanicals, many of which were produced by the Gould Botanic Garden, represents some of the medicinal plants that were once widely available in drugstores and country general stores. The Gould herb business was begun in 1840 in Petersborough, New Hampshire, and was carried on by three succeeding generations of Goulds at their drug mill and herb factory in Maldin, Massachusetts. At one time, the Gould "botanic garden" consisted of eight acres of herbs, and the factory employed more than fifty men and women. Many of their herbs were sold to the makers of patent medicines, and one of their best and largest customers was the Lydia Pinkham Company of Lynn, Massachusetts. Two of their popular products not shown were "Gould's Catnip Tea" and "The Catnip Meow.".

186. Witch hazel (*Hamamelis virginiana*) is a small tree or a large multibranched shrub with alternate, oval or egg-shaped leaves that have wavy or scalloped edges. An understory plant, witch hazel is usually found growing in or on the borders of moist woods or on the edges of streams. There are many examples of *H. virginiana* and related species and hybrids grown either as specimens or as understory plants at the Arnold Arboretum. A native witch hazel can be found growing in its typical habitat close by Rehder Pond, one of the three small ponds in the Arboretum. Although trees are usually thought of as being much longer-lived than shrubs, this large multi-stemmed specimen was collected as a young plant from Lenox, Massachusetts, on 20 September 1883.

woody, or aborescent, New England species selected from their materia medica would include a decoction of the bark of the white ash, *Fraxinus americana*, which they used to reduce fever; buds from the balsam poplar, *Populus balsamifera*, which was used to relieve congestion from colds; the berries of the bearberry, *Arctostaphylos uva-ursi*, a low, creeping shrub in the heath family (Ericaceae) similar to the cranberry, as an astringent and antiscorbutic; and the twigs and bark of the sweet birch, *Betula lenta*, both of which were used as an aromatic diaphoretic.

The bark of the black cherry, or wild cherry, *Prunus serotina*, which, as a medium-sized tree, is the largest of the native cherries, yielded a cough remedy for the Penobscots. They steeped its bitter, aromatic bark, which contains hydrocanic acid, in water and drank the resulting tea. The Mohegans used wild cherry fruits, which they let ferment for a year, for curing dysentery. The bark has been used as a sedative and a pectoral by druggists, and *P. serotina* has been officially recognized in the U. S. *Pharmacopeia* since 1820, but, today, wild cherry syrup is thought to be just a flavoring agent, and few people are aware of its historic medicinal use.

As its common name implies, the slippery elm, *Ulmus rubra*, has mucilaginous proprieties. The Penobscots chewed its bark and roots to obtain relief from an inflamed throat, and they drank a decoction of its bark to heal "bleeding lungs." They also ground up the bark of slippery elm and used it for poultices.

As an all-purpose home remedy, witch hazel extract (or hamamelis extract) has outlived many of the patent medicines of our great-grand-parents' day. Commercial manufacture of witch hazel extract began in 1866, when Thomas Newton Dickinson, a minister and entrepreneur,

187. Hamamelis is from the Greek *hama*, "together with," and *melon*, "apple" or "fruit," and it refers to the witch hazel's producing "flowers together with the fruit." Flowering begins just as the witch hazel's leaves start to turn from their dull green of summer to a translucent yellow, and it continues well after the leaves have fallen. It is not unusual to see the witch hazel's fragile-looking flowers, with their crinkled golden-yellow petals that look like miniature ribbons, covered by an early snowfall. Being the last of our native plants to flower, witch hazel is surely the last source of nectar for many insect pollinators. It is interesting that a plant with yellow flowers is the last to blossom, because many of our earliest spring-flowering trees and shrubs are also yellow. At the same time that they are in flower, the previous year's seed pods have matured. Each pod contains two shiny black seeds, and, when the pod has dried enough to split apart, the seeds will be expelled, with a popping noise, over a distance of twenty feet or more.

built a witch hazel distillery in Essex, Connecticut. Originally, witch hazel brush was cut locally and then transported either by boat or by horse and wagon to the distillery. The company has always obtained the witch hazel it needs from the forests of southern New England, and most of the harvest now comes from the northwestern corner of Connecticut. And today, as in the past, the brushcutters—farmers and woodcutters working their own land or land they have contracted to clear—sell directly to the distiller. Work begins in October and often continues until late spring. Sometimes only the branches are cut; otherwise, the plant is cut to the ground. But, because witch hazel quickly sprouts from stumps, only a few years will pass before a plant may be harvested again. The invention of the portable chipper allowed the refining process to begin right on site, and now the brush arrives at the factory ready to be distilled in stainless-steel vats, where steam is applied for more than thirty-six hours to the chopped brush. The vaporized essence, which comes from the cambium layer just under the outer bark,

is "scrubbed" in washing chambers, reheated to vapor, condensed, and filtered. Today's modern equipment and techniques still deal with three basic elements—witch hazel brush, water, and heat—and T. N. Dickinson's "formula." The clear liquid you see in a bottle of hamamelis extract is 86 percent "double distilled" witch hazel and 14 percent alcohol.

Witch hazel's applications seem to have changed as little as its manufacturing process. The explorer botanist Peter Kalm reported the use of *Hamamelis virginiana* by Native Americans in treating eye diseases as early as 1751. They called the plant "magic water," boiled the stems and used the liquid not only for their eyes but also to treat cuts, bruises, and scratches. The many modern-day applications of aqueous witch hazel approved by the Food and Drug Administration include treating sores, minor lacerations, sprains, and tired and puffy eyes.

There is also a mystical side to *Hamamelis virginiana:* its use in the occult arts. The common name witch hazel was given to *H. virginiana* by early English settlers be-

188. Witchal was a stronger mix of witch hazel and alcohol. A legend published by the Dickinson Witch Hazel Company places "a more attractive spirit" in the Witchal bottle. According to Dickinson's advertising, "In the early days it was believed that when the good witches boiled the Witch Hazel twigs in their cauldrons it was a sign that the potion was ready for use when the phantomlike shape of a beautiful young woman could be seen rising through the steam." Apparently, the batch in this illustration has not quite reached that stage.

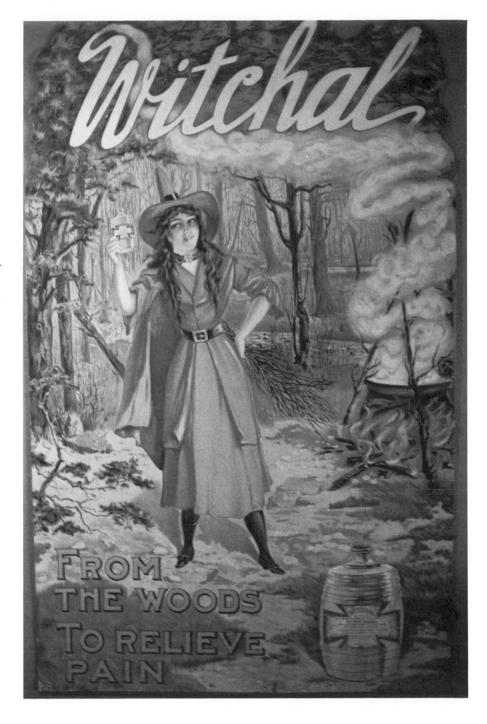

189. Birch bolts on their way to becoming toothpicks at the Forster Manufacturing Company in Wilton, Maine.

cause they believed it possessed the ability "to divine." Our native tree was not the first plant to be called witch hazel; the colonists brought the name with them across the Atlantic. Its application is an example of how often a common name reflects an association people make with a plant, rather than an accurate description.

In Great Britain, dowsers used their native elm, *Ulmus glabra*, which they called the "witch hazel tree," to find hidden veins of precious metal or underground springs. In Old English, *wice* meant "lively" or "to bend," and, as a dowser approached the site of, say, a potentially productive spring, the branch would become "lively" and begin to point to the source.

The pliant branches of the elm were also used by archers to make their bows. When it was reported that the "aborigines" made the same use of *Hamamelis virginiana* for their weapons, it seems that the colonists were convinced to transfer all the elm's associated powers to the New World plant. Although many plants were used for dowsing, witch hazel became the preferred one for use as a divining rod.

Wood in Everyday Life

Whereas the essence of witch hazel resides incognito in the medicine cabinet, we are just as unaware of the source and identity of the many wooden objects that make up a large part of our world. Birch and beech, along with maple, make up the trio of what many manufacturers consider to be "the hardwoods." Although these trees are quite distinct from one another botanically, and, in fact, each of these three genera (*Betula, Fagus,* and *Acer*) is the source from which its family name (Betulaceae, Fagaceae, or Aceraceae) is derived, the physical properties of their woods are very similar, and the uses that they are put to often overlap. Sugar maple, or, as lumbermen prefer, hard maple (*Acer saccharum*), with its pale cream to pie-crust-brown wood, is fine-textured, strong, and exceptionally hard, and it takes a fine polish. Its wood is slightly superior to the wood of birch and beech, and, although the woods of all three are often used interchangeably, hard maple is usually preferred by the makers of high-grade furniture and those who do fine

190. The finished product moving down the conveyor belt. Arthur J. Haug, President of the Forster Manufacturing Company, set the record straight on the wood used for making toothpicks in a letter to Abigail Van Buren in 1983. Apparently, a correspondent who had signed her letter "Vacationing" had raised some questions on oral hygiene, and Mr. Haug took umbrage with Abby's published reply. "And as for suggesting that the lady might pick up Dutch elm disease from chewing toothpicks—that is impossible. All domestic manufacturers of toothpicks (and I am one) use white birch. Please correct the record and reinstate your credibility. [signed] Arthur J. Haug, President, Forster Manufacturing Co., Inc., Wilton, Maine."

finish work. But the clear, light-colored wood of birch and beech are often used more extensively throughout our homes. Not only is much flooring, paneling, and furniture made of birch and beech, but these woods are also used for plywood, subflooring, and the framework of upholstered furniture—those necessary, but hidden, structural elements that we seldom see. There is another category of wooden products, little everyday things with which we are so familiar that we tend to overlook them: clothespins, brush backs, kitchen utensils, handles for knives, brooms, and small hand tools, as well as popsicle sticks and toothpicks, are also made from the lumber of these two trees.

Surprisingly, three-fourths of the lumber marketed under the name birch is actually yellow birch, *Betula alleghaniensis*, and its fine-grained wood is among the most valuable of northern hardwoods. Once mechanization allowed its hard wood to be separated into thin sheets, yellow birch became a sought-after species for decorative veneers and plywood. The process of bonding thin layers, veneers, or leaves of wood together in

191. These spring-clip clothespins were made at the National Clothes Pin Factory in Montpelier, Vermont, and are sold under the trade name Klos Klips. The company, located in a wooden building constructed in 1908 for the manufacture of clothespins, is one of the three remaining clothespin factories in the United States. Each week the company uses 10,000 board feet of wood to produce 750,000 clothespins—and they are still using some of the original equipment from 1908 to do so. According to the president of the company, although they also use maple and birch, "beech wood is the best type of wood for our purposes because it is harder, less porous, and tends to be whiter."

sandwichlike fashion to make a board similar to modern-day plywood has been known since ancient times. A wall painting that decorates the tomb of one of Egypt's Old Kingdom rulers depicts men constructing a box by gluing separate sheets of wood together, and a coffin discovered in the Saqqara Pyramid that dates from approximately 2750 B.C. was made with six layers of cypress, juniper, and cedar of Lebanon veneers; in this instance, rivets of gold, rather than glue, held the layers of these precious woods together. Using decorative face veneers of a more fine-figured wood to cover a less-attractive base wood is a method cabinetmakers have long employed to make the most economical use of rare, exotic, or expensive woods. Veneering is a labor-intensive craft, and, until modern machines allowed wood to be easily separated into thin sheets—called fletches in the industry—slicing logs into slender sheets of uniform thickness with hand tools was equally, if not more, laborious. A New Englander, John Dresser of Stockbridge, Massachusetts, mechanized the process in 1840 by inventing a hand-cranked veneer lathe. Veneers that are only one millimeter thick (one twenty-fourth of an inch) are now made either by positioning a block of wood, preheated by steam or hot water to soften it, on a carriage that moves back and forth beneath a huge blade and pressure plate, or by mounting a log on a machine that rotates it against a log-length, pressure-backed knife blade. The first method produces separate sheets; the second, which separates the veneer from the log as if unwinding a roll of paper, results in one continuous sheet. Cutting veneers with a saw rather than a knife is still used when the wood is exceptionally hard. This method wastes much of the wood because the kerf, the slit the saw blade creates as it cuts through the wood, is often the same width as the thickness of the veneer itself.

The latest methods for producing veneers allow the lustrous sheen and faint pinkish tones of the yellow birch's figured grain and its uniformly textured wood to be used to great advantage, and it is considered to be one of the best veneer species that grows in the United States. Because *Betula alleghaniensis* veneers—as little as one millimeter thick—can be cut at room temperature and can dry as fast or faster than those of any other hardwood, this species has become the standard against which other hardwood species are compared.

Michaux used the specific epithet *lutea*, Latin for "golden yellow," to describe this species of birch. At the same time, he cited the name *Betula excelsa*, a binomial a contemporary plantsman had proposed for yet another birch species, as a synonym for the yellow birch. Unfortunately, this rendered Michaux's name for the yellow birch incorrect, a nomenclatural faux pas that escaped detection until 1953. In 1904, Nathaniel Lord Britton, chief proponent and first director of the New York Botanical Garden and a botanist who specialized in the flora of North America, discovered what he believed to be another native birch, which he named *Betula alleghaniensis*. Britton's new species was, in fact, a form of the yellow birch, and, as the nation's chief forester, Elbert L. Little, pointed out in his *Checklist of the Native and Naturalized Trees of the United States*, by the rules of botanical nomenclature, *B. lutea*, the yellow birch, became *B. alleghaniensis*, the birch from the Allegheny Mountains. As a common name, the birch from the Alleghenies does not capture the imagination, nor does it speak for this species' most notable feature, its yellowish-bronze, shaggy, shiny bark. But, when the mavens of the *International Code of Botanical Nomenclature* adhere to the rules and correct mistakes that other botanists have committed, they help to make the language of plants more precise. So long as the plant's identity is correct, a nursery catalogue that lists plants by their current botanical names ensures that the plant ordered is precisely the plant being sought. Botanical binomials are exact, while common names are frequently confusing, regional in their application, suggestive of relationships that do not exist, and likely to become obsolete. Witness "yellow poplar" and "poor man's shirt tree" as common names for *Liriodendron tulipifera*. But, when a common name has become attached to a species of great commercial importance, as in the case of this yellow-barked birch, it is unlikely that a new common name will successfully supplant the old one.

Unlike the paper birch (*Betula papyrifera*), the yellow birch is not a circumboreal species: it is restricted to eastern North America. Yellow birches do, however, grow farther north than the gray, river, or sweet birches (*B. populifolia*, *B. nigra*, and *B. lenta*, respectively). *Betula alleghaniensis is* a common tree of the forests of southeastern Canada and of those of the northeastern states and and the Great Lakes region, and its range continues along the Appalachian Mountains southward into eastern Tennessee and northern Georgia. With the exception of Cape Cod and the islands of Martha's Vineyard and Nantucket, yellow birches can be found throughout New England, but they occur with greater frequency and attain their greatest size—reaching upwards of seventy feet in height, making them the tallest of our native birches—in eastern Canada and in northern New England and New York. Unlike the gray birch (*B. populifolia*), the yellow birch is not a pioneer species but is commonly associated with various stages of climax forests. The yellow birch is considered to be a "fugitive species," which means that it cannot compete with the more shade-tolerant climax species unless it can quickly occupy a habitat that offers a balance of sun and shade. An opening in the canopy caused by windthrows, or by the topping of trees in severe storms, presents the yellow birch with its

most optimal conditions for seeding, germination, and growth. The seeds need a dependably moist soil in which to germinate in a site that lacks a dense cover of leaves or forest litter. When the wind blows down a tree, yellow birch seedlings quickly occupy the mounds created by the upheaved roots. These disturbed areas lack substantial amounts of litter, and, by being able to tolerate the moderate shade that keeps the mounds moist, yellow birch seedlings can prosper and grow. This strategy for survival, the quick occupancy of gaps created in dense forests in which climax species are usually competing under relatively stable environmental conditions, keeps the yellow birch a transient or "fugitive" inhabitant of almost all stages in forest succession

The birch collection in the Arnold Arboretum is located on the north-facing slope of Bussey Hill. A grove of yellow birches grows amid an array of gray-, white-, reddish-, and black-barked trees that encompasses more than forty species, varieties, hybrids, and cultivars of birch. Collected in Bar Harbor, Maine, these yellow birches have grown on this grass-covered hillside since 1900. With their trunks firmly anchored to the dry, gravelly ground, these trees have attained impressive proportions as cultivated specimens, but they look sedate and tame in comparison with their wild counterparts in New England's north woods, and, without the benefit of a cool, moist climate, their bark is more of a silvery gray than yellow, and it holds only hints of the lustrous golden sheen displayed by wild trees.

The birch family, Betulaceae, contains five genera in addition to *Betula*. Taken together, the six genera consist of more than one hundred species; the beech family, Fagaceae, also consists of six genera, but this family has more than six times the number of species as the Betulaceae. North America is rich with birches. Of the fifty to sixty species in the genus *Betula*, fifteen or more are endemic to the temperate regions of this continent; of that number, fully a third grow in New England. There are only about ten species of beech throughout the world. North America has but two; the United States, one. *Fagus grandifolia*, the American beech, grows in the eastern United States from eastern Canada to the Gulf of Mexico, while *F. mexicana*, which some taxonomists believe to be a variety of the American beech, *F. grandifolia* var. *mexicana*, inhabits the mountainous regions of Mexico.

Beeches are exceptionally handsome, stalwart trees that light up the forest throughout the year. Clad in a luminous skin of smooth, thin, gray bark, they are the ghost trees that glimmer at night in the winter wood. On winter days, their sturdy gray trunks and limbs fuse

The New Yankee Forest

snow-covered earth to leaden skies. In spring, beeches glow with a tender green as their delicately fringed vernal leaves unfold like silken fans. More fully expanded, their leaves, sharp-toothed and a dark blue-green, shine in the summer sun. Then, in fall, their leaves turn a translucent yellow that can either trap the sparkle of sunlight on a clear, crisp day or illuminate a dark and somber sky. Long after the frosts of September and October have split their prickly burs and freed the two three-sided nuts, their leaves, bleached a pale tan, hang on. They cling to the twigs well into winter's whiteness, dry, brittle shells of leaves curled up within themselves.

Although they are companion species in the moist soils of cool, north-facing slopes, the beech, unlike the yellow birch, seldom perches on a rock or a log—it plants itself squarely on the ground and lays hold of the earth with elephantine roots. Beeches also fix themselves in place with a wide-ranging web of shallow roots. These roots may sucker, sending up thickets of growth that often remain small and shrubby. Characteristically, although as many as a dozen of these root sprouts, which arise from adventitious buds that form on the roots, will reach sapling size, most will never attain the status of trees during the life of the parent plant. Beech is a slow-growing, long-lived tree whose range includes almost all of eastern North America. The American beech is a mesophytic species, and, as such, it is a tree that requires only average moisture conditions. For example, drought-resistant oaks require only about five inches of water annually for growth; the beech consumes twice that amount. But it is also a species that can be quite sensitive to reductions and fluctuations in soil moisture. The largest beech trees occur on alluvial bottom land in the southern part of their range. When growing in these consistently moist environments, beeches seldom sprout root suckers. However, in the northern part of their range, where the moisture content of the soil may fluctuate, beeches sucker vigorously: having a large number of suckers greatly enhances the ability of the root system to absorb

any available water. Among the northern hardwoods, the beech is the most tolerant of shade and root competition, and it is considered to be, along with the sugar maple, whose tolerance equals, and whose longevity exceeds, that of the beech, a climax species of this forest type.

A fine grove of beeches graces the east bank of the Arboretum's Bussey Brook. With its characteristic mixture of the species' different stages of growth—understory root suckers forming a thicket beneath sapling-sized and mature trees—this grove exemplifies the appearance of a typical stand of native American beech growing in New England. Although its prominent location suggests that a plantsman with a keen sense of composition and a flair for the dramatic selected the site, it is not, in fact, a planted grove but a remnant of the native New England forest. Although Frederick Law Olmsted recognized the naturalistic effect that could be achieved by the use of this large forest tree and included only the native species in his planting plans for the Boston park system, there are relatively few planted stands of American beech in our cultivated landscape. Individual specimens of American beech planted in parks, gardens, or yards are also a rarity. Once the European beech, *Fagus sylvatica*, was introduced as a ornamental tree in the early 1800s, gardeners and horticulturists consistently favored the exotic species and its many attractive cultivars over the native one.

Colonial farmers clearing land for crops considered beech a nusiance: after cutting down these large trees, they still had to deal with the beeches' dense, brushy thickets. They quickly discovered that, when beech wood comes in contact with soil, it decays rapidly and cannot, therefore, be used for sills or foundations, or even for fencing. But, as they cleared stands of beech from their farmlands, they did come to appreciate the fact that beech burns well, and it is also an excellent wood from which to make charcoal. So, burn beech they did: cords of beech wood were consumed in fireplaces, and stacks of beech wood smoldered in charcoal pits. Lumbermen, too, found

192. Although they can endure a range of moisture and soil conditions, yellow birches (*Betula alleghaniensis*) make their best growth in hilly or mountainous terrain on the moist, rich, well-drained soils that are often found on the cooler northern and eastern slopes. In poorly drained areas, their seedlings can persist on moss-covered rocks, and they thrive on old mossy logs and stumps. Eventually, their roots (which are well adapted for dealing with exposure) reach the ground, and the stumps and logs that provided places for the seeds to germinate and a nursery area in which the seedlings could become saplings, rot and disappear, leaving the yellow birches to live on with their trunks suspended above the forest floor on curiously contorted spiderlike roots.

193. "A winter landscape in the Arboretum of which I never tire has for its dominant note the large clump of American Beech on the left bank of the Bussey Brook near the Arbor-vitae and opposite the northern end of the Hemlock grove. The parent tree is dead but from its far spreading roots scores of saplings have sprung up and form a large thicket. . . . In this setting the clump of Beech with its pale gray bark and myriads of slender, spreading branches suggests from a distance a billowy cloud of morning mists." (E. H. Wilson, *America's Greatest Garden; the Arnold Arboretum*, 1925.)

beech wanting; its wood was difficult to season, causing lumber sawn from it to warp, check, twist, and split. However, its wood did have some redeeming qualities. It could withstand friction under water, and millwrights put it to use making the axles and the shafts of waterwheels. Makers of other machines that had wooden parts that were constantly wet, such as old-fashioned washing machines, also used beech wood. Consequently, except in these few specialized situations, and in the making of such small items as brush backs or handles for cutlery and tools, beech wood was not utilized to a great extent until modern methods of kiln drying made it possible to control the rate at which beech lumber is seasoned.

Until the end of World War II, the production of finished wooden goods was a major component of the New England economy. While fuel wood, pulpwood, and lumber used for ties, poles, and beams left the forest or sawmill in rough form—but ready for use—the conversion of forest resources into "secondary" products sustained a thriving concentration of regional wood-using industries. Not only were the shuttles, spools, and bobbins that were manufactured for the textile mills and the lasts and fillers that were destined for shoe factories made and used in New England, they were exported worldwide. And out of mills from Maine to Connecticut came the pine crates and boxes and the fragrant excelsior in which New England's products, wooden or not, were packed and shipped.

By the 1960s, the textile and shoe manufacturers (like their predecessors in the tanning, naval-stores, shipbuilding, charcoal-making, and small-arms industries, all once great consumers of wood) had all but forsaken New England. But, just as large-scale manufacturing no longer plays a significant part in the New England economy, wood no longer plays an extensive role in production lines. New technologies have evolved: shuttleless looms

194. Excelsior—thin, curled, strands of wood commonly called "ribbon veneer" —was produced with a battery of machines that included a wood splitter, a cut-off saw, a barker, a knife-and-spur grinder, and a baling press. These vertical or upright knife-and-spur machines, the last step before the product is baled, were grinding out excelsior at a factory in Union, New Hampshire, during the early 1900s. Excelsior first appeared on the market in the middle of the nineteenth century. It was called "wood fiber," and its principal use was for mattress stuffing. An upholsterer used the trade name Excelsior in his advertising, and, as with kleenex and xerox, the trade name became synonymous with the product. As a packing material, which was its principal use, excelsior was preferred to sawdust, shavings, and hay because it was free from dirt and dust and it was also light and nearly odorless. It was also used to stuff carriage seats, automobile cushions, and furniture. Basswood (*Tilia americana*) was the wood preferred for its manufacturer and it brought the highest prices on the market. Poplars made up about half the wood used, followed by yellow pine.

are obviously no longer in need of fast-flying dogwood shuttles, and pocket calculators have completely replaced rock maple (and even plastic) slide rules. Technology has also generated synthetic materials that can be substituted for wood. We have moved from cedar and spruce canoes to ones made of Kevlar and fiber-glass; from bats made of ash to aluminum ones; and, unfortunately, from paper packing and its predecessor, excelsior, to the ubiquitous plastic "peanut." Since World War II, however, while both large wood-products companies and small cottage woodworking manufactories have declined in number, timber-based industries have increased their demands on New England's forest. While innovations enabled the lumber industry to make veneers out of birch wood and to control the drying process of beech, many wood products produced today transcend the characteristics and structure that is particular to the wood of each species. Formerly, working with wood meant dealing either with the whole tree or with products made from portions of its trunk, and the qualities of the wood of each species (its capacity to bend, its moisture content, its hardness, strength, or brittleness, as well as its ability to hold nails, take paint, and saw easily) determined which trees were used. Today, new methods for processing wood and tree products have influenced the ways in which many New England species are used. In many cases, these advances have enabled the substitution of one wood or a combination of woods for another. The development of durable synthetic-resin adhesives during World War II expanded and redefined an entire range of wood-based products. Glue-laminated timbers, exterior plywood, and sandwich panels—two thin facings of wood bonded to a thick core of a weak, low-density material, such as rubber foam, foamed glass, cloth, metal, or even paper—increased the capacity of wood to bend, weather, and provide thermal insulation, as well as making wood more fire resistant. Today, raw material from the forest no longer needs to be in log form: particleboard, flakeboard, waferboard, and oriented-strand board use wood that has been reduced to small fragments then bonded back together. Now sawmills no longer have waste; every part of a saw log is usable residue, even bark, chips, and sawdust. And coarse residues from secondary forest products, such as planer shavings, plywood mill waste, roundwood waste, and wood chips, have become important sources of raw material for fiber-based reconstituted woods. Insulation board, fiberboard, and laminated paperboard are but three products that use wood that has first been reduced to fibers or fiber bundles before being put back together by a process of manufacturing that produces panels of rela-

tively large size and thickness. Innovations such as these have necessitated the improvement of forest-management practices.

In 1884, when Charles Sprague Sargent, the Arnold Arboretum's young, ambitious director, submitted a *Report on the Forests of North America* to the Secretary of the Interior for publication as a separate volume of the nation's tenth (1880) census, the viability of the nation's forests was being questioned. Initially, timber had been thought to be an inexhaustible resource; but, by the nineteenth century, the fear that the nation's forest resources could soon be depleted had taken hold. Sargent viewed the project, which he began in 1880, as an opportunity to accomplish "the much needed work in showing the great wealth and value of our forests, and the dangers with which their destruction will threaten us." Sargent organized his report into three parts: a catalogue of 412 forest trees (which included remarks on taxonomy, distribution, economic value, and use), a critical examination of the physical and economic properties of the wood of each of these species, and a study (by state and territory) of the condition, extent, and economic potential of the North American forest.

The first distribution maps made for many native North American trees appeared in a portfolio issued to supplement the report, but the maps that accompanied the text best summed up the impact that lumbering had already made on many of these species. The multicolored maps depicted the type of forest and its density with "special reference to the lumber industry." The legend varied from map to map, but dark green usually indicated stands of virgin forest—whether hardwood or softwood—and lighter shades of green identified cutover areas and regions where the forest was less dense. The land from which all the merchantable timber had been removed was colored brown. Brown prevailed throughout the Northeast, where the original forest had been destroyed, but brown swatches, thousands of acres in extent, abutted the dark green of the pine forests of the Great Lakes region and those of the Southeast. Except for the lands of the trans-Mississippi West, the highways of the lumber industry along the nation's river systems — a vast network of broad, brown tentacles—penetrated deep into the country.

Before striking out on the series of field trips that would take him across the country to view firsthand the state of the forests, Sargent had sought advice from his friend and mentor Charles Perkins Marsh. Sargent would later attribute his interest in forests and his concern with their preservation to Marsh's seminal work, *Man and*

Nature: or, Physical Geography as Modified by Human Action. Marsh's treatise included chapters on wildlife, water, sands, and the effects of engineering projects. But it focused on the ecology of forests and the consequences of deforestation—especially along rivers and in watersheds. By undertaking the census report, Sargent had had the opportunity to test Marsh's theories. But what better place to start observing and documenting the inroads that logging had made than in New England? Sargent was optimistic. About southern New England's forests, he wrote of the promise that a second, third, and fourth growth of trees held for the future, and of the original pine and spruce forests of northern New England, he wrote, "The forests of Maine, once considered practically exhausted, still yield largely and continuously, and the public sentiment which has made possible their protection is the one hopeful symptom in the whole country that a change of feeling in regard to forest property is gradually taking place." Sargent concluded that "The forests of the United States, in spite of the great and increasing drains made upon them are capable of yielding a larger amount of material than has yet been drawn from them, even with our present reckless methods of forest management." He warned, however, that the nation would face more than a substantial loss in forest resources if the timber policies continued unchanged.

Sargent's investigations into the forest flora of North America tempered his early plans for the Arnold Arboretum's design. Mindful of the Arboretum's original indenture of 1872, to grow "all the trees, shrubs, and herbaceous plants either indigenous or exotic, which can be raised in the open air at the said West Roxbury," Sargent had been acquiring plants from throughout the world's North Temperate Zone for more than a decade. Concurrent with the acquisition of plants, Sargent had been working on a scheme for their arrangement with Frederick Law Olmsted. Negotiations with Olmsted for the design of the Arboretum had begun in 1874, and, by 1878, he had agreed "to furnish a plan." By 1884, Olmsted had prepared as many as thirteen studies for the design of the permanent arrangement of the collections.

On 5 February 1885, a year after the *Report on the Forests of North America* had been published, Sargent described his concept for the selection and siting of trees in a letter to Olmsted.

I should therefore propose to make a selection of North American trees with some of the most important foreign trees to serve as an illustration of the tree growth of the temperate portion of the world; arrange them in as large groups of species as space will permit with the view of allowing their full development and the opportunity for their satisfactory display; and consider this collection as the show part of the Arboretum for the general education of the public.

Later that year, Olmsted's design was completed and accepted, and Sargent went public with the plan in his annual report to the President of the University for the year ending 31 August 1885. The influence that his work on the native forest flora held in his concept of the role that a public Arboretum should play is evident in this excerpt from his report:

The selection of this type collection has only been reached after the most careful consideration and with many modifications of the plan which at first appeared practicable. It will contain, as now determined upon, representatives of all the genera of trees hardy in Eastern Massachusetts. Species of doubtful hardiness and all accidental and other varieties not permanently fixed by time or long cultivation will be excluded. Prominence will be given to the species of Eastern North America, and especially to those native of New England, because these species are better adapted to reach maturity in this climate than those of any other region; and because it is believed that the community, which will naturally have the closest relation with the Arboretum, will derive the greatest benefit from the examination of a collection of our native trees growing under favorable conditions and eventually fully developed. And this will doubtless be found true whether the collection studied in its scientific, industrial, or purely ornamental aspect."

Originally, Sargent had planned to represent each tree species in two different settings. A single specimen placed alone close by the roadway would show the form and shape of an open-grown tree. Behind this representative, a grove composed of several individuals of the same species would enable visitors to observe their appearance when growing in a "forest" situation. Initially having less than 135 acres in which to accommodate the imposing number of plants included in his and Olmsted's design for the Arboretum, the execution of this scheme must have appeared questionable even at the onset, and other events would soon radically alter Sargent's preliminary plans. In 1872, very little was known about the botanical and horticultural riches of the Asian flora. The wealth of the botanical diversity within western China, as well as the botanical similarities between the flora of eastern North American and that of eastern Asia, were just beginning to be discovered. Sargent would launch a series of botanical expeditions in eastern Asia when he visited Japan in 1892. Ernest Henry Wilson joined in this effort in the first decade of the twentieth century, and his introductions were to change the face of the Arboretum's collections and would enrich the gardens of North America.

Siting multiple representatives of a single species in the Arboretum's collection had to be abandoned within a few years; but, by taking advantage of the availability of native species, Sargent did manage to execute his plan in a few instances during the first years of planting. Today, amid the major collections, there remain scattered groves of the forest trees of New England that represent the vision of his original concept.

The examination of the management and productivity of New England's forests is a topic that does not lie dormant for long. In celebration of the nation's bicentennial, Charles H. W. Foster, Dean of the School of Forestry and Environmental Studies of Yale University, addressed the Society of American Foresters on the state of the region's forests, in Boston, on 11 March 1976. In his keynote speech, Dean Foster proposed that, in recognition of the "successive waves of utilization that first swept over early New England, then the Lake States, then the West, and most recently the South," New England's regenerated woodlands had become the county's Fifth Forest.

At no time since the arrival of the Europeans, until today, has so much of New England's landscape been forested. Eighty-one percent of the region's land surface—from the low, sandy hills of Cape Cod, where the wind sculpts the waist-high shrub oaks and twisted pitch pines, westward to Connecticut's stands of oaks and hemlocks, and northward into the "big woods" of Maine, the country of spruce and balsam spires—is, once again, reforested, a situation that even Charles Sprague Sargent could not have anticipated. This forest that constitutes Dean Foster's Fifth Forest is neither the colonist's "well-wooded earthly paradise" nor "a hideous and desolate wilderness." Rather, it is the new Yankee forest, which Lloyd Irland so aptly describes (in his paper of the same name) as being a patchwork of "wildlands and woodlots."

Today, more than 108,000 New Englanders work either in the forest or with the forest's products. Of that number, more than 61,000 people hold jobs associated with the paper industry. Lumber and wood products employ an additional 30,000 people, and nearly 17,000 workers make furniture and other wooden fixtures. Although synthetics are often used where wood once was, wood is still the best material for many of the things that we use daily. Although tradition and aesthetics influence our preference for using wood, in many instances, its durability, coupled with its renewability as a resource, make it a sound (and an economically and environmentally wise) choice. Thus, New England's forests continue to support a multitude of specialized industries and countless small, family-owned businesses that transform trees into durable goods. New Englanders are makers of paper and boxes, woodenware and picture frames, tennis rackets, tool handles, toys, and snowshoes, as well as musical instruments. Skilled operators working lathes, saws, and drills turn out cabinets, doors, windows, and millwork, as well as sash, trim, plywood, and pallets. And artisans ensure that many of our old ways with wood endure by practicing their crafts using hand tools—and, occasionally, even with ancient woodworking machines driven by waterpower—to make everything from custom-made furniture to hand-built boats.

BIBLIOGRAPHY

ILLUSTRATION CREDITS

INDEX

Ackerman, E. 1976. "Rediscovering hackmatack." *Wooden Boat* 9: 44–46.

Adams, J. T., ed. 1944. *Album of American History: Colonial Period.* New York: Charles Scribner's Sons.

Adney, E. T. 1944. "Native berries and fruits." *Acadian Naturalist* 9: 44–46.

Adney, E. T., and H. I. Chapelle. 1964. *The Bark Canoes and Skin Boats of North America.* Washington, D.C.: Smithsonian Institution.

Ahlgren, I. F. 1979. "New hope for eastern white pine." *American Forests* 85(9): 46–62.

Albion, R. G. 1926. *Forest and Sea Power: The Timber Problem of the Royal Navy, 1652–1862.* Cambridge, Massachusetts: Harvard University Press.

Allen, R. S. 1957. *Covered Bridges in the Northeast.* Brattleboro, Vermont: Stephen Greene.

Anagnostakis, S. L. 1978. "The American chestnut: New hope for a fallen giant." *Connecticut Agricultural Experiment Station Bulletin 777,* pp. 1–9.

———. 1981. "Knowledge of genetic barriers helps control chestnut blight." *Frontiers of Plant Science* 34: 6–7.

———. 1988. "Hypovirulence in chestnut blight in Connecticut improves the condition of chestnut trees." *Frontiers of Plant Science* 41(1): 1–8.

Anburey, T. 1789. *Travels through the Interior Parts of America in a Series of Letters by an Officer.* London: Printed for William Lane. [1969 repr. of 1789 ed. New York: Arno Press.]

Anderson, E. 1933. "Basswood bark and its use by the Indians." *Arnold Arboretum Bulletin of Popular Information* (Series 4) 1: 33–37.

Anonymous. 1891. "Rhododendron maximum." *Meehan's Monthly* 1:1–2.

Anonymous. 1892. *List of Large, Old and Interesting Trees.* Boston: Massachusetts Horticultural Society.

Anonymous. 1908. "The making of a hickory handle." *Hardwood Record* 25: 24–25.

Anonymous. 1914. "The chestnut bark disease: Control; utilization." *New Hampshire Forestry Commission Bulletin No. 6.,* pp. 16–40.

Anonymous. 1915. "The tulip or yellow poplar tree." *American Forestry* 21: 833–844.

Anonymous. 1942. "Need dogwood blocks for textile shuttles." *Journal of Forestry* 40: 876.

Anonymous. 1955. "Shuttles and bobbins." *Economic Botany* 9: 38.

Anonymous. 1957. "Yellow poplar (*Liriodendron tulipifera*): Yellow poplar, tallest among the broad-leaved trees." *U.S. Department of Agriculture, Forest Service Publication No. 27.*

Anonymous. 1980. "Pretty as it is useful." *InterEssence* 1(2): 1–6.

Anonymous. 1987. *Working Water: A Guide to the Historic Landscape of the Blackstone River Valley.* Providence: Rhode Island Department of Environmental Management, Rhode Island Parks Association.

Anonymous. n.d. *The American Elm: Its Glorious Past, Its Present Dilemma, Its Hope for Protection.* Washington, D.C.: American Forestry Association.

Ansel, W. D. 1983. *The Whaleboat: A study of Design, Construction and Use from 1850 to 1970.* Mystic, Connecticut: Mystic Seaport Museum.

Appleyard, D. 1978. "Urban trees, urban forests: What do they mean?" In *Proceedings of the National Urban Forestry Conference,* Vol. 1 (Session 1, Nov. 13–16), pp. 138–155.

Ascher, A. A. 1985. "The oldest seed company in America." *Green Scene* 14(1): 13–17.

Aughanbaugh, J. 1967. "All about hickory." *American Forests* 73(7): 28–29.

Axtell, J., ed. 1981. *The Indian Peoples of Eastern America: A Documentary History of the Sexes.* New York: Oxford University Press.

Back, E. A., and F. Rabak. 1922. "Red cedar chests as protectors against moth damage." *U.S. Department of Agriculture Bulletin No. 1051,* pp. 1–14.

Bagnall, W. R. 1893. *The Textile Industries of the United States, Including Sketches and Notices of Cotton, Woolen, Silk, and Linen Manufacturers in the Colonial Period.* Cambridge, Massachusetts: The Riverside Press.

Bailey, L. N. 1898. *Sketch of the Evolution of Our Native Fruits.* New York: Macmillan Publishing Company.

Baker, G. 1947. *Primary Wood-using Industries of Maine.* Maine Agricultural Experiment Station Bulletin No. 448.

Baker, W. A. 1973. *A Maritime History of Bath, Maine and the Kennebec River Region.* Bath, Maine: Marine Research Society of Bath.

Bardin, P. C. 1923. "The outline history of the sawmill." *Hardwood Record* 55: 35–36.

Barnhart, J. H. 1909. "Some American botanists of former days." *Journal of the New York Botanical Garden* 10: 177–190.

Bartram, J. 1751. *Observations on the Inhabitants, Climate, Soil, Rivers, Productions, Animals, and Other Matters. . . .*

London. [1895 repr. of 1751 ed. Geneva, New York: Humphrey.]

Batchelder, S. F. 1925. *The Washington Elm Tradition: "Under this Tree Washington First Took Command of the American Army." Is It True?* Reprinted from the *Cambridge Tribune*.

Battison, E. A. 1973. *The American Clock 1725–1865: The Mabel Brady Garvan and Other Collections at Yale University*. Greenwich, Connecticut: New York Graphic Society.

Baxter, D.V. 1967. "Disease in forest plantations: Thief of time." *Cranbrook Institute of Science Bulletin No. 51*. pp.1–251.

Beattie, R. K., and J. D. Diller. 1954. "Fifty years of chestnut blight in America." *Journal of Forestry* 52: 323–329.

Beauchamp, W. M. n.d. "Aboriginal use of wood in New York." *New York State Museum Bulletin No. 89*, pp. 87–272.

Belknap, J. 1812. *The History of New Hampshire . . . Containing A Geographical Description of the State*. 3 vols. Dover, New Hampshire: O. Crosby and J. Vaney.

Bennett, M. K. 1955. "The food economy of the New England Indian, 1605–1675." *Journal of Political Economy* 63: 369–397.

Bidwell, P. W. 1916. "Rural economy in New England at the beginning of the nineteenth century." *Transactions of the Connecticut Academy of Arts and Sciences* 20: 241–399.

———. 1925. *History of Agriculture in the Northern United States, 1620–1860*. Washington, D.C.: Carnegie Institution.

Bigelow, J. 1814. *Florula Bostoniensis: A Collection of Plants of Boston and Its Environs, with Their Generic and Specific Characters, Synonyms, Descriptions, Places of Growth and Time of Flowering and Occasional Remarks*. Boston: Cummings and Hilliard.

———. 1817–1820. *American Medical Botany*. 3 vols. Boston: Hilliard and Metcalf.

———. 1822. *A Treatise on the Materia Medica*. Boston: Charles Ewer.

Bloomfield, H. 1980. "New hope for the chestnut." *American Forests* 86(1): 14–17, 59–62.

Bogart, E. L. 1948. *Peacham: The Story of a Vermont Hill Town*. Montpelier: Vermont Historical Society.

Bolles, A. S. 1881. *Industrial History of the United States*. [1966 repr. of 3rd ed. New York: Augustus M. Kelley.]

Bolton, H. E., and T. M. Marshall. 1971. *The Colonization of North America, 1492–1783*. New York: Hafner Publishing Company.

Bourque, B. J. 1973. "Aboriginal settlements and subsistence on the Maine coast." *Man in the Northeast* 6: 3–20.

Bradley, W. T. 1936. "Medical practices of the New England aborigines." *Journal of the American Pharmaceutical Association* 25: 138–147.

Brasser, T. J. C. 1971. "The Coastal Algonkians: People of the first frontiers." In E.B. Leacock and N.O. Lurie, eds., *Indians in Historical Perspective*, pp. 64–91. New York: Random House.

———. 1978. "Early Indian–European contacts." In B. G.

Trigger, ed., of *Handbook of North American Indians*, Vol. 15. Washington, D.C.: Smithsonian Institution Press.

Braun, E. L. 1974. *Deciduous Forests of Eastern North America*. (Facsimile of 1950 ed.) New York: The Free Press.

Brayshaw, T. C. 1966. "The names of yellow birch and two of its varieties." *Canadian Field-Naturalist* 80: 160–161.

Bridenbaugh, C. 1955. *Cities in the Wilderness: The First Century of Urban Life in America, 1625–1742*. New York: Alfred A. Knopf.

———. 1955. *Cities in Revolt: Urban Life in America, 1743–1776*. New York: Alfred A. Knopf.

———. 1961. *The Colonial Craftsman*. Chicago: University of Chicago Press.

Briggs, M. S. 1932. *The Homes of the Pilgrim Fathers in England and America (1620–1685)*. London: Oxford University Press.

Britton, E. G. 1922. "Wild flowers needing protection: 14. Great laurel or rose-bay (*Rhododendron maximum* L.)." *Journal of the New York Botanical Garden* 23: 137–138.

Britton, N. L. 1904. "Four new North American birches." *Bulletin of the Torrey Botanical Club* 31: 166.

———. 1905. "The Hemlock grove on the banks of the Bronx and what it signifies." *Transactions of the Bronx Society of Arts and Sciences* 1(1):5–13.

Brooks, A. B. 1937. "*Castanea dentata*." *Castanea* 2: 61–67.

Brown, J. H. 1966. *Early American Beverages*. Rutland, Vermont: Charles E. Tuttle Company.

Brown, N. C. 1919. *Forest Products: Their Manufacture and Use*. New York: John Wiley & Sons.

Brown, S. C. 1978. "Beers and wines of old New England." *American Scientist* 66: 460–467.

Brush, W. D. 1918. "Utilization of elm." *United States Department of Agriculture, Forest Service Bulletin No. 683*.

———. 1922. "Utilization of basswood." *United States Department of Agriculture, Forest Service Bulletin No. 1007*.

———. 1927. "The wood industries of New England." *Forest Weekly* 3(3): 15–16.

Burk, C. J., and M. Holland. 1979. *Stone Walls and Sugar Maples*. Boston: Appalachian Mountain Club.

Burnham, C. R. 1988. "The restoration of the American chestnut." *American Scientist* 76: 478–487.

Burns, H. 1962. *Drugs, Medicine and Man*. New York: Charles Scribner's Sons.

Butler, E. L., and W. S. Hadlock. 1957. "Uses of birch bark in New England." *Robert Abbe Museum Bulletin* 7: 1–66.

Byran, E. W. 1900. *The Progress of Invention in the Nineteenth Century*. New York: Munn & Company.

Campana, R. J. 1978. "Dutch elm disease: Perspectives after 60 years." *Search Agriculture (Plant Pathology 1) 8(5): 1–52*.

Campbell, C., and F. Hyland. 1978. *Winter Key to Woody Plants of Maine*. Rev. ed. Orono: University of Maine Press.

Card, F. W. 1902. "The forests of Rhode Island." *Agricultural*

Experiment Station of the Rhode Island College of Agriculture and Mechanic Arts Bulletin No. 88, pp. 13–39.

Carroll, C. E. 1973. *The Timber Economy of Puritan New England*. Providence, Rhode Island: Brown University Press.

Carver, J. 1779. *Travels Through the Interior Parts of North America in the Years 1766, 1767, and 1768*. London: William Richardson.

Catesby, M. 1731–1743. *The Natural History of Carolina, Florida, and the Bahama Islands*. 2 vols. London.

Catton, B., and W. B. Catton. 1978. *The Bold and Magnificent Dream: America's Founding Years, 1492–1815*. New York: Doubleday Publishing Company.

Chamberlain, A.F. 1891. "Maple sugar and the Indians." *American Anthropologist* 4: 381–383.

Chamberlain, L. S. 1901. "Plants used by the Indians of eastern North America." *American Naturalist* 35: 1–10.

Chapman, H. H. 1952. "The place of fire in the ecology of pines." *Bartonia* 26: 39–44.

Clarence, A. D. 1963. *Blueberries: From Barrens to Farms: Farming in Maine, 1860–1940*. Orono: University of Maine Press.

Clark, C. E. 1983. *The Settlement of Northern New England, 1610–1763*. Hanover, New Hampshire: University Press of New England.

Cobb, C. M. 1917. "Some medical practices among the New England Indians and early settlers." *The Boston Medical and Surgical Journal* 177(4): 97–105.

Conkey, R. E., E. Boissevan, and I. Goddard. 1978. "Indians of southern New England and Long Island: Late period." In B. G. Trigger, ed., *Handbook of North American Indians*, Vol. 15. Washington, D.C.: Smithsonian Institution Press.

Cook, H. O. 1910. *How to Make Improvement Thinnings in Massachusetts Woodlands*. Boston: Wright & Potter Printing Company.

Cooke, S. F. 1973. "The significance of disease in the extinction of the New England Indians." *Human Biology* 45: 485–508.

Coolidge, P. T. 1963. *A History of Maine Woods*. Bangor, Maine: Furbush-Roberts Printing Company.

Coville, F. V. 1937. "Improving the wild blueberry." In *U.S. Department of Agriculture, Bureau of Plant Industry, Yearbook of Agriculture*.

Cowley, C. 1868. *Illustrated History of Lowell*. Rev. ed. Boston: Lee & Shepherd.

Cox, T. R. 1985. "Americans and their forests: Romanticism, progress, and science in the late nineteenth century." *Journal of Forest History* 29: 156–166.

Cox, T. R., R. S. Maxwell, P. D. Thomas, and J. J. Malone. 1985. *This Well-wooded Land: Americans and Their Forests from Colonial Times to the Present*. Lincoln: University of Nebraska Press.

Cromie, G. A., and W. O. Filley. 1912. "The planting and care of street and highway trees." *Documents of the Civic Federation of New Haven No. 8*, pp. 1–19.

Cronon, W. 1983. *Changes in the Land*. New York: Hill and Wang.

Crosby, I. B. 1928. *Boston Through the Ages: The Geological Story of Greater Boston*. Boston: Marshall Jones Company.

Crosby, S. S. 1974. *The Early Coins of America*. Lawrence, Massachusetts: Quarterman Publications.

Cruikshank, J. W. 1940. "The utilization of dogwood in the lower south." *Journal of Forestry* 38: 284–85.

Cummings, A. L. 1979. *The Framed Houses of Massachusetts Bay, 1625–1725*. Cambridge, Massachusetts: Belknap Press of Harvard University Press.

Cuno, J. B. 1926. "Utilization of dogwood and persimmon." *United States Department of Agriculture Department Bulletin No. 1436*, pp.1–42.

Curtis, J. D. 1946. "Preliminary observations on northern white cedar in Maine." *Ecology* 27: 33–36.

Cutler, Manasseh. 1785. "An account of some of the vegetable productions naturally growing in this part of America." *American Academy of Arts and Sciences Memoirs*. 1: 396–493.

Czestochowski, J. S. 1982. *American Landscape Tradition: A Study and Gallery of Paintings*. New York: E. P. Dutton.

Dame, L. L., and H. Brooks. 1902. *Handbook of the Trees of New England*. Boston: Ginn & Company.

Dana, H. S. 1889. *History of Woodstock, Vermont*. Boston and New York: Houghton Mifflin Company.

Dana, S. T. 1909. "Paper birch in the northeast." *U.S. Department of Agriculture, Forest Service Circular No. 163*, pp. 1–37.

Darling, Dr. 1846. "Indian diseases and remedies." *The Boston Medical and Surgical Journal* 34(1): 9–13.

Davidson, D. S. 1937. "Snowshoes." *Memoirs of the American Philosophical Society* 6:1–189.

Davis, R. B. 1960. "A late glacial pollen diagram from Taunton, Massachusetts." *Bulletin of the Torrey Botanical Club* 87: 258–270.

———. 1966. "Spruce–fir forests of the coast of Maine." *Ecological Monographs* 36(2): 79–94.

Davis, R. B., and G. L. Jacobson, Jr. 1985. "Late Glacial and early Holocene landscapes in northern New England and adjacent areas of Canada." *Quaternary Research* 23: 341–368.

Day, C. A. 1963. *Farming in Maine, 1860–1940*. Orono: University of Maine Press.

Day, G. M. 1953. "The Indians as an ecological factor in the northeastern forest." *Ecology* 34: 329–346.

———. 1962. "English–Indian contacts in New England." *Ethnohistory* 9: 24–40.

Day, J. 1979. "Harvesting hackmatack knees: A conversation with Frank Morse." *Wooden Boat* 30: 66–72.

Defebaugh, J. E. 1906. *History of the Lumber Industry of America*. 2 vols. Chicago: The American Lumberman.

DeForest, J. W. 1853. *History of the Indians of Connecticut from the Earliest Known Period to 1850*. Hartford: Connecticut Historical Society.

Del Tredici, P. 1981. "*Magnolia virginiana* in Massachusetts." *Arnoldia* 41(2): 36–49.

Dengler, H. W. 1967. "Bayberries and bayberry candles." *American Forests* 73(12): 5–7, 46.

Devlin, R. M. 1969. *Plant Psychology*. 2nd ed. New York: Van Nostrand.

DeWolf, G. P., Jr. 1975. "Common pines of Massachusetts." *Arnoldia* 35: 197–229.

Dexter, L. A., ed. 1982. *The Gosnold Discoveries*. Brookfield, Massachusetts: Published by the editor.

Diller, J. D. 1965. *Chestnut Blight*. U.S. Department of Agriculture, Forest Pest Leaflet No. 94. Washington, D.C.: U.S. Government Printing Office.

Dincause, D. F. 1971. "Prehistoric land use in the Arnold Arboretum." *Arnoldia* 31: 108–113.

———. 1972. "The Atlantic phase: A late Archaic culture in Massachusetts." *Man in the Northeast* 4: 40–61.

———. 1974. "An introduction to archaeology in the greater Boston area." *Archaeology of Eastern North America* 2: 39–67.

Dincauze, D. F., and M. T. Mulholland. 1976. "The Neville site: 8000 years at Amoskeag, Manchester, New Hampshire." *Peabody Museum Monographs* 4, pp. 1–150.

Doty, C. L. 1969. "River birch, *Betula nigra*." *The Morton Arboretum Quarterly* 5(4): 55.

Douglass, W. 1749–[1757]. *A Summary, Historical and Political of the First Planting, Progressive Improvements, and the Present State of the British Settlements in North America*. 2 vols. Boston: Rogers & Fowle.

Douthat, S. 1989. "Pinning their future on wood: Plant still makes beech clothespins." *Boston Sunday Globe*, 31 December, p. 35.

Downing, A. J. 1844. *A Treatise on the Theory and Practice of Landscape Gardening Adapted to North America: With a View to the Improvement of Country Residences*. 2nd ed. New York and London: Wiley and Putnam.

Dunwell, S. 1978. *The Run of the Mill: A Pictorial Narrative of the Expansion, Dominion, Decline and Enduring Impact of the New England Textile Industry*. Boston: David R. Godine, Publisher.

Dutky, E. M. 1983. *Controlling Plant Disease in Home Landscapes*. College Park: Cooperative Extension Service, University of Maryland.

Dutlinger, F. H. 1925. "The grey birch." *Forest Leaves* 20: 30–31.

Dwelley, M. 1980. *Trees and Shrubs of New England*. Camden, Maine: Down East Books.

Earle, A. M. 1898. *Home Life in Colonial Days: Illustrated by Photographs Gathered by the Author, of Real Things, Works and Happenings in Olden Times*. New York: Macmillan Company.

Ebeling, W. 1979. *The Fruited Plain: The Story of American Agriculture*. Berkeley, California: University of California Press.

Edlin, H. 1969. *What Wood is That? A Manual of Wood Identification*. London: Thames & Hudson.

Elias, T. S. 1980. *The Complete Trees of North America*. New York: Outdoor Life/Nature Books.

Eliot, C. W. 1914. "Town Forest" Contest. Rules of the Contest in order to encourage reforestation.

Elliot, F. R. 1868. *Popular Deciduous and Evergreen Trees and Shrubs for Planting in Parks, Gardens, and Cemeteries, etc., etc.* New York: Francis W. Woodward.

Elliott, S. B. 1912. *The Important Timber Trees of the United States*. Boston: Houghton Mifflin Company.

Ellis, G. E. 1880. *Memoir of Jacob Bigelow, M.D., LL.D.* Cambridge, Massachusetts: John Wilson and Son.

Elliston, J. E. 1981. "Hypovirulence and chestnut blight research: Fighting disease with disease." *Journal of Forestry* 79: 657–660.

Ellsworth, L. 1975. *Craft to National Industry in the 19th Century: A Case Study of the Transformation of the New York State Tanning Industry*. New York: Arno Press.

Emerson, A. F. 1981. *Early History of Naushon Island*. 2nd ed. Boston: Howland and Company.

Emerson, G. B. 1846. *Report on the Trees and Shrubs Growing Naturally in the Forests of Massachusetts*. Boston: Dutton and Wentworth.

Evans, J. G. 1975. *The Environment of Early Man in the British Isles*. London: Paul Elek.

Eyde, R. H. 1959. "The discovery and naming of the genus *Nyssa*." *Rhodora* 61: 209–219.

Fairbanks, J. L. 1982. *New England Begins: The Seventeenth Century*. (Catalogue of the exhibition held at the Museum of Fine Arts, May 5–Aug. 22, 1982. Department of American Decorative Arts and Sculpture.) Boston: Boston Museum of Fine Arts.

Fales, D. A. 1972. *American Painted Furniture, 1660–1880*. New York, New York: E. P. Dutton.

Fay, J. H. 1974. "Masting the fleets of Britannia." *American Forests* 80(10): 16–19.

Felt, E. P. 1938. *Our Shade Trees*. New York: Orange Judd Publishing Company.

Fergus, C. 1985. "Wild nuts: A gatherer's compendium." *Blair & Ketchum's Country Journal* 12(10): 23–32.

Fernald, M. L. 1922. "Notes on the flora of Nova Scotia." *Rhodora* 24: 166.

Fernald, M. L., and A. C. Kinsey. 1943. *Edible Wild Plants of Eastern North America*. Cornwall-on-Hudson, New York: Idlewild Press.

Fitting, J. E. 1968. "Environmental potential and the postglacial readaptation in eastern North America." *American Antiquity* 33: 441–444.

Flemer, W., III. 1980. "The remarkable witch hazel family." *Green Scene* 9(2): 21–22.

Fleming, R. L., and L. A. Halderman. 1982. *On Common*

Ground: Caring for Shared Land from Town Common to Urban Park. Boston: The Harvard Common Press.

Flint, H. L. 1983. *The Country Journal Book of Hardy Trees and Shrubs.* Brattleboro, Vermont: Country Journal Publishing Company.

Fowler, W. S. 1954. "Agricultural tools and techniques of the Northeast." *Massachusetts Archaeological Society Bulletin* 15(3): 41–51.

———. 1972. "Woodworking: An important industry." *Massachusetts Archaeological Society Bulletin* 35: 29–40.

———. 1976a. "A review of dugout–making." *Massachusetts Archaeological Society Bulletin* 37: 1–6.

———. 1976b. "Procurement and use of bark." *Massachusetts Archaeological Society Bulletin* 37: 15–19.

Fowles, H. A. 1965. "Silvics of forest trees of the United States." *U.S. Department of Agriculture, Forest Service, Agricultural Handbook No. 271.*

Fox, W. F. 1903. *Tree Planting on Streets and Highways.* (Seventh Report of the State of New York Forest, Fish and Game Commission.) Albany: J. B. Lyon Company.

Frick, G. F., and R. P. Stearns. 1961. *Mark Catesby: The Colonial Audubon.* Champaign: University of Illinois Press.

Frothingham, E. H. 1912. "Second growth hardwoods in Connecticut." *U.S. Department of Agriculture, Forest Service Bulletin No. 96,* pp. 14–47.

Fulling, E. H. 1954. "American witch hazel—history, nomenclature, and modern utilization." *Economic Botany* 7: 359–381.

Funk, R. E. 1972. "Early man in the Northeast and the late glacial environment." *Man in the Northeast* 4: 7–39.

Furnas, J. C. 1969. *The Americans: A Social History of the United States, 1587–1914.* New York: G. P. Putnam's Sons.

Gerard, W. R. 1896. "Plant names of Indian origin." *Garden and Forest* 9: 436–440.

Gifford, G. E., Jr. 1980. "Botanic remedies in colonial Massachusetts, 1620–1820." *Publications of the Colonial Society of Massachusetts* (57): 263–288.

Glubok, S., ed. 1969. *Home and Child Life in Colonial Days.* (Abridged from *Home Life in Colonial Days* and *Child Life in Colonial Days,* by Alice Morse Earle.) London: The Macmillan Company.

Goldenberg, J. A. 1976. *Shipbuilding in Colonial America.* Charlottesville: The University Press of Virginia.

Gookin, D. 1792. *Historical Collections of the Indians of New England.* [1970 repr. of 1792 ed.] New York: Arno Press.

Gould, M. E. 1942. *Early American Wooden Ware and Other Kitchen Utensils.* Springfield, Massachusetts: The Pond-Ekberg Company.

Gove, W. G. 1970. "Making wooden bowls." *Vermont Life* 24(4): 10–14.

Graves, A. H. 1943. "A brief historical survey of the use of plants in medicine." *Brooklyn Botanic Garden Record* 32: 169–186.

Grey, G. W., and F. J. Deneke. 1978. *Urban Forestry.* New York: John Wiley & Sons.

Grosselin, R. 1962. "The status of natural products in the American pharmaceutical market." *Lloydia* 24: 241–243.

Gutman, A. 1973. "Work, culture, and society in industrial America, 1815–1919." *American Historical Review* 78: 531–588.

Hallberg, M. C., and R. A. Clemente. 1971. *The Pulp and Paper Industry in the Northeast.* [Progress Report 313.] University Park: Pennsylvania State University.

Hallet, L. F. 1956. *Medicine and Pharmacy of the New England Indians.* Mansfield, Massachusetts: Published by the author.

Harder, K. B. 1976. *Illustrated Dictionary of Place Names.* New York: Van Nostrand Reinhold.

Harlow, W. M. 1970. *Inside Wood: Masterpiece of Nature.* Washington, D.C.: American Forestry Association.

———. 1979. *Textbook of Dendrology: Covering the Important Forest Trees of the United States and Canada.* 6th ed. New York: McGraw-Hill Book Company.

Harper, R. M. 1918. "Changes in the forest area of New England in three centuries." *Journal of Forestry* 16: 442–452.

Harris, S. K. 1942. "Spruce and balsam fir." *New England Naturalist* 14: 31.

Harrison, J. B. 1889. "The abandoned farms of New Hampshire." *Garden and Forest* 2: 573–574.

Hay, J. 1979. *The Run.* 3d ed. New York: W. W. Norton & Company.

Hemmerly, T. E. 1970. "Economic uses of eastern red cedar." *Economic Botany* 24: 39–41.

Hempstead, A. G. 1931. *The Penobscot Boom and the Development of the West Branch of the Penobscot River.* Orono: University of Maine Press.

Henderson, H. L. 1932. "Dry kiln practice." *Bulletin of the New York State College of Forestry. Technical Publication No. 38.* 5(2).

Henshaw, H. W. 1890. "Indian origin of maple sugar." *American Anthropologist* 3: 341–391.

Hepting, G. H. 1974. "Death of the American chestnut." *Journal of Forest History* 18: 60–67.

Hergert, H. L. 1983. "The tannin extraction industry in the United States." *Journal of Forest History* 27: 92–93.

Hicock, H. W. 1970. "An early history of forests and forestry in Connecticut." *Connecticut Woodlands* 35: 26–30, 40.

Higgennbotham, B. W. 1947. "Sassafras shaped history." *Natural History* 56: 159–164.

Hinde, T. 1985. *Forests of Britain.* London: Victor Gollancz Ltd.

Hindle, B., ed. 1975. *America's Wooden Age: Aspects of its Early Technology.* Tarrytown, New York: Sleepy Hollow Press.

———. 1981. *Material Culture of the Wooden Age.* Tarrytown, New York: Sleepy Hollow Press.

Holbrook, S. H. 1959. *The Golden Age of Quackery.* New York: Macmillan Publishing Company.

Holman, M. M. 1985. "The history of the rhododendron." *Rosebay*. [Massachusetts Chapter of the American Rhododendron Society] 14(2): 10–15.

Holmes, F. W. 1988. *New England Records of Champion Trees*. Amherst: University of Massachusetts Shade Tree Laboratories.

Holmes, F. W., and H. M. Heybroek, trans. 1990. *Dutch Elm Disease—The Early Papers: Selected Works of Seven Dutch Women Phytopathologists*. St. Paul, Minnesota: APS Press.

Hopkins, A. D. 1901. *Insect Enemies of the Spruce in the Northeast*. Washington, D.C.: U.S. Government Printing Office.

Horsfall, F., Jr. 1969. "Horticulture in the eighteenth-century America." *Agricultural History* 43: 159–167.

Hosie, R. C. 1979. *Native Trees of Canada*. 8th ed. Don Mills, Ontario: Fitzhenry and Whiteside Ltd.

Hough, R. B. 1907. *Handbook of the Trees of the Northern States and Canada East of the Rocky Mountains*. Lowville, New York: Published by the author.

Howe, H. F. 1943. *Prologue to New England*. New York: Farrar & Rinehart.

Huden, J. C. 1962. "Indian place names of New England." *Contributions from the Museum of the American Indian Heye Foundation* 18: 1–408.

Hugh, B. A., M. N. Straugn, C. G. Church, et al. 1917. "Maple sugar: Composition, methods of analysis, effect of environment." *U.S. Department of Agriculture Bulletin No. 466*.

Hume, E. P. 1971. "Hemlock—graceful conifer." *Morton Arboretum Quarterly* 7(4): 37–41.

Hunt, C. B. 1974. *Natural Regions of the United States and Canada*. San Francisco: W. H. Freeman and Company.

Hutchinson, J. 1980. "A taste for horticulture." *Arnoldia* 40: 31–48.

Huth, H. 1957. *Nature and the American: Three Centuries of Changing Attitudes*. Lincoln: University of Nebraska Press.

Illick, J. S. 1922a. "The maples." *American Forestry* 28: 12–19.

———. 1922b. "The sycamores." *American Forestry* 28: 145–150.

———. 1922c. "The birches." *American Forestry* 28: 355–364.

———. 1922d. "The beeches." *American Forestry* 28: 546–551.

———. 1922e. "The white oak." *American Forestry* 28: 586–592.

———. 1924. *Tree Habits: How to Know the Hardwoods*. Washington, D.C.: American Nature Association.

———. 1925. "The black oaks." *American Forestry* 31: 488–494.

Imbrie, J., and K. D. Imbrie. 1986. *Ice Ages: Solving the Mystery*. Cambridge, Massachusetts: Harvard University Press.

Irland, L. C. 1975. "Importance of forest industries to New England's economy." *Northern Logger and Timber Processor* 24(3): 16–17, 38–39.

———. 1981. "Taps for the Yankee forest? How to make sure that it doesn't happen." *Connecticut Woodlands* 46(3): 6–10.

———. 1982. *Wildlands and Woodlots: The Story of New England's Forests*. Hanover, New Hampshire: University Press of New England.

Jack, J. G. 1889. "*Magnolia glauca* in its most northern home." *Garden and Forest* 2: 363–364.

Jackson, K. T. 1985. *Crabgrass Frontier: The Suburbanization of the United States*. New York: Oxford University Press.

Jaynes, R. A. 1968. "Progress with chestnuts." *Horticulture* 46(12).

———. 1974. "The search for blight-resistant chestnuts continues." *Horticulture* 52(5) 42–43.

———. 1978a. "Selecting and breeding blight resistant chestnut trees." *Proceedings of the American Chestnut Symposium, West Virginia University, Morgantown, January 4–5*. New Haven: Connecticut Agricultural Experiment Station.

———. 1978b. "The late, great American chestnut." *Horticulture* 56(5): 27–30.

Jensen, J. H. 1945. *Lumber and Labor*. New York. Farrar & Rinehart.

Johnston, M. 1985. "Gardening in America, 1830–1910." *Garden* 9(2): 16–20.

Jorgensen, N. 1977. *A Guide to New England's Landscape*. Chester, Connecticut: Globe Pequot Press.

Josselyn, J. 1672. *New England's Rarities*. London: G. Widdowes. [1860 repr. of 1672 ed. in *Archaeologia Americana* IV.]

———. 1675. *An Account of Two Voyages to New England, Made During the Years 1638, 1663*. 2nd ed. Boston: William Veazie; London: G. Widdowes. [1865 repr. of 1675 ed. in Massachusetts Historical Society Collections, 3rd Series.]

Judd, R. W. 1984. "Lumbering and the farming frontier in Aroostock County, Maine, 1840–1880." *Journal of Forest History* 28: 56–67.

———. 1988. "Reshaping Maine's landscape: Rural culture, tourism, and conservation, 1890–1929." *Journal of Forest History* 32: 180–190.

Kalm, P. 1770–1771. *Travels into North America*. 3 vols. Trans. by J. R. Forster. London: Warrington, Eyres, Lowndes.

Kammerer, E. L. 1943. "Birches." *Morton Arboretum Bulletin of Popular Information* 18(2): 17–24.

Kappel-Smith, D. 1982. "Pipeline in the sugarbush." *Country Journal* 9: 66–75.

Karnosky, D. E. 1982. "Double jeopardy for elms: Dutch elm disease and phloem necrosis." *Arnoldia* 42: 70–77.

Kavasch, B. 1979. *Native Harvests: Recipes and Botanicals of the American Indians*. New York: Random House.

Kawashima, Y., and R. Tone. 1983. "Environmental policy in early America: A survey of colonial statutes." *Journal of Forest History* 27: 178–179.

Kaye, C. A. 1976. "The geology and early history of the Boston area of Massachusetts: A bicentennial approach." *U.S. Geological Survey Bulletin No. 1476*.

Keeler, H. L. 1904. *Our Native Trees.* New York: Charles Scribner's Sons.

———. 1920. *Our Northern Shrubs and How to Identify Them.* New York: Charles Scribner's Sons.

Keene, A. S. 1981. *Prehistoric Foraging in a Temperate Forest.* New York: Academic Press.

Kempton, H. B. 1903. "The planting of white pine in New England." *U.S. Department of Agriculture, Bureau of Forestry Bulletin No. 45.*

Kennedy, D. H. 1857. *The Art of Tanning Leather: By a New and Improved System Theoretically and Practically Considered in All Its Details.* New York: Baker & Godwin, Printers.

Kennedy, G. G. 1916. "Some historical data regarding the sweet-bay and its station on Cape Ann." *Rhodora* 18: 205–212.

Kennedy, J. T. 1971. *The Hitchcock Chair: The Story of a Connecticut Yankee—L. Hitchcock of Hitchcocksville—and an Account of the Restoration of his 19th Century Manufactory.* New York: Clarkson N. Potter.

Ketchum, W. C., Jr. 1974. *American Basketry and Woodenware: A Collectors Guide.* New York: Macmillan Publishing Company.

Kienholz, R. 1970. "Early logging." *Connecticut Woodlands* 35(3): 6–9.

Kingsford, W. 1851. *History, Structure, and Statistics of Plank Roads, in the United States and Canada with Remarks on Roads in General and a Letter on Plank Roads.* Philadelphia: A. Hart.

Klauber, C. 1908. "The making of a hickory handle." *Hardwood Record* 25(12): 24–25.

Knowlton, C. H. 1950. "*Rhododendron maximum* in New England." *Rhodora* 52: 215–217.

Kramer, P. J., and T. T. Kozlowski. 1979. *Physiology of Woody Plants.* New York: Academic Press.

Krochmal, A. 1971. "A Guide to Medicinal Plants of Appalachia." *U.S. Department of Agriculture Handbook No. 400.*

Kulik, G., R. Parks, and T. Z. Penn, eds. 1982. *The New England Mill Village, 1790–1860.* Cambridge, Massachusetts: MIT Press.

Kunkel, D., and B. J. D. Meeuse. 1987. "Pollen grains by electron microscope." *University of Washington Arboretum Bulletin* 50(2): 2–11.

Largy, T. 1984. "Analysis of botanical remains from Charlestown Meadows, Westborough, Massachusetts." *Archaeological Quarterly* 6(2): 1–17.

Larson, E. H. 1965. *The Forest Wealth of Maine.* Maine State Forestry Department.

Larson, G. J., and B. D. Stone, eds. 1980. *Late Wisconsin glaciation of New England.* Dubuque, Iowa: Kendall/Hunt Publishing Company.

Lavine, S. A. 1966. *Handmade in America: The Heritage of Colonial Craftsmen.* New York: Dodd, Mead and Company.

Lawall, M. R. 1936. "Apothecary shops of colonial times." *Journal of the American Pharmaceutical Association* 25: 230–240.

Lee, G. 1838. *Two Lectures on Tanning Delivered Before the Eclectic Fraternity on the 7th and 14th February, 1838.* New York: Eclectic Fraternity.

Leroi-Gourhan, A. 1982. "The Archaeology of Lascaux Cave." *Scientific American* 246: 104–112.

Lewis, R. G. 1914. "The commercial importance of birch." *Canada Lumberman and Woodworker* 34(1): 30–32.

———. 1914. "The commercial importance of beech." *Canada Lumberman and Woodworker* 34(6): 34–35.

Lowe, D. 1974. "Reflections on a seventeenth-century house." *Blair and Ketchum's Country Journal* 1(3): 22–27.

Lowenthal, D. 1958. *George Perkins Marsh: Versatile Vermonter.* New York: Columbia University Press.

Lutz, H. J. 1930. "Observations on the invasion of newly formed glacial moraines by trees." *Ecology* 10(3): 562–567.

———. 1972. "Veneer species that grow in the United States." *U.S. Department of Agriculture, Forest Service Research Paper 167*, pp.1–127.

Macaulay, R. 1987. *Dull Dejection in the Countenances of All of Them: Children at Work in the Rhode Island Textile Industry, 1790–1938.* Pawtucket, Rhode Island: Slater Mill Historic Site.

Malone, J. L. 1964. *Pine Trees and Politics: The Naval Stores and Forest Policy in Colonial New England, 1691–1775.* Seattle: University of Washington Press.

Mangelsdorf, P. C. 1974. *Corn: Its Origin, Evolution, and Improvement.* Cambridge, Massachusetts: Harvard University Press.

Mann, J. 1824. *Travels in North America: Particularly in the Provinces of Upper and Lower Canada, and New Brunswick, and in the States of Maine, Massachusetts, and New York: Containing a Variety of Interesting Adventures and Disasters, Which the Author Encountered in His Journey among the Americans, Dutch, French, and Indians. . . .* Glasgow: Andrew Young.

Manning, S. F. 1979. *New England Masts and the King's Broad Arrow.* Kennebunk, Maine: Thomas Murphy.

Manning, W. E. 1973. "The northern limits of the distribution of hickories in New England." *Rhodora* 75: 34–51.

Marchand, P. J. 1987. *North Woods: An Inside Look at the Nature of Forests in the Northeast.* Boston: Appalachian Mountain Club.

Martin, C. 1973. "Fires and forest structure in the aboriginal eastern forest." *Indian Historian* 6(4): 38–42, 54.

———. 1978. *Keepers of the Game: Indian–Animal Relationships and the Fur Trade.* Berkeley: University of California Press.

Marx, L. 1981. *The Machine in the Garden: Technology and the*

Pastoral Ideal in America. New York: Oxford University Press.

Mattoon, W. R. 1909. "The origin and early development of chestnut sprouts." *Forestry Quarterly* 7: 34–47.

Maunder, E. R. 1968. "The history of land use in the Housatonic Valley." *Connecticut Woodlands* 33: 10–14.

Maxwell, H. 1910. *A Study of the Massachusetts Wood-using Industries.* Boston: Wright & Potter Printing Company.

———. 1913. "Uses of commercial woods of United States: Beech, birches and maples." *U.S. Department of Agriculture Bulletin No. 12.*

———. 1915a. "The story of white pine." *American Forestry* 21: 34–46.

———. 1915b. "Commercial uses of sugar maple." *American Forestry* 21: 1022–1030.

———. 1918a. "Indian medicines made from trees." *American Forestry* 24: 205–211.

———. 1918b. "The uses of wood: Woods used in the manufacture of handles." *American Forestry* 24: 679–687.

———. 1919a. "Fencing materials from forests." *American Forestry* 25: 923–930.

———. 1919b. "The uses of wood: Wood used in the cooperage industry." *American Forestry* 25: 1208–1216.

———. 1920. "The uses of wood: Wood in agricultural implements." *American Forestry* 26: 148–155.

McBridge, B. 1983. "A special kind of freedom." *Down East* 24: 92, 114–115.

McGregor, R. K. 1988. "Changing technologies and forest consumption in the upper Delaware Valley, 1790–1880." *Journal of Forest History* 32: 69–81.

McKenzie, M. A., and W. B. Becker. 1937. "The Dutch elm disease: A new threat to the elm." *Massachusetts Agricultural Experiment Station Bulletin No. 343.*

McManis, D. R. 1972. *European Impressions of New England, 1479–1620.* Chicago: University of Chicago Press.

———. 1975. *Colonial New England: A Historical Geography.* New York: Oxford University Press.

Melder, K. 1979. *Life and Times in Shoe City: The Shoe Workers of Lynn.* Salem, Massachusetts: Essex Institute.

Mergen, F. 1958. "Distribution of reaction wood in eastern hemlock as a function of its terminal growth." *Forest Science* 4: 98–109.

Meyer, J. E. 1960. *The Herbalist.* New York: Rand McNally.

Michaux, F. A. 1819. *The North American Sylva; or, A Description of the Forest Trees of the United States, Canada and Nova Scotia, Considered Particularly with Respect to Their Use in the Arts, and Their Introduction into Commerce. To Which is Added a Description of the Most Useful of the European Forest Trees.* Translated from the French [by A. L. Hillhouse]. 3 vol. Paris; Philadelphia.

Millspaugh, L. F. 1887. *American Medicinal Plants.* 2 vols. New York: Boerike & Tafel.

Moloney, F. X. 1931. "The fur trade in New England, 1620–1676." *Harvard Undergraduate Essays.* Cambridge, Massachusetts: Harvard University Press.

Monardes, N. 1925. *Joyfull Newes out of the Newe Founde Worlde.* Translated from the Spanish by John Frampton. London: Constable and Company, Ltd.; New York: Alfred A. Knopf.

Montgomery, M. R. 1982. "The thing about clothespins." *The Boston Globe Magazine.* 23 May 1982.

Moore, G. T. 1924. "White-oak acorns as food." *Missouri Botanical Garden Bulletin* 12: 32–33.

Morfit, C. 1860. *A Treatise on Chemistry, Applied to the Manufacture of Soap and Candles.* Philadelphia: Henry Carey Baird.

Morison, S. E. 1971. *The European Discovery of America: The Northern Voyages, A.D. 500–1600.* New York: Oxford University Press.

Munson, W. M. 1901. "The horticultural status of the genus *Vaccinium.*" *Maine Agricultural Experiment Station Bulletin* 76: 113–158.

Murrill, W. A. 1906. "A serious chestnut disease." *Journal of the New York Botanical Garden* 7: 143–153.

Nearing, H., and S. Nearing. 1970. *The Maple Sugar Book: Together with Remarks on Pioneering as a Way of Living in the Twentieth Century.* New York: Galahad Books.

Nellis, J. C. 1914. "Uses for chestnut timber killed by the bark disease." *U.S. Department of Agriculture, Farmers' Bulletin No. 582.*

Nelson, R. M. 1932. "Growth and mortality of chestnut sprouts." *Journal of Forestry* 30: 872–873.

Nevel, R. L., Jr., and J. T. Bones. 1980. "Northeastern pulpwood, 1978: An annual assessment of regional timber output." *U.S. Department of Agriculture, Forest Service Resource Bulletin NE-62.*

Newbanks, D., D. N. Roy, and M. H. Zimmerman. 1982. "Dutch elm disease: What an arborist should know." *Arnoldia* 42(2): 60–69.

Nichols, G. E. 1913. "The vegetation of Connecticut: II. Virgin forests." *Torreya* 13(9): 199–215.

———. 1935. "The hemlock–white pine–northern hardwood region of North America." *Ecology* 16: 403–422.

Noss, R. F. 1985. "On characterizing presettlement vegetation: How and why." *Natural Areas Journal* 5: 5–19.

Novak, B. 1979. *American Painting in the Nineteenth Century: Realism, Idealism, and the American Experience.* 2nd ed. New York: Icon Editions, Harper & Row.

Olson, J. S., F. W. Stearns, and H. Nienstaedt. 1959. "Eastern hemlock seeds and seedlings: Response to photoperiod and temperature." *Connecticut Agricultural Experiment Station Bulletin No. 620.*

Olson, S. 1971. *The Depletion Myth: A History of Railroad Use of Timber.* Cambridge, Massachusetts: Harvard University Press.

O'Neill, S. D. 1981. "The flora of Cuttyhunk Island, Massachusetts: With an analysis of vegetational changes over the past half century." *Rhodora* 83: 25–55.

Ormsbee, T. H. 1930. *Early American Furniture Makers: A Social and Biographical Study.* New York: Thomas Y. Crowell Company.

Osborn, W. C. 1974. *The Paper Plantation: Ralph Nader's Study Group Report on the Pulp and Paper Industy in Maine.* New York: Grossman Publishers.

Paget, A. 1927. "They built a business from a bayberry: Now they dip over a million candles a year." *The Cape Cod Magazine and Cape Cod Life* 37: 18–20.

Palmer, E. 1870. "Food products of the North American Indians." *U.S. Department of Agriculture Report No. 15,* pp. 404–428.

———. 1878. "Plants used by the Indians of the United States." *American Naturalist* 12: 593–606, 646–655.

Palmer, E. J. 1934. "Indian relics of the Arnold Arboretum." *Arnold Arboretum Bulletin of Popular Information* (Series 4)2: 61–68.

Patterson, M., and R. Patterson. 1982. "Acorns: A forgotten food." *American Forests* 88(8): 20–23.

Peattie, D. C. 1950. *A Natural History of Trees of Eastern and Central North America.* Boston: Houghton Mifflin Company.

Peterson, B. S., C. E. Cross, and N. Tilden. 1968. "The cranberry industry in Massachusetts." *U.S. Department of Agriculture Bulletin No. 201.*

Pettis, C. R. 1909. "How to grow and plant conifers in the northeastern states." *U.S. Department of Agriculture, Bureau of Forestry Bulletin No. 76.*

Pfeiffer, C. B. 1975. *Shad Fishing.* New York: Crown Publishers.

Phillips, H. 1823. *Sylva Florifera:* Vol. II. London: Longman, Hurst, Rees, Orme, and Brown.

Pielou, E. C. 1988. *The World of Northern Evergreens.* Ithaca, New York: Comstock Publishing Company.

Pierce, N. R. 1976. *The New England States.* New York: W. W. Norton & Company.

Pierson, A. H. 1913. "Wood using industries of Connecticut." *Connecticut Agricultural Experiment Station Bulletin No. 174.*

Pinchot, G. 1911. *A Primer of Forestry. Part 1: The Forest* (Farmers' Bulletin 173). Washington, D.C.: U.S. Government Printing Office.

———. 1911. *A Primer of Forestry. Part 2: Practical Forestry* (Farmers' Bulletin 385). Washington, D.C.: U.S. Government Printing Office.

Pinto, E. H. 1969. *Treen and Other Wooden Bygones: An Encyclopaedia and Social History.* London: G. Bell & Sons.

Putnam, B. L. 1896. "*Hamamelis virginiana.*" *Botanical Gazette* 21: 170.

Rackham, O. 1980. *Ancient Woodland: Its History, Vegetation and Uses in England.* London: Arnold.

Randall, C. E. 1967. "Ivy league forest." *American Forests* 73(4): 24–27.

———. 1967. "Black walnut: Our vanishing money tree." *American Forests* 73(10): 14–17.

Rasmussen, W. D. 1975. *Agriculture in the United States: A Documentary History.* New York: Random House.

Raup, H. M. 1935. "Notes on the early uses of land now in the Arnold Arboretum." *Arnold Arboretum Bulletin of Popular Information* (Series 4)3: 33–38.

———. 1937. "Recent changes of climate and vegetation in southern New England and adjacent New York." *Journal of the Arnold Arboretum* 18: 79–117.

———. 1939. "The north meadow." *Arnold Arboretum Bulletin of Popular Information* (Series 4)7: 21–24.

———. 1940. "Old field forests of southeastern New England." *Journal of the Arnold Arboretum* 21: 266–273.

———. 1941. "An old forest in Stonington, Connecticut." *Rhodora* 43: 67–71.

———. 1966. "The view from John Sanderson's farm: A perspective for the use of land." *Forest History* 10: 2–11.

Rehder, A. 1940. *Manual of Cultivated Trees and Shrubs Hardy in North America.* 2d ed. New York: Macmillan Publishing Company.

Reidel, C. H. 1978. *The Yankee Forest: A Prospectus.* New Haven: Yale School of Forestry and Environmental Studies.

———. 1982. *New England Prospects: Critical Choices in a Time of Change.* Hanover, New Hampshire: University Press of New England.

Remington, S. B., and P. E. Sendak. 1989. *New England and New York's Timber Economy: A Review of the Statistics.* Burlington, Vermont: Northwestern Forest Experiment Station.

Reynolds, R. V., and A. H. Pierson. 1942. *Fuel Wood Used in the United States.* Washington: U.S. Department of Agriculture Circular No. 641.

Ritter, E. 1940. "The distillation of birch oil." *Journal of Forestry* 38: 517–518.

Rivard, P. E. 1974. *The Home Manufacture of Cloth, 1790–1840.* Pawtucket, Rhode Island: Slater Mill Historic Site.

Roane, M. K. 1986. *Chestnut blight, other Endothia diseases, and the genus Endothia.* St. Paul, Minnesota: APS Press.

Roberts, R. C. 1975. "The liberty tree." *American Forests* 81: 20–21.

Ronnberg, E. A. R., Jr. 1985. *To Build a Whaleboat: Historical Notes and a Modelmaker's Guide.* New Bedford, Massachusetts: Old Dartmouth Historical Society Whaling Museum.

Rosier, J. 1906. "True relation of the voyage of Captaine George Waymouth." In *Early English and French Voyages.* H. S. Burrage, ed. New York: Charles Scribners' Sons.

Ross, A. H. D. 1915a. "The commercial importance of hemlock." *Canada Lumberman and Woodworker* 35(12): 32–33.

———. 1915b. "The commercial importance of cedar." *Canada Lumberman and Woodworker* 35(13): 26–28.

———. 1915c. "The commercial importance of tamarack. *Canada Lumberman and Woodworker* 35(15): 36–37.

———. 1915d. "The commercial importance of oak." *Canada Lumberman and Woodworker* 35(17): 28–30.

———. 1915e. "The commercial importance of maple." *Canada Lumberman and Woodworker* 35(17): 36–37.

Roszkiewicz, R. 1984. *The Woodturner's Companion.* New York: Sterling Publishing Company.

Rouse, C. 1986. *Fire Effects in Northeastern Forests: Oak.* U.S. Department of Agriculture, Forest Service. North Central Forest Experiment Station General Technical Report NC-105.

Rowe, W. H. 1948. *The Maritime History of Maine.* New York: W. W. Norton & Company.

Rowlee, W. W. 1899. "Historic trees of North America." *The Plant World* 2: 125–127.

Rush, B. 1793. "An account of the sugar maple tree of the United States, and of the methods of obtaining sugar from it, together with observations upon the advantages both public and private of this sugar" *Transactions of the American Philosophical Society.* 3: 64–79.

Russell, H. S. 1976. *A Long, Deep Furrow: Three Centuries of Farming in New England.* Hanover, New Hampshire: University Press of New England.

———. 1980. *Indian New England before the Mayflower.* Hanover, New Hampshire: University Press of New England.

Santamour, F. S., Jr. 1983. "Woody-plant succession in the urban forest: Filling cracks and crevices." *Journal of Arboriculture* 9: 267–270.

Sargent, C. S. 1884. *Report on the Forests of North America.* [Vol. 9 of the Tenth Census of the United States.] Washington, D.C.: U.S. Government Printing Office.

———. 1890–1902. *The Silva of North America.* 14 vols. Boston: Houghton Mifflin Company.

———. 1905. *Manual of the Trees of North America (exclusive of Mexico).* Boston: Houghton Mifflin.

———. 1922. "The first fifty years of the Arnold Arboretum." *Journal of the Arnold Arboretum* 3: 127–171.

Savage, H., Jr., and E. J. Savage. 1986. *André and François-André Michaux.* Charlottesville: University Press of Virginia.

Schall, D. 1978. "Cape Cod's trees: The pitch pine." *Cape Cod Naturalist* 7(2): 38–39.

Scheffer, T. C., G. H. Englerth, and C. G. Duncan. 1974. "A technical comparison of red and white oaks." *Wooden Boat* 1: 48–57.

Schlesinger, A. M. 1933. *The Rise of the City, 1878–1898.* New York: Macmillan Publishing Company.

Schoef, J. D. 1787. *Materia Medica Americana Potissimum Regni Vegetabilis.* Erlangen, Germany. [1903 repr. of 1787 ed. *Lloyd Library Bulletin No. 6* (Reproduction Series No. 3). Cincinatti.]

———. 1911. *Travels in the Confederation, 1783–1784.* Ed. by Alfred J. Morrison. 2 volumes. Philadelphia: William Campbell.

Schreiber, L. R., and J. W. Peacock. 1975. "Dutch elm disease and its control." *U.S. Department of Agriculture Information Bulletin No. 193.*

Scott, E. 1980. *Working in Wood: The Illustrated Manual of Tools, Methods, Materials and Classic Constructions.* New York: G. P. Putnam's Sons.

Scully, V. 1974. *The Shingle Style Today: Or, The Historian's Revenge.* New York: George Braziller.

Sears, R. 1853. *A Pictorial Description of the United States Embracing the History, Geographical Position, Agricultural and Mineral Resources, Population, Manufactures, Commerce, and Sketches of Cities, Towns, Public Buildings, etc. of Each State and Territory in the Union.* New York: Published by the author.

Senn, T. L. 1969. "Farm and garden: Landscape architecture and horticulture in eighteenth-century America." *Agriculture History* 43: 149–157.

Sewell, J. 1800. *Collection of Papers on Naval Architecture: Originally Communicated through the Channel of the Wrapper of the European Magazine; . . .* Vol. 1. 3rd ed. London: Bunney & Gold.

Seymour, F. C. 1969. *The Flora of New England.* Rutland, Vermont: Charles E. Tuttle Company.

Shepard, H. N. n.d. *Statutes of the Commonwealth of Massachusetts, Relating to Trees.* Boston: Massachusetts Horticultural Society.

Sherman, C. F. 1944. "Habitations, summer and winter sites." *Massachusetts Archaeological Society Bulletin* 6: 10–14.

Shurtleff, H. R. 1939. *The Log Cabin Myth.* Cambridge, Massachusetts: Harvard University Press.

Simmons, J. R. 1919. *The Historic Trees of Massachusetts.* Boston: Marshall Jones Company.

Skehan, J. W. 1979. *Puddingstone, Drumlins, and Ancient Volcanoes: A Geologic Field Guide along Historic Trails of Greater Boston.* 2nd rev. ed. Dedham, Massachusetts: WesStone Press.

Skutch, A. K. 1929. "Early stages of plant succession following forest fires." *Ecology* 10: 177–190.

Sleeper, M. O. 1949. "Indian place names in New England." *Massachusetts Archaeological Society Bulletin* 10: 89–97.

Smith, D. C. 1970. *History of Papermaking in the United States 1860–1969.* New York: Lockwood.

———. 1972. *A History of Lumbering in Maine, 1861–1960.* Orono: University of Maine Press.

Smith, D. M. 1970. "Connecticut parks and forests in the 20th century." *Connecticut Woodlands* 35: 31–40.

Smith, J. J., ed. 1858. "Cranberry culture." *The Horticulturist and Journal of Rural Art and Rural Taste* 8: 114–116.

Smith, W. H. 1970. *Tree Pathology: A Short Introduction.* New York: Academic Press.

Snow, D. R. 1947. *Eastern Algonquin Block-stamp Decoration:*

A New World Original or an Acculturated Art. With an addendum: Butler, E.L. Some early Indian basket makers of southern New England. Trenton, New Jersey: The Archaeological Society of New Jersey.

———. 1978. "Eastern Abnaki." In B. G. Trigger, ed. *Handbook of North American Indians,* Vol. 15. Washington, D.C.: Smithsonian Institution Press.

———. 1980. *The Archaeology of New England.* New York: Academic Press.

Speck, F. G. 1915. "Decorative art of Indian tribes of Connecticut." *Canada Geological Survey Memoir, 75. Anthropological Series No. 10.*

Speck, F. G., and R. W. Dexter. 1952. "Utilization of animals and plants by the Malecite Indians of New Brunswick." *Journal of the Washington Academy of Sciences* 42(1): 1–6.

Spring, S. N. 1905. "The Natural Replacement of White Pine on Old Fields in New England." *U.S. Department of Agriculture, Bureau of Forestry Bulletin No. 63.*

Springer, J. S. 1851. *Forest Life and Forest Trees.* New York, N.Y.: Harper & Brothers.

Stafleu, F. A. 1967. "Carolus Clusius' Austrian flora." *Taxon* 16: 535–537.

Sterrett, W. D. 1915. "The ashes: Their characteristics and management." *U.S. Department of Agriculture Bulletin No. 299.*

———. 1917. "Utilization of ash." *U.S. Department of Agriculture Bulletin No. 523.*

Stewart, G. R. 1945. *Names on the Land: An Historical Account of Place-Naming in the United States.* New York: Random House.

Steyermark, J. A. 1956. "Eastern witch hazel." *Missouri Botanical Garden Bulletin* 44: 99–101.

Stilgoe, J. R. 1983. *Metropolitan Corridor Railroads and the American Scene.* New Haven: Yale University Press.

Stout, A. B. 1914. "Vegetable foods of the American Indians." *New York Botanical Garden Bulletin* 15: 50–60.

Strobel, G. A., and G. N. Lanier. 1981. "Dutch elm disease." *Scientific American* 245: 56–66.

Stuhr, E. T. 1931. *Medicinal Trees of the United States.* Portland, Maine: American Pharmaceutical Association.

Sturtevant, W. 1975. "Two 1761 wigwams at Niantic, Connecticut." *American Antiquity* 40: 437–444.

Svenson, H. K., and R. W. Pyle. 1979. *The Flora of Cape Cod.* [Brewster, Massachusetts]: Cape Cod Museum of Natural History.

Swaine, J. M., F. C. Craighead, and I. W. Bailey. 1924. "Studies on the spruce budworm (*Cacoecia fumiferana* Clem.)." *Canadian Department of Agriculture Bulletin.*

Swartz, D. 1971. *Collegiate Dictionary of Botany.* New York: Ronald Press.

Tattar, T. A. 1978. *Diseases of Shade Trees.* New York: Academic Press.

Thomas, P. A. 1976. "Contrastive subsistence strategies and land use as factors for understanding Indian–white relations in New England." *Ethnohistory* 23: 1–18.

Thompson, B. 1976. *Black Walnut for Profit: A Guide to Risks and Rewards.* Phoenix, Arizona: Walnut Press.

Thomson, B. F. 1977. *The Changing Face of New England.* Boston: Houghton Mifflin Company.

Traub, M. 1944. *Roller Skating through the Ages: The Story of Roller Skates, Rinks, and Skaters.* New York: William-Frederick Press.

Trelease, W. 1894. "Sugar maples and maples in winter." *Fifth Annual Report of the Missouri Botanical Garden* pp. 1–19.

———. 1895. "The Pignuts." *Bulletin of the Torrey Botanical Club.* 22: 331.

———. 1916. "The oaks of America." *Proceedings of the National Academy of Science.* 2: 626–629.

Trigger, B.G., ed. 1978. *Northeast.* Vol. 15, *Handbook of North American Indians.* W. C. Sturtevant, gen. ed. 20 vols. Washington, D.C.: U.S. Government Printing Office.

Trimble, H. 1895. "Oil of birch." *Garden and Forest* 388: 303.

Tryon, R. M. 1917. *Household Manufactures in the United States, 1640–1860; A Dissertation.* Chicago: University of Chicago Press. [1966 repr. of 1917 dissertation. New York: Johnson Reprint Corporation.]

Vaughan, A. T. 1964. *New England Puritans and the American Indian, 1620–1675.* Ph.D. Dissertation, New York: Columbia University.

Vogel, V. J. 1970. *American Indian Medicine.* Norman: University of Oklahoma Press.

Waister, P. D., and M. R. Cormack. 1981. "The American cranberry." *Garden* 106: 307–309.

Walters, R. S., and A. Shigo. 1978. "Tapholes in sugar maples: What happens in the tree." *U.S. Department of Agriculture, Forest Service General Technical Report NE-47.*

Warren, J. C. 1855. *The Great Tree on Boston Common.* Boston: John Wiley & Son.

Warren, R., and A. J. Fordham. 1978. "The fire pines." *Arnoldia* 38: 1–11.

Watt, A. 1890. *The Art of Leather Manufacture.* 3rd ed. London: Crosby Lockwood & Son.

Watts, M. T. 1975. *Reading the Landscape of America.* Rev. ed. New York: Collier Books.

Waugh, F. W. 1916. "Iroquois foods and food preparation." *Canada Department of Mines Memoir 86, No. 12* (Anthropological Series 1-227).

Weaver, R. E., Jr. 1974. "The shadbushes." *Arnoldia* 34: 22–31.

———. 1976a. "Sassafras: A neglected native ornamental." *Arnoldia* 36: 22–27.

———. 1976b. "The witch hazel family (Hamamelidaceae)" *Arnoldia* 36: 69–109.

———. 1978. "The ornamental birches." *Arnoldia* 38: 117–131.

Weeden, W. B. 1963. *Economic and Social History of New England, 1620–1789.* New York: Hillary House Publishers.

Weeks, L. H. 1916. *A History of Paper Making in the United States, 1690–1916*. New York: Lockwood Trade Journal Company.

Wells, S. D., and J. D. Rue. 1927. "The suitability of American woods for paper pulp." *U.S. Department of Agriculture Bulletin No. 1485*.

Whitehead, D. R. 1979. "Late-glacial and postglacial vegetational history of the Berkshires, Western Massachusetts." *Quaternary Research* 12: 333–357.

Wilbur, K. C. 1978. *The New England Indians*. Chester, Connecticut: Globe Pequot Press.

Williams, E. 1975. "8,000 wedges and 4,000 trunnels." *Wooden Boat* 3: 44–48.

Williams, M. 1980. "Products of the forest: Mapping the census of 1840." *Journal of Forest History*. 24: 4–23.

———. 1987. "Industrial impacts on the forests of the United States, 1860–1920." *Journal of Forest History* 31: 108–121.

Williams, R. 1643. *A Key into the Language of America*. London: Gregory Dexter. [New ed. 1973. J. Teunissen and E. J. Hinz, eds. Detroit: Wayne State University Press.]

Williams, T. 1984. "Getting the red out." *Sanctuary* 23(4): 7–9.

Willoughby, C. C. 1906. "Houses and gardens of the New England Indians." *American Anthropologist* 8: 115–132.

———. 1908. "Wooden bowls of the Algonquian Indians." *American Anthropologist* 10: 422–434.

———. 1935. *Antiquities of the New England Indians, with Notes on the Ancient Cultures of the Adjacent Territories*. Cambridge, Massachusetts: Peabody Museum of American Archaeology and Ethnology, Harvard University.

Wilson, E. H. 1925. *America's Greatest Garden: The Arnold Arboretum*. Boston: Stratford Company.

Wilson, H. F. 1936. *The Hill Country of Northern New England: Its Social and Economic History, 1790–1930*. New York: Columbia University Press.

Winkler, M. G. 1985. "A 12,000-year history of vegetation and climate for Cape Cod, Massachusetts." *Quaternary Research* 23: 301–312.

Winship, G. P. 1905. "Bartholomew Gosnold, 1602, Buzzards Bay." In *Sailors Narratives of Voyages Along the New England Coast, 1524–1624*, with notes by George Parker Winship. Boston: Houghton Mifflin and Company.

Wood, P. 1977. *The Salt Book: Lobstering, Sea Moss Pudding, Stone Walls, Rum Running, Maple Syrup, Snowshoes, and other Yankee Doings*. New York: Anchor Press/Doubleday.

Wood, R. G. 1935. *A History of Lumbering in Maine, 1820–1861*. Orono: University of Maine Press.

Wood, W. 1634. *New England's Prospect*. London: Tho. Cotes, for John Bellamie.

Wright, L. B. 1957. *The Cultural Life of the American Colonies, 1607–1763*. New York: Harper & Brothers.

Wynn, G. 1974. "On the history of lumbering in northeastern America." *Acadiensis* 3: 122–129.

Young, J. H. 1961. *The Toadstool Millionaires: A Social History of Patent Medicines in America before Federal Regulation*. Princeton, New Jersey: Princeton University Press.

———. 1967. *The Medical Messiahs: A Social History of Health Quackery in Twentieth-Century America*. Princeton, New Jersey: Princeton University Press.

Youngquist, W. G., and H. O. Fleischer. 1977. *Wood in American Life*. Madison, Wisconsin: Forest Products Research Society.

Zaitzevsky, C. 1982. *Frederick Law Olmsted and the Boston Park System*. Cambridge, Massachusetts: The Belknap Press of Harvard University Press.

Zeide, B. 1982. "The fugitive yellow birch." *American Forests* 88(11): 36–39, 58.

ILLUSTRATION CREDITS

114 Photograph by Istvan Racz. Photographic Archives of the Arnold Arboretum.

115 Courtesy of the Yale University Art Gallery, Mabel Brady Garvan Collection.

116 From John Warner Barber, *Connecticut Historical Collections* (New Haven, 1836). Courtesy of Widener Library, Harvard University.

117 Photograph by Christopher Burnett. Courtesy of John Tarrant Kenney.

118 Courtesy of the National Museum of American History, Smithsonian Institution.

119 Photograph by Istvan Racz. Photographic Archives of the Arnold Arboretum.

120 Photograph by Albert Bussewitz. Photographic Archives of the Arnold Arboretum.

121 By permission of *The Boston Globe*.

122 From Edward W. Byrn, *The Progress of Invention in the 19th Century* (New York, 1900). Courtesy of Cabot Library, Harvard University.

123, 124 Photographic Archives of the Arnold Arboretum.

125 Courtesy of the National Museum of American History, Smithsonian Institution.

126 Photograph by Istvan Racz. Photographic Archives of the Arnold Arboretum.

127 Photograph by Albert Bussewitz. Photographic Archives of the Arnold Arboretum.

128 Courtesy of the Pusey Library Map Collection, Harvard University.

129 Photographic Archives of the Arnold Arboretum.

130, 131 Photographs by Albert Bussewitz. Photographic Archives of the Arnold Arboretum.

132 Drawing by Dorothy Marsh. Generic Flora of the Southeastern United States Project, Arnold Arboretum. Courtesy of Carroll E. Wood, Jr.

133, 134 Photographs by T. E. Marr. Photograph Archives of the Arnold Arboretum.

135 From Charles Mason Hovey, *Fruits of America* (Boston, 1852). Library of the Arnold Arboretum.

136 Photograph by Christopher Burnett. Portrait Collection, Photographic Archives of the Arnold Arboretum.

137 By permission of the Century Association and the National Museum of American Art, Smithsonian Institution, Gift of Thomas M. Evans and Museum Purchase.

138, 139 Photographic Archives of the Arnold Arboretum.

142 Photograph by Istvan Racz. Photographic Archives of the Arnold Arboretum.

143 From William Cullen Bryant, ed., *Picturesque America Or, The Land We Live In* (New York, 1894). Courtesy of Widener Library, Harvard University.

144 From Edward W. Byrn, *The Progress of Invention in the 19th Century* (New York, 1900). Courtesy of Cabot Library, Harvard University.

145 Illustration by Winslow Homer, "Lumbering in Winter," from *Every Saturday*, 23 January 1871. Courtesy of Widener Library.

146, 147 By permission of *The Boston Globe*.

148 Photograph by Istvan Racz. Photographic Archives of the Arnold Arboretum.

149 Photograph by Sheila Connor.

150 Pennsylvania Chestnut Blight Commission, Photograph Album. Archives of the Arnold Arboretum.

151 Photograph by E. A. Richardson. Photographic Archives of the Arnold Arboretum.

152 Courtesy of the U.S. Department of Agriculture. Photographic Archives of the Arnold Arboretum.

153 Courtesy of Widener Library, Harvard University.

154 By permission of *The Boston Globe*.

155 Photograph by Istvan Racz. Photographic Archives of the Arnold Arboreum.

156 Photograph by Christopher Burnett. Courtesy of Nan Blake Sinton.

157 Photograph by Barth Hamberg. Photographic Archives of the Arnold Arboretum.

158 Photograph by Istvan Racz. Photographic Archives of the Arnold Arboretum.

159 Library of the Arnold Arboretum.

160 From Charles R. Skinner, *Arbor Day Manual* (Syracuse, New York, 1896). Library of the Arnold Arboretum.

161 Photograph by Ernest H. Wilson. Photographic Archives of the Arnold Arboretum.

162 Photograph by Albert Bussewitz. Photographic Archives of the Arnold Arboretum.

163 From the American Tree Association, 1932. Library of the Arnold Arboretum.

164–166 Photographs by Ernest H. Wilson. Photographic Archives of the Arnold Arboretum.

167 From Lorin L. Dame, *Typical Elms and Other Trees of Massachusetts* (Boston, 1890). Library of the Arnold Arboretum.

168 Photograph by Ernest H. Wilson. Photographic Archives of the Arnold Arboretum.

169 *Above,* from *U.S. Department Of Forestry Bulletin No. 45* (1914). Library of the Arnold Arboretum. *Below,* from Gifford Pinchot, *A Primer of Forestry* (Washington, D.C., 1911). Library of the Arnold Arboretum.

CHAPTER 4

140 Photograph by Albert Bussewitz. Photographic Archives of the Arnold Arboretum.

141 Photograph by P. P. Kormanik, U.S. Forest Service, Athens, Georgia.

170 Photograph by Sheila Connor.

171 Photograph by Barth Hamberg. Photographic Archives of the Arnold Arboretum.

172 From *Ballou's Pictorial Drawing-Room Companion,* Vol. 8 (1855). Courtesy of Widener Library, Harvard University.

173 Photograph by Ernest H. Wilson. Photographic Archives of the Arnold Arboretum.

174 Photograph by Albert Bussewitz. Photographic Archives of the Arnold Arboretum.

175 Photograph by Ernest H. Wilson. Photographic Archives of the Arnold Arboretum.

176 Photograph by Sheila Connor.

177 Photograph by Ernest H. Wilson. Photographic Archives of the Arnold Arboretum.

178 Photograph by Ethan Johnson.

179 Photograph by Christopher Burnett. Photographic Archives of the Arnold Arboretum.

180 Photograph by Alfred Rehder. Photographic Archives of the Arnold Arboretum.

181 From Mary Farwell Ayer, *Early Days on Boston Common* (Boston, 1910). Courtesy of Widener Library, Harvard University.

182 From M. A. De Wolfe Howe, *Boston Common: Scenes from Four Centuries* (Cambridge, Massachusetts, 1910). Courtesy of Widener Library, Harvard University.

183 Archives of the Arnold Arboretum.

184 Photograph by Ernest H. Wilson. Photographic Archives of the Arnold Arboretum.

185 Courtesy of the Shelburne Museum, Shelburne, Vermont.

186, 187 Photographs by Sheila Connor.

188 Courtesy of the Dickinson Witch Hazel Company, Essex, Connecticut.

189–191 Photographs by Sheila Connor.

192 Photograph by Istvan Racz. Photographic Archives of the Arnold Arboretum.

193 Photograph by Ernest H. Wilson. Photographic Archives of the Arnold Arboretum.

194 From Nelson Cortland Brown, *Forest Products* (New York, 1919). Library of the Arnold Arboretum.

COLOR PLATES

1 From Aylmer Bourke Lambert, *A Description of the Genus Pinus,* 2 volumes (London, 1828). Library of the Arnold Arboretum.

2 From Asa Gray, *The Forest Trees of North America,* illustrations by Isaac Sprague (Washington, 1891). Library of the Arnold Arboretum.

3 From P. W. Watson, *Dendrologia Britannica,* 2 volumes (London,[1823]–1825). Library of the Arnold Arboretum.

4, 5 From Franz Schmidt, *Osterreichs Allgemeine Baumzucht,* 4 volumes (Vienna, 1792). Library of the Arnold Arboretum.

6 From *Curtis's Botanical Magazine,* Vol. 52 (1825). Library of the Arnold Arboretum.

7 From P. W. Watson, *Dendrologia Britannica,* 2 volumes (London,[1823]–1825). Library of the Arnold Arboretum.

8 From Jakob Trew, *Plantae Selectae* (Nuremberg, 1750–1773). Library of the Arnold Arboretum.

9 From André Michaux, *Geschechte der Amerikanischen Eichen* (Stuttgart, 1802). Library of the Arnold Arboretum.

10–13 From Aylmer Bourke Lambert, *A Description of the Genus Pinus,* 2 volumes (London, 1828). Library of the Arnold Arboretum.

14, 15 From Mark Catesby, The *Natural History of Carolina, Florida, and the Bahama Islands,* 2 volumes (London, 1730–1734). Library of the Arnold Arboretum.

16, 17 From Franz Schmidt, *Osterreichs Allgemeine Baumzucht,* 4 volumes (Vienna, 1792). Library of the Arnold Arboretum.

18 From Mark Catesby, *The Natural History of Carolina, Florida, and the Bahama Islands,* 2 volumes (London, 1730–1734). Library of the Arnold Arboretum.

19 From Aylmer Bourke Lambert, *A Description of the Genus Pinus,* 2 volumes (London, 1828). Library of the Arnold Arboretum.

20 From Franz Schmidt, *Osterreichs Allgemeine Baumzucht,* 4 volumes (Vienna, 1792). Library of the Arnold Arboretum.

21 From Asa Gray, *The Forest Trees of North America,* illustrations by Isaac Sprague (Washington, 1891). Library of the Arnold Arboretum.

22 From Aylmer Bourke Lambert, *A Description of the Genus Pinus,* 2 volumes (London, 1828). Library of the Arnold Arboretum.

23 From Mark Catesby, The *Natural History of Carolina, Florida, and the Bahama Islands,* 2 volumes (London, 1730–1734). Library of the Arnold Arboretum.

24 *Prunus serotina* from Asa Gray, *The Forest Trees of North America,* illustrations by Isaac Sprague (Washington, D.C., 1891). *Betula lutea* from François André Michaux, *The North American Sylva,* 3 volumes (Philadelphia, 1865). Library of the Arnold Arboretum.

INDEX